GOOD BOOKS
FOR THE
CURIOUS TRAVELER

EUROPE

GOOD BOOKS FOR THE CURIOUS TRAVELER

EUROPE

Theodora Nelson
and Andrea Gross

Johnson Books: Boulder

For David and John

We find only the world we look for.
—Thoreau

© 1989 by Theodora Nelson and Andrea Gross

Cover design by Molly Davis

Library of Congress Cataloging-in-Publication Data

Nelson, Theodora, 1940-
    Good books for the curious traveler. Europe.

    Includes index.
    1. Europe—Description and travel—1971- . —Book reviews. 2. Europe—Civilization—Book reviews. I. Gross, Andrea, 1940- . II. Title.
Z2000.N35   1989   [D923]   016.94   89-1701
ISBN 1-55566-038-X

Printed in the United States of America by
Johnson Publishing Company
1880 South 57th Court
Boulder, Colorado 80301

CONTENTS

INTRODUCTION vii

ACKNOWLEDGEMENTS viii

GENERAL EUROPE
General 2   Architecture 10   History 11

ENGLAND
General 16   Anthropology and Archaeology 24
Art and Architecture 28   Cuisine 32   Folktales 35
History 37   Literature 42   Nature 48
Performing Arts 51   Young People's Books 53

SCOTLAND AND WALES
General 58   Anthropology and Archaeology 68
Art and Architecture 68   Cuisine 73   Folktales 73
History 75   Nature 78   Performing Arts 79
Young People's Books 80

IRELAND
General 84   Anthropology and Archaeology 91
Art and Architecture 93   Cuisine 98
Folktales 100   History 101   Literature 104
Nature 105   Performing Arts 106
Young People's Books 107

FRANCE
General 110   Anthropology 118
Art and Architecture 119   Cuisine 123
Folktales 126   History 127   Literature 134
Nature 136   Performing Arts 137
Young People's Books 141

IBERIA
General 146   Art and Architecture 154
Cuisine 157   History 159   Performing Arts 161
Young People's Books 163

ITALY
General 166 Anthropology and Archaeology 177
Art and Architecture 180 Cuisine 183
Folktales 185 History 186 Nature 190
Performing Arts 191 Young People's Books 193

GERMANY
General 198 Art and Architecture 203
Folktales 205 History 206 Performing Arts 207
Young People's Books 208

SCANDINAVIA
General 214 Anthropology and Archaeology 219
Art and Architecture 221 Cuisine 228
Folktales 229 History 229 Literature 232
Nature 232 Performing Arts 233
Young People's Books 233

ALPINE AND LOW COUNTRIES
General 238 Art 239 History 240
Nature 242 Performing Arts 243
Young People's Books 245

CENTRAL EUROPE
General 248 Art 256 History 258
Mythology 262 Performing Arts 263
Young People's Books 263

GREECE AND TURKEY
General 266 Anthropology and Archaeology 276
Art and Architecture 280 History 281
Nature 286 Young People's Books 287

SOVIET UNION
General 290 Art and Architecture 305
Cuisine 308 History 309 Nature 312
Performing Arts 313 Young People's Books 315

TITLE INDEX 319

AUTHOR INDEX 323

INTRODUCTION

Samuel Johnson once said that "in traveling a man must carry knowledge with him if he would bring home knowledge," and what was true in his day is even more true today. In a world where we can eat McDonalds hamburgers in Brussels, drink Coca Cola in Mozambique, and sleep at a Hilton Hotel in Istanbul, it's all too easy to take America with us on our trips abroad, to fly half way around the world without really leaving home at all.

To get the most out of our travels, we must *understand* the people and places we visit. We must delve beneath the surface and explore the meaning behind the sights, the history beneath the attractions. And that's why we've prepared this book, to help you do just that.

Good Books for the Curious Traveler is a natural outgrowth of Travel Source™, our information service for inquisitive travelers. Our customers—well-educated, curious, culturally-oriented folk—were having difficulty finding the exact reading material they desired. Oh, they could find guide books aplenty—many of them quite good— but the main purpose of a guide is to recommend restaurants and hotels, to give up-to-date information on the hours and costs of museums and attractions. Guides are able to give only cursory overviews of customs and traditions, art and history. There just isn't room for more.

And so we began looking for special books that provide background information on the different countries and regions of the world. We researched thousands of books—books on archaeology, anthropology, and architecture; art, music, and theatre; plants, wildlife, and history. Most of the books were non-fiction, but some, a special few, were fiction—we call them "place-set fiction"—of the type that offers insights about the people, customs, and history of a specific locale. Many of these books were from traditional publishers; but others were from small presses that offer more unusual material, and still others were imported.

Here, in **Good Books for the Curious Traveler**, we've reviewed approximately four hundred of our favorite books on Europe. We've arranged them first by country or region, then by topic. Inevitably there are books that resist categorization. We've cross-referenced in many cases, but please do browse through *all* related sections. If you are going to one country, for example, look also at the "General Europe" section which covers many books that may contain one or more chapters on the country you're planning to visit. And if you are particularly interested in history, look also at the section on archaeology, which after all, has been defined as "tangible evidence of the past," and at the one on architecture, which A.L. Rowse once called "history arrested in stone."

We're often asked what standard we apply when selecting books to recommend to travelers. First, we have a lot of help. Our Travel Source™ Advisory Board, men and women from recognized universities, is a wonderful resource. Fellow travelers, students, travel agents—all offer suggestions. (Note the lengthy acknowledgement section!) Then we haunt bookstores and libraries and we continually pore over book catalogues from nearly every publisher in the English speaking world. We obtain copies of books that we feel would be of special interest to the inquisitive traveler, and then we choose the best. We look for books that are neither text nor trash, those that inform and entertain at the same time.

We try to recommend only books that are currently available. Some of these books may not be in your local bookstore, but booksellers should be able to order them for you. If they have difficulty, have them give us a call. We'll try to help out.

In the final analysis, of course, it comes down to personal opinion. Countries vary greatly in the amount that is written about them. England and France, for example, seem to inspire authors. There are literally hundreds of wonderful books about these countries. We've tried to select the best. Scandinavia and Germany, on the other hand, are less well documented in English. We point out what is available.

Finally, in any undertaking such as this, there is bound to be controversy. We have possibly left out a book that is a favorite of yours or included one you found displeasing. Please write or call us at Travel Source™ and let us know. We'll take your suggestions into account in the next edition of Good Books for the Curious Traveler; then others will benefit from your ideas.

Thank you and Happy Traveling!

Theodora Nelson and Andrea Gross
January 1989

Travel Source™
20103 La Roda Court
Cupertino, CA 95014
(408) 446-0600

ACKNOWLEDGEMENTS

Researching, selecting, and reviewing these books has been a bigger job than we ever anticipated. Perhaps only two Virgos would have even attempted it! We're deeply grateful for the understanding and support of our husbands—Irv Green and Dor Hesselgrave—and for the patience and good humor of our children. Lindy Green in particular showed a great deal of maturity on those days when "Mom was too busy."

Eugene Ulansky, Peter Green, David Browman, and Valentina Broughter were quick to answer our pleas for help; and we thank them. In addition, we were fortunate to have suggestions and advice from a large number of friends and co-workers, many of whom helped with the actual writing: Kathy Skaggs-Rodriguez, Ruth Priest, Elizabeth Cheatham, Michael Green, Mireille Grovier, Rosalind Hutton, Debra Sloane, David Babb, David Brooks, Anne Cheng, Sandra Cortright, Denise Ellsworth, Wendy Franson, Douglas Green, Cindy Martin, Pamela Priest, Judas Riley and Patrick Siegman.

Valuable help and occasional reviews also were provided by Richard Beecher, Rita Breenen, Michael Condon, Roberta Cortilla, Michael Cummins, Vernon Cox, Kelly Ann Craigmile, Diana Di Pietro, Christie Fertal, Katherine Evans, Susanne Kibler, Ingrid Kessler, Anne Larson, Eric Larrivée, Julia Lavaroni, Nancy Layton, Doug Leadon, Wendi Lee, Kenneth McKeough, Kristine Merrell, Neli Moody-Berne, David Oline, Simon Oswitch, Stacy Pelinka, Tami Runyan, Sue Toorans, De Anne DeRosa, Denise Ford, Agnes Lee, Jeanne McMahon, Eileen Menteer, Faye Miranda, Steven Oddo, Madge Saksena, Andrea Sandke, Kevon Wade and Gloria Walker.

Thank you, everyone.

A.G. and T.N.

GENERAL EUROPE

GENERAL

Apple's Europe: An Uncommon Guide
R.W. Apple, Jr.

R.W. Apple is, in his own words, an "enthusiast" who has an "incurable case of wanderlust." Unlike most of us who are similarly afflicted, he has a job that allows—no, encourages—him to indulge his dreams. As a journalist, he has been traveling on all five continents for over twenty-five years.

In this, his first book, he concentrates on Europe, beginning with Britain where he lived for a good bit of time, touching lightly on France, and then stopping by Italy, the Low Countries, Austria and Germany, Spain, Eastern Europe, Scandinavia, and—although not technically in Europe—Morocco and southern Jordan.

"Inevitably," he says, "the shape of the book has been affected by my own passions and prejudices. My kind of travel centers on art and architecture, music and natural beauty, good food and good drink, [and] I see Europe's past as the key to appreciating its present."

Apple gives travel tips ("Barcelona . . . is the place to shop for leather goods of all kinds"), but he also imparts insight ("Apulia was once part of Magna Graecia—Great Greece, the network of Greek colonies in southern Italy—and Taras was its most opulent and exuberant city. Magna Graecia was to Greece as the New World is to the Old, it seems to many antiquarians, and if that is so, Taras was the New York of the fourth century before Christ.") As its subtitle suggests, **Apple's Europe** is a very "uncommon guide" that will enhance the trip of the curious traveler.

(Atheneum, 1986, ISBN 0-689-11607-1, hardcover, 264 pages, $14.95)

The City as a Work of Art: London, Paris, Vienna
Donald J. Olson

Using three major European capitals (London, Paris, and Vienna) to illustrate his point, author and history professor Donald J. Olson challenges the widespread view that everything urban is inherently evil and everything rural, virtuous. As he writes in his preface to **The City as a Work of Art:**

We can regard cities as complex but legible documents that can tell us something about the values and aspirations of their rulers, designers, builders, owners, and inhabitants . . . I have . . . approached my three cities as objects to be cherished and understood rather than evils to be exposed, as works of art rather than as instances of social pathology.

In his investigation of the three cities, Olson creates a fascinating tapestry of social history, art, architecture, and urban anthropology. He limits his study to the period of the cities' most significant growth, the century preceding 1914, suggesting that there isn't enough distance and perspective to accurately assess the events of the twentieth century. Separate chapters discuss the city as luxury, as monument, as home, as playground, and as document, revealing individual threads of each city's personality.

Why, for example, does the Londoner crave a home and garden of his own, while the residents of Paris and Vienna prefer flats? What about the tendency of the Parisian family to dine together in a restaurant, while the Englishman slips away from his family to eat at his club? How did the collective personality of each city's inhabitants contribute to the form of urban development, and how did the style of the city in turn shape the character of its people?

Olson examines questions such as these, all the while vividly evoking the spirit of each city. The book—oversized and amply illustrated with black-and-white and a few color photos—is beautiful enough to reside on a coffee table. But as a fresh and provocative look at these familiar cities, it won't just sit there and gather dust.

(Yale, 1986, ISBN 0-300-04212-4, softcover, oversized, 341 pages, $19.95)

Europe: A Tapestry of Nations
Flora Lewis

The chapter titles of Flora Lewis's **Europe: A Tapestry of Nations** have a charm all their own. For example, there's "France—The Reign of Intellectuals," "Portugal—Leaping Half a Century," and "Switzerland—The Quiet Cuckoo." Moving east there is "Poland—The Malady Is Geography," "Czechoslovakia—A Sullen Quiet," and "Yugoslavia—The Undone Puzzle."

With similar wit and incisiveness, Lewis characterizes the seventeen countries of Western Europe (she combines England, Scotland and Wales) and the eight of Eastern Europe in a book that couples the first-hand knowledge of a long-time resident with the objective perspective of a native American.

She approaches her rather formidable task on a country-by-country basis, showing each nation both as it sees itself and as its neighbors perceive it. Her text sparkles with anecdotes and quotations from a wide variety of sources as she investigates each country's history, geography, economy, and government to capture its distinctive national character. Topics of general concern are treated within the country they most affect, such as terrorism in connection with Italy and the rebuilding of industry following World War II in the chapter on West Germany.

Pointing out that the continent is truly united in many ways, Lewis notes that "there is such a place as Europe, such a thing as European, even though the moment you approach to look more closely it breaks up into kaleidoscopic fragments. My wish is to bring both the unity and the complexity within grasp." She succeeds remarkably in an overview that is as enjoyable as it is informative.

(Touchstone/Simon and Schuster, 1988, ISBN 0-671-66829-3, softcover, 592 pages, $10.95)

Europe 101: History, Art and Culture for the Traveler
Rick Steves and Gene Openshaw

European history doesn't have to be an endless tangled skein of Fredericks, Henrys, Charleses, and Louises interspersed with forgettable dates and battles. It can be a fascinating account of the artists, musicians, and politicians of the past who, with their talent and power, created the tourist sights of today's Europe.

The author-instructors, Rick Steves and Gordon Openshaw, prove this in **Europe 101**. Despite the title, they promise no tests; instead they offer practical knowledge of history and art especially for the traveler. From Albrecht Dürer ("Europe's first top selling artist" in the 15th century) to Versailles (unpopular in its time because "it was expensive to live there and keep up with the latest fashions") to Bismarck (who "united Germany as if he were reading from a great political recipe book,") European history and culture come alive through their discussion.

Steves and Openshaw explain the layout of the book, pointing out "there are two halves - 1) *Corpus* (Latin for 'body') and 2) *Tangents* (English for 'things you go off on when you're excited')." *Corpus* packs the basics of Europe's history and art into 200 pages. *Tangents* gives more specific descriptions of areas of special interest to travelers.

Steves and Openshaw spent sixty-five months traveling in Europe and have degrees in European history, art, and culture. Here they combine their practical experience with their academic knowledge to produce a readable but highly informative crash course in Everything European, specifically for the person who wants to remember what he's afraid he's forgotten.

(John Muir, 1985, ISBN 0-912528-42-7, softcover, 369 pages, $9.95)

The Europeans
Luigi Barzini

Meet the "Elusive Europeans." More specifically, meet the "Imperturbable British," the "Mutable Germans," the "Quarrelsome French," the

"Flexible Italians," and the "Careful Dutch." Then, just for good measure, learn how those people see us, the "Baffling Americans."

Luigi Barzini, Italian writer and graduate of the Columbia University School of Journalism, plays host at this international cocktail party. Although he introduces his guests with a genial combination of wit and charm, he is intent on thoughtful discussion: there are today, he says, "serious, sober, and objective reasons for the immediate creation of a European union," and now is the time to consider them.

The Europeans is a book that can be read on several levels. On the surface it's a breezy, almost irreverent, look at the characteristics that combine to form national identities. About the British he writes: "I studied the eminent, gray-haired, distinguished gentlemen in their offices . . . I studied them in their ancient clubs. They received me with stiff courtesy and some bewilderment. Some let their monocles drop in astonishment (nature too often imitates clichés), and let them oscillate at the end of black silk cords, at my more indiscreet questions. They cleared their throats. . . ."

In another sense the book is an intimate look at Europe's history, a study of the events that shaped its current habits and thought patterns. And beneath it all lies Barzini's concerns and the possibilities of a Soviet-American confrontation and Europe's role in such an event. He throws a party worth attending.

(Penguin, 1983, ISBN 0-1400-7150-4, softcover, 267 pages, $6.95)

Footsteps: Adventures of a Romantic Biographer
Richard Holmes

Richard Holmes was eighteen years old when he set off on foot to retrace the steps of Robert Louis Stevenson as chronicled in *Travels with a Donkey*. His odyssey was not an easy concept to explain to those he met on the rural roads of France. Accepting a ride with a Frenchman in a Citroën, he explained he was following a friend, a Scot who had walked through the region, and he showed the Frenchman his well-worn book.

"Ah, that!" broke in M. Crèspy with a shout, taking both hands from the steering wheel and striking his forehead. "I understand, I understand! You are on the traces of Monsieur Robert Louis Steamson. Bravo, bravo . . . I understand, I understand," repeated M. Crèspy. And I believe he was the first person who ever did.

Although few people could comprehend, let alone share, his penchant for retracing the paths of famous writers, Holmes's passion grew to encompass the roamings of other authors—Wordsworth, Mary Wollstonecraft, Shelley, Gérard de Nerval—and led him over the next twelve years to all parts of France as well as to Italy and England. **Footsteps**, in combining tales of his journeys with details of the famous authors' lives and works, becomes at once biography, detective story, adventure, and travelogue. It is an intelligent, imaginative, and altogether fascinating book.

(Penguin, 1985, ISBN 0-014-008860-1, softcover, 288 pages, $7.95)

Heidi's Alp: One Family's Search for Storybook Europe
Christina Hardyment

It all began when Christina Hardyment was reading *Wind in the Willows* to her two youngest daughters. She began to note a sensation of missing adventure, of lacking (in Toad's terminology) that "horizon that's always changing." Then Daisy, another daughter, wandered in, *Heidi* in hand, wishing for a life on a mountain raising goats. So after months of dreaming and planning, Christina and her husband Tom loaded their four daughters, aged five to twelve, in a motor home and set out "in search of the roots of the stories that linked our children with children all over Europe in a common imaginative heritage." Leaving their home in Oxford, England, their minds boggled at the possibilities:

We could hunt trolls in the Norwegian mountains, look for witches and wolves in the German forests. In Switzerland we'd rout out Heidi and William Tell, in Italy track down Pinocchio and Punch and Judy. What sort of a man could write a book like Struwwelpeter? *What was the true significance of Cinderella and Sleeping Beauty? Where did Don Quixote tilt at windmills? Was there a jackdaw at Reims, a hunchback at Notre Dame?*

For 4,000 miles through six countries they pursued legendary characters—Hans Brinker in the Netherlands, Babar in Burgundy, Hans Christian Andersen in Denmark and Germany, and, yes, Heidi in Switzerland. There the delighted family even found a present-day Alm Uncle who invited them to spend the night:

We looked at each other. To have come all these hundreds of miles with only the vaguest of directions, and find ourselves sleeping in a Heidi alpine attic seemed too good to be true. But the gods, as I said, were with us that day.

Their adventure is a touch of childhood magic, and for those who would like to duplicate it, Hardyment appends a list of "Useful Addresses" and a bibliography. Do you suppose her daughters know how lucky they are?

(Atlantic Monthly, 1987, ISBN 0-87113-178-1, softcover, 260 pages, $7.95)

Mean Feat: A 3000-Mile Walk Through Portugal, Spain, France, Switzerland and Italy
John Waite

A journey of a thousand miles, it's said, begins with a single step. John Waite took that first step in February 1981, embarking on a journey that was to take most of that year and span five countries, from Portugal to Spain, across France and Switzerland into Italy. **Mean Feat** is the saga of his trek across miles of raw countryside and dangerous snow-capped mountain passes, through torrential rains, and into picturesque villages.

As he traveled he conversed with people he met. In Spain a parent confided:

'It's so difficult, so expensive, to educate your children. Then, just a year before they have finished their studies they have to go and do their military service, wasting time playing soldiers, and when they do eventually come out with a degree there's no work for them. . .'

In France he paused to live and work for a bit in the remote village of Mas Bas, enjoying the simple, hard life of the country peasants. Then it was back on the road again, on to the spectacle of Switzerland.

Imagine waking to a very soft green light, the blue shadows in the valley gradually changing, turning green, the reflection of the mountains on the surface of the lake slowly crystallising, the sun about to break out over the tops, the spot peaceful and quiet.

He had treked, eaten, and wined his way through most of Italy when, within smell and sound of the Adriatic Sea:

My back was very stiff in the morning. I was in no hurry . . . I tidied things away, lifted my pack as I had done so many times before, then dropped it with a scream as a searing pain ripped up my back, leaving me gasping, breathless, broken.

Waite's odyssey ended with a pulled *Sacropinalis* muscle after he had walked exactly 2812 miles. Despite being forced to quit short of his goal, his accomplishment is impressive and his journal teems with the people he encountered and the places he experienced.

(Oxford Illustrated Press, 1985, ISBN 0-946609-19-5, hardcover, 288 pages, $12.95)

The Mermaids of Chenonceaux: An Anecdotal Guide to Europe
Phyllis Méras

• When he was young, Hans Christian Andersen wanted to be a dancer, but his dancing was "so bizarre and so dreadful that the ballerina thought him mad and screamed for help." It soon became clear that he would never meet success as a dancer, so he decided to try singing. "But this hope too was short-lived—his voice changed. And it was then that he decided to become a writer."
• In 1602 the city of Geneva was invaded, but a kettle of vegetable soup hurled from a window saved the day.
• A poem, read aloud on the patio of Sintra Palace, inspired King Sebastian of Portugal to invade Morocco. It cost him his own life as well as the lives of eight thousand others.

Phyllis Méras, travel editor of the *Providence Journal*, knows that it's the little stories—the exclamation points of history—that are remembered long after mere dates and names are forgotten. Here she relates 829 such tales, most of them only one or two paragraphs long.

Who preferred to become a nun rather than marry a bastard? Why did the Spanish ambassador spit in the face of his valet? And what happened while Talleyrand was waltzing at the Metternich Palace? The answers are all here, gossipy delights from the countries of continental western Europe.

(Congdon & Weed, 1985, ISBn 0-86553-038-6, softcover, 352 pages, $16.95)

The Three Romes: Moscow, Constantinople, Rome
Russell Fraser

Moscow, Constantinople (now Istanbul), Rome—three centers of civilization; three cities that have aspired to be spiritual, as well as temporal, kingdoms. "Rome, the City of the Seven Hills," writes Russell Fraser, author and English professor, "became a great power in the centuries before Christ. This power was physical but appealed to moral sanctions, and Rome ruled the world by right as well as might. You could say the same for Constantinople, also for Moscow, yesterday and today."

In **The Three Romes** Fraser describes life today in each of the three cities, interspersing his travel essays with historical musings. Careening through the streets of Istanbul in a taxi, for instance, he recalls that the poet Yeats, if given a month to spend in any place in antiquity "would spend it in Byzantium a little before Justinian opened Sancta Sophia. This was December 537. When the emperor came to the finished church, he held out his arms in prayer and said he had beaten King Solomon. In the Holy City, Yeats said, 'religious, aesthetic, and practical life were one.'"

In Moscow he notes that the lower stature of women harks back to Mongol times: "Women being prone to compassion, the Mongols shut them away. Russians did this too. In Cathedral Square they built the Terems, a very private place where they kept the Tsarina and her ladies. The Mongol idea that ladies are best when not seen and not heard hung on until the time of Peter the Great."

Yet he doesn't neglect the present. Frustrated in his attempt to view the mosaics in a small church in Rome, he offers a new name for such churches: "Santa Maria Sempre Chiusa. 'Chiusa' means closed."

Fraser shuttles easily between past and present, East and West, image and reality to tell the tale of three of history's most influential cities.

(Harcourt Brace Jovanovich, 1985, ISBN 0-15-190186-4, hardcover, 305 pages, $17.95)

Painted in Blood: Understanding Europeans
Stuart Miller

In spite of all the differences between its various provinces, Europe is a whole shaped by a common past.
—Czeslaw Milosz

In today's Europe a Dutch reporter whose father was a Nazi hallucinates that there are grenades exploding inside his car as he drives home. Road signs on the German *Autobahn* give two speed limits: one for cars and one for tanks. A law in militarily neutral Switzerland requires that households stock sixty days' worth of food in the house, in case of war. The ever-present memory of war on their home turf is a major factor in the European character; as Stuart Miller writes, "The background of collective violence, combined with other historical forces like memories of massive poverty, makes the European closed and defended in ways that are typically un-American."

This is a thoughtful, analytical and sympathetic book by an American author and comparative literature scholar who recently spent six years in Europe. Through deeply revealing anecdotes, Miller explores the European character in much the same way Europeans from de Tocqueville onward have studied Americans.

Many books on Europe engage in country-by-country description; Miller prefers to concentrate on similarities. "While it is obvious that Swedes aren't Spaniards and Belgians aren't even Dutch, at a certain useful level of analysis, all these people have much in common. In addition, the peoples of Europe are becoming more similar. Modern life has tended to dissolve many distinctions." For this reason he deliberately focuses on the "unexotic Europeans, the urban and suburban people" who, he says, are "plugged into the modern world by the market system, political parties, and a hundred other means."

His book has been called audacious, disturbing, profound, stunning, and totally unique by the critics. It is all these things and even more: it is a tool for understanding.

(Atheneum, 1987, ISBN 0-689-11531-8, hardcover, 255 pages, $17.95)

ARCHITECTURE

The Faber Guide to Twentieth Century Architecture: Britain and Northern Europe
Lance Knobel

Lance Knobel's innovative book, **The Faber Guide to Twentieth Century Architecture**, serves as a systematic overview of some of the great architectural works of modern times.

Knobel, an editor of *Designers' Journal*, is well versed in the area of contemporary architecture. His comprehensive guide covers 294 buildings in Great Britain, France, West Germany, Scandinavia, the Netherlands, and Belgium, and includes the works of some of this century's most distinguished masters. The very distinctive Le Corbusier, Hans Scharoun with his strong Expressionist influence, and art nouveau devotee Hector Guimard are but a handful of the 174 architects who are discussed in this book.

Featured buildings are all accessible to the public, although as Knobel notes, "many of them are off the beaten tourist track." This, he proclaims, is an "incidental reward [as] visitors have a chance to discover unknown, unspoilt areas of the major cities of Europe." Black-and-white photographs of each building are included, as well as a detailed and informative history. Knobel has thoughtfully included complete addresses for each site and a map for geographical reference.

"The idea for this book came from a personal need," explains Knobel. In answering that need Knobel has produced a superior guide that cannot fail to delight architecture buffs.

(Faber and Faber, 1985, ISBN 0-571-13556-0, softcover, 199 pages, $29.95)

HISTORY

The Book of the Medieval Knight
Stephen Turnbull

"This book is a celebration of a romantic ideal," explains author Stephen Turnbull, speaking of his delightful and informative work, **The Book of the Medieval Knight.**

Defender of the family, faith, and country, backbone of the crusading armies, follower of chivalric ideals, and sometimes mercenary, the knight was an integral part of medieval court and culture. Yet at no time was his presence more necessary and influential in his society than in the high middle ages. From the defeat of Edward II by King Robert the Bruce of Scotland in 1314 to the death of Richard II and the ascension of Henry Tudor at the Battle of Bosworth in 1485, the knight was the epitome of an age balanced between war and romance.

Over two hundred pictures and drawings interspersed throughout the book beautifully illustrate the fascinating and turbulent world of the knight and the medieval Europe in which he lived and fought. Often, the illustrations are paired to contrast the idealized image with the mundane reality. For example, one page bears the romantic drawing of a fifteenth-century jousting tournament performed by feathered and armor-clad mounted knights in front of a royal audience. On the facing page is an etching of a castle under violent siege; the defenders appear to be throwing everything, from bedsteads to bed pans, on their attackers.

An integral part of this book is, of course, the knights and knightly families themselves. That there is "a Henry Percy mentioned in nearly every chapter of the book, and each one seems to meet a violent death," says the author, is no accident. It is the lives of these fervent warriors that is the "thread running through the pages."

(Crown, 1985, ISBN 0-517-55863-7, hardcover, 192 pages, $17.95)

The Guns of August
The Proud Tower
Barbara W. Tuchman

The Great War of 1914-18 lies like a band of scorched earth dividing that time from ours. In wiping out so many lives which would have been operative on the years that followed, in destroying beliefs, changing ideas and leaving incurable

wounds of disillusion, it created a physical as well as psychological gulf between two epochs.
—Barbara Tuchman, Introduction, *The Proud Tower*

August, 1914. Liège, Tannenberg, Mons. . . . The guns of World War I began to take their toll. This month—hot, humid, and horrible—was one of the most critical in the history of the Western world, and historian Barbara Tuchman tells its story with a sense of you-are-there authenticity. Her recreation of these days, **The Guns of August**, won the 1963 Pulitzer Prize for General Non-Fiction; it is a tale of strategic maneuvers and military might, of strong generals and desperate politicians.

Yet the war whose results so changed the world did not come about entirely because of the actions, or non-actions, of these national leaders. It was not fought over treaties or alliances. In fact, she says, "the diplomatic origins, so-called, of the Great War are only the fever chart of the patient; they do not tell us what caused the fever. To probe for underlying causes and deeper forces one must operate within the framework of a whole society and try to discover what moved the people in it."

And probe she does in **The Proud Tower**, a masterful work that takes its title from Edgar Allan Poe: "While from a proud tower in the town/ Death looks gigantically down" (*The City in the Sea*). Tuchman climbs the proud tower of the prewar years to examine an epoch where self-confidence and extravagance were mixed with injustice and hypocrisy and where change was the norm. The world was a vast pressure cooker demanding release.

Although one chapter concerns the United States as it moved toward world power, the book concentrates on Western Europe: England where the aristocrats still governed, France where the Dreyfus Affair held center stage, and Germany where composer Richard Straus served as "a barometer of his native weather." Aristocrats and anarchists, heroes and fools, bigots and patriots people this vast panorama of European society in the twenty-five years before the outbreak of war.

Tuchman captures the mood as well as the facts of history in these two books that so clearly beat the rhythms of a century ago.

(Macmillan; The Guns of August, 1962, 1988, ISBN 0-02-62031-0, hardcover, 528 pages, $19.95; The Proud Tower: 1966, ISBN 0-02-620300-6, hardcover, 528 pages, $17.95)

Who's Who in the Ancient World
Betty Radice

You're standing in the Vatican Museum, gazing at the statue entitled *Laocoön*, and wondering about the identity of the man and the two youths struggling with those fearsome snakes. If you had a copy of **Who's Who in the Ancient World** handy, you'd soon know that Laocoön was a priest who tried to save Troy by keeping the Trojan Horse from entering the city gates; for his efforts Apollo or Athene sent serpents to kill him and his two sons.

This useful little book lists hundreds of classical references: rulers and heroes, gods and goddesses; places both real and legendary; and terms like "Gordian Knot" and "Golden Bough." It is fully indexed and cross-referenced and contains a chronology table and maps.

For those who want to know why Lapiths are doing battle with centaurs all through Greece, or why Hadrian's Wall was built, this book is a gem.

(Penguin, 1971, ISBN 0-14-051055-9, softcover, **336** pages, $6.95)

ENGLAND

GENERAL

The Beefeaters of the Tower of London
G. Abbott

What's the *real* story of the Beefeaters? Mr. G. Abbott is the perfect person to ask. As a member of the elite group that is more formally called "yeoman warders," Abbott spent eight years living and working in Her Majesty's Tower of London. And now he's written a book answering all the questions he was asked by the millions of tourists who visit the Tower each year.

No, he says, "we are not film extras or fancy dress salesmen . . . We do not commute to work in the Tower each day and travel home in the evening [and] we do not inherit the job from our ancestors . . . So what are we?"

He explains briefly: "We marshal the queues, assist the bewildered and guide the foreigners . . . We try to ensure that the tourists, despite their jetlag, aching feet, the crowds and the weather, still enjoy their visit to the Tower . . . And then, after the curfew bell has ushered out the last lingering tourist of the day, our duties still continue. For the Royal Palace and Fortress must be guarded as it has always been for over nine hundred years, by the yeoman warders."

Of course, these yeoman warders live "knee-deep in history." Even their nickname, "Beefeaters," has historical overtones. Although the exact origins are uncertain, the most likely story is that as members of the royal bodyguard they were permitted to eat as much beef as they wished from the king's table, even carrying on their daggers extra bits for their families.

Here is the complete inside story of what it's like to live within the brooding walls of the Tower of London. Full of anecdotes and little-known facts, generously spiced with tales of buried treasure and ghosts, *The Beefeaters of the Tower of London* is "everything you ever wanted to know about the tower but feared the Axe too much to ask!"

(David and Charles, 1985, ISBN 0-7153-8636, softcover, 96 pages, $6.95)

The Best of James Herriot: Favorite Memories of a Country Vet
James Herriot

James Herriot has done it again. The veterinarian-author has once more created a delightfully humorous and entertaining work in the tradition of his bestseller, *All Things Bright and Beautiful*.

Subtitled "Favorite Memories of a Country Vet," **The Best of James Herriot** is simply that—a collection of Herriot's own favorite stories from his original works. Newcomers as well as confirmed Herriot fans will enjoy meeting the fascinating people who inhabit the world of Herriot's Yorkshire: Helen, Herriot's loving and understanding wife; Siegfried and Tristan Farnon, his eccentric veterinary partners; Jock, the indefatigable, car-chasing sheepdog; and Mrs. Pumphrey and her perfectly pampered Pekingese, Tricki Woo.

The book also reveals Yorkshire's breathtaking beauty in more than 116 color photographs that adorn and illustrate various subjects—such as "Ancient Abbeys and Village Churches," "Dales and Moors," and "The Country Pub"—and when matched with appropriate chapters from Herriot's tales, give the reader a truly complete picture of Herriot-country.

Of special interest are the little "extras" in the book's margins, all of which relate to the stories. There are recipes for Yorkshire pudding, tea cakes, and bilberry pie; descriptions of country chores from cutting peat to lambing in the fields; and zoological information such as how to differentiate between Leicester, Lonk, and Teeswater sheep.

Born in Glasgow, Herriot says, "I was totally unprepared for the beauty of the Yorkshire Dales, but their wildness and peace captivated me instantly. I fell under an enchantment which has remained until this day." Through this book we can share the enchantment.

(St. Martin's Press, 1982, ISBN 0-312-07716-5, hardcover, 502 pages, $22.50)

Brit-Think, Ameri-Think: A Transatlantic Survival Guide
Jane Walmsley

Witty and irreverent, Jane Walmsley has written a book in which even the dedication is funny: "To my daughter Katie," she begins, "who has an American mother and a British father, and is—as she puts it—'haff and hawf.'"

But it's not only the accent, or even the fact that in England a *cookie* is a *biscuit* and a *truck* is a *lorry*, that divides us. It's the "separate habits of mind." For example, she explains, "Americans think that death is optional . . . That's the secret of America's fundamental optimism . . . You owe it to yourself to be beautiful, clever, skinny, sucessful, and healthy. If you fail, it's because you're not trying hard enough . . . (you didn't jog regularly, you should've eaten more bran)."

The British know otherwise. They "keep a weather eye on the Sword of Damocles, suspended above their heads. Lives are to be lived with a certain detachment, and a sense of distance preserved . . . Face-lifts and jogging geriatrics are vaguely obscene. One should grow old gracefully, bow to the inevitable."

Or take the American view of progress: "Americans are the world's greatest believers in progress. Life gets better all the time—or should . . . No point in clinging grimly to the past, or we'd never have traded gramophones for color TVs, buckshot for Star Wars, or headaches for coated aspirin."

The Brits think differently: "Brits loathe newness, and display a profound fear of change . . . Even small changes can cause Brit-trauma, with the nation shaken to its roots at suggestions that traditional red phone boxes may be painted yellow. Far better to preserve the status quo, to hope that custom and ritual will somehow counter the capriciousness of fate. Conclusion: change nothing unless forced. Remember that God usually gets it right the first time."

Walmsley tries hard to be even-handed ("If there's someone I haven't insulted . . . I'm sorry.") as she discusses topics of international importance (a telephone system that works, Caesar salads and soap operas). Read her book. If you're British you'll learn why Americans love the word *now*; and if you're American you'll find out why British toasters purposely burn bread on one side while leaving the other side raw.

(Penguin, 1986, ISBN 0-14-009367-2, softcover, 131 pages, $6.95)

Coasting: A Private Voyage
Jonathan Raban

It was 1982. The British Navy was sailing to war in the Falklands. Jonathan Raban, British travel writer, was sailing on his own long journey around the British Isles, a journey he describes as "a test, a reckoning, a voyage of territorial conquest, a homecoming." His goal was to know his country, and himself, more fully.

In his thirty-foot ketch, Raban traveled surrounded by an explorer's library—books on British people, history, and nature. He was also surrounded by his own preconceived notions:

> [The English] are famous for their insular arrogance and condescension. They love fine social distinctions and divisions and are snobbishly wedded to an antique system of caste and class. Yet the upper lips of this superior race are so notoriously stiff that they can barely bring themselves to speak, preferring to communicate in monosyllables interleaved with gruff silences . . .

Yet the colorful characters he meets are quite voluble: travel writer Paul Theroux, poet Philip Larkin, a host of sailors, tourists, politicians, priests, and even Pepe the talking parrot.

Raban finds a country that is not so much in decline as in flux. His book is exciting as an adventure and revealing as an autobiography, but most of all it is enlightening as the story of a country that is coasting toward the twenty-first century.

(Penguin, 1987, ISBN 0-14-010657-X, softcover, 302 pages, $7.95)

The English Channel
Nigel Calder

For hundreds of years the English Channel has been the scene of world-changing events. In 1066 the Normans crossed it to conquer England, and in 1944 the Allied forces crossed it in the other direction to crush Hitler's troops. Even today, "where full-rigged frigates used to shadow one another, American, British, French and Russian nuclear submarines play their all-too-earnest games of hide-and-seek."

As the world's busiest seaway, the English Channel has offered passage to traders and smugglers, pirates and conquerors, travelers and fishermen. For centuries it has challenged those who would swim across it or those who would fly over it in all manner of devices, from hot air balloons to bicycle-powered aircraft and, once, even an upside-down biplane.

Now it's our turn. Come along on a cruise with author Nigel Calder as he sails his way through the waters of history in **The English Channel**, an unusual book that follows the shore, pointing out historical and natural wonders. Off the coast between the South and North Forelands, for example, "is the maritime black hole called the Goodwin Sands, long known as the 'ship swallower.'" We see a ship there, half buried and lying on its side, serving as a warning to other ships.

Each port—Boulogne, Dover, Hastings, Plymouth, and Penzance—is a new and fascinating lesson. Geology and archaeology, history and political science, even the art of sailing are explored in masterful and captivating style. So come. Bring your lifejacket and your curiosity, and hop aboard the author's ketch. Whether you are a waterlogged sailor or a warm and dry landlubber, **The English Channel** is an invitation to listen, to learn, to laugh, and to fall in love with one of the world's most remarkable bodies of water.

(Viking, 1986, ISBN 0-14-010131-4, softcover, 384 pages, $8.95)

Hawksmoor
Peter Ackroyd

Hawksmoor is not ordinary reading, not comfortable before-bed relaxing reading. It's dark, spooky, chilling—and innovative. The action moves back and forth between the London of two centuries: the early eighteenth and the mid twentieth. The historical Nicholas Hawksmoor (1661-1736) was an architect who designed churches in London's East End. Here he is transposed into the fictional Nicholas Dyer who, orphaned by the plague and devoted to a satanic sect, haunts his twentieth century alter ego, a Scotland Yard detective. The detective, none-too-coincidentally named Nicholas Hawksmoor, is investigating a series of murders that have occurred on the sites of various churches built by his namesake.

As the story traverses the years, Ackroyd evokes the two periods. Dyer's London is one of slums and urchins, "a Nest of Death and Contagion" he says, speaking in the language of his time. "This Capital City of the World of Affliction is still the Capitol of Darknesse, or the Dungeon of Man's Desires: still in the Centre are no proper Streets nor Houses but a Wilderness of dirty rotten Sheds, allways tumbling or takeing Fire, with winding crooked passages, lares of Mire and rills of stinking mud . . ." Hawksmoor's London is tame by comparison.

Hawksmoor has become a cult phenomenon in England, where people have started touring the East London churchyards, expecting, no doubt, to see fictional young lads getting their throats slit by ghostly architects.

(Harper & Row, 1985, ISBN 0-06-091390-8, softcover, 290 pages, $7.95)

The Illustrated Counties of England
Edited by James Bishop

Come—come visit Bedfordshire and Berkshire, Cornwall, Somerset and Essex, Norfolk, Cumbria and Durham. Come with thirty-nine of England's most distinguished writers and visit the places they call home.

"Ask an Englishman where he comes from and he will give you the name of a county. It may not be where he is now living. It may be where he was born, but has not lived for many years, or it may be somewhere he has come to know in later life . . . So powerful is the Englishman's sense of identity with his county that a loyalty towards it can persist throughout his life," explains editor James Bishop.

Elspeth Huxley takes us to Wiltshire, the land of Stonehenge and "the great white Plain with its villages clustering along the shallow valley of chalk streams; thatched lime-washed cottages; tank-tracks scarring hillsides; and the spire of Salisbury Cathedral."

Phil Drabble leads us through Staffordshire "where some of the most delicate china in the world is still produced," and Stanley Baron walks with us through Surrey on "a route certainly older than Christianity [where] as early pilgrims would have varied their route according to weather and danger, so can we stop off at valley villages like Shere, through which the Tillingbourne meanders prettily."

These are not travel tours as much as personal reminiscences, a glimpse into the private places special to each author. The writings are accompanied by full-color photographs that, along with the text, portray the amazing variety of the English countryside.

(Facts on File, 1980, ISBN 0-8160-1157-5, hardcover, oversized, 248 pages, $24.95)

On Living in an Old Country: The National Past in Contemporary Britain
Patrick Wright

May Alice Savidge was "a bit fed up" when the authorities insisted that her house was in the way of urban redevelopment. As she said, "they keep destroying everything." So Miss Savidge moved, and she moved her house with her. Piece by piece, she had it dismantled, shipped in eleven lorry loads to the coast of north Norfolk and rebuilt. In a most tangible way, Miss Savidge held on to her past.

While she may be somewhat unusual, her preoccupation with the past is not. In Britain, the past is the present too, an integral of everyday life. Why? What is it about the British past that makes it so dear to ordinary English men and women?

This is the question Patrick Wright explores in a series of thoughtful essays about his homeland. Wright was away from England for five years and when he returned in 1979, he says, "I felt as if I had stumbled inadvertently into some sort of anthropological museum . . . I had come back to a country which was full of precious and imperilled traces—a closely held iconography of what it is to be English—all of them appealing in one covertly projective way or another to the historical and sacrosanct identity of the nation."

On Living in an Old Country assesses the bonds that hold a nation together, the shared experiences that differentiate it from its neighbors. It is a reflective book, one that enables the reader to view contemporary Britain through the prism of history.

(Verso, London, from Pantheon/Schocken, 1985, ISBN 0-86091-127-6, hardcover, 262 pages, $25.50)

The Radiant Way
Margaret Drabble

The Radiant Way is a plunge into today's England, a visit to a country that dreams of past glory while struggling with modern reality. It is "a radar-like penetration of the era we're still living through," says the *Daily Mail* of London, and "should be put in a time capsule for the benefit of future historians."

The Radiant Way, of course, is also a novel—a curl-up-in-bed, identify-with-the-characters sort of novel. It's the story of three mid-fortyish women, chums from college days, trying to cope with men, government budget cuts, AIDS, race riots, not-quite-adult children, murders, strikes, divorce—with the England of Margaret Thatcher, in other words.

The action begins with the lavish New Year's Eve party given by Liz Headland, successful psychotherapist, mother of five, the woman-who-has everything. The party is nothing fancy, just 200 guests: some friends of her children and step-children (to provide a mixture of ages), all five men she's slept with, and "a few publishers and poets and novelists, with an actress or two, with a clutch of psychologists and psychotherapists and art historians and civil servants and lawyers and extremely quarrelsome politicians." And there are some friends of her husband: Fleet Street journalists, television moguls, and the woman he's planning to marry.

Her two long-time friends are also present: Alex Bowen, crusader, trying to save the world and, for starters, teaching English literature to female prisoners; and Ester Breuer, arty and a bit eccentric, supporting herself by giving lectures on the Italian Renaissance.

So there it is—December 31, 1979. Ring out the old, bring in the new. A new decade, new opportunities, new beginnings, new problems: "A soap opera," says *Time* Magazine, "grafted onto a newsreel."

(Knopf, 1987, ISBN 0-394-56143-0, hardcover, 408 pages, $18.95)

The Selling of the Royal Family: The Mystique of the British Monarchy
John Pearson

For the British monarchy "its mystery is its life. We must not let in daylight upon magic," observed theorist and journalist Walter Bagehot over a hundred years ago. In the years since, the Royal Family has followed his advice, retaining a mystique and prestige unparalleled in other European countries.

Author John Pearson, former reporter and columnist for the *Sunday Times* of London, shows that their success is no accident. He begins his tale with Queen Mary, "the mainstay and mentor of the Royal House of Windsor," continues it through the wedding of Prince Charles and Princess Di and stops just short of Prince Andrew's marriage to Sarah Ferguson. Throughout the narrative he reveals how the British Royal Family keeps itself in the public eye, carefully avoiding overexposure, constantly changing its cast of characters, and providing a ready focus for a country eager to witness the tradition and the ceremony, the shock and the scandal.

Along the way he presents a captivating combination of fact and, most likely, gossip. As Pearson admits, the words of Cyril Connolly strongly apply: "Those who tell don't know; those who know don't tell." Much of what Pearson recounts is familiar—the drama of Edward VIII's abdication, the coronation of Queen Elizabeth, the ill-fated romance of Princess Margaret and Peter Townsend, the speculation surrounding Prince Charles's choice of a mate, and the worldwide infatuation with his eventual bride, Lady Diana Spencer—but he looks at these events from a different perspective, seeing them through the lens of Media Man.

His story is fascinating if not new, and it highlights the overwhelming importance of the Monarchy in a country where the queen, according to Enoch Powell, "is not a crowned president [but] a supernatural element."

(Jove, 1986, ISBN 0-515-09276-2, softcover, 334 pages, $4.50)

The Very Best of British
Nicholas Courtney

"It is confidence that sets [them] apart," says Nicholas Courtney, speaking of the British upper classes. "It's a state of mind . . . Money and power may largely have departed, but style remains; style teetering on the edge of vulgarity yet rarely tumbling over."

In this tongue-in-cheek guide to the British elite, Courtney provides insider's information as to what to do, what to wear when you do it, what to say, and to whom to say it. For example, there's the weighty matter of having your portrait painted. The first consideration is "when" (the light is best in the morning); second is "why" (several reasons here—perhaps the most important is the old family tradition of portraiture); and next is "by whom" (do you prefer a safe and sure "classicist" or would you be better off investing in an "innovative?")

The decisions, of course, continue: "how" (truly important people give many sittings because in the peace of the studio the telephone never rings), "what to wear" (suits of armour or angels' wings are out, undress for females is acceptable), and "what to serve at the hanging" (the best champagne, of course).

Courtney speaks as the true insider that he is, having been an estate manager in the hunt country of Leicestershire. He knows about country house tennis, shooting grouse, attending a gallery opening, and having tea at the House of Lords; and here he tells all. Whimsical cartoons by John Ireland lend added charm.

"Life as practised by the British upper classes is indeed elegant and correct," he says. "To some it may also appear vapid, artificial and socially irresponsible, but that, the British upper classes will explain, is a misapprehension based on jealousy. How could it not be, since the life led by the British upper classes is the Very Best of British?"

(St. Martin's Press, 1986, ISBN 0-312-83884-0, hardcover, 158 pages, $12.95)

ANTHROPOLOGY AND ARCHAEOLOGY

The Druids
Stuart Piggott

Dawn breaks over Stonehenge. A stately procession of white-robed men and women chant and worship around a rose and a flaming copper globe. History and imagination become entwined as modern Druids, a people steeped in myth and mystery, celebrate the Summer Solstice in the same way as they believe their ancestors did.

"Who [were] these Ancient People?" asks archaeology professor Stuart Piggott, recipient of the coveted Gold Medal award from the Society of Antiquaries. The answer "involves archaeology and ancient history; literary sources in classical and Celtic languages; the history of ideas and of literary and artistic fashions . . . It is bedevilled with almost unbelievably fatuous speculations and fantasies, and shot through and through with Moonbeams from the Larger Lunacy."

Druids, explains Piggott, claim unbroken descent from the Celtic priests of pre-Roman Gaul and Britain. He traces their history from these long-ago days, through their banning by Tiberius and Claudius "for superstitions and human sacrifices," and on to the 1908 initiation of the young Winston Churchill into the Ancient Order of the Druids. He takes us with him as he travels to the archaeological digs of ancient Gaul, reads the classical texts and examines the changing image of the Druids as reflected in art and literature.

The Druids delves into the story of a people who are an integral part of English folklore and who have "achieved a place in the average Englishman's mind as part of his heritage." Through this clear overview accompanied by 130 illustrations, Piggott brings into a focus an important part of English prehistory.

(Thames and Hudson, 1975, ISBN 0-500-27363-4, softcover, 214 pages, $11.95)

Pillar of the Sky
Cecilia Holland

Moloquin dreamt he stood on the open land, and before him was the embankment of the Pillar in the Sky, but instead of the sad untidy circle of stones, he saw within the circle of the bank a wonderful ring of great uprights . . . rising up toward Heaven.

Thus begins Cecilia Holland's tale of a demon-driven man leading his people on a colossal undertaking—Stonehenge. Beginning with Molonquin's ostracized childhood as "the unwanted," the novel depicts the clash of the resolute dreamer and the realities of life on the primeval Salisbury Plain. As Molonquin first instructs the Salmon Leap Society to shape the huge obdurate blocks and later provisions the workers with food supplies at the Pillar of the Sky, Holland recreates the difficulties of antiquity in the land that would become England. Her epic touches on disparate areas as she discusses everyday hardships and the wonders of metal as well as the political trials and engineering breakthroughs.

A masterful storyteller herself, Holland sees Stonehenge "as a piece of story, in an age when stories were the greatest power that people could bring to deal with the whirling universe around them." It is, she says, "an era that is on us still."

(Ballantine, 1985, ISBN 0-345-3336-5, softcover, 534 pages, $9.95)

Prehistoric Avebury
Aubrey Burl

The stone circles of Avebury "as much excel Stonehenge as a Cathedral does a parish church," wrote John Aubrey in the seventeenth century. Yet, while a list of books and articles about Stonehenge can easily run to over a hundred pages, comparatively little has been written about Avebury. Now Aubrey Burl, British archaeologist and professor of prehistory, has begun to remedy this situation:

How old is Avebury? How was it built? What techniques were used to heave stones over fifty tons in mass-weight upright? How was a ditch ten metres deep dug into rock-hard chalk? Which people built Avebury? What do we know, not only of their way of life, the places where they lived, the tools they used, but of the people themselves, what they looked like, how long they lived? And, in conclusion . . . what was Avebury used for?

Even with the wealth of archaeological and historical evidence that is available, Burl admits "it is like trying to touch shadows to see in the dark the people who have gone and who left no word or sound behind them . . . [They] lived in a world where reality and the imaginary reflected against each other like the shimmering of crystals." Burl considers, and largely discounts, theories of astronomical use; he feels the primary function of the circles was most likely to serve as performance areas for rituals of death and regeneration.

Generously illustrated with drawings and photos, both color and black-and-white, the book probes the mysteries of Avebury in a highly readable yet responsibly scientific way. Burl describes the design and construction of Avebury's multiple circles and earthworks and takes the reader back nearly five thousand years to explore the lives and beliefs of those who built a monument "equal to any of the noted wonders of the world."

(Yale, 1979, ISBN 0-300-03622-1, softcover, 275 pages, $12.95)

Stonehenge Complete
Christopher Chippindale

For centuries the collection of mysterious monoliths rising from the Salisbury Plain has stirred the imagination of visitors. Scientists have made measurements of Stonehenge and formed theories about its construction and use; artists have immortalized it in every known medium; writers have composed volumes analyzing its structure, admiring its ingenuity, and chronicling its history.

Christopher Chippindale, research fellow in archaeology at Cambridge, here brings together "everything important, interesting or odd that has been written or painted, discovered or imagined, about the most extraordinary ancient building in the world." A formidable task to be sure, but Chippindale is equal to it.

He begins with the first known written mention of Stonehenge. Translated from the Latin and dating from about 1130, it conveys the awe that Stonehenge always inspires: "Stanenges, where stones of wonderful size have been erected after the manner of doorways, so that doorway appears to have been raised upon doorway; and no one can conceive how such great stones have been so raised aloft, or why they were built there."

British architect Inigo Jones in the seventeenth century was equally amazed: "Who cast their Eyes upon this Antiquity, and examine the same with Judgment, must be enforced to confess it erected by People, grand Masters of the Art of Building, and liberal Sciences, whereof the ancient *Britains* utterly ignorant, as a Nation wholly addicted to Wars, never applying themselves to the Study of Arts, or troubling their thoughts with any Excellency."

The book is lavishly illustrated with a mind-boggling array of Stonehenge portraits, from scientific renderings and surrealistic paintings to an advertising photograph that inserts a monolithic cigarette pack into the structure. **Stonehenge Complete** is an impressive work of research, comprehensive and informative. Moreover, it is a great deal of fun.

(Cornell, 1983, ISBN 0-8014-9451-6, softcover, oversized, 296 pages, $24.95)

Wiltshire Village
Heather and Robin Tanner

Let Heather and Robin Tanner introduce you to the village of Kington Borel. Heather's text and Robin's meticulous line drawings, you must be aware, are the *only* means of meeting the townspeople and wandering the narrow, winding streets—for Kington Borel is fictitious, a composite of several villages in Wiltshire in the south of England. Yet this record of the imaginary town's customs and characters is an accurate reflection of life in Wiltshire at the time the book was first published, some fifty years ago.

You'll meet Joseph Gingell, thatcher, whose livelihood is disappearing as fire regulations mandate new roofing materials, and who has given up hope of seeing his son take up his trade. And you'll talk with Abel Wootton, basketmaker, who'll tell you about the long process of cutting, seasoning, and peeling the withies from which he forms bushel baskets. Wagon-makers, wheelwrights, blacksmiths, and sawyers—they all speak of their trades, imparting their secrets before automation renders the crafts, and the workmen, obsolete.

The Tanners also lead a tour through the countryside, pointing out the flowers that bloom in profusion: buttercups and moondaisies and sorrel, summer snowflake and lilies-of-the-valley and henbane. Then there are the birds, waking the villagers in the early hours of dawn: cuckoos and blackbirds and robins, corncrakes and thrushes and woodpeckers.

You also will learn of customs, like the "woosetting" to which an adulterous couple would be subjected. "The guilty pair were serenaded with a loud beating and rattling of pots and pans . . . The ceremony that followed savoured more of tribal witchcraft than of Christian England: the effigies of the two delinquents, that had been carried round in the procession, were solemnly burned."

Wiltshire Village is, as *House and Garden* says, a "delightful evocation of English rural life." It is a siren call not only to a gentler past but also, if you have the imagination, to a spot of enchantment: "a place where the bumblebees are called dumbledores, and even the men are Moonrakers."

(Impact Books, London, from Cupress Ltd., 1987, ISBN 0-245-54416-X, softcover, 179 pages, $13.95)

ART AND ARCHITECTURE

British Art Since 1900
Frances Spalding

"Twentieth-century British art represents, like many English gardens, an enclosed world which holds our attention, not so much through its immediate impact but through the slow revelation of the subtlety and complexity of species contained within it," says Frances Spalding as she prepares to lead us down the meandering pathways of modern British art.

Spalding, art critic and historian, opens with the "studied elegance" of the Edwardians before moving on to Post Impressionism which, as she says, marked the real beginnings of modern art. "A painting," she explains, "was now to have a vitality that was no mere reflection of external reality but inherent."

The following years were varied and exciting. The '20s were "a period of retrenchment, recovery and individual endeavour"; the '30s became more "progressive and dedicated to communal effort"; the '40s combined the English landscape tradition and Surrealism during the War years and experimented with "realism and angst" in the post-war era; the '50s marked a return to abstraction; and the '60s and '70s moved toward conceptualism and post-modernism. Spalding finds that "British art of this century is outstanding for its range of interest and style. A leaning toward the romantic and particular, the fanatical and self-obsessed can be discerned, but sufficient contradictions exist to keep talk of national characteristics at bay."

Spalding discusses sculpture and printmaking as well as painting, op and pop art. Her book is a concise overview, emphasizing major trends and placing art in the context of historical events. It contains 211 illustrations, fifty in full color, and a listing that gives the location of each work. **British Art Since 1900** is a most pleasant stroll through a delightful and diverse English garden.

(Thames and Hudson, 1986, ISBN 0-500-20204-4, softcover, 252 pages, $9.95)

British Design Since 1880: A Visual History
Fiona MacCarthy

British design is solid. Functional. Purposeful. And it works. It is based on the idea that "consistent standards are both practically possible and morally desirable, that design solutions can be measured against a sense of idea rightness, both functional and aesthetic," explains author Fiona MacCarthy.

In this light she begins her overview of a century of British design with an eclectic list of the ten most typically British designs of the past century. They include two pieces of fabric, three pieces of furniture, a radio cabinet, a piece of pottery, and a high speed train. Practical? Assuredly. But also handsome and stylish.

Through detailed text and an abundance of photographs, some in full color, McCarthy isolates the major influences on British design and weaves them into identifiable patterns. In addition, she provides a brief list of places—museums, galleries, archives, salesrooms, and historic houses—where British design can be viewed in context. "There is no substitute for looking at the thing before you," she says. True, but her book is a worthwhile vicarious experience—or, better yet, a preparation.

(Lund Humphries, London, from Humanities, 1982, ISBN 85331-447-0, softcover, oversized, 229 pages, $15.00)

English Architecture: A Concise History
David Watkin

A nation's history can be seen in its architectural structures by those knowledgeable enough to read the stones and mortar of its text. David Watkin, considered one of Britain's most brilliant younger architectural historians, is such a man. Thoroughly conversant with both history and architecture, he intertwines the disciplines and discusses, clearly albeit briefly, English buildings through the ages.

Beginning with the early structures of Anglo-Saxon and Norman times, Watkin moves through the centuries, for the most part stopping only at presently existing buildings. He studies grand Gothic cathedrals and impressive Tudor and Jacobean country houses, examines influential designs of Inigo Jones and Christopher Wren, gazes at the changes wrought by the Classical Revival, looks at Victorian architecture, and only rests when he reaches the buildings of the Modern Movement.

In each chapter he discusses characteristics of style, influences from outside England, and outstanding examples of the period. All are presented in the context of the social and political situation of the time and amply illustrated with black-and-white photographs and drawings. He avoids technical terminology, appending a glossary to explain the occasional unfamiliar term. His book is exactly what its title states: a concise history of English architecture.

(Thames and Hudson, 1979, ISBN 0-500-020171-4, softcover, 216 pages, $9.95)

English Painting: A Concise History
William Gaunt

"The general character of English painting is defined for us by the work of great individuals," states William Gaunt in the introduction to his overview of English painting. Those great individuals are ably represented: Hogarth, Gainsborough, Constable, Turner, and Blake among a host of other artists, both well-known and obscure. In highly readable text and 222 illustrations, forty-one of which are in full color, Gaunt presents the best and most representative examples of English painting from the Middle Ages to the present.

Placing the works in their historical settings, he shows the relative influence of other countries upon English art and emphasizes the clear separation of styles from one era to the next, as they alternated between conservatism and "individual ascents into freedom of expression." Yet overall, Gaunt sees a unity in English painting, one which links, "despite many transformations, the present with the past."

His book is a brief tour through the centuries and provides what *Art Review* calls "a highly informative though concise history which is illuminated both by a sensitive critical approach and a vast . . . knowledge of the historical background."

(Thames and Hudson, 1978, ISBN 0-500-20016-5, softcover, 288 pages, $9.95)

English Style
Suzanne Slesin and Stafford Cliff

Analyzing English style is as difficult as grabbing an octopus, and it has just about as many tentacles. One moment you think of it as something immensely grand and formal echoing our lost empires, the next, something comfortable, informal, and rather down at the heel. And then a stylish surprise, a terrifically elegant modern room with all the perfection and attention to detail that only the best designers can achieve.

These words by home-furnishings enterpreneur Terence Conran introduce **English Style**, a sumptuous survey of English interior design. Just as he states, everything is here: the formal, the comfortable, the elegant. Within these pages is a design tour of a vast range of English homes, a private showing to which you can return again and again.

There is the thatch-roofed cottage dating from the fifteenth century on the edge of the Cotswold region of central England—indeed, the oldest home in the village. It is owned by an architect and furnished with period antiques. Dinner guests are seated at an eighteenth-century refectory table under a beamed ceiling; the master bedroom is dominated by an intricately-carved four-poster bed, c. 1450, that belonged to Lord Stanley who "took the crown from Richard III and gave it to Henry Tudor."

Quite different in tone is a Chelsea residence designed in 1868 for a Victorian artist. This home has the "feel of a gracious country house" in the midst of a London neighborhood that was a "hotbed of artistic and literary activity" a century ago. The present owner restored the home to its original romantic ambiance. He decorated with overscale furnishings such as the dining room table and chairs that came from the boardroom of the Prudential Insurance Company, and used textiles by William Morris throughout the home. Antique lace covers one bed; a seventeenth-century embroidered cover and silk plush canopy grace another.

With chapters on town homes, flats and apartments, country houses and conversions, **English Style** beautifully describes and illustrates (with more than six hundred color photographs) just what it is that makes up "English Style."

(Potter, 1984, ISBN 0-517-55276-0, hardcover, oversized, 288 pages, $35.00)

Illustrated Handbook of Vernacular Architecture
R. W. Brunskill

England is rich in "everyday" buildings with colorful and eye-catching architectural modes: thatch-roofed cottages, timber walls infilled with wattle and daub, stone water mills, smithies and kilns. As interesting in its own way as the design of grandoise country manors or imposing cathedrals, this "vernacular" architecture is thoroughly but simply explained in R. W. Brunskill's delightful handbook.

There are chapters on walls (stone, flint, brick, timber, wattle and daub), roofs (hipped, gabled, single- and double-raftered), architectural details (windows, doors, ornamentation) and plan and section (the interior arrangement of rooms and the way this is often revealed on the exterior of the building). Separate chapters cover farm buildings and vernacular urban and minor industrial structures.

The book is designed to work well as a field manual, with photographs and short sections of descriptive text facing pages of diagrams with explanatory notes. Extensive appendices and a comprehensive bibliography provide information for further study.

Detailed but not forbiddingly technical, the book is written to "help the enthusiastic amateur to increase his own awareness of vernacular architecture." It is a fascinating approach that does just that.

(Faber and Faber, 1987, ISBN 0-571-13916-7, softcover, 256 pages, $12.95)

CUISINE

The Afternoon Tea Book
Michael Smith

Had Anna, seventh duchess of Bedford (1783 to 1857) in the very early years of the nineteenth century, not been incredibly greedy, afternoon tea as we knew it in England, and to some extent as we still know it today, might never have become our national habit.

With this tantalizing beginning Michael Smith, whom the *New York Times* has called "the doyen of English cookery," takes us on a tea-time trek through the very proper world of the British drawing room. Beginning with a brief history of tea-drinking in England, moving on to an explanation of essential ritual, and ending with a collection of "traditional tea-party tidbits," his book is a delightful ode to a not-so-distant past.

"A fireplace is an essential factor for an elegant afternoon tea," he says, "for where else would you toast muffins, crumpets, pikelets, or just plain bread? 'In a mechanical toaster,' you'll say, but that cuts out the romance of the occasion."

Of course, recipes for muffins, crumpets, and pikelets, as well as for muscatel-rum sandwiches and chelsea buns, are included. Of particular interest are the lettuce sandwiches, also "known as honeymoon sandwiches because they have a filling of lettuce (let us) alone." Why, how the Victorian ladies must have blushed behind their fans!

As Smith encourages us to taste the elegance of Afternoon Tea in our own homes, he reminds us that, elegant or not, tea drinking is a very British thing to do: "As you read this book, more than *20 million* cups of tea will be drunk in London alone—TODAY!"

(Atheneum, 1986, ISBN 0-689-11592-X, hardcover, 278 pages, $21.95)

British Cookery
Jane Grigson

Jane Grigson's **British Cookery** is far more than a collection of interesting, and often mouth-watering, recipes. It is a leisurely stroll through the cooking history of England, Ireland, Scotland, and Wales. Along the way there are conversations with farmers, grocers, restaurateurs, and chefs, all of whom offer nuggets of food lore as well as advice on where to find special ingredients and how to cook them.

We learn the cook's secret for Irish nettle soup:

In Joyce's Lives of the Saints, *he gave the story of . . . the saint [who] met an old woman picking nettles near his monastery, and asked her what she was doing that for. She said she was going to make nettle soup . . . He thought that if she could survive on so simple a diet, he could too. Nettles, oatmeal and water. The saint grew quite plump to everyone's surprise, and felt better than usual. He sent for the cook whose answers were evasive. Then he picked up the stick used for stirring the pot, and found it was hollowed out so that the cook could slip milk into the soup without anyone noticing.*

Grigson recommends a trip to the Lion Salt Works at Northwich. While there, she says, "you may also visit Arley Hall where the inhumanly energetic Mrs. Raffald [shares] ideas for sousing turkey and salting chops." Raffald's recipe for "Egg and Bacon Pie" is included.

The full-color photos of food, food factories, fields, markets, and country folk are outstanding; and if instructions to "put your sauce in a Bain Marie" are bewildering, a glance at the extensive glossary will clear up the confusion. And if you've a craving for Dittisham Plums, fear not; a Consumer Guide contains the names and addresses of food suppliers. Jane Grigson has thought of everything.

(Atheneum, 1984, ISBN 0-689-11524-5, hardcover, oversized, 232 pages, $24.95)

Great New British Cooking
Jane Garmey

When rumors of a "new British cuisine" reached the ears of author Jane Garmey, she began to investigate. Turning aside from the subject of her previous book, *Great British Cooking: A Well Kept Secret*, in which she paid homage to traditional English food, Garmey began a search that led her to some of England's greatest restaurants and most charming country inns. There she discovered that there had indeed been a "considerable change of culinary climate" in Britain.

This practical and entertaining book, the result of Garmey's findings, presents a French-inspired "nouvelle Anglaise cuisine" that combines the goodness of traditional English cooking with the best in innovative preparation. For example, there is the unusual "Turnip Colcannon," an Irish version of the English dish "Bubble and Squeak," so named for the sounds produced when the potatoes and cabbage are fried in hot oil. And even the most humble apple waxes exotic when prepared as "Apple Tart with Calvados, Brown Sugar and Tarragon," a delectable dessert which "presents slices of apple lying on a puree of apples and fresh puff pastry."

Each recipe is introduced with the dish's history or with information about the British restaurant or inn where the original dish can be sampled. It is this last feature that qualifies the book to double as a unique restaurant guide to some of Britain's most outstanding gourmet meals. According to Garmey, this is precisely what she has in mind: "My hope is not only that readers will be encouraged to try out some of these recipes but also that this book will lead them to many of the hotels and restaurants mentioned when next they visit Britain."

(Simon and Schuster, 1985, ISBN 0-671-53258-8, hardcover, 243 pages, $16.95)

Harrods Book of Traditional English Cookery
Hilary Walden

Think of England and you think of Harrods, the quintessentially British store known for quality and elegant understatement. Here, carrying that most illustrious name, is a cookbook that simply overflows with good taste (pun most definitely intended!). **Traditional English Cookery** is comfortable in size (8" x 8"), lovely to feel (heavy, semi-glossy paper), and delicious to look at (beautiful full-color pictures, pages nicely bordered).

Hilary Walden, author of eleven cookbooks, intersperses bits of English culinary history:

Until the sixteenth century and the Reformation the eating of fish on Fridays and other designated holy days was obligatory on religious grounds. After that, the State joined in and passed laws stating that fish only and not meat, should be eaten on Saturdays as well as Fridays—there was even an attempt to make Wednesday a fish-only day as well—to stimulate the fishing industry and in turn the shipbuilding industry and thus—with these industries—maintain England's prestige as a seafaring nation.

She also gives historical background for many of her recipes. She includes, for example, "Water-Souchy," a light fish stew named after the Belgian *waterzootje* and thus reminiscent of "the strong links that existed between England and the Low Countries from Tudor Times." And there is "Douce Ame," a chicken dish "based upon one that appeared in the 'Forme of Cury,' one of the earliest collections of manuscript recipes, written about 1390 by Richard II's cooks." (Even for these recipes of fourteenth-century origin, Walden makes sure that the ingredients and methods are appropriate for today's kitchens.)

Soups and light dishes, fish and shellfish, meat, roasts, poultry and game, vegetables, puddings, cakes and biscuits, traditional accompaniments—all are given their due in this delightful book. And in case you want the perfect settings for your meals, the china, cutlery, and menu cards displayed in the photos are all available from Harrods!

(Arbor House, 1987, ISBN 0-87795-839-4, hardcover, 96 pages, $12.50)

FOLKTALES

The Discovery of King Arthur
Geoffrey Ashe

"A conspicuous feature of Arthur's rebirth today is the interest in British legend in the United States," says Geoffrey Ashe in **The Discovery of King Arthur.** Arthurian novels have become American best-sellers and Arthurian travel tours are being sponsored by American universities. Why this interest in a figure commonly believed to be a mere myth? Perhaps, says Ashe, because "Arthur's kingdom embodies the notion of a far-away golden age." Indeed, to many people the story of King Arthur has become synonymous with the birth, or rebirth, of a better society—hence, for example, the "Camelot" image of John F. Kennedy.

The influence of the alleged fifth-century hero cannot be disputed. "But what about the real King Arthur?" questions Ashe. Was he, in fact, a real historical person? The answer, according to Ashe, is a resounding yes. He has rejected the standard method of looking into contemporary historical records to prove his theory. Rather, he says, "Arthur's legend itself must be brought back into the investigation . . . It must be sifted for clues. The right questions [are not] Who was Arthur? or Did he exist? but Where did the legend come from? and What facts is it rooted in? If we line up the legend side by side with history . . . the problem can be solved."

Aided by numerous pictures of Arthurian-related artifacts and places, such as the purported "Round Table" from Winchester Castle, Ashe reveals the facts behind the fiction and the history behind the myth. Yet he never dispels the magic of the legendary figure on whose tomb at Glastonbury Sir Thomas Malory, author of *Le Morte d'Arthur,* claims to have seen written, "Here lies Arthur, King that was, King that shall be."

(Anchor/Doubleday, 1985, ISBN 0-385-19032-8, hardcover, 226 pages, $18.95)

Folk Heroes of Britain
Charles Kightly

"Heroes attract myths as inevitably as magnets attract iron-filings; but just as the filings will eventually conceal the magnet, so at last the hero may be totally obscured by the myths," says Charles Kightly, author of **Folk Heroes of Britain**. The purpose of his book, then, is to look behind the fiction that surrounds many of the major heroes of England, Scotland, and Wales and to discover their historical cores.

Some of the heroes presented here are well-known, like the tenth-century King Alfred the Great. According to Anglo-Saxon legend, Alfred once hid from the Danes in the house of a cowherd. While there he became distracted and let the cakes burn, an act for which he was strongly rebuked by the cowherd's wife. (She apparently had no idea that her culinarily inept visitor was of royal blood!) Popular stories such as this, Kightly shows, may cause people to overlook Alfred's more important actions. He was, after all, a "formidable general and an unrivalled war-leader."

Other heroes, equally brave, are less famous. Followers of nursery rhymes may be surprised to learn that "Old King Cole" who was a "merry old soul" was in reality Old Coel the Splendid, the third-century "Founding Father of the North" who ruled in Scotland after the end of Roman Britain.

Kightly explains how these men and women attained mythical status. In many cases, he says, they were champions of the underdog in battles against Romans, Danes, Normans, and various other oppressing groups. As such, their heroic exploits in defense of a losing cause were elevated to the realm of legend.

Tales about these folk heroes have been passed down through the ages, but as Kightly says, "the real people on whom they were based [have become] increasingly difficult to discern: this book, it is hoped, will do something to restore them to their rightful place in history."

(Thames and Hudson, 1982, ISBN 0-500-27325-1, softcover, 208 pages, $10.95)

Haunted England: Royal Spirits, Castle Ghosts, Phantom Coaches, and Viking Ghouls
Terence Whitaker

"Either a large number of people have been victims of some kind of delusion—or ghosts really do exist," says spook-sayer Terence Whitaker, a man who is quite obviously comfortable with ghostly friends.

Here he creeps across England, chasing through ancient castles and ruined abbeys in search of silent, shadowy figures from the past. Ghosts, he finds, have different personalities. Emily Brontë's, for example, is a rather sweet little thing. Always smiling and giggling, she dresses in a crinoline and carries a wicker basket for her yearly appearances on the anniversary of her death.

Not so the ghost of Anne Boleyn, the second of Henry VIII's wives. This spiritual specter even caused one poor man to be court-martialed. It seems, relates Whitaker, that a guard in the Tower of London was found unconscious one morning in 1864. Accused of sleeping while on duty, he defended himself by stating he'd seen a strange white figure wandering through the early morning mist. In an attempt to do his duty he pointed his bayonet—and the body walked right through it. A flash of fire ran up his rifle barrel. The guard passed out.

His story was confirmed by other sentries who had seen the apparition. The court, upon learning that the ghost has appeared just below the room where Anne Boleyn had waited for her execution in 1536, cleared the guard—innocent by reason of phantasmagoria!

Whitaker provides anecdotal evidence for his eerie tales; and while many are somewhat abbreviated, they cast a deliciously spooky atmosphere over the foggy byways of England's past. Many, though not all, of the haunted locations are open to the public.

(Contemporary Books, 1987, ISBN 0-8092-4646-5, softcover, 222 pages, $9.95)

HISTORY

Daily Life in Johnson's London
Richard B. Schwartz

Bedbugs amongst your bedclothes? Call Andrew Cooke, first-rate exterminator. He rids over 800 beds of insects each year. Satisfaction guaranteed. Traveling from Ingatestone to London? Try walking. It's faster than coach and only fifty miles. Need money? Maim your children. It'll increase their success as beggars . . .

Eighteenth-century London was often explosive, repellent, brutal, and savage. It was also fascinating, a magnet for the intelligentsia. "You find no man, at all intellectual, who is willing to leave London," said Samuel Johnson in 1777. "No, Sir, when a man is tired of London, he is tired of life; for there is in London all that life can afford."

Richard B. Schwartz, Professor of English and Dean of the Graduate School at Georgetown University, uses London's most famous citizen and most articulate defender as a focus to examine the city in the vibrant period of the 1700s. "Johnson is an inseparable part of eighteenth-century London," he says. "[He] was there at a time of important change. He nearly spans the century and combines a love of the past, of history, and of tradition, with a keen and youthful eye on the future . . . He knows the worlds of the titled, the grand, the great, the rich, the squierarchy, the middle class, the industrious and the not-so-industrious poor, the desperate, and all the gradations in between them."

Here are cock-fights and brothels, hospitals and prisons, theatres, museums, and churches. Here is an uncensored London, dynamic and diverse. Schwartz captures the sights, sounds and, yes, even the smells in a small book that is educational and, at the same time, vastly entertaining.

(University of Wisconsin, 1983, ISBN 0-299-09494-4, softcover, 196 pages, $9.95)

A History of London
Robert Gray

London, says Robert Gray, "is an acquired pleasure, a town that invites discovery rather than demands admiration." With this in mind he assists the modern reader in discovering the panorama of London's history, using as his theme the city's gradual expansion from the inner core "City" of medieval times.

He begins with the early days when the Roman legions erected a bridge across the Thames and thus created a port for Continental traffic. The pivotal acts of Edward the Confessor who, in the eleventh century, rebuilt Westminster Abbey and established the seat of government on the Isle of Thorney are part of the narrative, as are details of the rise of Puritanism, the Plague, the Great Fire of 1666, and the World War II bombings.

In each era Gray paints London's portrait with honesty and candor. For instance, during the years between 1500 and 1650, which were the commercial high point of London's history, he describes the vibrant atmosphere on the Thames: "'A man would say, that seeth the shipping there,' wrote a contemporary, 'that it is, as it were, a very wood of trees . . . so shaded it is with masts and sails.'" But he also points out this same Thames "stank to such a degree that the Venetian ambassador complained that its 'odour remains even in clean linen.'"

The characters in his drama are the humble as well as the famous, the peasants as well as the kings, the ignoble as well as the noble. In fact, says Gray, "anyone coming to London instantly becomes a member of this mighty company; surely he will enjoy himself the more for some prior knowledge of the plot."

(Taplinger, 1978, ISBN 0-8008-3885-8, softcover, 352 pages, $7.95)

An Illustrated History of England
John Burke

"Two factors shaped England's political development," writes Sir Arthur Bryant in his introduction to John Burke's history of England. "One was the strong, unifying rule of her Norman and Angevin kings and the native Tudors who followed them . . . The other was the libertarian instinct of her people . . . which made it increasingly difficult for her kings to rule them without 'counsel and consent.'"

By basing his book on these broad concepts, Burke has produced a history that is more than just an account of the succession of kings and queens, more than a chronicle of battles and treaties. He spins a thread that connects events into trends, weaving in the parts played by politicians and soldiers, artists and craftspeople, scientists, and the "ordinary" men and women of England.

Enlivened by a multitude of illustrations, both black-and-white and full color, Burke's text moves briskly through the entire panorama of English history, from the Stone Age through nuclear-weapons protests in the early 1980s. It is an excellent overview and a resource to refer to again and again.

(Collins, London, from Salem House Ltd., 1985, ISBN 0-00-217535-5, hardcover, 382 pages, $19.95)

No. 10 Downing Street: The Story of a House
Christopher Jones

No. 10 Downing Street is the sort of house that makes you wish walls could talk. For over 250 years it's been the home, off and on, to the "demi-gods and goddesses of British politics." Sir Robert Walpole was the first notable to live there, moving in on September 22, 1735, and displacing a "mere mortal" named, most aptly perhaps, Mr. Chicken.

Other famous politicos followed: Disraeli, Gladstone, Balfour, Baldwin, Chamberlain, Churchill, Attlee, Macmillan, Wilson, and Callaghan, among others. "This place seeps into your blood," says Margaret Thatcher. "It becomes part of your life. It is, above all, a home—and it is a house of history."

BBC Parliamentary Correspondent Christopher Jones gives a delightful history of the house and its surroundings, beginning with a brief coverage of the area as it was in the eleventh century, long before Downing Street existed and the heretofore obscure Mr. Chicken was born.

"The man who gave his name to Britain's most famous, most respectable, most desirable address was," we learn, "an infamous, treacherous turncoat." Somehow, says Jones, young George Downing "wormed his way into the confidence of Oliver Cromwell himself, and in 1649 became the Commonwealth's Scoutmaster General in Scotland. A less delicate title would have been Cromwell's master spy." Downing married well, became a Member of Parliament, practiced blackmail, amassed a fortune, built houses on the street that would bear his name, let his mother die a near-pauper, and was imprisoned in the Tower of London.

Jones, aided by numerous photographs (some of which are in full color) and a sprinkling of architectural drawings, tells the story of this scoundrel and others as he presents history from a unique perspective. His book is the next best thing to talking walls.

(British Broadcasting Corporation, London, from Salem House Ltd., 1985, ISBN 0-563-20441-9, hardcover, 192 pages, $18.95)

Now I Remember: A Holiday History of Britain
Ronald Hamilton

English history is full of Williams and Richards and Henrys, plus all the Georges, I through VI. Of course, there are a few Marys and Elizabeths too.

If, like many of us, you find that these names tend to blur, **Now I Remember** is just the book you need. Its object is "not to *teach* but to *remind*," says author Ronald Hamilton, who is firmly convinced that "we have all been taught History, the trouble is that we have all forgotten. We go about the countryside, we look at churches, castles and houses . . . but we find ourselves saying: 'Who was on the throne then?'; 'How did Henry IV succeed Richard II?'; 'What *was* Henry VII's claim to the crown, and who *were* the Beauforts?'"

This book aims to answer these questions, to remind us of facts that were once familiar. Hamilton arranges history under architectural periods—Norman, Early English, Decorated, Perpendicular, Tudor, Elizabethan, Jacobean, Stuart, Georgian, Victorian, Twentieth Century—so that as we travel around the country looking at ancient buildings, we can relate architecture to history.

Now I Remember is thumbnail history, quick sketches designed to refresh the memory. Each section begins with a short (one to two paragraphs) explanation of the architecture and follows with brief biographical sketches of each monarch who presided during the period and the historical events that took place during his or her reign. Black-and-white photos and small line drawings show the architecture, furniture, and costume of the era.

The sales blurb on the front cover promises "All the English history you'll ever need." While it's true some may *want* more detailed coverage, this small book definitely allows the traveler to see England with the perspective and understanding afforded by history.

(Chatto & Windus, London, from Salem House Ltd., 1983, ISBN 0-7011-2669-8, softcover, 224 pages, $7.95)

Sarum: The Novel of England
Edward Rutherfurd

Take one aspiring author who was born in the history-rich area of England's Salisbury Plain. Give this author two pounds of admiration for James Michener and enough common sense to know that you always write about what you know best. The result? A panoramic saga about the South of England, with most of the strengths and weaknesses of a Michener blockbuster.

Rutherfurd focuses on several families: the Wilsons, a group of thieves and smugglers who through the years represent England's low-life; the Masons (named after their trade) who hark back to Nooma, a stonecutter helping with the mysterious Stonehenge, and his descendent who works on the Salisbury Cathedral; the Shockleys, whose members range from a Saxon warrior princess to a nineteenth-century feminist, and . . . You get the idea.

The land bridge to Europe disappears in a great flood, the Church gains and loses power, the system of English law is developed, monarchs come and go, wars are won and lost, generation follows generation. Beginning with the Paleolithic hunter of the Ice Age and ending with modern-day residents of today's England, **Sarum** offers a telescoped, fascinating, fictionalized, and factual overview of English history.

(Ivy Books/Ballantine, ISBN 0-8041-0298-8, softcover, 1038 pages, $5.95)

A Social History of England
Asa Briggs

"The dairymaid ought to be faithful and of good repute," states Walter of Henley in a thirteenth-century text on stewardship and husbandry.

"Servants are necessary for the preparation of lavish meals and for the keeping of a proper Victorian household," expounds Isabella Briggs in her 1861 *Book of Household Management*.

Asa Briggs (no relation) introduces us to many such experts on convention in his **Social History of England**, a comprehensive guide through the centuries which begins with the Romans and continues to Margaret

Thatcher. "Social history is the history of society," he explains. "It is concerned with structures and with processes of change. Nothing is irrelevant to it."

Briggs is intrigued with the rhythms of life, with the poetry in the story. He concentrates less on great events themselves than on the way in which those events affect people. For example, his discussion of World War I describes not the politics, not the battles, but the "industrial pressure" that led many children, even those under the age of fourteen, to work. This caused traditional discipline to slacken and gave youngsters more spending money. Therefore, one of the results of World War I was that it was more difficult than ever to "keep the home fires burning," he explains.

Through village and city, factory and field, war and peace, work and prayer, Briggs looks at the English people and at the forces shaping their lives. Accompanied by a plethora of full-color plates, line drawings and maps, this text illuminates "the experience of people who left no name behind them," as well as that of the people in power.

"The longer you look back, the farther you can look forward," wrote Winston Churchill. Briggs makes looking back a pleasure, and by helping us understand the past he helps us see the future.

(Penguin, 1983, ISBN 0-14-007492-9, softcover, oversized, 320 pages, $9.95)

LITERATURE

A D.H. Lawrence Album
George Hardy and Nathaniel Harris

Even more than most writers, D. H. Lawrence used his own life as the raw material of his fiction. His novels and stories are crowded with descriptions of places he knew, characters he had met, and incidents that had actually occurred . . . The materials Lawrence used most exhaustively—and most directly of all—were taken . . . from Eastwood, the Nottinghamshire mining town where he was born, and from the countryside he loved so much.

These people and places are brought vividly to life by George Hardy and Nathaniel Harris in their definitive pictorial record of Lawrence's early years. Lawrence's work often mimicked reality so closely, says Harris, that "he was lucky not to face actions for libel. (Such an action was in fact threatened by the husband of his friend Alice Hall, whom Lawrence put into *The White Peacock*, absurdly under-disguised as 'Alice Gall.')"

Well over a hundred photographs, collected by George Hardy and captioned with quotations from Lawrence's writings, depict people and locales that Lawrence immortalized in his works. For example, a gamekeeper's hut in High Park is almost certainly the one described in *Lady Chatterley's Lover*. "As she came out of the wood on the north side, the keeper's cottage, a rather dark, brown stone cottage, with gables and a handsome chimney, looked uninhabited, it was so silent and alone." Lawrence, as this album shows, preserved this past with amazing accuracy, using it when it suited his needs, diverging from it "when his art or vision demanded it."

(Franklin Watts, 1985, ISBN 0-531-15013-4, hardcover, 155 pages, $15.95)

Dickens's England
Tony Lynch

"I never knew an author's death to cause such general mourning. It is no exaggeration to say that this whole country is stricken with grief," said Longfellow upon learning of Charles Dickens's death in 1870. Already a world-famous author at the time of his passing, Dickens continues to enjoy popularity with each new generation.

Now fans can explore the England of his youth, aided by this fact-filled gazetteer which provides historical information on over two hundred of the locations frequented by the famous writer or popularized in his many novels. As author Tony Lynch explains, "It is essentially a tale of *two* countries—the England that [Dickens] knew in fact, and the 'Dickensland', whose locations were invariably borrowed from reality and then rebuilt in his imagination, and where lived all those memorable characters."

Dickens's England leads the tourist or armchair traveler to spots such as the Leather Bottle in Cobham, Kent, which is the scene of the Pickwicks' reunion with their friend Tracy Tupman in *The Pickwick Papers*. This "clean and commodious ale-house" was a "favorite wateringhole" of Dickens when he lived at Gad's Hill Place. Today, as a still-functioning inn, it displays the author's favorite chair in one of its dining rooms.

Nearly one hundred photographs enliven the book with a special charm and "reveal a surprising amount of Dickensian atmosphere still lingering" today, more than a century after the author's death. Concise street maps pinpoint the exact location of each of the settings mentioned, and two handy supplements, a "Checklist of Locations" (listed by novel) and "Travellers' Information," ensure ready access to each of the historical sites.

(Facts on File, 1986, ISBN 0-8160-1533-3, hardcover, 198 pages, $16.95)

The England of William Shakespeare
Michael Justin Davis

The London that Shakespeare knew in the late sixteenth century was a rough, brawling, lusty city:

[St. Paul's] Cathedral thrived as a centre for all kinds of business, however low. Idlers, thieves, hungry paupers, cheats, pimps and every sort of crook lounged in the nave and the aisles . . . Robberies were plotted and sexual liaisons arranged. Anything could be bought, sold or hired. 'I bought him in Paul's,' says Falstaff about his rascally man Bardolph in Henry IV Pt ii.

But aside from Oxford and Cambridge, it was the only town where printing was allowed, and thus it became the center of England's book trade:

This was the place to come not only to inspect large, handsome volumes . . . but also to thumb through trivial, little, unbound books which cost only a few pence . . . It was in this trashy format—in size a quarter of a sheet and so called 'quarto'—that Romeo and Juliet, Hamlet *and* King Lear *were first available to readers. The establishment did not think that plays had literary worth, but admired poetry.*

In this lovely book Michael Justin Davis explores the England that Shakespeare knew—not just London but also the many towns in which the playwright's works were performed in his lifetime. Ipswich and Cambridge, Bristol and Bath, Oxford, Shrewsbury and Coventry, and of course Stratford-upon-Avon are all here, described through eyewitness reports, enhanced with quotations from the bard and other writers and depicted in dramatic photographs (both full color and black-and-white) by Simon McBride as well as by numerous contemporary drawings.

In his writings Shakespeare "used landscape to place and illuminate people's actions, emotions and thoughts," remarks Davis. This book examines the landscape that served as inspiration for many of Shakespeare's settings, the events around which he created plots and the people who became his characters. In doing so it presents an intimate portrait of the customs and conditions of everyday life in Elizabethan England.

(Dutton, 1987, ISBN 0-525-24587-1, hardcover, 209 pages, $24.95)

Sherlock Holmes's London
T. Kobayashi et al.

What fan of Sherlock Holmes hasn't dreamed of making a pilgrimage to 221B Baker Street? To St. Bartholomew's Hospital (Bart's), where Watson first shook the hand of the great detective in *A Study in Scarlet*?

To Fleet Street, off of which were located the offices of the Red-Headed League?

Tsukasa Kobayashi, camera in hand, makes these dreams come true, leading the Holmes devotee to all the nostalgic sites. In this beautiful, oversized picture book, the haunts of Holmes and Watson are depicted in sepia prints from their own era and full-color photographs of modern days. Enough text, often interspersed with quotes from Holmes' creator, Sir Arthur Conan Doyle, is included to link the locales with their respective stories.

There are also the modern tributes to Doyle's immortal characters: Moriarty's Pub, the Sherlock Holmes Hotel, posters on the walls of the Baker Street Underground Station that depict scenes and characters from the books. Those looking for Holmes memorabilia will find plenty of it in a multi-page section on a Northumberland Street pub named "The Sherlock Holmes." A wax dummy of Holmes, his Stradivarius, various apparatus he used in his chemical experiments—they are all shown here.

There are disappointments too, like learning that 221 Baker Street is now a modern, multistoried structure occupied by the offices of the Abbey National Building Society. The authors theorize that the street has been renumbered, and the present No. 31 is the site of Holmes's former lodgings. Yes, Baker Street has changed, but "Sherlock Holmes has withstood the elements, surviving untouched for a hundred years."

(Chronicle, 1985, ISBN 0-87701-380-2, softcover, oversized, 128 pages, $14.95)

The Sixth Continent: A Literary History of Romney Marsh
Iain Finlayson

"I've heard say the world's divided like into Europe, Ashy, Afriky, Ameriky, Australy, an' Romney Marsh," says a character in Rudyard Kipling's *Puck of Pook's Hill*, and the pastoral area to which he refers does indeed assume continental importance in the literary world.

Romney Marsh, at the southeast borders of Kent and Sussex, seems to have a magnetic attraction for writers. Imagine this gathering at the turn of the twentieth century: "[H.G.] Wells at Sandgate just outside Folkestone, [Stephen] Crane at Brede Place, [Joseph] Conrad at Pent Farm . . . [Henry] James at Lamb House in Rye, and Ford Madox Hueffer [Ford] first at Aldington and later, from 1901, at Winchelsea. Rudyard Kipling lived further away, nearer to Brighton, though within driving distance of Rye and Romney Marsh."

What was (and is) the attraction of the area? It is certainly not universal. Paul Theroux found Rye "museum-like in its quaintness," and even resident

Henry James brooded that "both [church] tower and hill *would* have been higher if the place had only been French or Italian."

But free-lance writer and journalist Iain Finlayson determined to see for himself, and he took up residence in Romney Marsh. Through his first-hand experiences and the words of some of the famous (and infamous) other residents, he examines the lives of several of the notable inhabitants, shedding light on them as well as on the surroundings in which they lived and wrote. Finlayson delivers spicy details on Wells's numerous affairs, the luncheon at which Henry James was received by Guy de Maupassant and "a naked lady wearing a mask," and the *angst* that drove Conrad Aiken to a suicide attempt.

Gossipy, anecdotal, and witty, this book sketches a delightful portrait of Romney Marsh and its talented, though often eccentric, inhabitants.

(Atheneum, 1986, ISBN 0-689-11834-1, hardcover, 241 pages, $15.95)

Wordsworth & The Lake District
David McCracken

Although Wordsworth wrote much of his poetry about his home country, the Lake District of England, few works actually identified the particular locale that inspired them. David McCracken, Professor of English at the University of Washington, set out to connect the poems and the places and thus enable the traveler and scholar alike to better understand and appreciate the relationship between the two.

In researching the book, McCracken delved into Wordsworth's prose, letters and journals of the poet's friends and relatives, writings of early travel writers and scholars, and his own observations in the Lakes. The result is a thorough exploration of charming poetry and beautiful landscapes.

The book is divided into two sections. The first progresses geographically through the district, quoting poetry and noting the impact of place upon it. The second provides sixteen maps and walking guides, each corresponding to a chapter in the first section of the book. The maps—drawn especially for this book—are detailed enough to make it easy for the traveler literally to follow Wordsworth's footsteps through the countryside of the poet's home district.

"Considering particular poems that Wordsworth wrote about particular places," McCracken writes in his introduction, "will, I hope, help the eye to perceive and the heart to enjoy the poetry, the landscape, and the connections between them."

(Oxford, 1984, ISBN 0-19-281396-X, softcover, 300 pages, $7.95)

Writers at Home
Edited by Gervase Jackson-Stops

The trouble with any writer's house is, of course, that feeling which we always cherish, however subconsciously, that somewhere or other among its staircases and corridors we shall push open a door and stumble upon genius at work. A corresponding awareness that this can never be so creates a species of haunted, tomb-like sadness comparable to no other: the lovingly-amassed rows of first editions . . . the caricatures and signed photographs . . . the terrible collection of personal objects . . . none of these can bring back what we have come to find.

Nevertheless, we continue to visit the haunts of our favorite authors, searching for clues to their genius. The British National Trust has preserved many buildings because of their literary association, acting on the premise that "'historic interest' and 'natural beauty,' the two sides of preservation, [meet] in the written word." Several of the homes under the National Trust's guardianship are presented in this collection of essays, along with a discussion of the writers who lived and worked in them.

Wordsworth at Cockermouth and Allan Bank, Coleridge at Nether Stowey, Carlyle in Cheyne Row, Hardy, Henry James, Kipling, Shaw, T. E. Lawrence, Leonard and Virginia Woolf, and the "Bloomsbury Group"—each chapter explores an author's life and delves into the influence of place upon his or her writing. Numerous photographs and drawings, sixteen of them in color, give added interest; and the address of each home, as well as directions to it, is included.

Writers at Home introduces us to homes that, as Gervase Jackson-Stops says in his foreword, "may be modest architecturally . . . yet they can speak to us as many better known 'sights' cannot. In a simple view from a window across a cornfield, in a rickety bookshelf crammed with dog-eared volumes, a wind-up gramophone, or an abandoned eighteenth-century wig-stand, one can arrive at a fuller understanding of a mind already revealed to us with such intensity in another medium."

(Facts on File, 1985, ISBN 0-8160-1318-7, hardcover, 184 pages, $22.95)

NATURE

The Country Diary of an Edwardian Lady
Edith Holden

Imagine flipping through the yellowed pages of an old diary, a hushed feeling stealing over you as you realize you are looking into the inner world of someone's life. Well, this is precisely what happens when you read **The Country Diary of an Edwardian Lady**, a beautiful and nostalgic glimpse into the life of English artist Edith Holden.

One of seven children of an English paint manufacturer, Holden was a book illustrator by profession and a dedicated observer of nature by inclination. It was the combination of these two attributes that led her to write and illustrate this private diary for the year 1906.

Here, with all the detailed execution of a naturalist's eye, are watercolors of flowers, birds, and creatures of the village in which Holden lived. So lifelike are the paintings of soft blue-winged Kingfishers and Willow Warblers, they seem ready to fly off the very page!

Equally special are Holden's sentiments as she observes the passing of days, the changing of seasons in her country world. She delves into history to report that the Anglo-Saxons called September *gerst-monath*, "barley month," and that May Day comes from the old English tradition of meeting at dawn to welcome the advent of Spring.

Also fascinating are her insights into local folklore, such as her entry for June 24th, Midsummer Day, 1906:

The Cuckoo is beginning to change his tune, and a little later he will be saying 'Cuc-cukoo' instead of 'Cuckoo.' There is an old superstition concerning the Cuckoo's cry . . . If when you hear [it] you begin to run and count the Cuc-koo's cries, and continue running until out of ear-shot, you will add as many years to your life as you count calls . . .

This inspiring facsimile reproduction of an Edwardian woman's personal record remained undiscovered for seventy years. Now it beckons readers to explore the wonderful sanctuary of nature that is the English countryside.

(Holt, 1977, ISBN 0-03-059574-6, softcover, 192 pages, $9.95)

The Country House Garden
Gervase Jackson-Stops and James Pipkin

If the term "country house" conjures up images of a modest cottage with a little white picket fence and a small plot of wildflowers along the front walk, this book will be a great surprise. Pictured and described in this lavish volume are castles, conservatories, and estates surrounded by gardens containing acres of flowers ablaze with color, mazes of clipped hedges, and man-made waterfalls to rival Mother Nature's.

Architect and writer Gervase Jackson-Stops introduces his topic with a historical overview, explaining how attitudes about nature have evolved over the centuries and thereby influenced garden construction. Along with internationally acclaimed photographer James Pipkin he then leads us on a "grand tour," showing us parterres and knot gardens, lakes and bridges, flower gardens both formal and wild, herb and kitchen plots.

We meander through an Italian Renaissance arboretum at Crathes Castle where a copy of Verrocchio's "Boy With a Dolphin" cascades water into a wildflower-rimmed pool. In Sussex we stroll up a long, tree-lined avenue to reach a sumptuous estate, and in Wiltshire we cross a Palladian bridge based on "one of the architect's unexecuted schemes for the Rialto in Venice." Or we sit quietly and meditate admidst every conceivable shade of pink and purple in a peaceful Hampshire glade that has been carefully sculpted into a "wild" garden.

Informative text and brilliant color photographs combine in a book that portrays the grandeur and beauty of dozens of memorable country house gardens. (A map of those open to the public is appended.) Jackson-Stops and Pipkin have fulfilled the dream of an Englishman named John Evelyn who, in 1657, planned a book in which "persons of all conditions and faculties, which delight in Gardens, may therein encounter something for their own advantage." His book was never completed; but now, over three centuries later, it exists in **The Country House Garden.**

(New York Graphics Society/Little, Brown, 1987, ISBN 0-8212-1668-6, hardcover, oversized, 223 pages, $35.00)

God's Acre
Francesca Greenoak

A gentle watercolor depicts snakeshead fritillaries growing in a churchyard in Shropshire, a soft sketch shows an English partridge in Suffolk, and a full-page painting reveals house martins gathering over a churchyard in the Windrush Valley.

Clare Roberts's evocative illustrations and Francesca Greenoak's lyrical descriptions tell the story of the twenty thousand churchyards that dot the countryside of England and Wales. Within their walls plants and animals enjoy a protected environment, safe from encroaching urbanization or agricultural development.

"A new role for churchyards has emerged over the last decade—that of nature conservation," says Greenoak. "Churchyards have assumed an importance not only for the people of the parish but for its wildlife also." The churchyards, in short, have become unofficial nature reserves.

Greenoak and Roberts explore these sanctuaries, detailing the fragrant beauty of springtime blossoms and the scampering life of the graveyard mice. They speak of the past as well as the future and give a passionate plea that these oft-neglected and unappreciated spots, God's acres, be conserved.

(Dutton, 1985, ISBN 0-525-24315-1, hardcover, 192 pages, $19.95)

The Living Isles: A Natural History of Britain and Ireland
Peter Crawford

It's an enormous task, tracing ten thousand years of natural history, and Peter Crawford has done it superbly. As a senior television producer with the BBC's Natural History Unit at Bristol, he was author and executive producer of the ten-part television series, *The Living Isles*. This book, a companion to that series, is written in the same highly informative but almost conversational style that is the hallmark of such productions.

Crawford begins with the giant ice cap that linked the now-familiar masses of Britain and Ireland to Europe. He shows how, "in the brief timespan of two hundred human lives," the glacial emptiness was transformed into "an archipelago of islands and seas that, considering its size, has a greater diversity of scenery and wildlife than perhaps any other part of the globe." Two hundred full-color photographs portray this diversity, showing moist woodlands and dry heathlands, rocky shores and verdant pastures, and the creatures that inhabit them.

An eighty-page gazetteer at the end of the book lists nearly 450 sites, selected both because they reflect the character of a particular region and because they illustrate specific stages in the development of the area's landscape or wildlife. The sites are grouped geographically; all are open to the public.

The Living Isles is a useful guide and an erudite companion. It is also a visual delight.

(Scribner's, 1985, 1987, ISBN 0-684-18801-5, hardcover, oversized, 320 pages, $24.95)

PERFORMING ARTS

The Great Theatres of London: An Illustrated Companion
Ronald Bergan

"Archtecture and Drama are brother arts," says England's renowned actor Anthony Hopkins, and here these siblings come together in a celebration of the great theatres of London, "the glittering jewels in the crown that is this great capital city."

A potpourri of architectural details and theatrical lore are vividly illustrated by Kirsty McLaren's full-color photographs and a plentitude of black-and-white ones from days gone by. We visit the Barbican, which opened in 1982 and was named after the watch towers *(barbicans)* on Roman walls that were once nearby. "The whole building is a show in itself," says author Ronald Bergan. "As in most modern theatres there is no curtain, but at intervals a huge black stainless steel fire curtain rises from the floor to meet another descending from the ceiling." Jeremy Irons played in *Richard II* here, and Derek Jacobi triumphed in *Cyrano de Bergerac*. Of course, says Bergan, "it hasn't been bouquets all the way. There was the unhappy first night of *The Happiest Days Of Your Life*, when the juvenile lead forgot most of his lines. He turned to the audience at one stage and said, 'You've heard of actor's nightmare. Well, I'm living it.'"

In sharp contrast to this sleekly modern centre is the ornate and gilded Palladium, complete with six giant Corinthian columns and two cantilevered balconies. The original building was erected in 1871 as the home of Charles Hengler's Circus; when architect Frank Matcham was contracted to build a music hall, he incorporated parts of the former building. The Palladium opened on 16 December 1910 with a variety show and has since seen on its stage such notables as Yul Brynner, Jack Benny, Ethel Merman, Danny Kaye, Bob Hope, Bing Crosby, Duke Ellington, Frank Sinatra, Cyd Charisse, Judy Garland, and Liza Minnelli. "The play's the thing," of course, but in lieu of the actual play, Bergan's tour of forty-four of London's most fascinating playhouses is the stuff of dreams.

(Chronicle, 1988, ISBN 0-87701-571-6, softcover, 200 pages, $14.95)

Learning to Dream: The New British Cinema
James Park

Chariots of Fire—Oscar winner, 1982. *Gandhi*—Oscar winner, 1983. *Gregory's Girl, Educating Rita, The Killing Fields*. Do films such as these signal a revival of British film-making? Do they recognize cinema's ability to dream, "to explore the deeper levels of consciousness," or are they merely "the Emperor's new clothes?"

These questions are explored by James Park, film journalist for *Variety*. His slim volume assumes a familiarity with the industry; it is not for the novice. Park discusses various writers, directors, and producers with the ease born of long acquaintance; he makes references to multitudes of films, British as well as European and American. He observes, for example, that while *The Killing Fields* "shares the same English tradition of radical humanism" as does Michael Radford's *Another Time, Another Place*, its "thematic complexity" can be contrasted with "the simple logic" of *Casablanca*.

"The history of British cinema has been one of unparalleled mediocrity," he states. "In the past, with the exception of a few major directors, British film-makers generally lacked the strength of vision necessary to explore cinema's potential to chart the furthest reaches of fantasy and extremes of passion . . . To paraphrase a remark made by François Truffaut to Alfred Hitchcock, cinema and Britain have long seemed antithetical concepts." His book expresses the hope that this time is past, that it is now possible to celebrate the emergence of "a new generation of British film-makers determined to create a vibrant national cinema."

(Faber and Faber, 1984, ISBN 0-571-13401-7, softcover, 138 pages, $7.95)

New Grove Twentieth-Century English Masters
Edited by Stanley Sadie

Seven English musicians—Edward Elgar, Frederick Delius, Ralph Vaughan Williams, Gustav Holst, and William Walton—are discussed in this book, part of *The New Grove* Composer Biography Series. The biographies were orginally entries in *The New Grove Dictionary of Music and Musicians*; they have been expanded and updated for this volume. Yet they remain true to their original purpose: to impart a great deal of information in a concise and accurate manner.

Twentieth-Century English Masters is primarily a reference book and that "gives it a particular obligation to convey received knowledge and to treat of composers' lives and works in an encyclopedic fashion, with proper acknowledgment of sources and due care to reflect different standpoints, rather than to embody imaginative or speculative writing about a composer's character or his music." Each chapter concludes with a comprehensive work-list and extended bibliography.

Norton, 1986, ISBN 0-393-30351-9, softcover, 306 pages, $11.95)

YOUNG PEOPLE'S BOOKS

Ballet Shoes
Noel Streatfeild
For ages ten to thirteen

What child hasn't dreamt at some time of becoming a performer, dancer, or pilot? Well, enter into the London of the 1940s and meet Pauline, Petrova, and Posy Fossil, three young sisters whose lives revolve around the magical world of the stage. Add the fact that they are not really sisters, but three orphans who live with a wild and wacky assortment of characters, and you have Noel Streatfeild's delightful book, **Ballet Shoes.**

Streatfeild, long one of Britain's favorite writers of children's books, has produced a wonderfully entertaining story that all children, and especially girls, will enjoy reading again and again. But **Ballet Shoes** is more than just a clever story. It also conveys a wealth of information: first, about the world of the theater and second, about Britain—the Britain of little girls in their "frocks" and "knickers" who save their "shillings and pence" by walking rather than taking the bus to the Victoria and Albert Museum.

It all begins with Gum (short for Great Uncle Matthew), a crusty but kindly old adventurer with a wooden leg who travels around the world in search of fossils and other eccentric objects. During the few times he is home, he lives in a flat on the Brompton Road with his niece, Sylvia, and Nana, her devoted nanny. One day Gum brings home a different kind of "fossil": a baby! Before long he brings home another, and another! The last is delivered to Sylvia with a letter in which Gum says that he won't be home for at least five years.

So the little orphans—Pauline, Petrova, and Posy—grow up together as sisters, speaking reverently about the legendary Gum whom they can't remember seeing. But as the years pass and Gum fails to return, money becomes tighter and Sylvia is forced to open up their house to boarders: Doctor Jake, a professor; Mr. and Mrs. Simpson who come from Kuala Lumpur; and Miss Theo Dane, a dancer.

It is through the help and advice of these friendly boarders that all three girls grow to discover their special talents and to follow their dreams to become an actress, a dancer, and . . . well, you'll have to read and find out!

(Yearling/Dell, 1937, 1984, ISBN 0-440-41508-X, softcover, 294 pages, $3.50)

Discovering London
John Moyes
Discovering Shakespeare Country
Levi Fox
Discovering the Tower of London
Peter Hammond
For ages ten and up

"London is the most daunting city for a stranger and yet, only a little beneath the surface, the most friendly," says John Moyes at the beginning of **Discovering London**. Using fifth-grade vocabulary he embarks on a visit to England's capital, stopping at many of the major sites: the Houses of Parliament, Westminster Abbey, and Buckingham Palace among others. At each stop he presents a bit of history ("Buckingham Palace was purchased by George III for his wife and rebuilt in 1835 to a design by John Nash") and often a bit of tourist advice, presumably meant for the reader's parents ("You can travel all the way to Hampton Court Palace by water, but it's a long journey. You would be better to go by train from Waterloo.")

In similar fashion Peter Hammond zeroes in on **The Tower of London**, tracing its history from its predecessor, a timber fort that once occupied the same spot, to the forty (approximately) Yeoman Warders who guard the Tower today; and Levi Fox visits **Shakespeare Country**, seeing Stratford-upon-Avon as it was in the past (full of "very large streets" [and] buildings which were "reasonably well builded of timber") and as it is in the present ("Every Friday it has an open air market, and on Tuesdays farmers come to buy and sell their stock at the castle market.")

Small, compact, and with lots of color photos, this series offers quick tours of some of England's most interesting spots.

(Ladybird Books, hardcover, 52 pages, $2.50 each; London: 1986, ISBN 0-7214-0976-8; Shakespeare Country: 1987, ISBN 0-7214-1003-0; Tower of London: 1987, ISBN 0-7214-1002-2)

Robin Hood: His Life and Legend
Bernard Miles
For ages ten and up

"Myth is all too often history raised to a higher level, lifted into the realm of poetry," says author Bernard Miles. Intending to retell the Robin Hood story in its traditional fictional form, Miles searched through medieval ballads and journeyed through the lands of Nottingham and York. He began to see Robin as a true historical character, "just as solid as some of the great heroes of the American West." Now, in this colorfully illustrated and well-told tale, Robin Hood is brought to life, and his adventures are set against the backdrop of real villages and abbeys, churches, castles, and dungeons.

All the well-known characters are here: Robin, Maid Marian, Little John, Friar Tuck, Prince John, Will Scarlet, Alan a'Dale, and the Sheriff of Nottingham. In addition, Miles has added some new characters, such as Much, the miller's son, who becomes Robin's devoted friend, and the evil Sir Guy of Gisburn, who challenges Robin for Marian's love.

Miles strives to make the legend of Robin Hood as real and as meaningful as possible, even including a detailed map of the legendary region with the names of places mentioned in the early poems. Now, he says, "if ever you get to England you can go on a Robin Hood Holiday, visiting Robin's old haunts [and] using Robin as a sort of key to unlock the past."

(Rand McNally, 1979, ISBN 0-528-82340-X, hardcover, oversized, 125 pages, $11.95)

The Story of a Castle
The Story of a Main Street
The Story of an English Village
John S. Goodall
For ages four and up

John Goodall's books are gentle gifts—delicate watercolors that tell wordless stories, half-pages that alter the action and transport the viewer through the ages. In unique fashion they show the procession of English life from the Middle Ages to modern times.

Castle opens in the twelfth century when the Normans built a castle to use as a fortress. Goodall pictures the castle in subsequent years: the gentle days during the reign of Elizabeth I when it was filled with herb and pleasure gardens, the frightening era of the Civil War when it was attacked by Cromwell's troops, the social days in the early twentieth century when it was the host for elegant balls, the somber times during World War I when it served as a hospital for wounded soldiers, and finally the present when the castle is open to the public to raise money necessary for its upkeep.

Main Street and **Village** proceed in similar fashion, beginning with medieval days and moving through the Elizabethan, Restoration, Georgian, Regency, Victorian, and Edwardian periods to end with the bustling world of today. Architecture, activities, and fashion change with the ages, and Goodall records them all with authentic and colorful detail, presenting a panoramic view of village life.

Goodall's books are often categorized as children's, but they are ones adults will feel privileged to share. They travel through the centuries with grace and present history with picturesque charm.

(McElderry Books/Macmillan, hardcover, 60 pages each; Castle: 1986, ISBN 0-689-50405-5, $13.95; Main Street: 1987, ISBN 0-689-50436-5, $14.95; Village: 1979, ISBN 0-689-50125-0, $8.95)

The Tower of London
Leonard Everett Fisher
For ages six to ten

In 1078 William the Conquerer began building the Tower of London, to be "a symbol of his power, a fortress for his defense, and a prison for his enemies." The walls of this complex of buildings, if they could talk, could tell a fascinating and bloody history—in large measure the history of England itself. And with Leonard Everett Fisher as their guide, youngsters can eavesdrop on what the walls have to say.

They'll hear the echoes of happy voices and merry music from royal celebrations, the roars of lions and bellowing of elephants in the menagerie, the commotion of peasant revolts. They'll hear screams, too, of unfortunate prisoners being tortured and beheaded, including those of thirteen-year-old King Edward V.

The Tower witnessed the marriage of King Henry VIII and Anne Boleyn—and and her execution exactly three years later. It held Sir Walter Raleigh captive for twelve long years. It also served as refuge for the homeless during the Great Fire of London in 1666. All these historic events are told in simple language and illustrated with black-and-white drawings; each page also features a color illustration of the coat-of-arms of the ruling monarch of the time.

Fisher adds a final note about the six large ravens that are always within the Tower Walls. Legend says when the last raven leaves the Tower of London, the British nation will disappear. Fortunately, the big black birds are well cared for, and the future of England seems assured.

(Macmillan, 1987, ISBN 0-02-735370-2, hardcover, oversized, 28 pages, $13.95)

SCOTLAND AND WALES

GENERAL

The Crofter and the Laird
John McPhee

Twenty-five miles west of the Scottish mainland lies the island of Colonsay, a "fragment" of the Hebrides. It's not a large place. All told, 138 people live there. Colonsay has seven farms (a farm having more than forty-nine tillable acres) and seventeen crofts of eighteen acres each. These are tended by crofters who are, for the most part, "islanders," a title bestowed only upon folk who have a family history of several hundred years on the island. "Incomers" are those who, like the doctor, postman and schoolteacher, must remain for another century to establish credibility.

And then there's the laird, called the "new laird" as he only inherited Colonsay ten years ago. He's actually an absentee landlord, and as such unpopular though not unkind. In reality, he is "a quiet and benevolent man who wanted more than anything else not to have to listen to grumbling tenants during his short vacations on the island, so he was liberal in the allowances that he made for improvements in the real estate."

This then is the place John McPhee found when he went, with his wife and four daughters, to visit the land of his ancestors. And this book, with its tale of Donald McNeill, crofter, and the fourth Baron Stathcona, laird, is also the story of a wee bit of Scotland, its history, its legends, and its people. As the clansmen used to say, standing and lifting their cups high, "To the land of the bens and the glens."

(Farrar, Straus and Giroux, 1970, ISBN 0-374-1-3192-9, softcover, 159 pages, $6.25)

The Enigma of Loch Ness
Henry H. Bauer
The Loch Ness Mystery Solved: Making Sense of a Mystery
Ronald Binns

Does Nessie, the "diving dinosaur" of Loch Ness, lurk in the deep waters of northern Scotland or merely in the hyperactive channels of the imagination? Two books, both written by men with unimpeachable credentials, give opposing answers. Ronald Binns, a member of the Loch Ness Investigation Bureau, concludes that there is "no scientific evidence whatsoever of monsters in Loch Ness." Henry H. Bauer, professor of chemistry and science studies at Virginia Polytechnic Institute and State University, feels differently. "I happen to believe that the Loch Ness monsters (or

Nessies) are actual living animals," he says, although his book is not designed to prove, or disprove, this point. Rather, Bauer concerns himself with the sociological, psychological, and philosophical aspects of the case, asking not whether Nessies exist but why they exert such a strong hold on the fantasies of the world.

Binns starts by describing the setting and then, in rough chronological order, details the controversy since the first sighting in May 1933. "Strange Spectacle on Loch Ness" read the *Inverness Courier* headline. "Many monster-hunters have paid tribute to the item's historical significance," says Binns, "but no-one has ever examined the strange circumstances which lay behind the report, and no-one has ever bothered to go back and look at the *Courier's* files to see what sort of response the report drew from local people who knew Loch Ness well." This, of course, is exactly what Binns does and, if he does not convince the world, he certainly presents a strong case that the monster is illusory.

But why can't he convince the world? Why do so many people insist upon the existence of the monster, despite the fact that much of the evidence is suspect? This is the question that intrigues Bauer, and he devotes only the first two chapters of his book to a pro-and-con discussion concerning the reality of the monster. The remainder of his book shows "how controversy inevitably flows from the nature of the evidence, from the avocation of monster hunting, from society's attitude toward anomalous beliefs and claims, from the nature of science."

Both books have black-and-white photos that purport to show the monster; both have extensive bibliographies, although Bauer's is more thoroughly documented and also contains a brief (eight pages) chronology of the Loch Ness Story. His conclusion perhaps best summarizes the question of Nessie:

One should mention some awareness that one's own beliefs, though rational, may turn out to be wrong; and one ought to remember that the conflicting beliefs of others are not necessarily false, and that even if they are false they may nonetheless be quite rational.

(The Enigma of Loch Ness: University of Illinois, 1988, ISBN 0-252-06031-8, softcover, 264 pages, $9.95; The Loch Ness Mystery Solved: Prometheus Books, 1985, ISBN 0-87975-291-2, softcover, 228 pages, $9.95)

How Green Was My Valley
Richard Llewellyn

When Huw Morgan was a small boy in the prosperous South Wales countryside, life was full of the simple pleasures. He recalls, for example, a Saturday dinner:

There was always a baron of beef and a shoulder or leg of lamb on the dishes by my father. In front of him were the chickens, either boiled or roast, or ducks, or turkey or goose, whatever was the time of the year. Then potatoes, mashed, boiled and roast, and cabbage and cauliflower, or peas or beans and sometimes when the weather was good, all of them together.

Gold coins accumulated comfortably in the tin box on the mantlepiece, and Huw's father and mother gravely considered each expenditure:

My father always said that money was made to be spent just as men spend their strength and brains in earning it and as willingly. But just as they work with a purpose, so the results of that work should be spent with a purpose and not wasted. So . . . there was always thought before the tin was taken out of the kitchen.

But then things began to change. A monumental slag heap began to creep down to the valley and coal dust blackened the air. The day the union voted to go out on strike, Huw knew his life had changed forever:

"I could see you all day to-day," [father] said, "while they were talking and arguing . . . What is to happen to you I cannot tell. The ground is cut from under our feet. Nothing to be done. Nothing . . . It is your mother and the other women who will suffer," he said. "It is they will have the burden. I am shamed to go in and tell her."

Llewellen's fictional recollection of his childhood home won the National Book Award in 1940 and was made into a motion picture that won six Academy Awards in 1941. It is a beautiful and tender story, brimming with the spirit of Wales.

(Macmillan, 1940, 1986, ISBN 0-02-573420-2, hardcover, 495 pages, $30.00)

In the Footsteps of Johnson and Boswell
Israel Shenker

Imagine, as does Jan Morris in *The New York Times Book Review*, this conversation between Dr. Samuel Johnson, famous lexicographer and wit of the eighteenth century, and his friend, Mr. James Boswell:

Boswell: *Have you read, Sir, Mr. Israel Shenker's new book of travel, in which he follows the tour that you and I took together through the western part of Scotland in 1773?*
Johnson: *I have, Sir, and I have read it with admiration; for . . . it is instructive to pursue the journeys of our predecessors, . . . and to observe what changes have been wrought by the passage of time.*

Israel Shenker diligently retraced the path of Johnson and Boswell, setting forth from Edinburgh and spending a good deal of time in the

Hebrides. Although 205 years had elapsed, he desired to "go to the places Johnson and Boswell had been, see what they had seen, and seek out descendants of the people they had visited. If they had spoken with the local minister, so would I; if they had inquired into the customs of the country, so would I."

Shenker's journey was a mix of past and present. He declined to travel, as had his forerunners, by horseback, sensibly preferring an automobile. Yet he found himself waiting for the same ferry as had Johnson and Boswell, in the same pouring rain. For Shenker, as for Johnson, "there was no sign of ferry or ferryman. It seemed for all the world that the problem of crossing had not diminished since 1773." Much to his delight, he discovered one change: he need only pick up the telephone to summon the ferryman.

Did Shenker consider his trip a success? Suffice it to say that the former correspondent for *Time* and reporter for *The New York Times* is now a resident of Scotland.

(Oxford, 1982, ISBN 0-19-503470-8, softcover, 284 pages, $7.95)

Island: Diary of a Year on Easdale
Garth and Vicky Waite

It's a small white cottage some two hundred years old. You slip through the door and there, next to the binoculars on the plain wooden table, a book lies open. Curious, you venture closer. Its hand-lettered cover reads **Island: Diary of a Year on Easdale**; attracted by the vivid watercolors and detailed pencil sketches that adorn its pages, you begin to leaf through the quaint volume.

Jan. 4: A slight rise in temperature accompanied by a shower of rain has started a gentle thaw. Tiny oases of green grow larger and larger and the cushions of saxifrage in the garden look fresh and vigorous. Here and there a brave primrose is in flower as if to salute the hardy little daisies also blooming.

Mar. 10: Ivy—fidelity in friendship
Hazel—reconciliation
Willow—freedom

June 5: Vicky's birthday . . . Near some St. George's mushrooms we found a dor beetle and noted the metallic violet color of its underside.

The books's origins were in a chance meeting on a Scotland-bound train. Garth, a widower, and Vicky, a widow, exchanged pleasantries, then addresses, then correspondence; eighteen months later they were married. During their honeymoon on Easdale, an island off the coast of Scotland, Vicky suggested they take up permanent residence there.

Island, a simple record of unaffected pleasures, preserves their first year on Easdale. Garth's prose and Vicky's drawings reveal all the nooks and crannies of this beautiful, unspoiled island. Though amateurs, their collaboration produces a charming look at a very special couple living in a very special place.

(Century Publishing from David and Charles, 1985, ISBN 0-7126-0766-8, hardcover, 144 pages, $24.95)

John Prebble's Scotland
John Prebble

"The long brawl of Scotland's history began in the bloody cockpit of the lowlands eighteen hundred years ago," states author John Prebble in this, his eighth book about the Scots and Scotland. As he sweeps the reader through the centuries, Prebble is charming, provocative, at times pugnacious—but always entertaining.

He makes no attempt to hide his bias, so the reader is well-warned and can relax, enjoying the effect of skillfully aimed arrows hitting their marks. He puts, for example, the union of England and Scotland into what he considers proper historical prospective:

Its people had accepted the Union as an escape from famine and bankruptcy, and those who regretted the loss of their independence soothed their doubts with the truth that life was better now, and with the lie that they were joined in equality with a wiser and more experienced nation.

The book abounds with anecdotes as Prebble criss-crosses his adopted land, pausing now and again to reflect on historical events, to examine the present and to turn an admiring eye toward the grandeur of the landscape. Generously illustrated with thirty-two pages of full-color photographs, **John Prebble's Scotland** is a sardonic, biting history peppered with wry touches of humor. It is a grand Highland Fling across a craggy, misty country.

(Secker & Warburg Ltd., London, from David and Charles, 1984, ISBN 0-436-38634-8, hardcover, $29.95)

The Matter of Wales: Epic Views of a Small Country
Jan Morris

For this epic journey, Jan Morris brings Owen Glendower along as she investigates every nook and cranny of Wales. Morris is a very real and well-known travel writer and essayist; Glendower is a legendary medieval hero often confused with King Arthur. Still ever-present in Welsh consciousness, he represents "the Welshness in all Welshmen . . . the spirit of their origins." Through Morris's and Glendower's eyes, this small country's story does indeed assume epic proportions, combining elements of pride, heroism, tragedy, and hope.

Morris's exploration delves into history (social, political, religious, and economic), the arts (art, architecture, literature, and folklore) and modern everyday life. Much of the Welsh character derives, she theorizes, from the astonishing fact that, following the Roman occupation and introduction of Christianity, Wales was never again conquered by a foreign power:

England fell to the Angles, the Saxons, the Jutes and the Franks: Wales never did, and the Welsh accordingly came to see themselves as inheritors of Roman urbanity and Christian devotion, and as trustees of a lost Celtic civilization which was to become ever more marvellous in the imagination, peopled by ever more heroic heroes, inspired by saintlier saints, until the very dream of it became part of the whole world's consciousness in the legendary paragon of King Arthur. Wales was the folk-memory of Europe!

Morris is half Welsh herself (the other half is English), so the "matter of Wales" is especially near and dear to her heart. Her book is a passionate, and not entirely unbiased, portrait of a country that, as she says, "is not just a country on the map or even in the mind: it is a country of the heart, and all of us have some small country there."

(Oxford, 1984, ISBN 0-19-215846-5, hardcover, 442 pages, $22.50)

The Panther Book of Scottish Short Stories
Selected by James Campbell

What distinguishes the Scottish storyteller from his colleagues in other parts of Europe? It is his "keenness to investigate the dusty corners of other people's lives," says editor James Campbell. "This is an authentic ingredient in the Scottish personality. In a Scottish village you will find that by far the largest proportion of people are what we call 'ordinary' and, what's more, they expect the people they meet to be ordinary too . . . Scottish writers [are] aware that although their rightful place is at the world's keyhole, along with Joyce, with Chekhov, with Hemingway, some extra attention should be paid by them to the sights and sounds and smells of the kitchen."

Here then are sixteen tales, discovered by peeping through the keyhole at the lives of plain folk. Not all of the stories take place in Scotland (William Boyd writes of Los Angeles and Giles Gordon of Kashmir, for example) but all the characters are seen through the prism of Scottish sensibilities.

When [Jack Killeyan] had said he was minded to write to the Glascow Herald, exposing the injustices inherent in the present system of promoting teachers, [his wife] had been horrified. All the authorities in Scotland would read it, she'd whispered. His name would be marked . . . Best write nothing. Best give the impression you thought the system was fair enough. Best keep applying and hoping. That had been her advice, and he found it all the more insulting because of course he intended to follow it.

Teachers, thieves, hitch-hikers, time keepers, schoolboys, and fishermen inhabit the pages of this book and give a glimpse of what it is to be "ordinary folk" in today's Scotland.

(Panther Books, London, from Academy Chicago, 1984, ISBN 0-586-06165-7, softcover, 240 pages, $5.95)

Scotland: An Anthology
Compiled by Paul Harris

"The first thing to understand about the Scots is that they are not English," says Moray Mclaren. True enough, but who exactly are the Scots? And what is the nature of Scotland? Paul Harris has compiled a multitude of answers in **Scotland: An Anthology**, a collection of writings from both natives and visitors, famous and obscure, serious and whimsical.

There are, of course, excerpts from classic writers like Daniel Defoe, Robert Burns, and Robert Louis Stevenson:

My tea is nearly ready, and the sun has left the sky;
It's time to take the window to see Leerie going by;
For every night at tea-time and before you take your seat,
With lantern and with ladder he comes posting up the street.
                    —Robert Louis Stevenson, *The Lamplighter*

and from modern writers like David Daiches and H. V. Morton:

You can feel the Sabbath in the Highlands of Scotland just as in cities you can feel a fall of snow: the world is wrapped in a kind of soft hush; normal early morning noises are muffled or absent.
                                        —H. V. Morton

Much of the book is arranged geographically. In the chapter on the Lowlands, for instance, there are three traditional old rhymes, a piece on Selkirk in the days of Bonaparte by Andrew and John Lang, blank verse on the Kelso horse show by Maurice Lindsay, a rousing description of a Galloway fox hunt by Andrew McCormick, some poems and a prose excerpt by Sir Walter Scott, a poem entitled "The New Tay Bridge" by William McGonagall, and an excerpt from Morton's "In Search of Scotland."

In all well over one hundred writers are represented, and their words help paint a multi-hued canvas of the land of kilts and bagpipes.

(Little, Brown, 1985, ISBN 0-316-34830-9, hardcover, 252 pages, $19.95)

Scotland Forever Home
Geddes MacGregor

According to Geddes MacGregor there is not one Scotland, but three: "the never-never land of Brigadoon," the Scottish Homeland in northern Britain, and the "Scottish Diaspora"—the millions of expatriates who fondly look back to the homeland of their fathers. It is primarily for the latter group that MacGregor has written **Scotland Forever Home**, although non-Scots, too, will enjoy his insights.

In this highly entertaining book are all the essentials for appreciating the Scotland of past and present. History, education, religion, varieties of local speech, cuisine, local events, whisky, and songs are just a few of the topics explored through MacGregor's humorous eye.

Learning has never been so much fun. In the chapter entitled "Kilt, Clan, Tartan, and Bagpipe," MacGregor explains that the word "clan" comes from the Gaelic word "clann," meaning children. As most people know, the formal dress for the male members of the clan is the kilt, a tartan skirt. But surely it would be more natural for the female to wear the kilt, you suggest. Not so, MacGregor says, for "to Celtic eyes, a woman in a kilt is as ridiculous a spectacle as a man in a bra."

Equally fascinating are the stories to be found in the chapter on "Ghosts, Monsters, and other Ferlies." "Ferlie," MacGregor says, "is a good old Scots word for any sort of wonder or mysterious happening, sight, or sound." While virtually anything of note (including two American sailors in MacGregor's native seaside town) could constitute a ferlie, ghosts and monsters would always qualify "par excellence." At the end of the chapter MacGregor offers his readers some helpful advice:

A final word of warning: never ask a Lowlander about ghosts. He is unlikely to know unless he has Highland blood in him. Better still, ask no one. Just listen and look. Ghosts do not like to work through diplomatic channels.

(Dodd, Mead, 1980, ISBN 0-396-08733-7, softcover, 276 pages, $11.95)

Talking of Wales
Trevor Fishlock

I can feast on the landscape and I sometimes feel that I can quarry stories from the land itself. I am a Cymruphile, but well aware of the country's creaks and blemishes . . . Few small countries have been so persistently skinned and probed by writers, but the magic and the enigma endure.

The speaker is Trevor Fishlock, Welsh Affairs Correspondent of *The Times*, describing his "beat." Writing as a "resident visitor," he probes Wales from the black coal pits of Maerdy to the executive suites of skyscrapers; the result is an entertaining and informative primer on this mystifying country.

With Fishlock as our guide we visit pubs in Cardiganshire, walk the hill paths across the Brecon Beacons, and tour Camarthen and its still flourishing coracle-building industry. A coracle, he tells us, is an ancient, specialized form of fishing craft, "frail-looking, but . . . really very tough and waterworthy. Recently, two Teifi river coracles were paddled by intrepid men, the Welsh navy, across the English Channel, to the amazement of the English and the French." We learn the secret of finding good Welsh whisky, the mystique of rugby and the institution of the *eisteddfod*, which Fishlock defines as "a sort of annual general meeting of Welsh Wales . . . a stockade into which people can retreat and bolt the gate against English . . . an open house for all of Wales . . . a major culture festival."

Talking of Wales is intended as "a briefing, an entertainment, a broad, but not comprehensive, look at the country, the people and their mood." This lively and humorous book succeeds in all this and at the same time proves Fishlock to be a learned and very funny penman.

(Granada Publishing, London, from Academy Chicago, 1978, ISBN 0-586-04555-4, softcover, 191 pages, $4.95)

Wales: The Imagined Nation
Edited by Tony Curtis

"How do we imagine ourselves to be Welsh and where do we imagine Wales to be?" asks editor Tony Curtis. For answers he turns to a collection of his countrymen's essays and poems that depict the cultural and national identity of Wales through the media.

About half the book focuses on literature. Prys Morgan examines legends, James A. Davies discusses Dylan Thomas, and Tony Bianchi analyzes R. S. Thomas; Dai Smith and Curtis scrutinize Anglo-Welsh novels and poetry:

Writing in Wales, as far as the majority of outsiders are concerned (and certainly as far as the Wales Tourist Board is concerned), means Dylan Thomas . . . The genius of Dylan and his friend and fellow visionary Vernon Watkins created an enduring body of work located in a Swansea and Laugharne of the imagination.

—Tony Curtis

Other essays cover art, cinema, television, the "culturally invisible" Welsh women, and theatre:

In effect theatre says: "This is who we are, these are the things that worry us, these are our neighbours, these are our gods, our dreams, this is how we live and this is our language." . . . *There is a subterranean tunnel that connects theatre and the national consciousness.*
—Carl Tighe

"If nationality is not necessarily linked to language," Curtis asks, "if it is neither simply a matter of geographical residency, then is it a matter of rugby and singing? Is Welshness a thing to be opted into, or out of?" He raises a multitude of questions, and his thought-provoking book comes up with at least some of the answers.

(Poetry Wales Press, Wales, from Dufour Editions, 1986, ISBN 0-907476-54-6, softcover, 306 pages, $13.95)

Welsh Dylan
John Ackerman

It is indeed a wise man who knows himself. "One: I am a Welshman; two: I am a drunkard; three: I am a lover of the human race, especially of women," commented Dylan Thomas in a bit of humorous insight. It is worth noting that the renowned writer of lyric poetry and compelling prose puts his "Welshness" first, for it is through Dylan Thomas's works that many readers throughout the world have become aware of Wales as an entity separate from the rest of the British Isles. As John Ackerman writes, "His Swansea stories, his Laugharne-charted poems, his glimpses of Eden and of eternity in the landscapes of West Wales, and *Under Milk Wood's* evocations of warm, gossiping incorrigibly human Welsh life have captivated the popular . . . imagination."

Ackerman, himself a Welshman, has studied and written about Dylan (as he calls him) for many years; this biography incorporates some of his previous work as well as the results of his continuing research. He recreates the poet's life, beginning with a secure, confident childhood in Swansea, moving through the time of on-and-off Bohemianism in London, and ending with the years Dylan spent in a small shack by the sea in Laugharne exemplifying "the voice of the lyric poet passionately learning to grow old." Ackerman links the writer's works to the scene of their inspiration, quoting him often and illustrating passages with photographs of significant people and places.

Welsh Dylan is a fascinating look at a twentieth-century literary giant. It is also a unique guidebook to the Wales that produced him.

(Granada Publishing, London, from Academy Chicago, 1979, ISBN 0-586-08350-2, softcover, 143 pages, $6.95)

ANTHROPOLOGY AND ARCHAEOLOGY

The Druids
Stuart Piggott

See England—Anthropology and Archaeology

Scotland: Archaeology and Early History
Graham and Anna Ritchie

The Scottish countryside abounds with remnants of ancient times: *souterrains* (stone-built underground structures), *crannogs* (timber houses built on an artificial, or partly artificial, island), *brochs* (dry-stone towers), and *duns* (small forts with thick dry-stone walls); chambered tombs, henge monuments, and stone circles. Through these structures and artifacts such as tools and pottery Graham and Anna Ritchie recreate the pageant of Scottish history.

From the days when fishermen worked the calm fjords and sheltered bays of the west coast and hunters sought the deer and boar that roamed the forested hinterlands, the peoples of early Scotland left clues to tell of their lives. The Ritchies, both acknowledged experts on historical monuments and archaeology, examine these clues in an archaeological expedition through the centuries, beginning in the seventh millennium B.C. and continuing to A.D. 843 when the Scots and Picts were united. Their book, though scientifically accurate, largely avoids technical jargon, and the 149 photos and drawings show present-day views of many of the sites discussed.

(Thames and Hudson, 1985, ISBN 0-500-27365-0, softcover, 192 pages, $10.95)

ART AND ARCHITECTURE

At Home in Scotland
Lesley Astair and Roddy Martine

Scottish weather may oftentimes be gloomy, but the houses—oh, the houses are grand indeed! Imagine joining Ewan and Sandra Macpherson at Glentruim House in the Scottish Highlands. Macpherson tartan rugs, perfect for wrapping around chilly shoulders, are draped casually over the chairs; a roaring fire beckons cozily.

Or for a more formal atmosphere there is Manderston, the home of Adrian and Cornelia Palmer. The interiors are "sensationally opulant. The staircase is a replica of the Petit Trianon at Versaille, and the rails are plated in silver. Everywhere are silk damask wall coverings."

A modern look dominates the Kelvin Court flat of Ken McCullough, a successful restaurateur and hotel-owner. Again there is a fireplace, but this time it is in Art Deco style. Flickering flames encourage the visitor to sink into the Le Corbusier chairs.

It's no accident that many Scottish homes have names; they have personalities too, and **At Home in Scotland** provides the introductions. "Some of the houses," say the authors, "are grand, some are masterpieces of understatement, some are erratic and others are relatively modest, but made special by the inventiveness of their owners. There are properties which have been devotedly restored and maintained, and others which have weathered the passing of years with magnificent defiance. Whether they be country mansion, historic tower house or town flat, they are all individual, exciting and a joy to explore."

To aid in the exploration Fritz von der Schulenburg's splendid color photography shows each home in all its glory, and text by Lesley Astaire and Roddy Martine gives the background. This is a grand tour into the homes—and lives—of the Scottish elite.

(Abbeville, 1987, ISBN 0-89659-767-9, hardcover, oversized, 240 pages, $45.00)

Chambers Guide to Traditional Crafts of Scotland
Jenny Carter and Janet Rae

The time-honored skills of weaving, knitting, and coopering are intertwined with Scottish history until it's difficult to imagine the country without tweeds, Fair Isle sweaters, and fine whiskey aging in oak barrels. This wonderful book by Jenny Carter and Janet Rae celebrates these artforms and many others, both cottage arts and those that are now industrialized.

Carter and Rae delve into the history of each craft as well as its present status, often finding actual craftspeople to discuss harness-making and tanning, spinning, weaving and knitting, pottery, glass manufacture, blacksmithing and carving, gunmaking and fly tying. They look at musical instruments too, exploring the workings of harps, fiddles, and of course, bagpipes. Alastair Sinclair, a third-generation pipe maker, explains some of the fine points of the instruments' construction: "The drones are turned on a lathe to a rough finish, then holes are put through using big hand drills. We have to make a lot of our own tools because nothing is in standard sizes. The size of the hole is important, but in my opinion it's the *relationship* of all the sizes in the drone which gives the sound, and the finish."

Highland dress comes in for its fair share of attention, and this leads to an examination of the clan system and the "myth" of the tartan: "There is evidence to show that the close family of some of the chiefs began to wear tartan of similar colourways by the end of the eighteenth century and the beginning of the nineteenth, although there is no evidence that use of a *clan* tartan was widespread." Perhaps the most important use of the tartan, the authors add, was as a "uniform" for the eighteenth-century Highland regiments, and since that time the "wearing of the tartan was patchy."

More than one hundred photographs and drawings in both color and black-and-white amplify the text, showing both the artisans at work and their products. **Traditional Crafts of Scotland** is a book to be enjoyed on many levels; but mostly, as the authors intended, it pays homage to "the age-old skills of the land, the way in which they have changed and survived."

(W & R Chambers Ltd., Edinburgh, from Cambridge, 1988, ISBN 0-550-20000-2, hardcover, 128 pages, $24.95)

The Historic Architecture of Wales
John B. Hilling

The walls of our buildings ring with voices from the past; the shout of triumph at Raglan, the cry of despair at Castell y Bere, the poetry of love at Ystrad Fflur, the hymn of hope at some Salem and the babble of children in the tyclom.

So says architect John Hillings as he surveys the gamut of Welsh architecture from prehistory to the early twentieth century. He includes structures of many varieties: Celtic and Roman fortifications, medieval churches and towns, castles, vernacular architecture, country mansions, and industrial buildings.

Intertwined in his architectural overview are tidbits of the social and political history of Wales. For example, in discussing the castles of the Middle Ages he explains that "the chief reason for the profusion of castles stems from the very different reactions of Wales and of England to the French (i.e. Norman) invasion . . . They symbolise on the one hand the persistent pressure of the invaders, and on the other, the determined opposition and tenacity of the Welsh princes in the defence of their country."

Photos, illustrations, and floorplans accompany text; maps indicate the distribution of various types of structures. Hilling's book demonstrates that Welsh history is, in the words of David Bell *(The Artist in Wales)*, "written clearly on the stones."

(University of Wales Press, Cardiff, from Humanities, 1975, ISBN 0-7083-0626-8, hardcover, 234 pages, $15.00)

Kinkell: The Reconstruction of a Scottish Castle
Gerald Laing

"The final approach was by way of a rough grassy track, deeply rutted by the spinning wheels of tractors on wetter days than this. Overgrown hedges crowded the car on either side, scratching at the paintwork. We could feel the high, grassed ridge in the centre of the track, scraping at the sump and exhaust pipe. After about a quarter of a mile the track widened and swung away to the left. Straight ahead was a dilapidated barbed wire fence; beyond it lay the warm, grey bulk of Kinkell Castle." It had been uninhabited for decades, save for generations of jackdaws who had built nests in every cranny.

This is the building that Gerald and Galina Laing decided to call home. They worked for a year—laboring, improvising, learning—and at the end of that time they had turned a sixteenth-century castle into a twentieth-century home.

Kinkell is the story of that effort; it is a testament to the Laing's determination and perseverance. But it is also the story of a castle and of a region. First a home and fortress for the chief of the Mackenzie clan, then a country house, a farmhouse, and finally a Civil Defense training station during World War II, Kinkell reflects the history of Highland life.

The castle, which was perfectly designed for the life of its original owner, is now equally well suited for modern living. "The crumbling ruin had been replaced by a new and stronger reality," says Laing as he views his new home, "stronger partly because it gave no premonition of imminent collapse but mainly, I think, because its original design and concept were no longer compromised ... The new beams at Kinkell will discolour, crack and warp in their own time, part of the continued life of the building."

Laing, a renowned painter and sculptor, combines architecture and history, past and present into this account of a castle's renovation and makes Scotland's history come alive in very personal way.

(Ardullie House, Scotland, from International Specialized Book Services, 1974, 1984, hardcover, 180 pages, $17.95)

Mackintosh Architecture
Edited by Jackie Cooper

The buildings and interiors of Charles Rennie Mackintosh are imaginative, innovative, intriguing. For twelve years, from approximately 1897 when he won his first major commission (a new building for the Glasgow School of Art) until 1909 when his career began to decline, Scottish-born Mackintosh was an influential figure in the world of architecture, helping to develop the designs and trends that, according to David Dunster, "took Scotland, and England, into the twentieth century." The cornerstone of his work was his firm belief in usefulness, or as he expressed it, that "construction should be decorated, and not decoration constructed."

Rarely content to design just a building, Mackintosh preferred to plan total environments including the interiors: furniture, curtains—even tablecloths and cutlery. This volume catalogs his architectural accomplishments in terms of completed buildings, interiors, alterations, unexecuted designs, and competition entries. It is a startling collection. One example is Hill House, built in Helensburgh, Dunbartonshire, in 1902-03 and widely considered to be the finest of Mackintosh's domestic creations. He designed the building (in the Scottish baronial tradition), the landscape (trees clipped just so), the fireplaces (complete with a set of pewter fire tongs), and the walls (generally white, some with pastel stencil designs).

Each structure and project is fully illustrated with drawings and photographs (some in full color) and accompanied by notes that indicate its present condition. In addition, there is a guide to Mackintosh collections in Scotland and a map of Glasgow showing the location of existing buildings. It has taken us half a century, says editor Jackie Cooper, "to come to terms with the innovations and with the discrepancies that combine so sensitively in Mackintosh's style." At last, there is a book that celebrates them.

(St. Martin's Press, 1984, ISBN 0-312-50244-3, softcover, oversized, 112 pages, $19.95)

Painting in Scotland: The Golden Age
Duncan Macmillan

In the history of art in Scotland, 1707, the year of the union of the English and Scottish parliaments, was not really a beginning and 1843, the year of the Disruption in the church of Scotland, was not really an end. Nevertheless these two events, moments of crisis in the still turbulent wake of the spiritual and political upheavals that followed the Reformation, are milestones in Scottish history and they frame the period of imaginative and intellectual excitement in Scotland known as the Scottish Enlightenment.

Duncan Macmillan, Curator of the Talbot Rice Art Center at the University of Edinburgh, discusses this "Golden Age" in his handsome book, **Painting in Scotland**. It was, he says, the time when Scottish painting achieved its own clear identity, largely because of the natural portraiture of Allan Ramsay and Sir Henry Raeburn and the social naturalism of Sir David Wilkie. Macmillan relates the work of each of these influential artists to that of the others as well as to that of lesser-known painters like Gavin Hamilton, Alexander Runciman, and Alexander Nasmyth. Moreover, he presents the artists in the political and social context of their day and traces the connection between painting and other forms of artistic expression, such as literature and music.

Originally prepared as a catalog for a 1986 Edinburgh art exhibit, the text is detailed and complete. More than 150 illustrations, nearly one-third in full color, show the work of many artists, providing a gallery in which the reader can view some of Scotland's finest paintings.

(Phaidon Press Limited, Oxford, England, from Salem House, 1986, ISBN 0-7148-2401-1, hardcover, oversized, 206 pages, $35.00)

CUISINE

British Cookery
Jane Grigson

See England—Cuisine

FOLKTALES

Folk Heroes of Britain
Charles Kightly

See England—Folktales

Gypsy Folk Tales
Edited by John Sampson

Come, sit by the campfire on the slopes of Foel Fawr above the small village of Abergynolwyn and hear the haunting stories that have captivated generations of Welsh gypsies. Perhaps the story-teller is "Black Ellen" herself, known as the Romani Shahrazad—a descendent of Abraham Wood, seventeenth-century "king of the Gypsies." Be sure not to drop off to sleep though, for in the midst of the story she will suddenly exclaim *"Tshiocha!"* (Boots!), and unless her listeners immediately respond *"Cholova!"* (Stockings!), she will break off the tale, never to resume.

But if that should happen, you can do the next-best thng and find twenty-one of these tales collected by the late Dr. John Sampson (often described as "the greatest Romany Rye of all") in his **Gypsy Folk Tales**. Giants and fiery dragons, beggars and travelers, fairy brides and the Devil roam through the pages of this captivating book, cursed and aided by witchcraft and magic. In most of the stories the hero is Jack: "always the youngest brother and generally despised as a fool, he is cunning and fortunate rather than wise and deserving and, while possessed of courage, somewhat of a braggart and a liar. His virtues are reverence for his mother, generosity in sharing food with strangers and helpfulness to men or animals in distress."

Through such delightful tales as "The King of the Herrings," "The Green Man of No Man's Land," "The Eighteen Rabbits" and "The Maid of the Mill" you'll "breathe the atmosphere of the Welsh 'Plas' and the Welsh farm," and come to better understand the spirit of Romany life.

(Salem House, 1984, ISBN 0-88162-061-0, softcover, 108 pages, $5.95)

More Mysterious Wales
Chris Barber

Myths and legends have hidden meanings. We are becoming increasingly aware that they are like cryptograms waiting to be decoded. In spite of everything they remain a fragile link between us and a remote past.
—Fernand Niel, *The Mysteries of Stonehenge*

Chris Barber takes special delight in roaming the hills and valleys of Wales decoding its cryptograms, interpreting its legends, unraveling its web of folklore. His interest in hill walking, caving, and mountaineering has led him to remote monoliths, hidden burial chambers, holy wells, and mystic mounds. In his enticing book **More Mysterious Wales,** as in its predecessor, *Mysterious Wales*, he shares the most intriguing of his finds and helps explain this country that is so haunted by its past.

Barber lingers predominantly in the fifth and sixth centuries—"the golden age of the Celtic saints; the time of Arthur and Maelgwyn Gwynedd, a period of Welsh history that is post-Roman and pre-Norman"—spinning tales of giants and magicians, the devil and warrior princes. Illustrated with his own black-and-white photographs, the book shows sites, discusses the historical and legendary significance of each, and identifies their locations for those who wish to make their own journey into the myth-shrouded past of Wales. For, as R.S. Thomas observed, "You cannot live in the present—at least not in Wales."

(David and Charles, 1986, ISBN 0-7153-8736-7, hardcover, 242 pages, $25.95)

HISTORY

A Concise History of Scotland
Fitzroy Maclean

The land of kilts and bagpipes has had a tumultuous history. For his **Concise History of Scotland,** Fitzroy Maclean leaves the "mists of antiquity" to the archaeologists and antiquarians and begins his account in A.D. 81 with the Roman invasion.

The Romans, harassed by the Picts and Scots, eventually left the area and in A.D. 844 Kenneth MacAlpin, King of the Scots, became King of the Picts as well. Centuries of violent conflict ensued: Malcolm II killed Kenneth III who killed Constantine III, and Malcolm III killed General Macbeth who murdered Duncan I. If all this sounds a bit confusing, it is—but Maclean sorts it all out and in only 218 pages brings the land we know today as Scotland up to present times.

His text is complemented by an abundance of photographs and illustrations—an average of one per page (not counting the index). From a Stone Age dwelling at Skara Brae, Orkney, to a General Assembly of the Church of Scotland attended by Queen Elizabeth, the Duke of Edinburgh, and Princess Anne, the story of Scotland comes vibrantly alive through Maclean's words and pictures.

(Thames and Hudson, 1983, ISBN 0-500-27224-7, softcover, 231 pages, $10.95)

Edinburgh
David Daiches

Sir Walter Scott called it "mine own romantic town"; Benjamin Robert Haydon termed it the "wild dream of a great genius"; and Dorothy Wordsworth announced that "high as my expectations had been raised, the city of Edinburgh far surpassed all expectation." Here literary critic and historian David Daiches portrays the city's colorful story, beginning with its origins as a Celtic fortress, witnessing its preeminence as the "Athens of the North," and following as it grows into a modern city of the mid-1970s.

While discussing the city's political, social, and economic development, Daiches offers glimpses of her talented inhabitants. Many of the individuals who helped shape the city also were those who mirrored it to the world—John Knox, David Hume, Robert Burns, Robert Louis Stevenson, and, of course, Sir Walter Scott, to name just a few.

Edinburgh is a lively, fast-paced history that illuminates the city's past to provide "the clue to the appeal of its present."

(Academy Chicago, 1978, ISBN 0-586-05237-2, softcover, 256 pages, $6.95)

Edinburgh Portraits
Michael Turnbull

"Edinburgh's history and geographical location," says author Michael Turnbull, "provided a many-levelled stage for the actors in [a] human drama." Indeed, **Edinburgh Portraits** reads like a casting director's Rolodex: artists and architects, businessmen, criminals and detectives, musicians and dancers, ghosts, witches, doctors, inventors and scientists . . .

Here is Sir Harry Lauder, a comedian and singer who sold enough records to be considered in the same league as Caruso. Lauder entertained troops during both World Wars and maintained a simple philosophy: "If, by bein' a simple Scots comic, and singin' bonnie humorous songs, I can do my wee bit to help make the world a brighter place, and help mysel' along the road at the same time, well, then, I'm richt glad to lend a hand."

And here are Joseph Lister, who conducted experiments in blood coagulation in an Edinburgh slaughterhouse in the 1850s; Robert Louis Stevenson, whose *Dr. Jekyll and Mr. Hyde* was derived in part "from the mixed experience of affection for Edinburgh and reaction against its oppressive Presbyterian respectability"; and Andy Irvine, the great rugby player, who "was probably the most exciting and lethal attacking full-back in the world and could change the course of a match with his thrilling acceleration and an armoury of unexpected jinks and deceptive swerves."

Turnbull gives brief sketches of a great many people, all of them characters who have participated in the Edinburgh drama over the last five hundred years. He allows them a quick, but rewarding, curtain call, and the reader can comfortably anticipate an encore as Edinburgh's stage attracts more and more performers.

(John Donald Publishers Ltd., Edinburgh, from Humanities Press, 1987, ISBN 0-85976-135-5, softcover, 313 pages, $9.95)

Glasgow
David Daiches

Situated on the banks of the Clyde, Glasgow seemed destined from the beginning to be successful in commerce. As early as the twelfth century it was known as a "bishop's burgh and a market town," and in 1726 Daniel Defoe confirmed the well-known fact that "Glasgow is a city of business":

Here is the face of trade, as well foreign as home trade; and I may say, 'tis the only city in Scotland at this time, that apparently encreases and improves in both ... The share they have in herring-fishing industry is very considerable, and they cure their herrings so well ... that Glasgow herring is esteem'd as good as a Dutch herring.
—Tour Thro' the Whole Island of Great Britain

But Glasgow is a city of contrasts, and today it is known as much for its architecture and Victorian music halls as for its position in business.

In his introduction David Daiches (an Edinburgh man) tells us this book is "the view of one who, in walking Glasgow's streets, talking to its citizens, reading and pondering the multifarious and often fascinating written sources of its history ... and steadily acquiring the 'feel' of the city century by century and even decade by decade, has developed a deeply affectionate understanding of its character as it defined itself throughout the ages." He passes along this understanding in *Glasgow*, an affectionate portrait of a multi-faceted city.

(Granada Publishing, London, from Academy Chicago, 1982, ISBN 0-586-0537-3, softcover, 272 pages, $7.95)

Scotland's Story
Tom Steel

The small country of Scotland is hardly homogeneous. Lowland, Highland, and Norse Scots are of Anglo-Saxon, Gaelic, and Scandinavian heritage respectively, and their history was dominated by conflict. Today the land is still a patchwork quilt of different languages, customs, and traditions, and the common thread that connects the Scots, says author Tom Steel, is a fierce sense of independence.

In **Scotland's Story**, Steel tells the stories of the disparate cultures and that of the country as a whole, beginning with the earliest origins and continuing to present times. A dominant theme in Scotland's history, and thus in the book, is the enduring love-hate relationship between the Scottish and the English. As Steel points out, the Scots fought the English for longer than the almost three hundred years they have been united with them. "This Union that is seen as permanent and sacrosanct is still a new thing and should be treated with care," he says.

His book is a provocative look at a "poor and inhospitable land [that] has bred people of remarkable talent." The country's poverty has caused many of those talented people to emigrate, and a portion of the book is given over to an account of the impact Scots have had on the rest of the world.

In his introduction Steel writes, "Scotland's story has been for the most part a bloody one, always lively and never dull." The latter part of that description is equally applicable to Steel's informative book.

(Collins, London, from Salem House, 1984, ISBN 0-00-216351-9, hardcover, 358 pages, $22.95)

NATURE

God's Acre
Francesca Greenoak

See England—Nature

The Living Isles
Peter Crawford

See England—Nature

My Small Country Living
Jeanine McMullen

Open **My Small Country Living** and you'll meet Doli, the doddering old draft horse who turns into a "prancing, shameless hussy touched by love's burning flames," or Dolores and Nana, a pair of goats whose favorite pastime is "whipping off and eating the hats of startled guests."

Jeanine McMullen, the owner of these unlikely critters, was a city-living BBC broadcaster when she bought her small farmhouse nestled in the verdant Welsh countryside. Eventually she and her mother found themselves mistresses of an incredible assortment of beasts and fowl. The book that resulted from this bucolic life is a whimsical tale about animals and the country scene, gusting with vibrant humor.

In the beginning, McMullen reports, "[we] lived in a kind of wonderland of our own dreams, getting to know at last the fields and woods, or sitting snug by the roaring fire as the gales shook the very bones of the cottage." But those were the days of innocence. Soon enough McMullen was engaging in encounters with her goat, Nana, in which she found herself "sticking my tongue out and rudely chucking sticks and stones at her . . . It simply confirmed her worst suspicions about the sheer nastiness of the human beast and she took off up the nearest tree and spat at me."

From the joy of a first foaling to the tragedy of a beloved animal's death, Jeanine McMullen has written a raucous celebration of country life among her animals. If, like the author, you've ever contemplated giving it all up and homesteading, here is your mentor. If not, then the book still serves as a delightful chronicle of life in the Welsh countryside.

(Warner, 1984, ISBN 0-446-38305-8, softcover, 219 pages, $8.95)

PERFORMING ARTS

Traditional Dancing in Scotland
J. P. Flett and T. M. Flett

Reels, Schottishches, and the Highland Fling are as Scottish as kilts and bagpipes, but they are just a few of the Scottish dances that were popular in the early days of this century. Prior to World War I, "public and private dances of one sort or another played a more significant part in social life than they do today, for they provided almost the only social occasions on which young people of both sexes could mix freely," say authors J. P. Flett and T. M. Flett.

Now interest in these traditional dances, which had declined for decades, is being revived by the Royal Scottish Country Dance Society; and to bolster this interest the Fletts have probed the memories of many of the people who once performed them. "Ye had to be verra mannerly when lifting your pairtner, no' likes as if ye were drawing a hog oot o' a ditch," reports one elderly man.

The authors discuss history and techniques as well as performers and performances, and they investigate how dancing on the islands of Orkney and Shetland differed from that of the mainland. But the bulk of the text is made up of a detailed look at many of the dances themselves. These descriptions, diagrams and step-by-step instructions explain the Highland fling, the Reel of Tulloch, the Everlasting Jig, the Jacky Tar, and the Duke of Perth among others.

Traditional Dancing in Scotland is practical instruction but it is also social history from an unusual perspective. As it trips the light fantastic it recreates a time when the sound of fiddles was enough to brighten the grey Scottish skies.

(Routledge, Chapman and Hall, 1964, 1985, ISBN 0-7102-0731-X, softcover, 313 pages, $8.95)

YOUNG PEOPLE'S BOOKS

Argyle
Barbara Brooks Wallace
For ages three to seven

"Once upon a time, somewhere in Scotland, there was a sheep whose name was Argyle . . ." What happens when Argyle eats some colored flowers? Why, he grows colored wool, of course—perfect for knitting stockings that are a beautiful plaid; an Argyle plaid, in fact!

Argyle becomes very famous, and his owner, the sheepherder MacDougal, becomes very, very rich. But his celebrity brings unforseen troubles.

In this delightful tale of fame, fortune, and plaid stockings, young children can learn a bit about the vicissitudes of a life of distinction while they catch a glimpse of the Scottish highlands, lowlands, and midlands. John Sandford's illustrations are bright and strong; Barbara Wallace's text is simple and clear. Together they abound with Scottish merriment.

(Abingdon Press, 1987, ISBN 0-687-01724-6, hardcover, 32 pages, $10.95)

Castle
David Macaulay
Cut & Assemble a Medieval Castle
A. G. Smith
For children and adults

The plot of **Castle** is simple: the King of England wants to build a castle and a town in northwest Wales. The purpose for creating the town is to provide opportunity to the settlers, thereby leading to well-being and peace; and the purpose of the castle is to protect the town.

David Macaulay's execution of the plot is masterful. With clear text and marvelously detailed line drawings as his tools, he builds the thirteenth-century castle stone by stone, discussing structural significance, military tactics, and social activity. When on the last page, the castle is shown two hundred years later, neglected except as a quarry for new buildings, we want to weep, so involved were we in its construction.

And so, for those who want an authentic replica to call their own, there is A. G. Smith's wonderful **Cut & Assemble a Medieval Castle.** The walls, towers, gates, courtyards, and ramps of Caernarvon Castle (still standing in northern Wales) are reproduced in color on stiff paper; step-by-step instructions and easy-to-understand diagrams explain how to cut, fold and assemble them into a three-dimensional model. Cutouts of scale-sized armored knights, humble peasants, and crested flags are also included. While too complex for a third-grader to tackle by him or herself, it's a wonderful parent/child project for younger children and a solo activity for those nearing their teens.

Two talented artists, both captivated by the legends of medieval times, have used very different means to depict the days of brave knights and heraldic banners, and both have succeeded in capturing the history, as well as the architecture, of those long-ago days.

(Castle: Houghton Mifflin, 1977, ISBN 0-395-32920-5, softcover, oversized, 80 pages, $6.95; Medieval Castle: Dover, 1984, ISBN 0-486-24663-9, softcover, oversized, 40 pages, $4.50)

Discovering Scotland
Eric Melvin
For ages ten and up

Scotland is Edinburgh Castle and Robert Burns's lyric poetry; it is bagpipes and Highland dancing and Skara Brae, a Stone Age village on one of the Orkney Islands. It is also the oil capital of Europe and an electronics center termed "Silicon Glen." It is soccer and gold, beautiful *lochs*, and a monster, "Nessie," that is said to inhabit one of them. And this handily-sized (4¾" x 7") little book covers all its many personalities in color photographs and text geared especially to the youthful traveler.

Eric Melvin rambles over Highlands and Lowlands, contributing bits of history and local lore to help explain today's Scotland and its romantic charm. His book is a picturesque, portable summation of a country with a "rich past and an exciting future."

(Ladybird Books, 1986, ISBN 0-7214-0946-6, hardcover, 53 pages, $2.50)

IRELAND

GENERAL

Belfast Diary: War as a Way of Life
John Conroy

Belfast, 1980. Two children, one Catholic and one Protestant, are thowing stones at each other. "One of them shouts, 'Sean, I've got to go home now for my tea. I'll be back about six.' 'Okay, Billy,' says the other one. 'Cheerio.'"

War is normal in Northern Ireland. Children consider lobbing rocks at each other to be an everyday pastime, one that can be casually discontinued for dinner and just as easily resumed afterwards. Bombings, police raids, fire—they are just "inconveniences," says Bridgit Barbour, who lives on Springfield Road in a Catholic working-class district of Belfast. Like one of Sean O'Casey's stoical Dubliners, she is a survivor. She elects to stay in her old neighborhood, long after it is safe to do so.

John Conroy, a journalist who has been to Northern Ireland six times and written countless articles about it, places human faces on what appears to be an endless war. He speaks with private citizens as well as government officials; he learns firsthand what it is like to be held captive while the Provos try to detonate a bomb in the next building.

This is a street-level view of people who "don't need any practice" in suffering, of their land where the "Troubles" are routine.

(Beacon Press, 1987, ISBN 0-8070-0205-4, softcover, 256 pages, $8.95)

The Best of Irish Wit and Wisdom
Selected and edited by John McCarthy

"Love of laughter is an Irish heritage," says John McCarthy, quoting an old Irish proverb, and here he proves his point with an anthology of tales, toasts, and songs that illustrate the wry humor and outright blarney for which the Irish are famous.

McCarthy, who although "a Yank [is] not a bad chap" according to his Irish comrades, begins with twenty stories—including "The Boarding House" by James Joyce, "The Fur Coat" by Sean O'Faolain, "The Last of Mrs. Murphy" by Brendan Behan, and "A Journey to the Seven Streams" by Benedict Kiely—all of which juxtapose humor and tragedy with typical Gaelic flair.

He then moves on to chuckle with Celtic comedians, relate "cute cracks" of friends and acquaintances, and retell the tales of a hodgepodge of "interesting characters," from politicians and statesmen to "Grady the Cabman" (who spends his time trying to keep people *out* of his taxicab). Irish-Americans are not forgotten—Leonard Wibberly and former Senator Eugene McCarthy are among those who have a chance to speak their mind—and two special essays pay homage to a pair of Ireland's most famous literary sons, Oscar Wilde and George Bernard Shaw.

Of course, there is a chapter devoted to that most celebrated form of Irish wit—the toast. And although an ancient Hibernian legend warns that the toast won't work "unless the glass you lift contains gentle Irish Whiskey," it's still worth a try. So . . .

May you have warm words on a cold evening,
a full moon on a dark night,
and a smooth road all the way to your door.

(Dodd, Mead, 1987, ISBN 0-396-08998-4, hardcover, 324 pages, $17.95)

In Search of Ireland
H. V. Morton
In Search of Modern Ireland: An American Traveler's Odyssey
Bryce Webster

When inveterate traveler and prolific writer H. V. Morton first arrived in Ireland in the early 1920s, he was intrigued with the "unorganized parties that just happen night after night. It must be impossible to be alone in Dublin," he declared. "The Irish have a genius for improvisation and—they hate to be alone!"

In his quest to find the "real" Ireland Morton meandered around the island, rejoicing in the lush landscape and reveling in conversation with common folk. **In Search of Ireland**, first published in 1930, is the account of his wanderings. Through it he takes the reader with him into Lienster, down to the magic of Cork and Kerry, then onward to the stone walls of Connemara and into Northern Ireland.

More than half a century later, American writer Bryce Webster retraced Morton's footsteps (and blazed some new trails) on her own voyage of discovery. Entitling her follow-up work **In Search of Modern Ireland**, she wrote of her experiences, often comparing them to those of her predecessor.

She found, for instance, on the road to Limerick, "three structures, seemingly built in a straight line, that illustrate what modern Ireland is all about." The first was the ruins of a castle tower, representing the past; the second was a modern motel, testimony to a present that relies largely on tourist trade; the third was a pair of radar towers, heralding the technologically-oriented future. "Limerick," she wrote, "is trying to blend the three. As a result, it has growing pains."

Both writers meld historical detail, contemporary fact, personal observation, and gossipy anecdote to give a prismatic view of a country and its people. Morton leans to the poetic while Webster is more to-the-point, but both are obviously under the spell of the Emerald Isle.

"When my feet first trod Irish soil I felt I had come to a magic country and now, as I said good-bye, I knew it truly as an enchanted island," wrote Morton. And Webster echoed, "And when I had completed recounting all of Ireland's glories, we'd raise our glasses together in a toast to that magical land and plan our next trip back."

(Dodd, Mead; In Search of Ireland: 1958, ISBN 0-396-08344-7, softcover, 276 pages, $9.95; In Search of Modern Ireland: 1986, ISBN 0-396-08695-0, softcover, 205 pages, $12.95)

Ireland
Dervla Murphy

Ireland, says author Dervla Murphy, is a "jigsaw puzzle . . . a tiny Island, blessed with an astounding variety of natural beauty, where half the citizens are under twenty-five and many of the dwellings are brand new . . . [with] a shockingly high rate of inflation, a temperamental telephone service, an agreeable if capricious climate, poorly maintained roads, one of the highest unemployment rates in Western Europe, indifferent food, excellent fishing where the rivers and lakes have not been polluted, a conspicuous population of tinkers, an astonishingly talented rural amateur theatre, magical sky-scapes like you get nowhere else, a unique national sport (hurling), prodigious quantities of litter including rusty car-skeletons strewn around beauty-spots, lively traditional music, architecturally boring small towns, a distinctive equine sub-culture based on hunting and racing, an intense pub life, and natives who occasionally seem crafty and mean in the busier tourist centres but elsewhere are generously helpful."

Murphy, a travel writer who has toured the globe from South America to Asia, at last turns her perceptive eye and jaunty pen homeward and, joined by German photographer Klaus Francke, presents a verbal and pictorial survey of her native Ireland. She looks at the past to ascertain its influence on the present, at the people to probe the social divisions amongst them, and at the North to determine its relationship with the South. Her informative, yet simply-written prose is the perfect complement to Francke's photographs. Ireland comes across as a kindly, if sometimes crochety, old uncle—comfortable and familiar, albeit of another time and place. And, it must be said, with many a tale yet to be told.

(Salem House, 1985, ISBN 0-88162-099-8, hardcover, oversized, 208 pages, $24.95)

Irish Life and Traditions
Edited by Sharon Gmelch

"Life and traditions" is a far-reaching topic and a difficult one to capture on paper, but cultural anthropologist Sharon Gmelch does an admirable job. Her method is simple: she lets thirteen experts, mostly Irish born and bred, speak for themselves to provide "an insider's understanding of Irish culture."

The natural environment always shapes the manmade one, and Gmelch's book begins with a discussion of the land and the sea, followed by a chapter on flora and fauna. Then archaeologist Joseph Raftery outlines early Ireland while architect Patrick Shaffrey talks about five modern cities: Dublin, Belfast, Cork City, Derry City, and Limerick.

The people—warm, delightful, gregarious—enter in Part Two, a collection of essays on "Growing Up in Ireland." Here a historian, a Protestant archbishop, a writer, and a feminist reveal different facets of Irish culture and show "the regional, religious, class and generational experiences that cross-cut an otherwise homogeneous population."

The magic of Ireland comes alive in Part Three, the section concerned with tradition: Fairs and Pilgrimages; The Sporting Tradition; Words: Written, Spoken and Sung; and Festivals. It's "all the fairy stories and pantomimes brought to life," says contributing author Maeve Binchy.

Sean MacBride, 1974 recipient of the Nobel Peace Prize, concludes the book by "Looking Forward" and visualizing Ireland's role in tomorrow's world.

The words of these thirteen essayists are complemented by numerous black-and-white pictures, and the combination is a rewarding overview of modern Ireland.

(Syracuse University, 1986, ISBN 0-8156-0201-4, paperback, 256 pages, $17.50)

No Country for Young Men
Julia O'Faolain

"That is no country for old men," said Yeats at the beginning of his poem, "Sailing to Byzantium." The Ireland depicted in Julia O'Faolain's compelling novel is, as the title states, no country for young men either. Or even for young women.

Set in present-day Dublin and involving frequent flashbacks to village life in the 1920s, the story focuses on two families, the Clancys and the O'Malleys. The central character is Sister Judith Clancy, who as a young woman fervently supported the struggle for an independent Ireland and who now is a half-mad nun, wrestling with flickering memories.

The plot moves back and forth, involving love and murder, history and politics. Like so many Irish novels, it is a story of the "Troubles," and perhaps it matters little that American publishers took a long six years to "discover" the book after its 1980 release in England. After all, as San Francisco editor Pat Tompkins says, "Change is slow in Ireland; the story in **No Country** is no older than yesterday. That is good news for readers and bad news for Ireland."

(Carroll & Graf, 1986, ISBN 0-88184-354-7, hardcover, 420 pages, $8.95)

Nothing Happens in Carmincross
Benedict Kiely

"History is a nightmare from which I am trying to awaken" says James Joyce, and Benedict Keily agrees. His novel, **Nothing Happens in Carmincross**, is his attempt to put the Irish Troubles into perspective.

Set in 1973, the story centers on Mervyn Kavenaugh, a balding, lovable Irishman whose name subtly underscores his spiritual affinity to the mythical Merlin. After years in America Mervyn returns to Ireland for a family celebration where he is immediately confronted with the reality of his strife-ridden homeland. "The object of terrorism is to terrorise. Kill or maim people so as to make them free," he is told.

A man relates the latest news: "A British soldier. Booby-trapped in a house in Derry at the corner of Foyle Road and Brooke Street. Searching for explosives and the explosives found him, three of them. Lost both legs." Later the radio announces "a sixteen-year-old boy, Tommy Kinsella, an apprentice gardener from Cork City has blown himself to bits on the Border while laying mines for Ireland." This is delivered in a matter-of-fact voice, sandwiched between weather reports and sports news.

Keily, whom *Publishers Weekly* has called "quite simply the finest writer out of Ireland today," triumphs in this, his seventeenth book. As intricate as a design in the Book of Kells, his narrative intertwines centuries of ancient myth and modern reality. Mervyn's visit to Carmincross, a town "as much North as it is South, as in-between as are most of the Irish," gives him an unflinching look at modern Ireland, a country where children are orphaned in the name of political freedom, while men drink in a Dublin pub, and ballads are sung in memory of a more peaceful time.

(Godine, 1985, 1987, ISBN 0-87923-725-2, softcover, 280 pages, $8.95)

O Come Ye Back to Ireland: Our First Year in County Clare
Niall Williams and Christine Breen

Niall Williams and Christine Breen actually did what many merely dream of doing: they escaped the urban rat race to return to the (supposedly) simpler life of their ancestors—in this case by moving to the tiny village of Kilmihil on the west coast of Ireland. Niall was a native Dubliner, Christine had gown up in New York; the two met as graduate students in Dublin and thereafter lived the good life in Manhattan—"an aspiring young couple with good jobs and lofty expectations," says Niall.

When they decided to "quit everything to go and live on a farm in the wild West of Ireland . . . to make our 'fame and fortune' when Irish emigration was at its highest in years," they both knew it was crazy. But they went, they struggled, and they triumphed. By the second year the overgrown land was a recognizable farm with fine, healthy cattle and potato stalks a foot high; the turf fire burned brightly; and Niall and Chris were accepted members of the small community.

O Come Ye Back to Ireland is the story of their adaptation to the bleakly beautiful land of west Ireland, a region "on the very point of change." In alternating voices they tell of life without washing machines, without telephones, without bacon cheeseburgers, or mushroom pizzas. Aah, but the "withs." They live with the past, with the seasons, and with the traditions of Ireland—and they plan to stay.

(Soho/Farrar, Straus and Giroux, 1987, ISBN 0-939149-07-9, hardcover, 233 pages, $16.95)

Round Ireland in Low Gear
Eric Newby

A bicycle would be just the thing for touring Ireland, decided English sexagenarian Eric Newby. Walking would be too slow, driving too stressful, and touring by bus too limited. His wife Wanda didn't share his enthusiasm, but elected to come along to be sure he didn't "get into trobble." And so clad in thermal underwear to ward off the December winds and perched on new mountain bikes, they set off in an ominous "torrential rain that turned day into night." And it got worse—on much of their trip they rode through rain, sleet, snow, and gale force winds, which on one instance reached a speed of seventy knots. But like dedicated mail carriers, nothing deterred them for long.

The trip, which was planned as a three-month venture, stretched into several expeditions over a year's time. They began in Limerick, toured the southern coastal regions of Wexford, Waterford, and Cork, and explored the Dingle peninsula. "Ahead of us now was Mount Eagle," wrote Newby, "and from this point onwards I experienced a feeling of unreality about the twentieth century that I had hitherto experienced nowhere else in the western world. I find it impossible to analyse, or even begin to write about it, but the memory remains with me still. Here we entered an area which contained within it one of the greatest concentrations of ancient remains in Ireland, an area so rich in them that even the minds of scholars must reel."

Continuing in June's better weather, they went to Dublin, "a city in which the inhabitants were, as I remembered, completely indifferent to the march of time . . . to the weather, to what is commonly regarded as edible food, and to their surroundings, but capable of talking the hind legs off the biggest herd of donkeys ever conceived." From here they crossed westward to Galway Bay and the Aran Islands, where Newby mused about the stone fort Dun Aengus: "[to] bring some sort of freshness to it is rather like trying to perform a similar service for Stonehenge: so many people have attempted it before that one is tempted to give up." The final stage of the trip took the couple to the north-west counties of Mayo, Sligo, and Donegal, including Shannon Pot, the supposed source of the River Shannon.

Throughout the trip Newby keeps up a patter consisting of anecdotal accounts of historical events, commentary on the Irish character, reviews of a wondrous variety of stouts, and wry analyses of the passing scene. He entertains as he educates, enlightens as he enchants, and the result is a thoroughly delightful book.

(Viking, 1988, ISBN 0-670-82244-2, hardcover, 308 pages, $18.95)

ANTHROPOLOGY AND ARCHAEOLOGY

The Druids
Stuart Piggott

See England—Anthropology and Archaeology

Knowth: And the Passage-Tombs of Ireland
George Eogan

Imagine being the first person in milennia to enter a structure that predates the Egyptian pyramids by several hundred years. "That is precisely what George Eogan did . . . when he located the stone-built passageway which led a distance of 34m into the western side of the great earth mount at Knowth, and discovered the megalithic tomb at its centre, hitherto unknown to science." These words by Professor Colin Renfrew of the University of Cambridge introduce **Knowth**, a vivid first-person account of the excavation of this five-thousand-year-old burial complex in the Boyne Valley north of Dublin.

Here clusters of burial mounds rise like giant anthills against the green landscape. Who built the tombs, and how, and why? Eogan, professor of archaeology at University College, Dublin, gives us the opportunity to accompany him on his excavation, uncovering the answer to these and many more questions as he goes.

He discusses not only the tombs at Knowth, but also the wealth of similar neolithic Irish burial mounds. Nothing escapes his attention, from construction materials and methods to the significance of the ritual offerings in the chambers. He also takes a look at nearby houses and settlements and describes the life of the villagers. A plentiful assortment of color and black-and-white photographs and drawings illustrate the text.

"For the late Stone Age Knowth was one of Europe's greatest public buildings," Eogan concludes. "To describe it as a massive and majestic megalithic masterpiece that reflected the pride and pomp of contemporary society is not an exaggeration." Professor Eogan's book, it must be added, does it full justice.

(Thames and Hudson, 1986, ISBN 0-500-39023-1, hardcover, 247 pages, $29.95)

Nan: The Life of an Irish Travelling Woman
Sharon Gmelch

I had a very hard life. I was poor and I made mistakes. Still, I done me best and I'm proud of meself. I never regretted. Whatever I done, I put up with it. Because it's all for life, it's all left out for you—that's how I look into it. I think from the day you're born, it's left there—marked down for you—and you just have to go through it . . . You just go through whatever the Lord leaves you. And for me, I was a Traveller on the road.

These words were spoken by Nan Donohoe, one of Ireland's "Travelling People." Impoverished and on the lowest rung of the social ladder, these gypsy folk formerly roamed the countryside making and repairing tinware, sweeping chimneys, performing odd jobs, and spreading news and gossip. Forced by lack of work into collecting scrap metal and welfare, they are urban dwellers now, living as pariahs in government-built housing and roadside trailers.

Sharon Gmelch, an American anthropologist, met Nan in the early 1970s in the course of doing research on the Travellers. Each became both student and teacher as they shared experiences over the next decade, and here Gmelch recounts Nan's life story, as told to her during their conversations. It was, as Nan says, a hard life, with more than a good measure of pain, but not without its pleasures too, as she roamed through countryside and city slums, worked for a bit as a kitchen maid and raised—and buried—children. During her lifetime, from 1919 to 1983, the Travelling People's way of life changed as dramatically as did Ireland itself.

In helping Nan tell her story Gmelch combines the sensitivity of a friend with the objectivity of an anthropologist; the result is a moving narrative that rings with truth.

(Norton, 1986, ISBN 0-393-02331-1, hardcover, 239 pages, $15.95)

Peig: The Autobiography of Peig Sayers of the Great Blasket Island
Peig Sayers

Eoin McKiernan, President of the Irish-American Cultural Institute, states: "In the bayous of literature rest many books whose humanity occasionally recalls them to the mainstream of thought. **Peig** is one such. In books such as these the quality of honesty and sincerity, of life lived at the bone, is the conduit through which the thought of one generation passes to illuminate the problems of another age or place."

Peig, who came to be recognized as one of the last of Ireland's traditional storytellers, lived on the Great Blasket Island off the Southwest coast of Ireland. Here she gives us a story as unforgettable as it is simple:

I am an old woman now, with one foot in the grave and the other on its edge . . . Had I known in advance half or even one-third of what the future had in store for me, my mind and heart wouldn't have been as gay and courageous as they were in the beginning of my days.

It is the story of many of the Irish, poverty and hardship leavened with indomitable spirit, courage and faith:

I remember well when I was trying to work while at the same time the heart in my breast was broken by sorrow, that I'd turn my thoughts on Mary and on the Lord, and on the life of hardship they endured.

Irish resiliency, spirit, and traditions are described; the pulse of the community is felt. Yet Peig realizes she is part of a vanishing world, that ". . people like us will never be there again." She died in 1958 at the age of 85. With her death a chapter in Irish history was closed, and her autobiography "can be seen for what it truly is—one of the great heart-cries of the Irish people."

(Longwood, 1983, ISBN 0-86167-092-2, softcover, 212 pages, $6.95)

Runes
R. I. Page

See Scandinavia—Anthropology and Archaeology

ART AND ARCHITECTURE

Castles of Ireland
Brian de Breffny

Castles are everywhere in Ireland. "County Limerick alone once boasted over four hundred medieval castles," says author Brian de Breffny, "Cork over three hundred, Tipperary, Galway, and Clare each between two and three hundred, and Kilkenny nearly two hundred." So, when de Breffny teamed up with photographer George Mott to give a verbal and pictorial survey of Irish castles, he had an abundance from which to choose.

The ninety-four he selected represent many architectural styles. There are those built for defense, those that just look as if they were, and "even those toy-castles that just have a 'castle' look." Likewise, they have met a variety of fates. Some are National Monuments, some private residences, some abandoned ruins, some commercial or government buildings. Regardless of their history or present use, all are intriguing.

There is, for instance, Carrickfergus, the most complete early medieval castle in Ireland. Begun in the 1180s by an Anglo-Norman adventurer, its story includes numerous sieges, cannibalism, and repeated renovations. It now houses a military museum. And there is Kilcolman Castle, granted on a perpetual lease to Edmund Spenser in 1586 because of his loyalty during a bitter battle against Italians and Spaniards. Here were written many of his works, including parts of *The Faerie Queen*, and here some of his manuscripts doubtlessly burned in a fire in 1598. The building is not known to have been inhabited since that time.

A brief but informative introduction covers the history of castle building and their architectural evolution. Individual sites are arranged alphabetically, and each listing includes a history and photographs (most in black-and-white, some in color). A map and a county-by-county index provides additional help. De Breffny has written a book that combines history and architecture, yet has an aura of fairytale magic as well.

(Thames and Hudson, 1977, 1985, ISBN 0-500-27398-7, softcover, 208 pages, $12.95)

A Concise History of Irish Art
Bruce Arnold

Ireland's art has always taken a back seat to her literature in the public's awareness, and many Irish painters "have been forced by circumstance, or persuaded by ambition, to seek a better fortune in London," says author Bruce Arnold. Yet the richness of her art, from illuminated manuscripts and metalwork to paintings, sculpture, and architecture, deserves greater attention.

Arnold outlines in **A Concise History of Irish Art** the most important developments in this country's artforms from the Celtic era to the twentieth century. "Irish art begins as abstract art," writes Arnold, "the ritual decoration by early Bronze Age man of the tombs of his ancestors. His art is a complex pattern of loops and spirals, diamonds, zig-zags, triangles and squares, pecked out in the granite kerb-stones, and cut into the pillars and stone slabs of passage graves and burial chambers." Irish art became "meagre and fragmentary" after the Viking invasion as the country faced nearly eight centuries of strife, but it enjoyed a resurgence in the 1700s as the realism of portraiture and landscape art took precedence. These trends continued well into the twentieth century when, moving full circle, many artists once again began turning to the abstract. Photographs, both black-and-white and color, illustrate the characteristic art of each period and complement the historical and stylistic overview.

"Which of the two Yeats brothers was the greater artist, Jack the painter, or William the poet?" asks Arnold rhetorically. His book helps show that in Ireland the visual arts deserve equal stature with the literary.

(Thames and Hudson, 1977, ISBN 0-19-519962-6, hardcover, 180 pages, $19.95)

Contemporary Irish Art
Compiled and edited by Roderic Knowles

In practically every medium one could name—drawing, painting, sculpture, photography, even kinetic art—says editor Roderic Knowles, "there has been a visual arts renaissance in Ireland during the past decade. It has been happening quietly, almost unobserved, not yet in any fullness of flourishing; it is still in its birth. But it is here."

And Knowles, in compiling what a reviewer for the *Sunday Independent* calls "an 'imaginary museum' between covers," puts this art on exhibit. He reproduces works of ninety-five artists (another 139 are detailed in the directory), each of whom is introduced by an authoritative art critic. Only current artists are included; the focus is on those who have been working in the years since 1975.

Various forms and styles of visual arts are displayed in nearly three hundred photographs, both color and black-and-white. Many of the works are realistic; others are stylized; a few are outlandish. There are, for example, the landscape oils of Tim Goulding, so realistic that at first glance they appear to be photographs; the figurative and often humorous works of John Devlin who says "I paint what I think I would like to see"; and the Human Sculpture of Vernon Carter: "A group of players, not more than twelve, dressed as toy musicians, is arranged to form a sculptural group . . . Each player . . . is responsible for observing any passers-by walking in this direction and playing his or her instrument in time with the rhythm of their footsteps."

Irish artists, it is clear, refuse to be categorized; they refuse to be relegated to one "movement" or "type." Instead, with typical Irish energy and exuberance they are opening the doors to the world of art and insisting the world take notice.

(Wolfhound Press, Dublin, from Irish Books and Media, 1982, ISBN 0-86327-001-8, softcover, oversized, 232 pages, $29.95)

The Houses of Ireland
Brian de Breffny and Rosemary ffolliott

I, the poet William Yeats,
With old millboards and sea-green slates,
And smithy work from the Gort forge,
Restored this tower for my wife George;
And may these characters remain
When all is ruin once again.

These words are posted on the wall of Thoor Ballylee, a four-story sixteenth-century tower-house in County Galway, that Yeats restored in the 1920s. Although not all do it so plainly, many a home can speak of the people who have lived within its walls and the events that have taken place there.

Brian de Breffny and Rosemary ffolliott, experts in history, architecture, and geneaology, and co-directors of the journal *The Irish Ancestor*, know how to wrest the secrets of the ages from eternally silent walls. They write, "The history of a house should not be separated from that of the people who built and lived in it, and thus domestic architecture cannot be divorced from family history, social history or political events." Proving their point, **The Houses of Ireland** offers a lively, anecdotal history of Ireland via a tour of its residences.

Presented chronologically, beginning in medieval times, are castles, farmhouses, country estates, and town-houses—each important in its own way. The authors present each building in its historical setting and give a detailed account of its construction and decoration. Black-and-white and color photos (278 in all) by accomplished photographer George Mott illustrate the text, while outline maps of the country show the relative location of each home, most of which are still in existence.

In Ireland, where domestic architecture includes great medieval castles from the past and little terrace-houses of the present, the murmurings of the walls are a gossipy review of the country's history.

(Thames and Hudson, 1980, ISBN 500-27351-0, softcover, 233 pages, $11.95)

Ireland's Traditional Crafts
David Shaw-Smith

• *Within sight and sound of the wild Atlantic Ocean, Bessie Morrisson engages in the age-old craft of spinning, her wheel turning rhythmically in time to the high lonely cry of the sandpiper, 'knittyneedle, knittyneedle.'*

- *There is probably only one remaining country cooper who still follows his trade, Edward Gavin . . . In 1938, at seventeen years of age, he made his first churn. This was regarded as the highpoint of the craft.*

- *Eugene Lambe began playing the pipes when he was ten years of age . . . He now lives and works as a full-time uilleann pipe maker in the old schoolhouse at Fanore, Co. Clare, an area where traditional music has always been strong.*

It's easy, admits author Shaw-Smith, to romanticize these folks, but traditional crafts were rooted in hard economic realities. As technology improved, handmade crafts tended to give way to mass produced creations. "The price paid, in terms of the country's cultural heritage," says the author, "has been high."

In this beautiful book containing 440 illustrations, 125 of which are in full color, Shaw-Smith records that heritage. He assembles his own photographs of craftsmen and women at work, accompanies them with his wife's explanatory drawings and adds text by acknowledged experts. More than forty traditional crafts are represented, from textiles to stonework, from basketry to glassware. A map shows the locations of craftspersons mentioned in the book.

Like the Irish patchwork that "mirrors the lives of those who made it," **Ireland's Traditional Crafts** reflects the life of a nation.

(Thames and Hudson, 1984, ISBN 0-500-27416-9, softcover, oversized, 224 pages, $14.95)

Irish Spinning, Dyeing and Weaving
Lillias Mitchell

Lillias Mitchell has a twofold mission: to teach and preserve a traditional craft and to promote weaving as a part of the Irish economy. To this end she set up a Department of Spinning, Dyeing and Weaving in the National College of Art in Dublin, and much of the research she has done is collected in this anthology of writings on the weaver's art.

It is an unusual book, part weaver's manual and part reminiscence. Mitchell begins with a discussion of the raw materials—wool, flax, and silk. Next she describes the processes of carding and combing, spinning, weaving, and dyeing, and discusses historical textiles. Much of the information is given by oldtimers. Mrs. Betty Robb, for example, has some advice about dyeing: "I didn't ever use lily roots but got a black dye from the bog," she says, while an old Dooagh woman insists that "socks dyed with *dar-na-gcloc* were always considered healthier to wear than any other kind."

The latter half of the book is given over to a chapter called "In Living Memory Traditions," excerpts from many sources dealing with every aspect of fibre arts: instructions on how to make and dye the traditional *cota dearg* (red petticoat), a description of the *crios* (woven belt from the Aran Islands) and the special loom on which it is woven, a recollection of a visit to the center of the tweed industry in Donegal.

One of the few male contributors, Father M. Dermot, perhaps echoes the thoughts of all weavers, no matter what material they use. "Silk," he asserts, "has an attraction of its own; once you get tangled in it, it is hard to escape."

(Dufour Editions, no date [approximately 1980], ISBN 0-85221-101-5, hardcover, 80 pages, $12.95)

CUISINE

British Cookery
Jane Grigson

See England—Cuisine

Great New British Cooking
Jane Garmey

See England—Cuisine

Irish Country Cooking
Malachi McCormick

"Laughter is brightest when food is best," states one of the proverbs that are sprinkled throughout Malachi McCormick's **Irish Country Cooking**, and a look at the twinkle in McCormick's eye will convince you that the food he talks about and the recipes he gives must be the best.

McCormick doesn't just give recipes. He can't. "Each one would remind me of a particular person, an exploit, a bit of family lore, an apt proverb or quotation, some lovely place in Ireland, a historical connection, or a piece of etymological trivia," he says, and these are every bit as much a part of his book as are the recipes.

Take colcannon, for instance. That, according to McCormick, is Ireland's true national dish. A down-home combination of potatoes, cabbage, leeks, milk, butter and garlic, it stimulates his memories as well as his appetite:

Every year my father planted a garden of potatoes, and it was a thrill to see the vigorous tuber, with its elegant flower, celebrate summer as it waxed large in its rows . . . The popular varieties of the day, Aran Banner, Kerr's Pink, or even British Queen (I used to wonder if this last was not so named because Queen Victoria's profile seemed to bear a striking resemblence to that of a spud stood on end), now seem in short supply. Today, who knows the name of their favorite variety?

And then he wonders, "Why do we never see gooseberries anymore? Must this ancient and venerable berry, known to Chaucer and Shakespeare, yield, on the whim of fashion, to such usurpers as the kiwi, itself hardly more than a steroid-bloated gooseberry?" But McCormick is nothing if not practical. Although he prefers fresh gooseberries for the Gooseberry and Fennel Sauce that accompanies Roast Goose on the Irish Christmas table, he will settle for gooseberry jam or preserves if necessary. Just omit the sugar.

His book is charming, authentic, and useful. Full of hearty recipes—from corned beef and cabbage to plum pudding with brandy butter—it is also full of Irish wit and wisdom. "Hunger is a good sauce," say the Irish, and McCormick is a good source.

(Potter, 1988, ISBN 0-517-56314-2, hardcover, 146 pages, $16.95)

The Joyce of Cooking: Food & Drink from James Joyce's Dublin
Alison Armstrong

Forget the "way to a man's heart" routine. Alison Armstrong is concerned about the way to a man's mind, "man" in this case including woman as well. Here she dissects and digests James Joyce, providing a *Ulysses* guide for the kitchen: recipes for hundreds of the dishes and libations mentioned in Joyce's fiction.

"Hot mockturtle vapour and steam of newbaked jampuffs rolypoly poured out from Harrison's. The heavy noonreek tickled the top of Mr. Bloom's gullet," (*Ulysses*, p. 157) reads the excerpt before Pungent Mockturtle Soup (1 large calf's head, 1½ quarts of veal or mutton broth, brains from the calf's head, chopped fine . . .); and "—What say you, good masters, to a squab pigeon pasty, some collops of venison, a saddle of veal, widgeon with crisp hog's bacon, a boar's head with pistachios, a bason of jolly custard, a medlar tansy and a flagon of old Rhenish?" (*Ulysses*, p. 337) introduces dishes of similar names.

Admittedly, some of the ingredients are hard to come by, but the majority of the recipes have been adapted to a contemporary American kitchen.

Using recipes from turn-of-the-century Ireland, Armstrong has come up with Joycian dishes such as Adulterer's Delight with Shamefaced Peaches, DeQuinceys Rainbow Salade and Molly's Breast Enlarging Mixture (eggs, confectioners' sugar, and Marsala wine.)

Her book transports the reader viscerally to the days of Joyce's Dublin, to the world of Molly and Poldy Bloom, Stephen Dedalus and Buck Mulligan, Gerty MacDowell, Blazes Boylan, Shem, Maria, and Gabriel. **The Joyce of Cooking** exemplifies Joyce's words, expressed through the mouth of Bloom: "Know me come eat with me." (*Ulysses*, p. 175).

(Station Hill Press, 1986, ISBN 0-930794-85-0, hardcover, 272 pages, $18.95)

FOLKTALES

Fairy & Folk Tales of Ireland
Edited by W. B. Yeats

On these pages William Butler Yeats captures as varied an assortment of strangely interesting creatures as has ever been assembled. Witches, giants and fairies, ghosts, devils, and leprecauns romp and creep through **Fairy & Folk Tales of Ireland.**

"Fallen angels who were not good enough to be saved, nor bad enough to be lost," describes the unique position of fairies in Irish legend. The *deenee shee* (fairy people, or *daoine maithe* (good people) as you must call them when they might be listening, "take what size or shape pleases them. Their chief occupations are feasting, fighting, and making love, and playing the most beautiful music."

They also enjoy putting a scare into people, as a traveling tinker named Pat Diver found out late one night. Sleeping in a barn, Pat was awakened by fairies in the form of four immense men. The men had with them a body they wanted to cook, and they persuaded Pat to help them. "Now Pat," they said, "you'll turn the corpse, but if you burn the corpse you'll be roasted in his place."

Such mischief is hardly limited to the supernatural beings in these stories. Bill Dawson, a blacksmith, swindles the Devil not once but three times in *The Three Wishes*, and makes Satan so mistrust him that Dawson is turned away at the Gates of Hell after he dies.

Retribution is dealt out in many a satisfying incident. Witch Sarah Kennedy assumes a supernatural form to steal milk from her neighbors but suffers a horrible death when confronted by an angry priest: ". . . the old wretch's pains increased; her body swelled to an immense size; her eyes flashed as if on fire, her face was black as night, her entire form writhed in a thousand different contortions; her outcries were appalling, her face sunk, her eyes closed, and in a few minutes she expired in the most exquisite tortures."

In **Fairy & Folk Tales of Ireland**, Yeats preserves a unique portion of the culture of his native land. Although a book for adults, it delights the child in all of us.

(Macmillan, 1983, ISBN 0-02-055640-3, softcover, 387 pages, $8.95)

HISTORY

Dublin
Peter Somerville-Large

"There's no beatin' the ould town," comments a visitor to Dublin in Peter Somerville-Large's overview of Ireland's capital. The "ould town" he shows us has many facets: the city "fought for by conquerors and died for by patriots; . . . the shabby, genteel, intimate city famous for taverns and wit and rich Dublin talk; . . . the lovely city dominated by castle, spire and brewery, lying along the banks of the Liffey . . ."

We visit medieval Dublin where "outside St. Audoen's the smell of malt comes from Guinness' brewery and cold wind from the river gushes up the steps," and we see the Lord Deputy, Sir Henry Sidney, as he leaves the Castle in Elizabethan times. There, heads are displayed on poles:

These trunckles heddes do playnly showe
Each rebelles fatall end
And what a haynous crime it is
The Queen for to offend.
–from an engraving by John Derricke

Later we enjoy plays at Smock Alley theater—"a stage, pit, boxes, two new galleries, lattices and music loft, all well lit with lamps and candles." We learn that along with this flowering of art, music, and theatre during the Restoration, Dublin remained "the city of the wine flasks." There were 1,180 ale-houses and ninety-one public brew houses to provide Dubliners with amusement and pleasure—after the theatre, of course!

Dublin takes us on a cultural and sociological journey through history, from the days of the Norse invader Brian Boru, through the Easter Rising of 1916, and into the present. Somerville-Large assures us that Dublin, with its "air of informality, indolence and leisure," is still an exciting, vital city, one in which "the only constants are the sea, the play of light and the same green curve of hills the Vikings saw when they arrived."

(Granada Publishing, London, from Academy Chicago, 1979, ISBN 0-586-05236-4, softcover, 330 pages, $7.95)

Ireland: A Concise History from the Twelfth Century to the Present
Paul Johnson

Order is an exotic in Ireland. It has been imported from England, but it will not grow. It suits neither soil nor climate.
–J. A. Froude, *The Two Chiefs of Dunboy*, 1889

Paul Johnson, former editor of the *New Statesman* and author of highly acclaimed histories and biographies, tackles the turbulent history of a land where order may be not simply exotic but nearly unknown. From the first arrival of the English through siege, rebellion, and civil war to Home Rule and the "Troubles" of the present era, Johnson presents Ireland's story through his vivid depiction of influential personalities and by quoting their own words. A section of black-and-white illustrations, complete notes of sources, and full index add to the book's appeal and usefulness.

Ireland is brief, compact, and informative. In short, it is exactly as its subtitle states: "A Concise History from the Twelfth Century to the Present Day."

(Academy Chicago, 1980, 1984, ISBN 0-89733-123-0, softcover, 272 pages, $6.95)

The Road Wet, The Wind Close: Celtic Ireland
James Charles Roy

Immerse yourself in Celtic Ireland as you travel with James Charles Roy through thousands of years of Irish history, from 7000 B.C. until the Norman invasion of the late twelfth century. During this era Ireland remained separate from the rest of Europe, developing her own way, relatively free of outside influence.

Roy's innovative approach to presenting the rich and colorful history of those years is to visit historic sites around the island and tell, in an informed but conversational manner, the story of the period each represents. He begins with a monastery from *c.* A.D. 640 at Skellig Michael, where he discusses the "cult phenomenon" of the druids. "Druids, quite simply," he writes, "were an order of priesthood. They were specifically Celtic, coming to Ireland *c.* 300 B.C. when their tribes migrated from Continental Europe . . . Druids looked to nature for guidance and rulings. They too were seers and prophets."

Along the way he debunks those sites that he feels are overrated like Tara, outside of Dublin:

For an age that should know better we seem to be losing . . . our ability to sort through fiction and arrive at some bearing that approximates reality. People come to Tara . . . to speculate over the glories of days gone by, glories that in truth hardly existed. Few spots in the world have been, in popular imagination, more abused.

And he ends with Mellifont Abbey, which witnessed the end of the Celtic era. "The purest Celtic Age could never survive intact. It would, over the centuries, squirm, fall back, revive, crumble. Mellifont predicts this clearly, "It is Irish, but not Celtic." Roy illustrates his journey through Irish Celtic antiquity with numerous black-and-white photographs, drawings, and maps.

If it is true, as Eleanor Hull said in 1908, that one of the Irish historians' greatest difficulties is "to discriminate where the imaginary ends and the actual begins," Roy deserves great praise for sifting through the myths and enchantment to find the actual.

(Dufour Editions, 1988, ISBN 0-8023-1283-7, softcover, 232 pages, $15.95)

Trinity
Leon Uris

"In Ireland there is no future, only the past happening over and over again," says Leon Uris, adapting the words of Eugene O'Neill. And here he tells the story of the past, focusing on the seventy-five-year period from the famine of the 1840s to the Easter Rising of 1916. Within this time he depicts the conflicting forces that "over and over again" bring strife to this troubled land.

Using three families, the "trinity" of the book's title, to exemplify the strands of Irish society, he personalizes differences so that all positions are understandable. To begin, there are the Larkins, hardworking Irish Catholics, struggling to bring forth food from the land. Then there are the Hubbles, noble British aristocrats, determined that Ireland is but an English colony, and the MacLeods, devout Presbyterians, loyal to the claims of their Scottish ancestors.

The story moves from a small Donegal village to the slums of Londonderry and on to the ports of Belfast, capturing at each locale different elements of Irish life. Of course there is a love story—the young Catholic rebel and the heroic Protestant girl and . . .

But that would give away the ending. Suffice it to say that fact and fiction mingle in a drama that explains as it entertains and holds out hope while it speaks of despair.

(Bantam, 1976, ISBN 0-553-25846-X, softcover, 815 pages, $4.95)

LITERATURE

A Writer's Ireland: Landscape in Literature
William Trevor

The trees are in their autumn beauty,
The woodland paths are dry,
Under the October twilight the water
Mirrors a still sky . . .

With these words of W. B. Yeats we step back in time and walk the paths of Coole Park, a Galway rendezvous for the writers of the 1920s that has since been designated a national shrine by the Forestry and Wild Life Service.

In **A Writer's Ireland** William Trevor takes us to this spot and others in his native land through the anonymous sagas of the early Celts and the meticulous chronicles of the monastic scribes, through the prose of nationalism and the poetry of exile.

We read of the hardships of the nineteenth century that caused some to emigrate:

Adieu to Belashanny! where I was bred and born
Go where I may I'll think of you, as sure as night and morn . . .
–William Allingham

and others to despair:

Weary men, what reap ye?—'Golden corn for the stranger.'
What sow ye?—'Human corses that await for the Avenger.'
–Lady Wilde

And in the last chapters we come to the more recent masterpieces of Synge, Yeats, and Joyce—all revealing bits and pieces of the story of Ireland. Trevor weaves these pieces together and intersperses them with relevant quotes, illustrations and photos. The result is a sensitive tapestry in which Irish authors and poets speak for themselves, delineating the history and character of their beloved Erin.

(Penguin, 1984, ISBN 0-1400-7704-9, softcover, oversized, 192 pages, $12.95)

NATURE

The Gardens of Ireland
Michael George and Patrick Bowe

Greens of every shade (including emerald, of course) provide a background for a riot of color in **The Gardens of Ireland.** A remarkable variety of plants, even subtropical species, thrive in Ireland's coastal valleys, and this book of sumptuous photographs and illuminating text by Michael George and Patrick Bowe highlights twenty-one of Erin's gardens, each outstanding in its own way.

Richard Grove Annesley, they note, helped finance an expedition to China and Nepal in 1924 to bring back wild plants and seeds for domestication in genteel gardens. His garden in County Cork, now in the care of his grandson, continues to exhibit specimens from that trip.

Birr Castle in County Offaly boasts 150 acres of gardens, still owned and managed by the family that acquired the property in 1620. Sir William Parsons, the owner in 1841, built what was then the largest telescope in the world with a tube over fifty feet long and seven feet wide. Feeling that the instrument was somewhat out of place in an ornamental garden, he "dressed up its supporting walls with Gothic arcading and battlements." Eventually ramparts, a gatehouse, and iron gates were added—and the entire structure remains to this day.

Most of the featured gardens are open to the public; the book includes a list of these and a map to help locate them. There is also a horticultural index, making it easy to find examples of a favorite plant. Whether to plant a seed of inspiration to visit Ireland, or for help in making your own garden look like a "piece o' the auld sod," this book is a nature lover's delight.

(New York Graphic Society/Little, Brown, 1986, ISBN 0-8212-1619-8, hardcover, oversized, 191 pages, $39.95)

The Living Isles
Peter Crawford

See England—Nature

PERFORMING ARTS

Irish Traditional Music
Ciarán Carson

*There are three ways of telling every story
but a thousand ways of singing every song.*

—Irish Proverb

   This small (3½" × 7½") pocket guide to **Irish Traditional Music** may not list a thousand ways of singing even one of Ireland's many traditional songs, but it does a remarkable job of explaining, with wit and brevity, the living tradition of Irish music. Enlivened with quotations from musicians and writers from several centuries and illustrated with line drawings, the book discusses what traditional music is, typical instruments, and even the etiquette of listening to music in a pub:

To the casual observer, a pub session of traditional music may appear haphazard and undisciplined: tunes are struck up at seemingly random intervals . . . some punters (i.e., non-musicians) may, at unpredictable moments, utter inarticulate cries of what might be encouragement . . . In reality, the session, like any form of social or artistic discourse, is governed by a complex set of implicit rules.

   What are these rules? How do the Irish uilleann pipes differ from Scottish bagpipes? What is a bodhrán, and should it really be played with a penknife? And is it true that the theme from "Dallas" and the Beatles's song "Hey, Jude" have been made into Irish dance tunes? All these questions and more are answered in this wee gem of a book.

(Appletree Press, Belfast, from Irish Books and Media, 1986, ISBN 0-86281-168-6, softcover, $5.95)

100 Irish Ballads

   The familiar tunes of "Botany Bay," "Cockles and Mussels," "The Last Rose of Summer," "When I Was Single," and other Irish melodies both familiar and obscure ring forth from this delightful audio tape. Accompanied by a small songbook, it features Anne Byrne, The Druids, and other traditional musicians singing and performing the first verse and chorus of ninety songs on bazooki, bodhrahan, flute, banjo and fiddle.

Lively and spirited, this is music guaranteed to set your toes tapping and your hands clapping.

(Soodlum Music Co., Ltd., Dublin, from Music Sales, 1985, ISBN none, softcover plus audio tape, 112 pages, $14.95)

YOUNG PEOPLE'S BOOKS

A Family in Ireland
Tom Moran
For ages seven to ten

Páid (pronounced Pawd) O Neachtain is nine years old. He plays hurling (a sport similar to hockey), speaks Gaelic rather than English when he's with his family, and likes to play old tunes on the Irish tin whistle. On weekends he goes into the bog near his home to cut bricks of peat to burn in the fireplace. His life is modern, but he tries to remember the traditions of the past.

Tom Moran travels to Ireland via words and pictures, taking young readers along with him to meet Páid and his family. He blends the familiar and the unusual, allowing children to enjoy and understand their counterparts across the sea.

(Lerner, 1986, ISBN 0-8225-1668-3, hardcover, 32 pages, $8.95)

Ireland: Land of Mist and Magic
Kathleen Allan Meyer
For ages ten to thirteen

Ireland's patron saint, St. Patrick, was actually British by birth. He was kidnapped at age sixteen by a Celtic king who brought the lad to Ireland. Although Patrick escaped, he later returned to spread the Christian faith. His preaching brought him into conflict with the Druids and eventually, legend has it, into a contest of faith with the chief Druid. When Patrick caused the Druid's snow to melt and his darkness to become light, he was allowed to preach throughout the kingdom. "He had a more lasting effect than any invader," states author Kathleen Meyer, who then goes on to mention other Irish heroes in a short overview of Irish history.

But history is just a small part of this tale of the "land of mist and magic." Other sections are devoted to Irish character and families, festivals and celebrations, schools and sports. And, of course, no book on Ireland would be complete without a chapter on leprechauns and the Blarney Stone. According to Irish folklore, says Meyer, leprechauns "are real mischief-makers. [They] don't like pointed fence posts, though. Many fences in the countryside were built this way to keep these nosy creatures from getting into trouble."

While the black-and-white photos aren't able to show the hues of the rainbows or the greens of the countryside, they do add interest to the text. A map of Ireland and a glossary are also included.

"There are only two kinds of people," goes an old Irish saying, "those who are Irish and those who want to be." Both will enjoy this book.

(Dillon, 1983, ISBN 0-87518-228-3, hardcover, 144 pages, $12.95)

Voices of Northern Ireland: Growing Up in a Troubled Land
Carolyn Meyer
For ages twelve and up

What's it like to be a teenager in a country torn apart by racial or religious strife? Carolyn Meyer, an oft-published writer for young people, had already answered that question as regards South Africa when, in 1986, she set out for six weeks in Northern Ireland.

"I was not happy in Northern Ireland," she says honestly. "Part of it was the weather, so awful that people boast about its awfulness . . . But is wasn't just the weather. It was the distrust, the suspicion, the anger always simmering just below the surface. People talked about 'having a good crack,' but they seldom seemed really to be having fun. How could they? They were too busy deciding whether a stranger is Catholic or Protestant, and if it was 'the other one,' then bracing for trouble, for dislike, maybe for anger or hatred, possibly for violence."

But Meyer liked the people, and she talked to a lot of them—not only teens but also children and adults, both Catholic and Protestant. She intersperses tales of her encounters with historical background and, always, with questions. Why, she wonders for example, is there no such thing as compromise in Northern Ireland? "Exploring similarities," she concludes, "is not the way people think here; harping on differences is."

Meyer's style is clear and direct, her manner warm and friendly. Although she says her book is intended for teens, adults can learn from it as well.

(Gulliver/Harcourt Brace Jovanovich, 1987, ISBN 0-15-200635-4, hardcover, 212 pages, $15.95)

FRANCE

GENERAL

Baron Philippe
Baron Philippe de Rothschild and Joan Littlewood

Yachts, racing cars, wine, and women—these were the interests of Baron Philippe de Rothschild, and not always in that order! Here he collaborates with Joan Littlewood in "a very candid autobiography" that traces his life from its non-humble beginnings through his emergence as a pre-eminent wine-maker.

Baron Philippe began life in a thirty-room home with doors "big enough to admit four tall giraffes, walking abreast." Yet he was most happy when visiting his grandmother's neglected estate, Mouton. There he feasted on onions and garlic, drank wine, and tramped through mud. "It was my idea of paradise," he says.

At the age of twenty he became manager of Mouton and began its conversion into one of the world's leading producers of fine wines. It's amazing that he had the time, considering his passions for architecture, poetry, astronomy, theater, yachts, and racing cars—not to mention his detention and imprisonment by the Nazis during World War II. And certainly not to mention the time he spent pursuing women: "I earned the title of 'womanizer.' I would have preferred 'woman lover' but there it is, seducers can't be choosers, and I really didn't care a damn what they said—I loved the game."

Exuberant, hedonistic, and above all, eminently likeable, Baron Philippe tells his story in a book that bubbles like the finest champagne.

(Ballantine, 1984, ISBN 0-345-33040-4, softcover, 330 pages, $8.95)

The Chateau
William Maxwell

The time is the late 1940s; the place, the château country of the Loire Valley. Barbara and Harold Rhodes, a young American couple, have arrived for a three-month vacation. Naive and impressionable, they are eager to become fast friends with France and the French. During a two-week stay in the village of Brenodville their lives become involved with those of the proprietress of their pensione, Mme Viénot, several members of her family, and some of the other boarders, including the mysteriously aristocratic Mme Straus-Muguet, who inexplicably takes them under her wing when they visit Paris.

But in the post-war atmosphere of rebuilding and rationing, many look at the Americans with a mixture of envy and distrust:

"Do I imagine it," he asked, "or is it true that when they speak of the Nazis . . . the very next sentence is invariably some quite disconnected remark about Americans?"

Separated by language and culture from their would-be friends, Harold and Barbara are sometimes dismayed, sometimes delighted and often puzzled by the reactions to their earnest attempts to win international friendship.

The Château is a gentle novel, "beguilingly old fashioned" says the *New York Times Book Review*. It shows, through the eyes of Barbara and Harold, the pleasures and pitfalls of total immersion in another culture.

(Godine, 1985, ISBN 0-87923-600-0, softcover, 402 pages, $10.95)

The English Channel
Nigel Calder

See England—General

France High-Tech
Edited by Mark Hunter

Computers, robots, and nuclear reactors in the land of Notre Dame, *haute cuisine*, and peaceful vineyards? *Mais oui!* In today's France, high tech is high chic.

Consider: Skiers ride to the top of Saulire Mountain in the French Alps via a computer-controlled cable car that is one of the fastest and safest in the world.

Consider: France produces sixty percent of her electricity through nuclear power and soon expects to fulfill half of her energy requirements domestically, a dramatic increase in energy independence.

Consider: At the distribution center for IBM France, a fleet of French-built robotic trucks runs along an underground cable, collecting and delivering orders.

And there are still more Gallic breakthroughs: "The sorting of letters at the Post Office is choreographed on streams of air. Actors in a holographic camera seem to break through the screen. The world's smallest cameras find their way into robot hands . . ."

France High-Tech includes eye-opening essays on current happenings in biotechnology, telecommunications, computing, manufacturing, and robotics, proving that France is once again a leader in the avant garde. Today, of course, the avant garde is technological.

(Autrement, Paris, from Bookpeople, 1985, ISBN 2-86260-149-7, softcover, 257 pages, $17.95)

The French
Theodore Zeldin

For many Americans the French are one of the puzzles of Europe. We copy their food, envy their culture, shake our heads at their arrogance, and wonder at their humor. Who are these French? Will we ever understand them?

Historian Theodore Zeldin answers these questions partly by using various articles and statistics, but mostly by letting the French speak for themselves. Through a remarkable series of interviews he talks with the famous and the ordinary about their passions, what makes them happy, how they treat others and what they believe.

Here are Brigitte Bardot the star and Saint-Laurent the designer, as well as Jean Marq the baker and Philippe Yverneau the farmer. And there is Noelle—wife of an electrician and, at last, a homeowner. "I may not have any diplomas, but with my own hands I've been able to get this," she says, gesturing toward her small house. "I have something of my own and something to leave the children; they'll have a less tough time than we did; it'll be butter on their spinach."

Here also is the duc de Brissac who is lord of a magnificent castle in Anjou as well as three other homes. "He could be regarded," says Zeldin, "as one of the country's leading experts on privilege." The duc does not dispute this but adds modestly, "No one gets what he deserves; we know that."

Illustrated with fifty cartoons that prove Gallic humor can be understood even by the non-French, **The French** is a book for anyone interested in the "real France"—not the monuments, museums, and churches, but the people who live around the corner and pass by on the bus or in their limousines on their way to work.

(Vintage, 1984, ISBN 0-394-72421-6, softcover, 538 pages, $9.95)

Inspector Maigret Stories
Georges Simenon

It's early morning in Paris, and Prosper Donge is bicycling to the hotel where he works as a chef. In the damp, cold air he pedals across the Pont de Saint-Cloud, passes through the Bois de Bologne, and notes with consternation that his back tire is flat when he reaches the Porte Dauphine. Slowed to a walk, he passes other landmarks—Avenue Foch, the Arc de Triomphe, the Champs-Elysees . . . Then, he finds a body in the hotel basement, and Inspector Jules Maigret is called to investigate.

In this case the book is **Maigret and the Hotel Majestic**, but the inspector is the lead character in more than one hundred novels and short stories by Georges Simenon. All are enthralling detective yarns that, as an added bonus, are steeped in French lore. For those who combine a love of France with a passion for mystery, a taste of the Maigret stories may lead to an addiction.

(Maigret and the Hotel Majestic: Harcourt Brace Jovanovich, 1982, ISBN 0-15-655133-0, softcover, 176 pages, $2.95)

A Little Tour in France
Henry James

"I traveled with two companions during my October visit to France last year, one living and one dead. My quick comrade was (and is) my husband. My ghostly friend was Henry James, who lives on in the pages of a book titled **A Little Tour in France**," writes Mary Ann Hoberman of *The New York Times*.

Henry, as he liked to be called, took this "little tour" over one hundred years ago and has been dead for nearly seventy; yet in this book he proves himself to be "far more alive than most of the flesh and blood guides whose rote recitals so often [reduce] fascinating monuments to dreary inanimate piles."

With relaxed charm and infectious delight, Henry begins his tour in Tours ("perhaps as a pun," suggests Leon Edel in the introduction, "but more likely because it is the birthplace of Balzac, whom [Henry] considered 'the father of us all—the fountainhead of the modern novel'"). He travels in and around the château country and the Midi, full of lively curiosity and mischievous good humor.

"We have entered the court, by the way, by jumping over the walls. The more orthodox method is to follow a modern terrace," explains Henry as he explores the Château de Blois. "Here, as elsewhere, lightness and grace are the keynote; and the recesses of the windows, with their happy proportions, their sculpture, and their colour, are the empty frames of brilliant pictures . . ." and he goes on, pointing out architectural highlights, relating bits of history, digressing on "pardonable flights of fancy."

Ever the erudite guide, Henry looks for the picturesque and discovers the characteristic. His enjoyment is contagious, his observations and reflections illuminating—in short, he is the perfect traveling companion.

(Farrar, Straus and Giroux, 1983, ISBN 374-51807-60970, softcover, 247 pages, $9.95)

Note: A Little Tour in France is also available in a deluxe edition, replete with lustrous Impressionist paintings of the era (reproduced in full color) as well as with watercolors by Joseph Pennell and sketches by Dechemant. In a 9" × 7½" format, small enough for comfortable reading yet large enough for table-top display, this is a book to return to again and again.

(Weidenfeld & Nicolson, 1900, 1987, ISBN 0-283-99464-9, hardcover, 255 pages, $20.00)

Permanent Parisians
Judi Culbertson and Tom Randall

Paris is famous for her croissants, her art treasures, and her general cachet, but perhaps she is less well knwon for her necrography. Yet nothing illustrates the slender line between life and death so well as the cemeteries of Paris. Stone figures seem to start up from their beds as if hearing a noise, or dance as if they had been turned to marble without warning. To visit these burial grounds is to be struck with wonder.

So begins **Permanent Parisians**, an off-beat tour of the cemeteries of Paris. More than a guidebook, it is a blending of history and biography, covering the wide range of notables buried in the City of Lights. The authors visit the graves of both the famous and infamous from France's Voltaire, Rousseau, and Marie Antoinette to America's Isadora Duncan, Jean Seberg, and Jim Morrison.

Each of the deceased is listed in the index, making it easy to locate the cemetery in which he or she rests and the page on which a thumbnail sketch and anecdotal tidbit appear. For example, we learn that "it took Jacob Epstein three years to sculpt [Oscar Wilde's] monument, done in an Egyptian art deco style. When Epstein arrived to put the finishing touches on the statue, he found it shrouded and guarded by a gendarme; the cemetery conservateur had found it 'indecent' and had it banned." Photos of some of the memorial momuments and gravestones are included.

Permanent Parisians provides an unusual way to become involved with the people of Paris. With its help you may find you agree with Balzac, who said, "What I feel myself flagging I go and cheer myself up in the Père Lachaise [cemetery] . . . While seeking out the dead I see nothing but the living."

(Chelsea Green, 1986, ISBN 0-930031-03-02, softcover, 230 pages, $15.95)

The South of France
Edited by Laura Raison

Laura Raison's book transports the reader to the Mediterranean climes of Southern France: to olive and orange groves, pristine beaches, medieval towns, and bustling modern cities.

Raison collected letters, prose extracts, short stories, and even recipes from those who lived in or visited Provence through the centuries. These bits and pieces speak for themselves, explaining the area's magnetic attraction. The clear sharp light, for example, has always challenged artists, and Van Gogh's description of Arles is as vivid as the blazing colors he used:

Of the town one sees only some red roofs and a tower, the rest is hidden by the green foliage of fig trees . . . and a narrow stripe of blue sky above it. The town is surrounded by immense meadows all abloom with countless buttercups—a sea of yellow—in the foreground these meadows are divided by a ditch full of violet irises . . . What a subject!

Mark Twain, however, was considerably more prosaic in his observation of Marseille:

These Marseillaise make Marseilles hymns, and Marseilles vests, and Marseilles soap for all the world; but they never sing their hymns, or wear their vests, or wash with their soap themselves.

Quotes from notables as varied as Emile Zola and Ezra Pound, Francesco Petrarch and Noel Coward, Brigette Bardot and the Countess of Die combine to form a composite picture of one of France's most unforgettable regions. **The South of France** is a verbal album that begets dreams of a trip-to-come as well as memories of one recently completed.

(Beaufort, 1985, ISBN 0-8253-0334-6, hardcover, 248 pages, $19.95)

Through Parisian Eyes
Melinda Camber Porter

There is a very ancient French tradition which is this respect for a small class of people who are very cultivated, and are often very highly developed, intellectually . . . These intellectuals created the illusion for the rest of the world that France is made up of cultivated people . . . And it's not true.

—Françoise Giroud

Although Giroud may feel that France is no longer the capital of western culture, Melinda Camber Porter seems to prove otherwise in **Through Parisian Eyes**, aptly subtitled "Reflections on Contemporary French Arts and Culture."

Her book is a collection of thirty-three interviews with some of the most prominent figures in modern France including François Truffaut, Eugène Ionesco, Louis Malle, Marguerite Duras, Françoise Sagan, Yves Montand, Jean-Paul Sartre, Roger Vadim, and André Malraux. Writers, philosohers, directors and actors—they all reveal themselves under Porter's trenchant questioning on many subjects.

On politics: director Costa-Gavras *(Z, Missing)* states that "the real impediment to understanding is extremism. People (in France) catalogue you as being Left or Right Wing. Automatically. And that makes absolutely no sense . . . It's a dogmatic fanaticism."

On feminism: Delphine Seyrig says, "We oppress women by offering them an image which is impossible to live up to. We set up envy. But that, again, is typical of man's attempt to sow discord among women."

And on intellectualism: Jean Anouilh is outspoken in his view that "one can appear to be intelligent in modern terms while remaining essentially stupid. The intellect has been popularized and mass-produced."

Porter leads her subjects through a kaleidoscopic array of topics, and in so doing uncovers not only the personalities but also the ideas that make France a country on the cutting edge of international cultural and intellectual life.

(Oxford, 1986, ISBN 0-19-504104-6, hardcover, 244 pages, $18.95)

Two Towns in Provence
M.F.K. Fisher

It is a special treat to travel with a friend—someone who acts as a guide, taking you to delightful out-of-the-way places, entertaining you with anecdotes, introducing you to surprising new foods and to lively, interesting people. It is even more wonderful if that friend happens to be adventurous, witty, observant and articulate.

Such a person is M.F.K. Fisher, and her portraits of **Two Towns In Provence,** Aix-en-Provence and Marseille, are just such a treat. Fisher begins in Aix-en-Provence on a holiday visit with her daughters, and returns again and again, drawn by "the sounds of its fountains in the early hours, by the melodious play of the pure clear sunlight of Provence through its summer cave of leaves." Their sojourns involve misunderstandings and frustrations as well as moments of deep contentment as they have ongoing adventures with lodgings, schooling, meals, language, and customs.

In Marseille they at first tread gently, wary of a city with a reputation for "dope, whores, and street violence." Yet Fisher finds the city to have a "special karma," and she reaches back into history to find the roots of Marseille's special mystique.

This is not, says Fisher, "a guidebook, the kind that tells how, with a chart to be got free from the driver of the tour, to follow a green line from A to G . . . I am not meant to tell anyone where to go . . . All I can do in this explanation about my being there is to write something about the town itself, through my own senses."

That, of course, is more than enough. Aix-en-Provence and Marseille should be proud to have been "explained" by such a delightful writer.

(Vintage, 1964, ISBN 0-394-71631-0, softcover, 212 pages, $7.95)

When in France
Christopher Sinclair-Stevenson

Take the legendary prowess of the French as lovers and their equally renowned abilities in the kitchen. Throw in a dash of history, an evocative tour of the châteaux in the Loire Valley, and a short course in wine-making. Round it all out with an examination of the typical Frenchman's chauvinism—or lack thereof—and you have the delightful **When in France.**

Written by Briton Christopher Sinclair-Stevenson, this penetrating view of France is an entertaining blend of fact and opinion, full of humor and warmth. He comments on Paris:

Parisian drivers are the worst in the world, Parisian waiters the most supercilious, Parisian concierges the greediest . . . but [Parisians] are also as courteous and helpful as any other inhabitant of any other capital city throughout the world.

remarks on "designer water":

The war of the waters is ferocious and never-ending. Water has always been drunk with meals in France, sometimes to dilute a strong red wine but generally in order to help the long-suffering liver to combat too much rich or heavy food. But water has become big business . . . And the French manufacturers . . . cannot be blamed if they make a great deal of money in the process.

and describes the intense beauty of Provence:

. . . the glowing red of the roof tiles, the bleached bone-white of the rocks which Cezanne so miraculously caught, the stark green of the umbrella pines, the scarlet and yellow of the canna lilies, the purple bougainvillea, the intense blue of the sky and the sea . . . glimpsed through the grey olive trees and the black cypresses.

Sinclair-Stevenson is an admitted Francophile and his book is a labor of love. John Kenneth Galbraith puts it best when he says, "Americans were once thought about equally divided between those who wanted in the hereafter to go to heaven and those who wished to go to Paris. [This book] could shift the balance dangerously toward Paris—and France."

(Simon and Schuster, 1987, ISBN 0-671-41644-8, hardcover, 223 pages, $15.95)

ANTHROPOLOGY

The Horse of Pride: Life in a Breton Village
Pierre-Jakez Hélias

Since I am too poor to buy any other horse, at least the Horse of Pride will always have a stall in my stable.
—Alain le Goff, the Elder

Alain le Goff, the Elder, was speaking for all his neighbors when he said these words, words that were never forgotten by his grandson, author Pierre-Jakez Hélias. Nearly fifty years later, Hélias recreated the world of his childhood, a Brittany which was then much as it had been five hundred years earlier. The power of the Church was all encompassing, the Breton language was spoken exclusively, the forces of nature were often harshly unrelenting, and most important of all, the people possessed the quiet pride and dignity of which his grandfather spoke.

Brittany has recently been studied—some would say invaded—by hordes of anthropologists, most of whom were unable to give what Hélias considers to be a true picture of his culture. "Although I went along rather often into the rural Breton-speaking areas with researchers from all countries," he says, "I suggested that they beware of taking tall stories, told with the utmost seriousness, as tribal revelations. There were a number of people around who had recently become rich and had forgotten they had ever been poor . . . In contrast to the Horse of Pride, they are symbolized by the Ass of Vanity."

To rectify this, Hélias (now a distinguished ethnologist and president of the National Folklore Commission) has written this memoir of the Brittany that was. He introduces us to the people and lets us join in their activities. We go with him to masses, to weddings, to funerals and to the fields; and through his eyes we are able to witness France's peasant past.

(Yale, 1978, ISBN 0-300-02036-8, hardcover, 384 pages, $34.00)

ART AND ARCHITECTURE

Art Works Itself into a Region: Visual Arts in France
Dominique Frétard

The visual arts are in Fashion. In fashion in France. Will we soon be seeing artists present their collections twice a year, like fashion designers? At the rate young artists in France's provinces are working, nothing is impossible . . . Brushes and scissors spring to work as a creative fever grips the provinces. Paris is no longer the artistic center . . . instead there's Lyon, Bordeaux, Lille and Marseille. Painting reckons it can be shamelessly figurative. Sculpture practically explodes in free-wheeling installations. Video's light brightens every field. Photography and comics leave their inferiority complexes behind, and new technology is shaping the next generation of artists in pilot schools. If you don't believe it, just hop on a train . . . or dip into this book. The author's already made the trip on your behalf. And she had a very good time.

With obvious enthusiasm, Dominique Frétard gallivants through the provinces, investigating the political and social climate that sustains the arts. She quotes Daniel Nouaille, president of FRAC (Regional Fund for Contemporary Art), Limousin: "We live in a society in which creativity can no longer be separated from economic and industrial problems."

The photographs are more often portraits of the artists than of their work, although a thirty-page color section at the end of the book does feature the art itself. This is followed by a five-page listing of important galleries and museums, complete with addresses and phone numbers.

This book is currently available only in a bilingual edition. The French text is set in type more than twice the size of the English and is reproduced in black whereas the English is in hard-to-read gray. Many of the captions, and indeed the table of contents, are only in French, which makes the book unnecessarily difficult for the English reader. Yet **Art Works Itself into a Region** (or *L'Art dans toutes ses Régions*, as it prefers to be called) is both unusual and worthwhile. People with a strong interest in contemporary French art may find the language problem to be an affront and an inconvenience, but not an insurmountable obstacle.

(Autrement, Paris, from Bookpeople, 1986, ISBN 2086-260-156-X, softcover, oversized, 176 pages, $19.95)

French Style
Suzanne Slesin and Stafford Cliff

Like the French woman, the quintessential French interior always looks put together as if by magic, projecting a thoughtful nonchalance, a refined elegance. It is composed without being self-conscious; a composition of shapes, a range of textures. It is quiet and serene without being dull; it can celebrate traditional values without being formal; it can be modern without being trendy.

French Style is a warm invitation to stroll through paneled foyers, admire elaborately carved mantels, and sniff herbs in classic country kitchens. Four hundred fifty full-color photographs provide entrance to more than twenty-five homes—city and country houses, apartments, lofts, ateliers and châteaux—and document the Gallic flair for design. Whether charmingly rustic as in the French country look or gracefully understated for a high-tech ambience, the interiors reflect the vitality and elegance of contemporary French life.

An ivy-covered iron staircase leads to an Art Deco living room in the villa of Maimé Arnodin and Denise Fayolle while fantasy dominates the Parisian studio of Louise de la Falaise. There nearly sixty candles twinkle in a magnificent eighteenth-century chandelier, recreating the glitter and sparkle of French court life.

Comfort is the theme of Pacha Bensimon's sixteenth-century home in the Touraine. An old coat rack displays a collection of antique country jugs; a claw-footed bathtub is decorated with a trompe-l'oeil marble-like effect; and bundles of grass and heather are hung on the walls to remind one of the surrounding countryside.

Dirand's photographs are superb; Slesin's and Cliff's words provide the necessary explanation. For those of us who can't wangle personal invitations to the premier French homes, their book is the next best thing.

(Potter, 1982, ISBN 0-517-545802, hardcover, oversized, 288 pages, $35.00)

The Impressionists at First Hand
Edited by Bernard Denvir

Degas worried about more than paints and palettes; he was also concerned about a new lease for his flat. And Renoir, despite the joys of painting lovely women, had to make sure his steam tricycle would get from Saint-Cloud to Paris.

These men, along with their fellow impressionists, were "individually various," says Bernard Denvir. It is their humanity, rather than their painting, that he seeks to emphasize in his collection of writings by and about these artists, **The Impressionists at First Hand.**

Here are Degas's comments on a visit to America; Cassatt's admission of strain and depression; Renoir seen through the eyes of his brother; and Manet from the viewpoint of his friend and supporter, Emile Zola.

Many writings give clues to the artists' interactions with each other, as when Manet in 1875 asked mutual friends to help Monet with his perpetual financial difficulties:

I went to see Monet yesterday. I found him in great distress, and at his wits' end. He asked me if I could find someone who would buy at choice ten or twenty of his paintings at 100 francs each. Do you think that we could fix him up between ourselves, each of us contributing 500 francs? Of course it must be understood that nobody, and he least of all, should know that we are arranging it ourselves. I had thought of a dealer or a collector, but I have been frightened of a refusal.

or when Renoir rebelled at exhibiting with fellow artists whom he considered to be of an unfortunate political persuasion:

To exhibit with Pissarro, Gauguin and Guillaumin would be as if I were exhibiting with some Socialist group. Before long Pissarro will be inviting Lavrof [a Russian anarchist] or some other revolutionary.

The Impressionists at First Hand lets the artists paint themselves in words as they painted others in oils. It is a fascinating, revealing, and completely impressionistic portrait.

(Thames and Hudson, 1987, ISBN 0-500-20209-5, softcover, 224 pages, $9.95)

Louis XIV's Versailles
Guy Walton

The château Louis XIV inherited from his father was a modest hunting lodge built on land described by the Duke de Saint Simon as "that most dismal and thankless of spots, without vistas, woods or water, without soil even, for all the surrounding land is quicksand or bog, and the air cannot be healthy."

Under Louis's administration this unpromising piece of real estate became the palace of Versailles, a "resplendent complex of buildings that ultimately set the standards for art and design in all of Europe." It is now the most-visited monument in France, an incredible architectural achievement and the epitome of "civilized living on a grand scale."

This comprehensive one-volume history takes a penetrating look at the lengendary palace in its political and historical setting. In particular, Walton investigates the period during which Louis XIV lived at Versailles, influencing greatly the design and decoration of the buildings: "No detail of interior decoration was too small to interest him. There was a standing order that everything was to be submitted to the king with alternative propositions, and either the king himself or his superintendent then noted the royal decision."

Louis XIV dreamed of creating a palace that "would represent at once the personal dignity and the political glory of the king and the ascendance of French art and design over Italian." Versailles is his expression of that dream.

(University of Chicago, 1986, ISBN 0-226-87255-6, softcover, 256 pages, $14.95)

Mont Saint Michel and Chartres
Henry Adams

Mont Saint Michel and Chartres is the record, not of a literal journey across the Atlantic Ocean and France, but of a meditative one across strange seas of thought and feeling. It is the narration of a voyage of the imagination across interior landscapes.

Thus does Raymond Carney of Middlebury College speak of Henry Adams's intriguing essays that, by focusing on the two structures of the book's title, bring together art, philosophy, religion, history, and architecture. In Adams's view the cathedrals of Mont Saint Michel and Chartres bring one close to truth and beauty: "If you want to know what Churches were made for, come down here on some great festival of the Virgin, and give yourself up to it; but come alone! That kind of knowledge cannot be taught and can seldom be shared . . . For us, the world is not a schoolroom or a pulpit, but a stage, and the stage is the highest yet seen on earth." And so he takes us along on his study of "the theatre of life," as represented in the medieval European world, and demonstrates a rare ability to share his experience.

Henry Adams, of the American family that engendered two presidents, was a man of intrepid intelligence and delightful verbal facility. His many talents (journalist, professor, writer, and diplomat) and avid curiosity enabled him to "breathe life into what others might see merely as monuments."

Mont Saint Michel and Chartres includes black-and-white photographs and line drawings that transport readers back into the thirteenth century. There, book in hand, they can roam the passages of two of the world's great cathedrals and hear the echoes of those who have gone before.

(Penguin, 1904, 1986, ISBN 0-14-3-9054-5, softcover, 398 pages, $6.95)

Paris Arts on Seine
Edited by William Mahder

- *A highly individual cinema, freed from the molds of realism and literature, is emerging in Paris . . .*
- *The new French architecture, far from forming a school, is a variegated and cosmopolitan milieu . . .*
- *Paris has steadily strengthened its claim as a world city of performing arts . . .*
- *One thing is sure: French dancers are riding a wave of renewed self-confidence . . .*

Paris Arts on Seine is a collage, an assemblage of articles about the movements and personalities that dominate the diverse world of Creative Paris. Nearly a hundred journalists, critics, illustrators and photographers—French, English and American—combined forces to "capture the essence of contemporary creation."

Sixteen sections explore modes of expression: architecture, art, cinema, cuisine, dance, fashion, graphics, interior design, jazz, literature, media, music, photography, rock, theater, and video. Eighteen interviews probe the minds of people like composer Iannis Xenakis, director Patrice Chéreau, and photographer Jacques-Henri Lartigue.

Photos and illustraions abound. The book vibrates with energy, hyperventilates with excitement. Arts on Seine, you realize, is where it's at.

(Autrement, Paris, from Bookpeople, 1985, ISBN 2-86260-073-3, softcover, 429 pages, $14.95)

CUISINE

Between Meals
A. J. Liebling

The first requisite for eating well, according to veteran writer and eater A. J. Liebling, is a good appetite such as his friend and mentor M. Mirande possessed. Mirande would dispatch "a lunch of raw Bayonne ham and fresh figs, a hot sausage in crust, spindles of filleted pike in a rich rose *sauce Nantua*, a leg of lamb larded with anchovies, artichokes on a pedestal of foie gras, and four or five kinds of cheese, with a good bottle of Bordeaux and one of champagne"—and then begin instructing the cook about preparations for dinner.

Next Leibling suggests you "put in your apprenticeship as a feeder when you have enough money to pay the check but not enough to produce indifference to the size of the total . . . The optimum financial position for a serious apprentice feeder is to have funds in hand for three more days, with a reasonable, but not certain, prospect of reinforcements thereafter . . . The man of appetite who will stint himself when he can see three days ahead has no vocation."

In **Between Meals,** Liebling looks back at a golden age of eating and drinking in Paris, "a legendary Paris," writes James Salter in his introduction, "parts of which no longer exist." The book was inspired by Liebling's reminiscences on the year (1926-7) he spent studying at the Sorbonne, where he attended few classes but learned lessons that were even more valuable than those taught in the classroom. The book is a nostalgic ode to excess, to memorable meals and great wines, and to the undiscovered bistros and neighborhood restaurants that served them.

(North Point, 1986, ISBN 0-86547-236-X, softcover, 185 pages, $10.95)

Blue Trout and Black Truffles
Joseph Wechsberg

Today it is sometimes difficult to get a reservation for one of Michelin's three-star restaurants, but in the early days of *La Tour d'Argent*, the oldest restaurant in Paris, "[a] cavalier who had neglected to make his reservation would pull up his horse, walk in, challenge one of the guests to a duel, kill him with a sword or lance and take his place."

Once inside, he would find most people eating with the first three fingers of their right hand. A contemporary journalist was amazed at the elegance of "four gentlemen who not once touched their meat with their fingers. They carried forks to their mouths," he wrote, "and bowed deeply over their plates."

With or without forks, connoisseur Joseph Wechsberg consumed thing but frankfurters and cocoa as a child. But now he has expanded his repertoire of acceptable foods and written a paean of praise for fine European dining, with emphasis on the eating-places and vineyards of France.

Blue Trout and Black Truffles is neither guide nor cookbook. It is instead a celebration of *la haute cuisine*, both past and present, and a fine gastronomic adventure. The reader is introduced to some of the greatest practitioners of the culinary arts and is encouraged to savor the delights of an epicurean heaven.

(Academy Chicago, 1948, 1985, ISBN 0-89733-134-56, softcover, 288 pages, $8.95)

Dining in France
Christian Millau

"France is the birthplace and kingdom of gastronomy," says Pierre Salinger, and **Dining in France** underscores the truth of his statement. Renowned food critic Christian Millau and photographer Philippe-Louise Houze spent a year traveling around France to meet its greatest chefs and learn about their cooking styles and philosophies, their methods of choosing wines and foods. Here they share with the reader the flavors of France's varied regions.

At the outset, Millau explains *haute cuisine, nouvelle cuisine*, and regional cooking, and offers suggestions on practical matters from making reservations to tipping. With these details out of the way, the tour begins.

We start with the historic French restaurants: Maxim's, La Tour d'Argent, and Le Grand Vefour, to name a few. Millau divulges gossipy tidbits: for instance, he claims that after prodigious meals at Lucas-Carlton, turn-of-the-century political and financial wizards "would climb discreetly to the small private rooms on the upper floor, to tipple champagne in far more amusing company." He discusses the strong points of each restaurant's menu and includes exquisite-sounding recipes. Houze's richly beautiful photographs amplify the text and do their own part to tempt the palate.

Chapters on modern classics, innovators, country inns, and bistros follow, all with a similar format. The final chapter gives a brief overview of French wine. There is an appendix assessing recent vintages of Bordeaux and Burgundies and one listing great wines of Bordeaux. Also appended are the addresses and phone numbers of restaurants named in the text.

Definitely a book for gourmets (or gourmands) on their way to France, **Dining in France** could cause an armchair traveler to do something rash—like run immediately to the nearest French restaurant!

(Stewart, Tabori & Chang, 1986, ISBN 0-941434-87-7, hardcover, oversized, 175 pages, $19.95)

The Taste of France
Robert Freson

Region by region, dish by dish, **The Taste of France** takes the reader on a sumptuous culinary tour of one of the world's leaders in fine cuisine. Robert Freson's luscious photographs, all 375 in full color, capture the flavor of the country and its people, as well as the foods.

Normandy and Brittany, Anjou and Touraine, Languedoc, Perigord—each region has its own character and specialties. The text, contributed by well-known European food writers, describes the history and features of each area as well as taking a detailed look at the typical cuisine. Mouth-watering recipes can easily be duplicated in American kitchens.

Even within regions there can be distinct differences; in Burgundy, for instance, Dijon and Morvan offer quite different styles. "However, if one must generalize about Burgundian cooking, it is often said that it is based on four principles: wine, cream, pork fat, and pastry." Here we find such regional staples as *escargots au chablis* and *coq au vin*. For dessert, *"pain d'epices* and *nonnettes* . . . are commodities that conjure up the thought of medieval fairs and the belief that no man was really famous until his effigy had been constructed in Dijon gingerbread."

For something quite different, "the high-spirited, playful Provençal cuisine . . . with its staples of tomatoes, garlic, saffron, sweet and hot peppers, salt anchovies, olives, olive oil, and the native wild herbs . . . is much closer to that of other Mediterranean countries than to any other regional French cuisine." Here we sample *soupe au pistou, gardiane d'agneau* (lamb stew), and *fougasse*, a flat, pierced loaf drizzled with olive oil.

The Taste of France is beautiful enough for the coffee table but will surely make many forays into the kitchen.

(Stewart, Tabori & Chang, 1983, ISBN 0-941434-36-2, hardcover, oversized, 288 pages, $45.00)

FOLKTALES

Folktales of France
Edited by Geneviève Massignon

Mme. Joly was a seventy-three-year-old peasant woman from Saint-Maurice des Lions when, in the spring of 1961, she related an earthy version of "la Cendroulié" to folklorist Geneviève Massignon. Mme. Joly's Cinderella is befriended by a benevolent "Holy Virgin" and a milking cow which, when tapped on the behind with a hazel wand, releases bread and cheese for Cendroulié but cowpat for the ugly stepsister!

M. Ganachaud was a seventy-four-year-old farmer when he told the story of "The Sleeping Beauty," whose princely rescuer must slay a seven-headed monster; but Marie-Renée Baudouin was only ten when she recounted the adventures of "Puss in Boots" as told to her by an elderly neighbor.

Massignon traveled throughout France in search of tales that had been handed down from the past. To keep them as faithful as possible to the original, she recorded them as she heard them, in a manner that "embraces the teller, the style, the dialect, and the milieu as well as the text."

Here she presents seventy of these stories, arranged geographically and revealing regional differences. The narrator's style, she points out, varies with the area: storytellers from Brittany give long, descriptive passages while those from Limousin are brief and to-the-point; folks from Poitou, the home of Puss in Boots, revel in animal tales while those from western France often include rhythmic sequences.

The tales are thoroughly indexed, not only by region but also by motif and type, and Massignon's commentary gives additional insight. Her **Folktales of France** is a masterful work, enabling readers to use folktales as a means of glimpsing a nation's character.

(University of Chicago, 1968, ISBN 0-226-50965-6, hardcover, 315 pages, $14.00)

HISTORY

The Birth of France
Katharine Scherman

The birth was bloody, attended by "warriors, bishops and long-haired kings," but out of the darkness of the Mergovingian centuries was born the beginnings of Europe as we now know it. The story reads like a grand opera complete with improbable saints and savage kings, poisoned knives and sweeping slaughters.

"The universal Roman Empire was dissolving," explains author Katharine Scherman. "Into the gap stepped the floating barbarian populations that had been alternately harassing and buttressing the failing giant. Gradually they settled, if uneasily and changeably, within definable boundaries that would later be called national."

Covering roughly the fifth to eighth centuries, Scherman illuminates the period often called "The Dark Ages." It is a tale rich in drama, cunning, and cruelty: Attila, king of the Huns, dying on his wedding night from an overabundance of revelry; Clovis, king of the Salian Franks, axing the skulls of his enemies and embracing Christianity; Brunhild, queen of Austrasia, being tied to the tail of an unbroken horse and merrily trampled to death. It is the story too of spiritual bishops and educated abbots, men who carried Christianity to the pagan Franks and helped form the nation that we now call France.

Scherman occasionally inserts asides of particular interest to the traveler. For example, she explains that "Tours today is a big bustling city of industry, agriculture and tourism. The old city, between the Loire and the Cher, is overlaid by the new, and the remnants of earlier centuries are hard to see. Martin's Tours has vanished benath sixteen centuries of building. Two beautiful eleventh- to thirteenth-century towers, the Tour Charlemagne and the Tour de l'Horloge are the only remnants of the great Romanesque Basilica of Saint Martin which replaced the fifth-century sanctuary leveled by the Normans."

Her book brings to life a period which is generally considered to be a low point in the history of Western Civilization. "The Dark Ages are dark indeed if one looks for traces of classical learning, poetry and dialectic, refined sculpture or noble architecture," she says. "It was a disordered time, as any period of extreme change must be . . . But out of it arose a new world."

(Random House, 1987, ISBN 0-394-56089-2, hardcover, 324 pages, $22.50)

Confessions of a Concierge
Bonnie G. Smith

Witty, gritty, shrewd Madame Lucie, the concierge, has seen it all, and in Bonnie Smith's book she shares reminiscences of her colorful life. Born in the 1890s, she describes the stirring and shattering events of the twentieth century from her special perspective. She tells of her childhood during the Belle Epoque, how World War I claimed her fiancé, the gaiety of the '20s, and the grimness of World War II, when circumstances reduced her to service as a concierge.

She was glad to find a place for herself and her husband, but she says, "My heart sank at the humiliation of it all. Hauling garbage cans, cleaning common toilets, serving as the butt of ridicule and intrigue—that's what the future as a concierge would hold. For once I was glad that my parents were dead and couldn't see what had become of me. I was never raised to be a concierge."

But she adjusted, and these experiences, too, added to her repertoire of fascinating stories. **Confessions of a Concierge** contains nearly a century of oral history, a view of the significant events in history against a backdrop of personal ups and downs. History is seldom this entertaining.

(Yale, 1985, ISBN 0-300-03316-8, hardcover, 156 pages, $14.95)

The Contentious French
Charles Tilly

Charles Louis Monique got up early on the morning of July 22, 1789. He left his Tournai lodging house around 4:30 A.M., intending to go to his job as threadmaker. He later reported to officials that he saw "a lot of tumult around the house of M. Martel [a grain merchant]. People were throwing all the furniture and goods out the window." The elegant walking stick he was carrying, said Monique, had been lying in the street, one of M. Martel's former possessions.

The police didn't believe Monique; they thought he had been part of the "awful populace" that had sacked not only Martel's house but also three others. Monique was hanged immediately, one of the ordinary people who, says author Tilly, "fight injustice, challenge exploitation, and claim their own place in the structure of power . . . by actions that authorities call disorder."

The Contentious French is the story of four centuries of disorder, or "contention," as Tilly prefers to call it. By tracing the reactions of common folk to the increasing power of the national state and to the growth of capitalism, he provides a unique view of both French history and the French character. "A new era [begins] not when a new elite holds power or a new constitution appears, but when ordinary people begin contending for their interests in new ways," he says, and to prove his point he intersperses details of actual events with discussions of historical patterns.

In a scholarly yet lively tone, he uses the experiences of ordinary French men and women to clarify what Yale University's John Merriman calls "the historical impact of the processes of statemaking, industrialization, urbanization, and proletarianization."

(Harvard University, 1986, ISBN 0-674-16695-7, hardcover, 456 pages, $25.00)

The Course of French History
Pierre Goubert

The Course of French History is a zesty narrative that begins a thousand years ago with the coronation of the first Capetian king and ends with the presidency of François Mitterand. Goubert describes the founding of France's economic and social structure, commenting from the sidelines as the procession of kings, generals, artists, and philosophers marches across time. His fresh—and often iconoclastic—remarks maintain a fast pace. He writes, for example, "At first glance it appears that Charles VI ruled for forty-two years . . . In reality his reign consisted of six years of childhood and thirty of insanity, with a few years and rare moments of lucidity in between."

His work has been termed satirical, profound, entertaining, impassioned, and "irony-etched." Goubert's credentials are impressive (one of France's most influential social historians, former professor at the Sorbonne) and his research impeccable. Moreover, he has an unquenchable belief that history's most important aspect is the way it affects the everyday life of ordinary people. He searched through records of births, marriages, and deaths, interviewed elderly people and studied ancient archives in order to make history come alive through the people who lived it.

Translator Maarten Ultee explains that "the English-speaking public should understand that Goubert is engaged in dialogue both with his readers and with the tradition of general histories of France. Too often these histories have been highly romantic, obsessed with national glories, insensitive to the role of the people. In France, histories are political statements."

Goubert's statement is informed, entertaining, and well worth reading.

(Franklin Watts, 1984 in French, 1988 in English, ISBN 0-531-15054-2, hardcover, 495 pages, $26.95)

The Crazy Years: Paris in the Twenties
William Wiser

Between 1919 and 1920, F. Scott Fitzgerald's annual income soared from $800 to $18,000, due to the first profits from *This Side of Paradise*. He and his wife Zelda moved to Paris where the downward spiral of the franc made them even richer. An America dollar would buy a month's supply of bread, and the glamorous Fitzgeralds became "a symbol of carefree high-living [and] ambassadors of the jazz age."

Artists, writers, musicians, and dancers from all over the world converged on Paris. *Le jazz hot, le cocktail,* and *un dancing* became part of the language. Not only Scott and Zelda, but also Gertrude Stein, Alice B. Toklas, Ernest Hemingway, Coco Chanel, Pablo Picasso, James Thurber, Igor Stravinsky, and Isadora Duncan—they were all there, drinking, talking, plotting, and laughing in Parisian cafés. These were indeed "the crazy years."

Award-winning novelist William Wiser describes the decade of the twenties in a book that, in the words of *New York Times* reviewer James Mellow, "has the velocity of a high-speed train." He describes the Fitzgeralds splashing through a fountain in evening clothes, E. E. Cummings arriving in Paris determined to lose his virginity, Joan Miró wandering the city "as a displaced person, overwhelmed by a turbulence of images and impressions," and Ezra Pound sending T. S. Eliot to deliver a pair of second-hand brown shoes to James Joyce—a not-so-subtle hint that Joyce replace his "startling pair of dirty tennis shoes."

When the American stock market crashed in 1929, "the cafés and hotels of Montparnasse emptied out; letters addressed to those who had already left for home piled up in the patrons' mail rack at the Dôme, unread." The crazy years had come to an abrupt halt.

(G. K. Hall, 1985, ISBN 0-8398-2859-4, softcover, 256 pages, $9.95)

A Distant Mirror
Barbara Tuchman

Curiosity about the Black Death's effects on society led historian-journalist Barbara Tuchman deep into the "calamitous" fourteenth century—"a violent, tormented, bewildered, suffering and disintegrating age, a time, as many thought, of Satan triumphant." It was indeed a time of chaos, when the chivalric ideal was crumbling and peasants were revolting against the ruling class, when Christianity was torn asunder and the plague struck repeatedly and mercilessly. But, as Tuchman warns, history is like the daily newspaper: "the normal does not make news." Life went on, even in those tumultuous times; and there were festivals and tournaments, gaiety and romance, the Sorbonne and Oxford, Petrarch and Chaucer.

To evoke this world for present-day readers, Tuchman built her history around the life of Enguerrand de Coucy, a French nobleman who was born in 1340. Orphaned by the plague, he inherited a grand barony of magnificent castles and 150 towns, had a brilliant military career, and eventually was killed in waning days of the century during the final crusade against the Turks.

His life offers Tuchman a chance to profile the chivalry and cruelty, pageantry and filth of this contradictory era. She explores the details of daily life from the point of view of both serf and nobleman, touching on courtship, marriage and child-rearing, religion, taxes and war; and she also examines the political and economic aspects of treaties and battles. Throughout she holds high a **Distant Mirror** and captures clear reflections of the pivotal fourteenth century.

(Knopf, 1978, 1980, ISBN 0-394-40026-7, hardcover, 720 pages, $25.00)

The Great Cat Massacre
Robert Darnton

"If we want to understand [other people's] way of thinking, we should set out with the idea of capturing otherness," says Robert Darnton, professor of history at Princeton University. And he sets out to do just that, journeying with us to eighteenth-century France. "Nothing is easier than to slip into the comfortable assumption that Europeans thought and felt two centuries ago just as we do today—allowing for the wigs and wooden shoes," he says as he begins to disabuse us of this notion.

Darton leads his tour through the Age of Enlightenment by "wandering through the archives"—exploring stories, police records, letters, and obscure documents in order to enter the minds of the people who wrote them. Folktales, for example, "show parents laboring in the fields while the children gather wood, guard sheep, fetch water, spin wool, or beg. Far from condemning the exploitation of child labor, they sound indignant when it does not occur."

A 1730s manuscript by Nicolas Contat tells of the time he and his fellow print-shop apprentices held a series of mock trials and then hanged every unfortunate cat they could find. Through an examination of this "Great Cat Massacre" Darnton is able to explain early labor relations and eighteenth-century ceremonies as well as the symbolic meaning of cats.

Darnton wants "to show not merely what people thought but how they thought—how they construed the world, invested it with meaning, and infused it with emotion . . . the inquiry leads into the unmapped territory known in France as *l'histoire des mentalités.*" And a most interesting territory it is.

(Vintage, 1984, ISBN 0-394-72927-7, softcover, 298 pages, $7.95)

Montaillou: The Promised Land of Error
Emmanuel Le Roy Ladurie

Jacques Fournier, Bishop of Pamiers, was only trying to detect sinful behavior and save souls when, in 1318, he initiated an elaborate Inquisition in Montaillou, a small village in the Pyrenees. He was the "very devil of an Inquisitor," according to the 114 people whom he accused of heresy, and his lengthy interrogations covered every aspect of daily life. Yet devil though he may have been, he kept careful records of the proceedings; and it is upon these records that Emmanuel Le Roy Ladurie, one of France's leading historians, based **Montaillou.**

One townsperson, for example, told Fournier of his quite practical reasons for marrying:

It is better for a man to attach himself to a definite woman than to fly from one to another like a bee among the flowers . . . moreover, when a man frequents several women, each of them tries to lay hold of something, and between them all they will turn a man into a pauper.

Another gave advice on how to avoid ghosts:

When you are walking, do not throw your arms and legs about carelessly, but keep your elbows well in, or you might knock a ghost over.

The villagers spoke of all aspects of life: love and marriage, the status of women, childhood, death, friendship, concepts of time and space, religion, morality, and magic. Through their words Le Roy Ladurie was able to recreate the feelings and beliefs as well as the activities of medieval life. It is a fascinating study—a bit of good rising from the evils of religious persecution.

(Vintage, 1979, ISBN 0-394-72964-1, softcover, 383 pages, $5.95)

The Old Regime and the French Revolution
Alexis de Tocqueville

Liberté, egalité, fraternité—those were the watchwords and the battle cry of the uprising that has been called the keystone of modern European history. But why did revolution erupt in France, when the rest of Eruope was seething as well? Why did the French monarchy, which had survived so many crises, collapse so suddenly? Was revolution truly inevitable, and if so, why?

In this definitive study, written more than 125 years ago, the great political thinker Alexis de Tocqueville addresses these questions as he investigates the origins of this pivotal event. "If we wish to get a true understanding of the French Revolution and its achievement," he says, "it is well to disregard for the moment the France of today and to look back to the France that is no more."

Tocqueville's analysis is absorbing and still relevant in today's world. He writes, for instance, on political apathy: "If the French people had still played an active part in politics (through the Estates-General) or even if they had merely continued to concern themselves with the day-to-day administration of affairs through the provincial assemblies, we may be sure that they would not have let themselves be carried away so easily by the ideas of the writers of the day; any experience, however slight, of public affairs would have made them chary of accepting the opinions of mere theoreticians."

Tocqueville should be required reading for concerned citizens of any nationality.

(Doubleday/Anchor, 1955, ISBN 0-385-09260-1, softcover, 300 pages, $5.95)

Pleasures of the Belle Epoque
Charles Rearick

Streets were bedecked with flags and bunting, and in some places banners and garlands . . . Parts of central Paris became a gala stage set, a sparkling mosaic of red, white, and blue. At night, gas lamps and electric lights and Venetian lanterns brought a rare cheering radiance to main streets and squares. Fireworks from six locations emblazoned and bombarded the night sky. No one could take July 14, 1880, as just another day.

It was the centennial celebration of Bastille Day, a magnificent premiere that kicked off the era known as the Belle Epoque, a period extending from 1880 to 1914. Following decades of war, instability, and economic depression, the Belle Epoque was a time of rest, prosperity, and pleasure. The middle class was emerging, shortened workdays allowed more leisure time, and new technology provided mass entertainment.

Pleasures of the Belle Epoque is an historical overview of these years, illustrated with marvelous color and black-and-white photographs as well as with renditions of posters and paintings. Charles Rearick, history professor at the University of Massachusetts, takes us on a romp through Parisian entertainments: Moulin Rouge, Folies Bergère, Comédie Français, Paris Hippodrome (with movable roofs), Oller's Piscine Rouchechouart (Paris's first heated swimming pool), Palais de Glace (skating rink), music halls, the World's Fair, cafés and concerts, cabarets, and fêtes.

This was the France of Toulouse-Lautrec and Jules Chéret, a time when the new leaders of the Republic promoted festivals as a means of unifying the people. Rearick shows us the problems of the era as well as the pleasures, but most of all he shows us its significance—the way in which "the leisure-time innovations of the Belle Epoque . . . left an imprint on popular culture that has lasted up to the present day."

(Yale, 1988, ISBN 0-300-04381-3, softcover, 255 pages, $17.95)

LITERATURE

Paris: A Literary Companion
Ian Littlewood

"'Was it fun in Paris?' asks Zelda Fitzgerald in a letter to Scott. 'Who did you see there and was the Madeleine pink at five o'clock and did the fountains fall with hollow delicacy into the framing of space in the Place de la Concorde, and did the blue creep out from behind the Colonades in the rue de Rivoli through the grill of the Tuileries . . .?' It scarcely matters whether we have noticed these things before—or whether they are still there to be noticed," says author Ian Littlewood. "Zelda's words are not intended to describe a place but to cast a spell. And the spell is stronger than the reality."

This collection of Parisian impressions casts its own spell through observations, descriptions, and reactions to that magical city. Littlewood intersperses the words of writers from the past five hundred years with his own commentary, guiding the reader to places half real, half imagined, for as he says, "The dull reality of the boulevard Montparnasse will never be quite enough to triumph over the romantic associations of its name."

Littlewood stalks the streets of Paris, sometimes following the trail of American expatriates on the Left Bank, other times listening for echoes of degenerate royalty in the Tuileries gardens. Here is Emile Zola, commenting on the Seine:

. . . the bridges, their arches cutting across the satin sheets of the river; the Cité covered with shadow, dominated by the yellowing towers of Notre Dame . . . the broad avenues, the buildings on either bank, and between them, the Seine, with all the lively activity of its laundry-boats, its baths, its barges.

and Henry Miller visiting Montmartre:

Suddenly the street opens wide its jaws and there, like a still white dream, like a dream embedded in stone, the Sacre-Coeur rises up. A heavy, somnolent whiteness, like the belly of a jaded woman.

Yet not everyone is aglow with praise; Saul Bellow, for instance, registers his disappointment with recent developments:

A certain decrepit loveliness is giving way to unattractive, over-priced, over-decorated newness. Dense traffic . . . requires an alertness incompatible with absent-minded rambling. Dusty old shops in which you might lose yourself for a few hours are scrubbed up now and sell pocket computers and high-fidelity equipment.

Paris: A Literary Companion titillates the senses, evoking the romance and the mystery, as well as the reality, of a city that has attracted literary luminaries through the centuries.

(John Murray Ltd., London, from Franklin Watts, 1988, ISBN 0-531-15079-8, hardcover, 246 pages, $16.95)

NATURE

The Gardens of Provence and the French Riviera
Michel Racine, et al.

"Landscape gardening is probably the most ambiguous, difficult, and elusive art of all," said Roger Caillois in *Pierres réfléchies*, and here Michel Racine, Ernest J. P. Boursier-Mougenot, and Françoise Binet, founding members of the French Association for the Art of Landscapes and Gardens, present some of the most beautiful examples of this art in Southern France.

The first sections of the book discuss terrain, microclimates, garden design, and history, aided by photographs, paintings, line drawings, and quotations from the literati. The remainder is given over to a detailed look at fifty individual gardens, from geometrical Renaissance-style designs through the softer lines of Victorian and naturalized plots. Some have existed for centuries virtually unchanged; others are mere decades old.

The authors lead us to the remains of Tourves, once a lush park and the scene of grand fêtes—now a jungle of plants overgrowing the ruins of fountains, the Vacherie (dairy), and the chateau owned by an eighteenth-century count. Despite the state of disrepair, "Once the nostalgia that inevitably accompanies the sign of ruins wears off, another feeling takes its place, that of summoning the power to make the park come to life again."

And then on to the Villa Noailles in Provence, which from a distance "appears to be just another olive grove, yet in this garden lies a suite of compositions born of a true gardener's inspiration, memories, and love of plants." Built by Viscount Charles de Noailles, patron of the arts and consultant to French National Museums, the formal gardens near the house soften towards natural landscaping as they move farther away "and the garden finally melts into the surrounding countryside."

There are more than five hundred illustrations in the book (375 of which are in full color); but handsome as the oversized volume is, it is meant for reading, not merely browsing. The text is a wonderful blend of nature, history, architecture, and philosophy and, combined with the pictures, makes a stirring garden tour. Since many of the featured gardens are not open to the public, it is an exclusive one as well.

(MIT Press, 1987, ISBN 0-262-18128-2, hardcover, oversized, 317 pages, $50.00)

Views from a French Farmhouse
Text by Julian More, photographs by Carey More

Views From A French Farmhouse is a love song to Provence, to "High Provence, Provence of the plains and the sea coast and the rivers . . . [a place where] elements and people are unpredictable, yet there is an inevitability that circumscribes the surprises: the roundness of the days; changing light at each hour; the rotation of crops—olive, wheat, lavender, peach, tomato, melon, grape. A sense of season prevails," says Julian More, writer and lyricist.

Julian's prose accompanies his daughter Carey's photographs—more than a hundred images that flow through the year, beginning with delicate flowers gracing springtime fields and progressing to barren trees framing St. Sauveur Cathedral on a cold winter's day.

The beauties of the Provençal landscape have beckoned to the famous and the not-so-famous. To the west of More's farmhouse is the country of Robert Louis Stevenson as well as that of Arthur Young and Henry James. To the east is the land of Jean Giono, while the south is associated with Alphonse Daudet, Van Gogh, Ezra Pound, Cézanne, and Stendhal, among others. More draws liberally on the works of these authors, quoting from books, poems, and letters to more fully evoke the region's mystique.

Provence, he says, "is a mongrel, a mixture of races related not by nationality but by nature . . . all things which unite and absorb us all. From Giono, the last words: "There is no Provence. Whoever loves it, loves the world."

(Holt, Rinehart and Winston, 1985, ISBN 0-03-005007-3, hardcover, 142 pages, $16.95)

PERFORMING ARTS

DramaContemporary: France
Edited by Philippa Wehle

"The increasing internationalism of our age now links world societies more closely, not only economically, but culturally as well," say the publishers of the DramaContemporary series. "[Now] the American public can have the opportunity to learn about other cultures—the speech, gestures, rhythms and attitudes that shape a society—in the dramatic life of their plays."

Toward that end acknowledged expert Philippa Wehle has chosen six contemporary French playwrights, writers whose "widely divergent experiments in technique, style and content . . . have produced a number of artistically venturesome plays," and presented them for our edification. "Some (Marguerite Duras and Michel Vinaver) have broken new aesthetic ground; others (Gildas Bourdet and Jean-Claude Grumberg), while relying on more established forms, are equally venturesome in terms of subject matter and content. And finally, all (including Nathalie Sarraute and Enzo Cormann) have found a new richness in the 'here and now'," she says.

DramaContemporary: France raises the curtain on the Gallic mind and for that it deserves applause.

(Performing Arts/Farrar, Straus and Giroux, 1986, ISBN 0-9337826-94-X, softcover, 233 pages, $9.95)

The Folies Bergère
Charles Castle

The most famous music hall in the world, the Folies Bergère, opened in 1869, "to inaugurate a new kind of spectacle composed of different elements: lyrical *opérettes-fantaisies*, pantomimes, music entertainments, acrobatic acts." The hall was large and sumptuous, with an open garden and a semi-circular balcony protruding over the stall. At the rear of the auditorium was a promenade where "ladies whose virtue was more obvious than real" could ply their trade.

The statistics concerning this giant pleasure palace are staggering. More than fifty million people have passed through its doors; its 1600 seats are sold out for every performance. It has its own workrooms for costumes, its own carpenter's shop, iron foundry, and laundry. It requires a staff of more than three hundred, including eighty dressmakers and thirty *pailleteuses* who sew beads and sequins on the costumes; two women spend eleven days to hand-sew sequins on a single costume, and a feathered costume requires four dressmakers and a total of about four hundred hours. Each artist averages forty costume changes per performance, and some forty-five sets are used for each show.

This fascinating book is a mixture of theatrical and social history, a gossipy peek into the lives of hundreds of performers (Maurice Chevalier, Anna Pavlova, and Charlie Chaplin among them) and an examination of the changing fashions and standards of feminine beauty over the past century.

Castle's text, accompanied by wonderful period posters and photographs, is as intriguing, entertaining, and occasionally shocking as the pleasure palace he writes about. **The Folies Bergère** is history from front row seats.

(Franklin Watts, 1985, ISBN 0-531-09774-9, hardcover, 319 pages, $18.95)

French Cinema
Roy Armes

If we were artists
We wouldn't say cinema
We'd say ciné
But if we were schoolteachers from the sticks
We wouldn't say ciné or cinema
But cinematograph.

–Appolinaire, 1917

The fledgling French film industry has always been beset not only by changing vocabulary but also by changing viewpoints and styles. Roy Armes documents this well in **French Cinema**, his stylistic and historical analysis of French filmmaking.

From the premiere cinematic performances arranged by Louis Luminere before the turn of the century to the commercialistic trend of the early '80s spearheaded by Alain Delon, he chronicles the craft's evolution and ultimate independence of a dominant Hollywood. Photographs provide added interest illustrating, for example, Jean Gremillon's masterful technique in the 1934 film, *Lumiere d'Ete*.

Armes, film critic for *London Magazine* and author of a book on British cinema, measures and interprets films based on their time periods, their directors' attitudes, and their resulting intellectual exchanges with the French mind. He proves himself to be as knowledgeable about cinema in France as he is about the art on his own side of the channel.

(Oxford, 1985, ISBN 0-19-520472-7, softcover, 310 pages, $10.95)

New Grove Twentieth-Century French Masters
Jean-Michel Nectoux, et al.

Fauré, Debussy, Satie, Ravel, Poulenc, Messiaen, Boulez—all are discussed in this collection of biographies taken from the comprehensive *New Grove Dictionary of Music and Musicians*. These musicians were selected to give a well-rounded view of the scope of French music "from the profoundly sensitive word-setting of Fauré and Poulenc, through the glittering textures of Ravel and the coolly ironic ones of Satie, to the prophetic celebration of religion and nature in the music of Olivier Messiaen and the profound intellectual refinement of Pierre Boulez."

There is a chapter on each composer that includes a definitive biography and discussion of his style and music, as well as bibliography for further reference and a more comprehensive listing of his works. The material was enlarged and updated for this edition, mostly by the original authors, and retains the encyclopedic format.

The information is detailed although concise and will be most appreciated by readers who already have some background in twentieth-century French music.

(Norton, 1986, ISBN 0-393-30350-0, softcover, 291 pages, $11.95)

Paris: The Musical Kaleidoscope 1870-1925
Elaine Brody

"Hector Berlioz died on the afternoon of 8 March 1869. As always, his timing was poor." Although Berlioz was virtually unknown at the time of his death (and disliked by those who did know him), he was later appreciated as one of the originators of the romantic movement in France. Alas, he missed the vibrant period when France emerged as the musical capital of Europe.

The late Elaine Brody, prominent musicologist and teacher, chronicles the development of a vital café society and the rise of French musical nationalism, "once the yoke of Wagner had been cast aside." This period, she says, was a time of ferment in all of the arts:

> ... *when poets animatedly discussed and sometimes even wrote music, when musicians regularly attended literary events, and people like Cocteau not only wrote but also illustrated their own works . . . these were the last years of* la vie de Boheme, la vie de café, *of occultism, mysticism, spiritualism, and exoticism—"isms" all present in the musical experience of composers of that day.*

The magnetic attraction created by the Parisian phenomenon drew the artistically-inclined from around the world; some of the most talented musicians from Spain, Russia, and America came to France, and trends like "le Japonisme" and "l'Orientalisme" extended beyond the visual arts and into music. Brody discusses the close connection between music and other art forms before concluding with a look at some of the preeminent composers of the period: Debussy, Bizet, Chabrier, Faure, Gounod, Offenbach, Ravel, and Saint-Saens among them.

Combining scholarly insight and sprightly anecdote, each chapter can stand on its own. But together they offer a perceptive look at the people, events and trends of turn-of-the-century Paris.

(George Braziller, 1987, ISBN 0-8076-1176-X, hardcover, 359 pages, $19.95)

YOUNG PEOPLE'S BOOKS

Cathedral: The Story of Its Construction
David Macaulay
For ages eight and up

It took the people of the imaginary town of Chutreaux eighty-six years to build their grand cathedral, and author/illustrator David Macaulay details every step of the ambitious undertaking. With clear text and elaborate pen-and-ink drawings, he builds a thirteenth-century French Gothic cathedral à la Chartres.

First an architect/builder is hired, than an assortment of master craftsmen: quarrymen, stone cutters, sculptors, mortar makers, masons, carpenters, blacksmiths, roofers, and glass makers. Each workman fulfills his own role, using the tools of his trade. The first foundation stone is lowered, the supporting columns erected, the tower bells cast and the stained glass windows installed. The building, presented in words and pictures, takes shape page by page.

Macaulay makes complicated concepts easy, and his book intrigues children and adults alike. **Cathedral** has won numerous awards including those from *The New York Times*, Caldecott, ALA, and the German Jugendbuchpreis. It deserves them all.

(Houghton Mifflin, 1973, ISBN 0-395-31668-5, softcover, oversize, 80 pages, $6.95)

A Family in France
Mary Regan
For ages seven to ten

Meet Pascal and Stéphane Gué, brothers (aged ten and eight) who live in Rennes, in the region of France known as Brittany. Their lives are often similar to those of American youngsters with small exceptions: they go to school on Saturday mornings rather than on Wednesday afternoons, and they have their big meal at lunch rather than at dinner. And, while birthdays are celebrated in France, for Stéphane, who was named after St. Stephen, his saint's feast day is just as important.

Mary Regan's clear text takes youngsters through a day in the life of the Gué family, but it is the plentiful, full-color photographs, showing mail carriers on bicycles and outdoor food markets, that are most likely to lead American children's imaginations across the Atlantic. Maps, a pronunciation guide to common French words, and a page of important facts provide additional help.

(Lerner, 1985, ISBN 0-8225-1651-9, hardcover, 32 pages, $8.95)

France: The Crossroads of Europe
Susan Balerdi
For ages ten to thirteen

Let's imagine I'm a magician who can make people's ideas appear before them. And suppose someone in the audience asked me to bring forth a typical French person . . . I'd snap my fingers and a middle-aged man wearing baggy pants and a beret, and riding a bicycle would appear. Strapped to his bike rack would be a baguette (a long loaf of French bread), a round of camembert cheese, and a wine bottle. By now my audience would no doubt be applauding. They would be sure that this man must live somewhere among France's fifty-four million people. But he is not at all what French people are like. He is a stereotype. That is, he's what the audience thinks a French person should look like. Some people say the French are great lovers . . . Still others think the French are very witty. To me, they are the trait d'union, or 'hyphen,' of Europe. For just as a hyphen joins two words, the French unite Europe's people and cultures.

With easy-going charm, Susan Balerdi introduces young folks to the people, land, and traditions of France. She covers history and geography but emphasizes those facets of French life that are most likely to interest preteens: holidays, food, school, and sports.

The book has numerous photographs, both color and black-and-white, and features pronunciation tips, a glossary, and a bibliography. Ms. Balerdi is the mother of three and it shows—she knows how to capture a child's attention and let the learning slide in.

(Dillon, 1984, ISBN 0-87518-248-8, hardcover, 144 pages, $12.95)

Linnea in Monet's Garden
Christina Björk
For ages seven and up

Linnea has a mischievous grin, all-seeing eyes, and a passion for flowers. She has read about Monet and his home at Giverny, where he spent much of his life painting and establishing a spectacular garden. She has even dreamed of standing on the Japanese bridge over his water-lily pond—so imagine her delight when Mr. Bloom, her upstairs neighbor, invites her to accompany him on a visit to Paris and nearby Giverny.

Everything fascinates Linnea: Monet's life ("When Monet was pleased with his paintings, then the whole household was happy. But when he was not pleased, everyone suffered."), his painting technique (The water lilies look "splotchy when you get up close [yet] when I stepped away again, they turned into real water lilies floating in a pond—magic!"), and of course his garden ("I never could have imagined all *this*! *This* big and *this* many flowers!")

The illustrations comprise a somewhat cluttered pastiche of reproductions of Monet's watercolors, illustrations by Lena Anderson, and photographs from Monet's time and the present. Together they show Linnea—always studying, sketching and photographing—and they reveal a child's-eye view of Monet—his work, his family, and his surroundings. **Linnea in Monet's Garden** brings horticulture and art, history and biography together in a colorful blend that imparts the charm of France and depicts the life of one of her greatest artists.

(R & S Books, Stockholm, from Farrar, Straus and Giroux, 1987, ISBN 91-29-58314-4, hardcover, 53 pages, $10.95)

One Summer at Grandmother's House
Poupa Montaufier
For ages six to ten

Oma (Grandmother) lives in a small village a nine-hour drive from Paris. She wears a black shawl and braided-straw hat, goes to church the minute she hears church bells, and worries about making dinner while breakfast is still on the table.

In this delightful book, translated from the French by Tobi Tobias, author-illustrator Poupa Montaufier recreates a 1950s summer with her grandmother in the Alsace region of France. Wonderful full-color paintings done in primitive style perfectly capture the gentle pace of an earlier time.

(Carolrhoda, 1985, ISBN 0-87614-238-2, hardcover, 32 pages, $12.95)

The Red Balloon
A. Lamorisse
For ages four to eight

In the mid 1950s a French director made a short film about a boy and his red balloon. Its plot was simple but it had a certain magic, and it was nearly as popular with adults as with children. This book is made from photographs taken during the production of that movie.

Pascal and his friend—an untethered red balloon—walk together through the streets of Paris. There's really nothing so surprising about the fact that the balloon follows Pascal everywhere because, after all, "Friends will do all kinds of things for you. If the friend happens to be a balloon, it doesn't fly away."

Taking place on the streets of Paris, this book evokes a Parisian atmosphere. After all, it's magic.

(Doubleday, 1956, ISBN 0-385-14297-8, softcover, oversized, 40 pages, $4.95)

IBERIA

GENERAL

The Alhambra
Washington Irving

Of all the "castles in Spain" that have inspired daydreamers everywhere, none is more romantic or more spectacular than the Alhambra. Through long centuries in medieval times the castle was the center of impassioned conflict between Christians and Moslems. Now fully restored as a historic monument (largely because of the attention gained through Irving's book), it attracts visitors from around the globe—many of whom arrive carrying Washington Irving's classic **The Alhambra** as a very special guidebook.

Though best known to Americans for such stories as "Rip Van Winkle" and "The Legend of Sleepy Hollow," Irving spent many of his happiest and most productive years in Spain. On his first visit there the spectacular Moorish fortification charmed and fascinated him into writing this delightful mixture of fanciful tales, history, and travel-essay. And if he embroiders the facts a bit as he practices the story-teller's art, who are we to quibble as we join him "nestled in one of the most remarkable, romantic and delicious spots in the world"?

This edition is a faithful facsimile of the original, with borders around each page and original engravings by Felix O. C. Darley; the cover is handsomely tooled and gold-stamped. An introduction by noted Irving scholar Dr. Andrew B. Myers gives valuable background information.

Irving wrote, as he took one last parting look at the Alhambra: "I will hasten from this prospect before the sun is set. I will carry away a recollection of it clothed in all its beauty." Through his book we can carry his recollections with us and make them our own.

(Sleepy Hollow Press, 1982, ISBN 0-912882-48-4, hardcover, 425 pages, $23.95)

The Dangerous Summer
Ernest Hemingway

The editor of *Life* magazine had an idea. "Wouldn't it be great if we could get Hemingway to write an article on bullfighting?" Hemingway must have liked the suggestion when it was proposed to him in 1959, for he returned to Spain to follow a succession of *mano a mano* bullfights between two world-famous rivals. Antonio Ordóñez and his brother-in-law Luis Miguel Dominguín.

He wrote 120,000 words that summer when only ten thousand were needed. This version runs about 45,000 words and brilliantly chronicles the rivalries and the friendships, the beauty and the gore of that very "dangerous summer."

As Hemingway follows Ordóñez and Dominguín from one Spanish town to the next, he captures the time, place, and season with descriptions that are uniquely Hemingway:

> ... *the Miramar Hotel where the bar and terraces that looked out on the sea were crowded with summer people, the rich of the town and a mixture of bullfight fans, followers, fighters, . . . nobility, nice people in jeans, un-nice people in same, old friends, ex-old friends, drink cadgers and characters.*

A comprehensive introduction by James Michener elaborates on the rituals—the bulls, costume, arena, various parts of the fight itself, and the trophies of *musica, pañuelos,* and *peticiones* that are presented to the matadors. Hemingway's own glossary further explains Spanish traditions and customs, and over twenty black-and-white photos portray the choreography of this elaborate "dance of death."

Hemingway's genius provides vivid imagery of the bullfighter's craft as well as of Spain's people and places. He does honor to the country that, he says, "I love more than any other except my own."

(Scribner's, 1960, 1985, ISBN 0-684-18355-2, hardcover, 228 pages, $17.95)

Fabled Shore: From the Pyrenees to Portugal
Rose Macaulay

"Spain is different," boasted the tourist slogan for Francoist Spain, and Rose Macaulay wanted to investigate its differences. So in 1949 she set out along the Catalonian, Valencian, Andalucian, and Algarve coasts of Spain and Portugal, a spirited and learned Britisher with a background in classical history.

"All the way down this stupendous coast," she wrote, "I trod on the heels of Greek mariners, merchants and colonists, as of trafficking Phoenicians, conquering Carthaginians, dominating ubiquitous Romans, destroying Goths, mangificent Moors, feudal counts, princes and abbots." Perhaps so, but the local populace wasn't yet used to outsiders, and a woman traveling alone by car was an object of great wonder. "The inhabitants stare and point," she observed. "A foreigner is 'a strange outlandish fowl, a quaint baboon, an ape, an owl.'"

Her sharp eye and quick wit provide a delightful commentary:

The Barcelonese are, indeed, a vivid and a tireless people: one sees why they have always had so many revolutions, bombs, commotions, aspirations, political movements, industries and wealth. Their spirit and energy are tremendous. Directly General Franco began his revolution, the Barcelona incendiaries rushed jubilantly round their churches and set them on fire.

Today's traveler to Spain will cluck with amazement at Macaulay's difficulty finding "petrol" and sigh with envy at her descriptions of deserted beaches. Of course, Macaulay herself is partly to blame for the now-crowded sands, for **Fabled Shore** quickly became a classic of travel literature and inspired a great many tourists to follow her footsteps. And it's still not a bad idea.

(Oxford, 1986, ISBN 0-19-281483-X, softcover, 248 pages, $9.95)

Farewell Spain
Kate O'Brien

Novelist Kate O'Brien was only twenty-four when, in the early 1920s, she first fell in love with Spain. She revisited often, and her acclaimed travel essay, **Farewell Spain**, is a nostalgic look at a country she feared was disappearing forever. Here she recalls the way it was in the early days of the Civil War when she visited Madrid ("gay, leisurely and *moqueur*"), Avila ("a mixture of granite and sandstone . . . blond and sun-washed"), Castile, Segovia, and Billalba. "The good taste of Spain when she isn't trying," she observes, "is only equalled, in my experience, by her bad taste when she is."

She was, as artist Mary O'Neill writes in the preface, "a most individual traveller combining wide reading and knowledge with a lively interest in the accidental event, in the odd, amusing and sometimes exciting encounter." Take, for instance, her encounter with the barber of Salamanca, who told O'Brien during an interminable train journey "the seating capacity of every restaurant and cinema in Salamanca. He told me the names of all the films which had come to those cinemas since their inception—and his own opinions on them. He told me the names of all the cafés and hotels, of all the doctors, dentists, lawyers, chemists and shoeblacks. He told me everyone's income, and the make of everyone's car . . ."

But signs of war are everywhere; it "strikes not merely for the death of Spain, but at every decent dream or effort for humanity everywhere." And so, mournfully, Kate O'Brien recalls and records the Spain she has loved, and to which she now bids farewell.

(Beacon Press, 1985, ISBN 0-8070-7025-4, softcover, 230 pages, $8.95)

Iberia
James Michener

"There's not much phoniness in Spain," Michener once said to his biographer John Hayes. "It's a rugged, to-hell-with-you-country—a first-rate country that makes little concession to the artist. That's why the artist has always liked it . . . certain men just vibrate to certain environments."

Michener had been to Spain several times when he decided in 1966 to organize his impressions into a book. "I wanted to know about its enduring quality, not its current preoccupations," he says, listing several questions that perplexed him:

- Why, for most of her history, was Spain "emotionally confined to her peninsula" whereas Italy, similarly peninsular, took part in continental movements?
- Why did she "fritter away" her important holdings in other parts of the world; reverse her pre-1492 tolerance for various cultural, religious, and ethnic groups; and repeatedly turn to dictatorial forms of government?
- How did she, once one of the richest countries in Europe, become one of the poorest; lose her preeminence in manufacturing, world trade, and agriculture; and abandon her leadership in the fields of art, music, drama, poetry, the novel, and philosophy?
- What does Catholicism mean in a country that is passionately devoted to it yet quick to oppose the Pope and "save Rome from itself?"
- What explains the Spaniard, at once "so outgoing, so earthy, so in love with the trivia of daily existence" and yet at the same time "so withdrawn and inwardly mystical?"

With typical thoroughness Michener attempted to answer these questions by traversing the country accompanied by a researcher and a photographer and by becoming steeped in Spanish history and traditions, surrounding himself with people who could give insight into *flamenco, toreo, zarzuela,* and *quinillas*. Once his first draft was completed, he had it reviewed by renowned Spanish authority Professor Kenneth Vanderford, and after receiving nearly seventy single-spaced pages of suggestions, he corrected and revised extensively. The result was published in the spring of 1968 and quickly became a fixture on the non-fiction best-seller lists. Spanish officials, noticing the number of tourists who used the book as a guide, released their own censored version.

Iberia is a hefty volume that captures both the history and the vibrancy of Spain. This is a personal book—a travel-essay by a sharp observer, a prodigious researcher, and a master writer. It is a rich, panoramic overview that probes the mysteries of a complex and contradictory land.

(Fawcett Crest/Ballantine, 1968, 1984, ISBN 0-449-20733-1, softcover, **960** pages, $5.95)

Matador
Barnaby Conrad

In 1947 Barnaby Conrad was a struggling young writer passionately attracted to bullfighting. Seriously injured while trying to learn the sport, he was in awe of the seemingly invincible Manolete, Spain's premier matador and a celebrated national hero. Then, in August, the twenty-nine-year-old Manolete was fatally gored. "He died such a beautiful dramatic Spanish death," wrote Conrad, "that I swear, in spite of the great funeral, the week of national mourning, the odes, the dirges, the posthumous decorations by the government, that in his heart of hearts every Spaniard was glad that Manolete had died. They, the Spaniards themselves, murdered him."

The irony and tragedy of Manolete's life haunted Conrad and inspired him to create Pacote, a fictional hero modeled on the great bullfighter. **Matador**, published in 1952, quickly became a best-seller and Book-of-the-Month-Club selection, and has now earned the status of a modern classic. This new edition includes an afterword by Conrad describing how he came to write the novel as well as a short biography of Manolete.

The action takes place in just twelve hours, on the day of Pacote's final bullfight. It begins in the dressing room where the famous matador wrestles with his ever-present fear, moves into the ring where the excitement and tension build to their tragic conclusion, and ends in the infirmary where Pacote regains consciousness long enough to learn that he has won at the same time he has lost: "They gave you everything . . . Everything. Ears, tail and hoof. The first time they've ever given a hoof in the Maestranza."

The pageant and majesty, the ritual and ceremony, the screaming crowds and snorting bulls, and above all, the quiet loneliness of the matador—all are powerfully evoked in Conrad's masterpiece.

(Capra Press, 1988, ISBN 0-88496-286-5, hardcover, 249 pages, $18.95)

Red Doll
Juan Luis Cebrián

Love story and spy thriller combine in this gripping novel of post-Franco Spain. The story's central character is Juan Altamirano, a hero who helped depose the remnants of Franco's regime after the dictator's death. Now a middle-aged political advisor in Paris, he becomes romantically entangled with a titian-haired university student with strong leftist political leanings—the "red doll" of the book's title.

Despite their attempts to keep the affair secret, their relationship becomes embroiled in international political dealings involving a Basque terrorist group, national security, and the KGB. Enmeshed in a complex world of duplicity and treachery, Juan finds himself in the dangerous position of being unable to trust his closest friends—or his own government.

Written by a prominent Spanish journalist, **Red Doll** was a best-seller in Europe. As a dramatic and fast-paced look at the complexities of modern-day Spanish politics, it is a chilling reminder of the fragility of newly acquired democratic institutions.

(Weidenfeld & Nicolson, 1987, ISBN 1-55584-145-7, hardcover, 162 pages, $15.95)

Spain
Nikos Kazantzakis

"I am not making Art. I am only letting my own heart cry out." While it's possible to contest the first part of Nikos Kazantzakis's statement, there is no doubting the last. **Spain** is an undeniable cry from the heart, a passionate and poetic record of a country in throes of a devastating civil war.

Kazantzakis first went to Spain as a reporter and observer before war broke out, visiting Miranda and Salamanca, Toledo and Cordova, Madrid and Seville. In a town on the Mediterranean he attended a bullfight:

For a moment [the bull's] horns flashed straight under the horse's belly. With all his might the horseman managed to stick his lance into the nape of the bull's neck and get away in time. The bull bellowed from the pain, then rushed toward the horseman. But now the capeadores surrounded it with their red capes waving. The bull veered and rushed on them. But with a light movement, the supple young men stepped out of the way, and the bull butted its horns at the empty cloth in vain.

Later at the height of the war he returned to record his impressions of the battle:

On the 19th of September, when we were leaning from the fortress early in the morning, we could see the fire engines speeding toward us, with their hoses ready to spray the gasoline in sheets. 'They're going to burn us alive, the devils!' we whispered in terror. And the gasoline actually began pouring all over the fortress.

In the same penetrating style he evidenced in *Zorba the Greek*, Kazantzakis captures the soul of the Spanish character, depicting at once the violence and the beauty, the terror and the pride of a people at a critical time in their history.

(Creative Arts, 1983, ISBN 0-916870-54-5, softcover, 254 pages, $7.95)

Spain
Jan Morris

Spain is a hierarchal country: on the farm, from the grave old paterfamilias at one end to the turnips in the field at the other; in the nation, from the grandees of Church and State, the brilliant young men at the Feria, or the debutantes showing their knees in the noisy sports cars of Madrid, to those simple people of the thatched huts, with their huddle of blankets on the earth floor, and their piglets in sacks beside the fire.

With her customary energy, enthusiasm, insight and wit, travel writer Jan Morris travels through the centuries to explore Spain's hierarchies as well as her scenery, her arts as well as her people, her past as well as her present. Beginning in the north at Roncesvalles, "the most heroic of the ten defiles that pierce the Pyrenees," she works her way south to Gibraltar, commenting continuously on all facets of Spanish life.

She remarks on bread ("It is the best bread I know, and its coarse, strong, springy substance epitomizes all that is admirable about Spanish simplicity"), gypsies ("If they are not the salt of Spain, they are the spiciest of sauces"), bridges ("Scarcely a Spanish town cannot boast a fine bridge"), and the city of Madrid ("The height of human happiness, infatuated Madrileños like to say, must be to go to that part of Heaven from which there is a view of Madrid").

This special reprint of a 1964 book (revised in 1979) features charming watercolors by Cecilia Eales, oil paintings by various Spanish artists, and Miró-like chapter openings. The juxtaposition of different styles can be jarring, yet like Spain herself they blend fantasy and reality, boldness and serenity. They complement Morris's lively text to provide a book, that, like a fresh-baked loaf of Spanish bread, leaves one delightfully satisfied.

(Prentice-Hall, 1964, 1988, ISBN 0-13-824152-X, hardcover, 207 pages, $24.95)

A Stranger in Spain
H. V. Morton

The *encierro de los toros*, the "shutting-up of the bulls," had realized all of the aficionado's expectations:

Suddenly, I hear shouts! I hear women scream! Then the screams and shouts get nearer and I see men running—running for their lives . . . and just behind them come the bulls, six or possibly eight, big and black and galloping as fast as horses, sometimes twisting their horns right and left. It is terribly exciting! Sometimes, when a man knows the bulls are gaining on him, he falls flat on his face and lies still and the bulls go past or he may do something that can be most perilous—he can step into a doorway and keep still; but there is a chance that a bull will stop and gore him! . . . it is all very barbaric, very pagan . . .

All Pamplona shares the frenzied excitement. Everything is closed but the cafés and bars; men dressed in white with red scarves and sashes roam the streets, drinking from *botas* as they pause to dance a few steps. The whole town is tipsy.

And veteran travel writer H. V. Morton provides front row seats for this Fiesta of San Fermín at Pamplona, offers a tour of the mosque of Córdoba, tells the story of the Black Virgin of Montserrat. He takes us through the lazy, fertile plains of Andalusia; over hills fat with olives; across the barren ridges of Castile and to the green and blue of San Sebastian, the jewel of Basque country. All the while he intersperses the twentieth-century narrative with tales of the Christian kings and the caliphs of Córdoba, of the Hapsburgs and of Columbus, of Cortes and Goya for, he says, "the stranger who wishes to approach Spain with sympathy and appreciation must do so through its history."

Yesterday and today—Morton reflects on it all, and in so doing captures the spirit and the glory of Spain.

(Dodd, Mead, 1955, 1986, ISBN 0-396-08797-3, softcover, 372 pages, $10.95)

White Wall of Spain
Allen Josephs

In order to understand Andalusia, whose civilization predates that of Phoenicia, Greece, and Rome, you must have "passion," says novelist Carlos Fuentes. And, he adds, Allen Josephs's learned and provocative exploration of the region, **White Wall of Spain**, possesses this quality in abundance.

In the beginning—*before the written word—fable, legend, oral history, myth, and religion were so intertwined that we can seldom separate their individual threads. So it was with Andalucia, known to the Hebrews as Tarshish and to the Greeks as Tartessos. Tarshish-Tartessos was a city, a river and a kingdom, a mythic place, land's end, a country of fabled resources. It was famous enough that trading ships became known to the Hebrews as 'ships of Tarshish.'*

Josephs analyzes sources from classical literature, history, mythology, and archaeology to explore this civilization that stems "in no small part from the ancient mysteries of the East." Upon this oriental base, he found, were added overlays of elements from the civilizations that repeatedly invaded and conquered the area through the centuries. The resulting rich and complex culture exists nowhere else on earth. "The frenzy of tuna fishing off the coast of Cádiz, the music and dance known as *flamenco*, religious celebrations such as Holy Week in Seville or the pilgrimage called the Rocio, and, of course, *toreo*, which we erroneously call bullfighting—these are unique phenomena which are native to southern Spain and have virtually no counterpart in our culture."

Enlisting the aid of writers and artists as varied as Federico Garcia Lorca, Ernest Hemingway, and Pablo Picasso, Josephs makes a plea that the "sterility, alienation, dehumanization" of modern society not be allowed to displace the tambourines and castanets of this distinctive region.

(Iowa State, 1983, ISBN 0-8138-1921-0, hardcover, 187 pages, $21.95)

ART AND ARCHITECTURE

Castles in Spain
Fernando Chueca Goitia

Reinhart Wolf pays glorious homage to Spain in a volume of golden pictures, often spread over two pages, depicting the massive fortifications that once dotted the countryside. His criteria were admittedly subjective; he photographed thirty-two of the more than two hundred castles in Spain, and chose those with "emotional, lyrical or dramatic" impact. Yet, despite the fact that he overlooked many with greater claims to historical importance or architectural uniqueness, his book reflects castles of differing styles and shows those from all sections of the country.

The text by Fernando Chueca Goitia, professor of art and architecture at Escuela Técnica Superior de Arquitectura in Madrid, is often overshadowed by the giant pictures, but it gives a brief history of castle-building in Spain and takes a look at the historical and geographical lore behind the various fortresses.

From the primitive ruins of Monasterio de Rodilla in the north (dating from the eleventh century) to La Calahorra in the south (one of the few models of Renaissance castle-palaces), Wolf and Goitia evoke the romance of Spain that is suggested by the very words, "castles in Spain."

(Abbeville, 1983, ISBN 0-89659-390-8, hardcover, oversized, 111 pages, $60.00)

Churches of Portugal
Carlos de Azevedo

It was Portugal that, during the age of discovery, first revealed the actual shape of our world and opened new horizons to European culture and commerce. Then, two and a half centuries later, it was again Portugal that indirectly financed the early industrial revolution. Portuguese history thus lies at the foundations of the modern age. And, as one of the world's great civilizing forces, this history finds its richest expression in those of its buildings that honour God: namely, its churches. Each of these historic shrines is therfore a reflection of its era, representing, so to speak, a thread in the fabric of world history.

Architecture and history are woven together in **Churches of Portugal**, a joint effort of two accomplished art historians: Carlos de Azevedo, former Portuguese Minister of Education, and Chester Brummel, American photographer. Azevedo's text journeys briefly through the ages, placing different architectural styles into their historical context, from the "Visigothic Beginning," "Romanesque Strength," and "Gothic Majesty" to "Manueline Extravagance," "Renaissance Order," and "Baroque Splendor."

Brummel's photographs, a mix of color and black-and-white, make up over three-fourths of the book. From the relative simplicity of the Gothic church at Coimbra, Santa Clara-a-Velha, to the Baroque exuberance of the Convent Church of Jesus in Aveiro (now a museum), the photos evoke a sense of wonder for past ages.

Several typographical oversights jar the reader, and the photographs would benefit from more detailed captions. Yet Azevedo and Brummel have provided an enjoyable overview of a worthy and neglected topic.

(Scala Books/Harper & Row, 1985, ISBN 0-9357-48-66-0, hardcover, oversized, 199 pages, $35.00)

Country Manors of Portugal: A Passage Through Seven Centuries
Marcus Binney

There is a poetic and timeless sense about a Portuguese manor house. Difficult to define, it is often accompanied by the scent of freshly waxed floors, flowers, and eucalyptus. Grand or modest, inhabited or abandoned, it reflects a sense of continuity and presence that says more about Portugal than any historic document.
—Nicolas Sapieha, Introduction

Portugal has been goaded by the Spanish, occupied by the Moors, influenced by the Italians and the French. Her architecture reflects all of these sources, yet blends them into something distinctively Portuguese. British conservationist and architectural historian Marcus Binney examines

Portuguese architecture through the ages, beginning with the austere towers of medieval days and continuing through the baroque period when the country house reached its apex.

Dividing the country into six regions—greater Lisbon, Sintra and surroundings, the Tagus River, between the Tagus and the Douro, the Douro region and the Minho region—Binney visits forty-five historic Portuguese country manors, indigenously known as *solares* or *quintas*. Here is Solar dos Pinheros, a starkly simple example of Gothic and Romanesque architecture that dates from the fourteenth century; Solar de Mateus (the silhouette of which is easily recognizable to those who enjoy the *rosé* wine of the same name) with its richly decorated interior and patterned gardens; and Quinta da Bacalhoa, an elegant Renaissance villa that would be at home in the hills of Tuscany but for the Moorish influence revealed in areas of intricate geometric patterns. Concluding sections show architecture in Madeira, the Azores, and Brazil.

Country Manors of Portugal is, as the subtitle suggests, "a passage through seven centuries." Approximately 250 color photographs from Nicolas Sapieha and Francesco Venturi aid in making it a most charming stroll through homes that pay homage to Portugal's past.

(Scala/Harper & Row, 1987, ISBN 035748-47-1, hardcover, oversized, 232 pages, $50.00)

Spanish Folk Ceramics
J. LL. Artigas and J. C. Matheos

Fearing that traditional pottery would soon be replaced by mass-produced objects, authors J. LL. Artigas and J. C. Matheos traveled throughout Spain to document their country's craft heritage. After opening with an explanation of potting technique, their book proceeds to a region-by-region examination of artisan communities. In Aragón, where the ancient art is rapidly disappearing, we meet José Arellano Castelló, a "pleasant, cordial man without any sons" to whom he can teach his craft. Castelló makes everyday objects, the *cántaros* and *botijos*, which he decorates in a simple, linear manner.

In Basque Country we visit Jesús Rodríguez Garrido, who makes the unique black ceramics from Llamas de Mouro. He talks freely about the supposed "secret" of the black pottery: "We put the objects in the kiln and cover them with 'tapines' (pieces of sod). Later, when the objects are fired, the tapines melt. Once the pottery is well 'baked,' everything is covered with earth from the kiln itself, including the door from which the fire is poked. This makes the smoke accumulate inside, and turns the objects black."

Artigas and Matheos continue throughout the country, visiting potters in small towns and villages along the way. F. Català Roca is responsible for the nearly two hundred black-and-white photos and thirty-six full-color plates, which show the potters and their way of life as well as their work. Together words and pictures provide a comprehensive and authoritative overview of Spanish ceramics, those beautiful and distinctive works that are threatened by modern technology.

(Editorial Blume, Barcelona, from International Specialized Book Services, 1974, ISBN 84-7031-362-2, hardcover, oversized, 235 pages, $35.00)

CUISINE

The Food of Portugal
Jean Anderson

Although Jean Anderson is a born and bred American, she considers Portugal her second home and visited there fifty-four times in a twenty-five-year period. Its attraction was more than slightly gustatory, judging from the the tantalizing recipes in this gem of a book.

Having once sipped a typical savory, thick *sopa* (soup); tasted a slice of home-baked crusty *pão* (bread) still warm from the brick oven; or dined on the freshest of seafood, bursting with tomato, garlic, and olive oil, it would be hard to stay away from these delights. Happily, Anderson makes it possible to duplicate them in the American kitchen—and by way of explaining the differences between Spanish and Portuguese cuisine, she offers a history lesson as well.

When Vasco da Gama returned from his explorations bearing curry, cinnamon, cloves, nutmeg, and pepper, these unfamiliar spices were quickly incorporated into the cuisine. "And as Portugal's overseas empire expanded, the other exotics of the East (among them rice and tea), of Africa (coffee, broad beans and peanuts), not to mention New World pineapples, peppers sweet and incendiary, tomatoes and potatoes found their way into local kettles too."

One chapter is devoted to explaining Portuguese cooking terms and discussing fine points of local foods and ingredients. Another discusses the many fine wines of Portugal—regrettably few of which are exported to the United States. And then there are scores of recipes—from *Pasta de Alho* (Garlic Paté) through *Sopa de Camarão* (Shrimp Soup), *Vieiras a Moda do Algarve* (Scallops Algarve-Style) and *Carne de Vinho e Alhos* (Pork with Wine and Garlic) to *Bolo de Amendoa* (Almond Cake). To add eye-appeal there is a sixteen-page section of beautiful color photographs by the author.

A peppering of history, a smidgeon of geography, and a *soupçon* of commentary on the countryside, people, and culture of Portugal add spice to the recipes and provide the seasonings for a first-class meal.

(Morrow, 1986, ISBN 0-688-04363-1, hardcover, 304 pages, $24.95)

The Wine and Food of Spain
Jan Read, Maite Manjón and Hugh Johnson

The region encompassing New Castile and Madrid "is Don Quixote country," comment veteran British writers Jan Read, Maite Manjón, and Hugh Johnson on their leisurely tour of Spain. "Its empty, rolling plains, bitterly cold in winter and unsheltered from a pitiless sun in summer, are relieved only by the occasional whitewashed village or clustered windmills." After a brief history of the area, highlighted with photographs, the authors plunge into a discourse on its *vino*. An 1845 description of the wines of Baldepeñas still pertains to today's vintages: "The red blood of the grape issues from this valley of stones. This delicious wine is the produce of the Burgundy vine, transplanted into Spain."

After discussing potables in some detail the authors move on to food: "In the country districts and small towns of New Castile the fare is as simple as it was in the days of Don Quixote. It is based on the fruits of a barren land given over mainly to wheat and vines, or on the proceeds of Sunday expeditions when the silence of the rolling sierra is punctuated by the crack of guns, and little groups of hunters return with their pouches full of rabbit, partridge and quail." Brief descriptions of a dozen restaurants follow and for those who favor a "do-it-yourself" approach, there are regional recipes—for *Tortilla a la Española* (Spanish Omelette), *Carne de Membrillo* (Quince Sweetmeat) and *Pepitoria de Gallina* (Chicken with Almonds).

Each of Spain's ten regions is revealed in the same way: an overview of history, geography, and architecture; a discussion of wines; comments on cuisine; suggestions of restaurants and two or three recipes. All are enhanced with photographs that bring life and immediacy to a land of varied gastronomic delights.

(Little, Brown, 1987, ISBN 0-316-73584, hardcover, 217 pages, $19.95)

HISTORY

Blood of Spain
Ronald Fraser

> *Friday. 17 July, 1936*
> *"Have faith in me! Load! Aim!" I shouted, looking at my men . . . The legionnaires aimed their rifles at the policemen; my pistol pointed straight at the police lieutenant's heart. In our eyes they saw our determination. One of the policemen, with a look of terror, dropped his rifle. "Lieutenant, don't shoot! We've got families!"*
> *"Surrender! Drop your weapons!"*
> *They did. Neither we nor they could imagine the full consequences of our first victory.*
> —Lt. Julio De La Torre, Spanish Foreign Legion

Julio De La Torre was one of more than three hundred people who spoke to Ronald Fraser, reminiscing about the Spanish Civil War. In this oral history of the war Fraser concentrates on the memories of the "ordinary" people, "people who, historically speaking, would otherwise remain inarticulate." Here are Koni Aguirre, blacksmith's daughter; José Alvarez, grocer's son; Ramón Calopa, teacher; Luis Michelena, clerk; José María Codón, student; Francisca de León, glassworker; and Juana Sánchez, railwayman's wife.

By recording the perceptions of people who actually participated in the dailyness of the war, Fraser provides a perspective far different than that gained by an examination of military movements. As he says, "The cause of the civil war lay deep within the formations of Spanish society; though rapidly internationalized, the war was fought out very largely by classes and sectors of that society." His book allows personal access to members of those "classes and sectors" and lets us meet those who shed the **Blood of Spain.**

(Pantheon, 1986, ISBN 0-394-73854-3, softcover, 628 pages, $12.95)

Homage to Catalonia
George Orwell

In 1936 George Orwell went to Spain to write about the Civil War; instead he joined it, becoming a soldier fighting the Fascists. Later he recorded his experiences, affording us a view of Spain and the Spanish people at a crucial time in their history. He describes the landscape:

The scenery was stupendous, if you could forget that every mountain-top was occupied by troops and was therefore littered with tin cans and crusted with dung. To the right of us the sierra bent south-eastwards and made way for the wide, veined valley that stretched across to Huesca . . . Often in the mornings the valley was hidden under seas of cloud, out of which the hills rose flat and blue, giving the landscape a strange resemblance to a photographic negative.

and revels in the people:

They have, there is no doubt, a generosity, a species of nobility, that do not really belong to the twentieth century. It is this that makes one hope that in Spain even Fascism may take a comparatively loose and bearable form. Few Spaniards possess the damnable efficiency and consistency that a modern totalitarian state needs.

Intrigued by politics as well as the people, Orwell gradually became disillusioned with Communism. **Homage to Catalonia**, therefore, is more than a history of the Civil War and a portrait of a people. It traces the developing philosophy of an important author and reveals some of the experiences that shaped his later books *Animal Farm* and *Nineteen Eighty-Four.*

An eighteen-page introduction by Lionel Trilling presents background detail for the book, which he calls "one of the most important documents of our time." By analyzing, in direct and simple prose, the conflicting ideals that exploded in the Spanish Civil War, Orwell gives insight into not only the Spain of the past, but into the one of the present as well.

(Harvest Books/Harcourt Brace Jovanovich, 1952, 1980, ISBN 0-15-642117-8, softcover, 232 pages, $4.95)

Spain: The Root and the Flower
John A. Crow

When the Carthaginians arrived on the Iberian peninsula around 300 B.C., not the least of the gifts they brought was their language. Their name for the peninsula was *Ispania* (land of the rabbits), which soon replaced the earlier Greek appellation *Hesperia* (land of the setting sun). Author John Crow, for one, finds the name most fitting. "The rabbit, like the Spaniard, never moves in a straight line, nor at a steady speed," he says. "It leaps about at a rapid but jerky pace, hurling itself first in one direction, then in another."

Here Crow, Professor Emeritus of Spanish at the University of California, Los Angeles, follows the similarly "rapid but jerky pace" of Spanish history in a compelling and comprehensive work, **Spain: The Root and the Flower.** Digging deep into the country's past, Crow begins with

Roman Spain and continues to the post-Franco years, adding this last section to update his original 1963 study. Although the essential political and military facts are included, he is more interested in presenting "the main currents in the ebb and flow of Spanish life." Therefore, he says, "There are no long lists of all the kings, queens, and ministers of Spain, nor any detailed account of every war or political change . . . My purpose has been to emphasize the underlying feelings and *mores* which bring about these events."

Crow's obvious affection for Spain and his enthusiasm for her culture has absorbed his entire professional life and has resulted in numerous visits over a fifty-year period. In fact, he probably agrees with the unknown wag who stated, "If God were not God he would be the King of Spain, and the King of France would be his cook."

(University of California, 1963, 1985, ISBN 0-520-05133-5, softcover, 455 pages, $12.95)

PERFORMING ARTS

DramaContemporary: Spain
Edited by Marion Peter Holt

The enormous political and social transition in Spain between 1974 and 1982 is eloquently reflected in the works of its artists. Here editor Marion Holt, a recognized authority on Spanish performing arts, presents four works that he feels exemplify "the larger perspective" of post-Franco Spain:

• *The Foundation* by Antonio Buero-Vallejo—Although set in an unnamed country, it reflects Buero's experiences during six years of imprisonment at the end of the Spanish Civil War. It is, says Holt, "A melding of a theatre of images and sound with dramatic discourse . . . [and] a universal warning that sudden liberation at a point in time does not signify the end of a struggle."

• *The Inmates of the Convent of Saint Mary Egyptian* by José Martín Recuerda—Award-winning playwright Recuerda re-creates the imprisonment and execution of Mariana Pineda, an event that took place during the reactionary reign of Fernando VII. His theme of torture for dissident political acts caused the play, first produced in 1977, to become a call to the new Spanish government for political amnesty.

• *The Cock's Short Flight* by Jaime Salom—In his characteristic mode of flowing from past to present, real to imaginary, Salom depicts the liberal-conservative schism that existed in Spain in the days preceding the Civil War.

- *Coronado and the Bull* by Francisco Nieva—Nieva is a prime practitioner of "Furious Theatre," a "theatre of conscience" that satirizes rigid adherence to tradition. He challenges preconceived notions about an "insular, ritualized" Spain and gleefully embraces the creativity and nonconformity that so often characterizes Iberian art.

Like the other volumes of DramaContemporary, **Spain** is intended to give Americans "the opportunity to learn about other cultures—the speech, gestures, rhythms and attitudes that shape a society—in the dramatic life of their plays."

(Performing Arts/Farrar, Straus and Giroux, 1985, ISBN 0-933826-86-9, softcover, 229 pages, $9.95)

Out of the Past: Spanish Cinema After Franco
John Hopewell

Most artists reflect, at least in part, the traditions of their childhood, and Spanish film directors are no exception. But in Spain, says author John Hopewell, the uniqueness of the cinema is rooted in more than the vibrant Spanish temperament and rich cultural heritage; it also springs from the traumas of Spanish history. The pain and destruction of the Civil War, the forty years of isolation under Franco's rule, the difficult transition from authoritarianism to democracy—all are reflected in contemporary film.

While Hopewell opens his book with a brief examination of the silent films of the late nineteenth century, the emphasis is on today's cinema, how it grew "out of the past" to reflect a "vague but identifiable 'Spanishness' of films made in Spain." He shows how directors including Carlos Saura and Juan Antonio often "explore Spanish themes using accessible Spanish styles, such as that mixture of fantasy and reality which foreigners can interpret as a kind of Spanish surrealism"; the manner in which filmmaker Fernando Fenrán Gómez "embodies Spaniards' quixotism, their tenacious holding on to illusions through the most trying of circumstances"; the ways in which Francisco Regueiro is more specific in his 1985 film *Padre nuestro* (Our Father), which portrays the desolation of Castilian rural life.

Hopewell's writing is both detailed and clear, his sources are well-documented, and a thirteen-page "Dictionary" gives biographical data on post-Franco film-makers. **Out of the Past** is a perceptive analysis of Spanish life as seen from second row center.

(University of Illinois, 1986, ISBN 0-85170-188-4, softcover, 295 pages, $15.95)

YOUNG PEOPLE'S BOOKS

Exploits of Don Quixote
Retold by James Reeves
For ages twelve and up

"Quixote is the embodiment, even though he is also the exaggeration, of a great idea. This idea is that there is more in life than the humdrum routine of everyday affairs; that true greatness is to be found only in the spirit of service to an ideal," says James Reeves, a storyteller who has taken Cervantes's greatest book and retold it for young readers. "Sancho Panza," he continues, "the simple yet shrewd squire, the lover of creature-comforts and material well-being, is the perfect foil to his master. Sancho is the ordinary man [who represents] the peasant virtues."

Together, knight and squire show many of the qualities that the Spaniards hold dear. Quixote, for example, has perfect manners, but they arise not from a surface desire to please but from a deep sense of honor, a belief that he deserves respect but must also accept responsibility. He is also an idealist, believing that a perfect world is not only desirable, but also possible. Quixote's fight for justice is often mirrored in Spanish history—it doesn't always work out but it is a brave attempt.

Reeves has selected episodes that he felt would appeal to young readers and yet remain true to the original. The result is a book that introduces children to a significant piece of literature, entertains them with the exploits of an impractical adventurer, and—for the more sophisticated—gives insights into many of the characteristic traits of the Spanish people.

(Blackie & Son Limited, London, from Peter Bedrick, 1977, ISBN 0-216-90466-8, softcover, 219 pages, $5.95)

Shadow of a Bull
Maia Wojciechowska
For ages eight and up

Manolo Olivar's father was the bravest matador the town of Arcangel had ever seen; he died a hero's death in the arena. Now eleven-year-old Manolo is expected to follow in his footsteps. But even though the townspeople are convinced that the boy's destiny lies in fighting the bulls, he isn't so sure:

It's not like wanting any other thing . . . You're either born with it or, if you're not, somewhere, someplace you get infected. And there it is. You have afición, *which just means that you'll never be happy doing anything else.*

In fact, Manolo is afraid he is a coward. He is afraid to jump from the top of a haystack; he is afraid to swim; he is even afraid to ride a bicycle. How can he ever hope to step into the bullfighting ring?

As Manolo learns that courage comes in many forms, this Newberry Medal-winning novel communicates the excitement of fiesta, the mystique of *toreo*, and the flavor of centuries-old customs and traditions of Andalusia.

(Aladdin Books/Macmillan, 1965, ISBN 0-689-71132-9, softcover, 151 pages, $3.95)

Spain: A Shining New Democracy
Geraldine Woods
For ages ten to thirteen

"Who says 'Spain' says everything" goes an old Spanish proverb, and Geraldine Woods explains the meaning of "everything" in her clear overview of a proud and beautiful country. She knows her readers well and makes her points through anecdotes sure to appeal to preteens. For example, in order to demystify the Spanish concept of "honor," she tells the following tale:

A professor at the University of Madrid once showed his sense of honor when he arranged an overnight field trip for his students. Because of a mixup in the hotel reservations, there were not enough rooms for everyone. Although he was nearly eighty, the professor insisted on giving up his room to a student. He spent the night on the bus. "A gentleman cannot rest when those he is responsible for are uncomfortable," he explained.

She explores Spanish geography, arts, history, legends, holidays, daily activities, education, and entertainment—using examples whenever possible to clarify and entertain. Wonderful pictures, mostly in full color, attract attention; and a map, pronunciation guide, glossary, and bibliography provide additional information. Her book takes a diverse country and makes it understandable.

(Dillon, 1987, ISBN 0-87518-340-5, hardcover, 166 pages, $12.95)

ITALY

GENERAL

All-Italy: The Book of Everything Italian
Frank Bianco et al.

"A man who has not been in Italy, is always conscious of an inferiority," said Samuel Johnson, and here to correct that is a host of authors, each expert in different aspects of Italian life and style. From cuisine to music, from crafts to sport, these ten men and women offer a crash course in All Things Italian.

Richard Horn begins with interior design, an apt beginning since, as he says, "You do not have to spend much time in Italy to realize just how much emphasis is placed on the visual aspect of things." Be it the bold patterns and bizarre shapes of the Memphis/Milano collaborative or the sleek simplicity that results from "a super-sophisticated technology merged with natural materials," Italian design is distinctive, individualistic, and sensual.

Italy's literary tradition is explored by Gabriella Dosi Delfini who goes back in time to speak of Dante, the first writer to compose in Italian rather than Latin, and progresses through the years to talk not only of contemporary authors but also of today's filmmakers, men like Roberto Rossellini, Federico Fellini, and Marcello Mastroianni who use celluloid rather than paper to express their ideas.

In honor of visitors who, while bent over guidebooks, "visualize the metamorphosis of leather thongs into Gucci loafers," there is a chapter on fashion with a section devoted to "shoes, shoes, shoes"; and for those who are intrigued by the "panorama of Renaissance palaces, Gothic churches, and baroque monuments" there is one on architecture.

Mixed with the text, perhaps even overshadowing it, is a panoply of full-color photos that create a kaleidoscopic array of impressions. **All-Italy** is an unusual book, a potpourri of short pieces that combine to give a words-and-pictures definition of a country.

(Running Press, 1986, ISBN 0-89471-386-8, softcover, oversized, 207 pages, $14.95)

Any Four Women Could Rob the Bank of Italy
Ann Cornelisen

Hermione Hendricks was the woman who was going "to liberate her sex and make men like it . . . She could turn men to stone or to jelly in any one of four languages without so much as a misplaced adverb." A bona fide celebrity, Hermione turned heads wherever she went. What better distraction if someone wanted to commit a robbery?

Kate Pound, wife, mother, and political analyst, was "exasperated, tired, and, as she recognized, on the verge of hysteria . . ." A robbery was just the thing to divert her from her problems.

And Lacey Wright, "thwarted Italophile," was grumpy and bored. With her friend, Eleanor Kendall, she went to Calabria for a vacation. "Neither was fit company for a normal person . . ."

Every afternoon, returning from the beach, El and Lacey ran into a police roadblock. Every afternoon, they were waved on by the police. The police, it seems, were not looking for women. "Any four women could rob the Bank of Italy," said El, "and the police would still go around looking for four men." Thus, the idea for a robbery was born.

Vassar-educated Ann Cornelisen, who lives in Tuscany, created in **Any Four Women** a lusty, witty, sexy, feminist novel. Her characters ramble around the Tuscan countryside taking advantage of the Italian male belief that women are incapable of plotting and executing a crime. Steeped in Italiana, this story bubbles with rollicking good fun.

(Penguin, 1983, ISBN 0-1400-7599-2, softcover, 291 pages, $5.95)

Florence: A Traveller's Companion
Selected and introduced by Harold Acton

Tuscany: An Anthology
Compiled by Laura Raison

"For most of us, Tuscany is the quintessence of Italy, the distillation of all those elements of the country that we think of as being most specifically Italian," says John J. Norwich in the foreword to **Tuscany**. True, perhaps, but why?

These two anthologies answer that question in the words of an assortment of writers, all of whom have been charmed by Tuscany and its capital city of Florence. These men and women have, through their works, created the composite image we have come to think of as "Italy." Michelangelo, Leonardo, and Dante, for example, were Tuscan natives who achieved much of their best work there; Shelley, the Brownings, Dylan Thomas, Robert Lowell, Mark Twain, and Henry James were among those travelers who, attracted by the area's beauty, visited and immortalized the region.

Florence provides an historical overview of the city from its earliest days, through its reign as a prosperous city-state and birthplace of the

Renaissance, up to the present century. Ghiberti comments on designing the Baptistry doors, Boccacio tells of the devastation of the Black Death, and D. H. Lawrence describes the impact of the massive statues in the Piazza della Signoria. The extracts are arranged by site, such as the Duomo, Palazzo Medici, Palazzo Pitti, San Lorenzo, and the Uffizi, offering the traveler the opportunity to compare his experiences with those of assorted previous visitors.

Tuscany also explores the region through the eyes of others, using poetry, prose excerpts, letters, drawings, paintings, and even recipes of many who found inspiration here. The works are arranged topically: Travelers, The Arts, Everyday Life, Encounters, *Pane e Vino*, and so forth. From its Etruscan beginnings to the present day, the region is depicted so thoroughly "that whether you are sitting under a cypress near Poppi or on a bench in Paddington Station, Tuscany and all her splendours never need be far away."

Both books are eclectic collections of facts and impressions, invocations of the elusive spirit of place.

(Florence: Atheneum, 1986, ISBN 0-689-70713-4, softcover, 333 pages, $9.95; Tuscany: Facts on File, 1984, ISBN 0-87196-858-4, hardcover, 262 pages, $19.95)

The Hill Towns of Italy
Carol Field

"Remember," he concluded, "that it is only by going off the track that you get to know the country. See the little towns—Gubbio, Pienza, Cortona, San Gimignano . . . and don't, let me beg of you, go with that awful idea that Italy's only a museum of antiquities and art."
—E. M. Forster, *Where Angels Fear to Tread*

Off the track and into the country is precisely where journalist Carol Field and photographer Richard Kauffman went to capture the sights, sounds, and feel of **The Hill Towns of Italy.** Through a hundred pages of text and sixty-four of beautiful full-color photographs, they give an intimate look at the ancient lands of Tuscany and Umbria, first settled as early as the eighth and seventh centuries B.C.

Traveling the back roads, they stop at towns such as Siena ("The Sienese make art of everything they touch, and their city has the feel of eternity"), Montepulciano ("aloof from any controversy as it sits, somewhat reserved and withdrawn, on a hilltop"), Assisi ("a splash of white spilling lightly down the hillside . . . all soft pinks and grays, its buildings formed of rosy limestone"), and Spoleto ("within its dense medieval center shadowed streets and dark passages alternate with sudden open spaces, small splashes of green in filmy trees and hidden gardens and in the vivid umbrellas of outdoor cafés"). They find that much has changed since their previous trips: "Unfortunately," says Kauffman, "the oxen were gone; the towns were bustling with automobiles. The medieval architecture, on the other hand, was mostly untouched."

Kauffman records the sights on film, Field with words. Interspersed as captions are quotations from writers who once lived in or visited the area: D. H. Lawrence, Hawthorne, Huxley, Montaigne, and Goethe, among others. The result is an unabashed love song to a richly multi-faceted region.

(Dutton, 1983, ISBN 0-525-93259-3, hardcover, oversized, 164 pages, $35.00)

Italian Hours
Henry James

Henry James—perceptive, witty, and urbane—gives us twenty-two "notes" on his various visits to Italy during the 1870s. From Venice to Florence and Siena, from Genoa and Pisa to Rome and Naples, James finds much that is delightful, some that is deplorable. His eye is sharp but affectionate, and the account of his wanderings is rich in detail. He writes of Venice:

The creature varies like a nervous woman, whom you know only when you know all the aspects of her beauty. She has high spirits or low, she is pale or red, grey or pink, cold or warm, fresh or wan, according to the weather or the hour. She is always interesting and almost always sad; but she has a thousand occasional graces and is always liable to happy accidents.

and about the festival for St. Margaret that he observes at Cortona:

The contadini from near and far had congregated in force and were crowding into the church or winding up the slope. When I arrived they were all kneeling or uncovered; a bedizened procession, with banners and censers, bearing abroad, I believe, the relics of the saint, was re-entering the church. The scene made one of those pictures that Italy still brushes in for you with an incomparable hand and from an inexhaustible palette when you find her in the mood.

and concerning the Italian style of discourse:

. . . almost any uttered communications here become an acted play, improvised, mimicked, poportioned and rounded, carried bravely to its denouement. The speaker seems actually to establish his stage and face his foot-lights, to create by gesture a little scenic circumscription about him; he rushes to and fro and shouts and stamps and postures, he ranges through every phase of his inspiration.

Whether the subject is history, art and architecture, or human nature, James's observations are nearly as timely today as when they were written over a century ago.

(Ecco Press, 1987, ISBN 0-88001-147-5, softcover, 376 pages, $10.50)

Note: **Henry James on Italy** combines selections from *Italian Hours* with evocative drawings and full-color paintings by Corot, Roberts, Turner, and Lear, among others. In a 9"x7½" format, this lovely volume packages James's erudite words in elegant wrappings (Weidenfeld & Nicolson, 1988, ISBN 1-55584-238-0, hardcover, 223 pages, $22.95)

Italian Journey
Johann Wolfgang von Goethe, translated by W. H. Auden and Elizabeth Mayer

By his thirty-seventh birthday, Goethe was a highly successful novelist and respected civil servant. No one, not even his closest friends, realized how close he was to a breakdown until suddenly he wrote a letter requesting a leave of absence and, without waiting for approval, departed for Italy at three o'clock one morning. The journals he kept on this and a subsequent trip, supplemented by letters to friends and relatives, form the basis for **Italian Journey**, translated and judiciously edited by Auden and Mayer.

Goethe's expedition was one of discovery and delight, and as the warm Italian sun and sunny Italian nature healed his troubled spirit, he reveled in the rich array of sights:

In other places one has to search for the important points of interest; here they crowd in on one in profusion. Wherever you turn your eyes, every kind of vista, near and distant, confronts you—palaces, ruins, gardens, wildernesses, small houses, stables, triumphal arches, columns—all of them often so close together that they could be sketched on a single sheet of paper. One would need a thousand styluses to write with. What can one do here with a single pen?

As Goethe visited Venice, Rome, Naples, and Sicily his incisive comments on the land and people are as interesting as his analytical musings. In Venice, for instance, he was appalled at the filthy streets and therefore devised plans for trash disposal, going so far as to carry on imaginary conversations with government officials about the subject.

Italian Journey paints dual portraits: one of eighteenth-century Italy and another of a brilliant man experiencing a troubled mid-life. Each is fascinating; together they are enthralling.

(North Point, 1982, ISBN 0-86547-076-6, softcover, 507 pages, $15.50)

Italian Labyrinth
John Haycroft

Forget all your preconceived notions about Italy: lecherous men pinching women in the streets, picturesque peasants treading barefoot in wine barrels, the love of *la dolce vita* that keeps Italians from achieving economic success, Mafia dons benevolently keeping order over a workforce of prostitutes and drug dealers. Well, forget most of them, anyway. John Haycroft has wound his way through the labyrinth of Italian byways in search of the real Italy, which is infinitely more complex and fascinating.

British-born Haycroft knows Italy well, as is obvious from this compelling exploration of the land and the people. Although billed as "an authentic and revealing portrait of Italy in the 1980's," his book also brings in considerable history against which to analyze contemporary Italy. Haycroft skips lightly from the linguistic influences on Sardinia to the effects of the Roman tradition of slavery upon today's labor relations to the films of Lina Wertmuller. He covers the land, institutions, and economy; the family and "broader families" (the Mafia), the Church, and the arts; and such everyday "challenges" as housing, education, medicine, and law and order.

Lively, authoritative and highly entertaining, **Italian Labyrinth** is, as Robert Fox of the *London Standard* says, "the ideal overture for newcomers to Italy, a *divertimento* for the better acquainted."

(Penguin, 1985, ISBN 0-14-006918-6, softcover, 314 pages, $6.95)

The Italians
Luigi Barzini

Nothing in Italy is quite what it appears to be, suggests Luigi Barzini. Churches were designed not really for prayer but as a display of Catholic power, politicians posture rather than plan, and even the passion of the Italian male is often calculated in advance for its effect.

Subtitled "A Full-Length Portrait Featuring Their Manners and Morals," **The Italians** touches on everything from the education of children to the quality of Italian prostitutes. But between the witty and unfailingly entertaining anecdotes, Barzini accuses his countrymen of a serious flaw. There is, he says, a "theatrical quality" to Italian life, an addiction to make-believe.

For instance all tickets, to opera and railroads alike, are priced at double what the company intends to collect. Why? An image must be maintained. The Italian must at all times be made to feel that he is, "sometimes for intricate and improbable reasons, one of the gods' favoured sons."

An accounting problem? Of course. But does it really matter? Barzini argues that it does. This preference for appearance over reality, he says, has far-reaching consequences. Inevitably it leads the people to believe their own half-truths, to neglect the very real problems that face them, and live, instead, with their illusions. He supports his thesis with examples from the last five centuries of Italian history. Michelangelo, Moravia, and Mussolini are all shown fooling themselves even as they fool the populace.

The Italians is a fascinating book, the more so because Barzini is not only a native son and honored journalist but also a member of the Chamber of Deputies. When he criticizes his compatriots, he is criticizing himself as well. By so doing he performs a valuable service: he reveals what's going on backstage.

(Atheneum, 1964, 1985, ISBN 0-689-70540-9, softcover, 360 pages, $8.95)

Memories of Mistresses
Luigi Barzini

Luigi Barzini, author of *The Italians*, was a master both of observation and of setting these perceptions down in writing. In this collection of twenty-two essays, published posthumously, he addresses a variety of topics, including the class of ladies remembered in his title:

When dining out with one of them, for instance, a man did not salute ladies he knew entering the restaurant. This was embarrassing, because she knew the man, knew the ladies, knew why he did not get up and bow, and knew why the ladies went by his table with raised chins and eyes forward.

Often providing telling views of larger-than-life figures, he recalls the time he was introduced to Benito Mussolini:

'. . . and this is Luigi Barzini.' At last, after a rather long interval, the Duce *spoke. Dragging out the syllables, he said: 'Ju-ni-or.' I was then little more than a boy, at least thirty years younger than the far more famous "Senior," my father, and felt like answering: 'Obviously,' but checked myself. Dictators have no sense of humor.*

He examines the aristocracy, Italian craftsmanship, *masochismo all'Italiana*, the Mafia, Italian Christmas Eve, Americans, the cities of Milan and Venice, and in a moving final essay, an account of his own heart attack. No matter what the topic, his wit and insight make for stimulating reading. Those who would know the Italian mind more intimately will come away from **Memories of Mistresses** much richer for the experience.

(Collier Books/Macmillan, 1986, ISBN 0-02-013080-5, softcover, 311 pages, $12.95)

On Persephone's Island: A Sicilian Journal
Mary Taylor Simeti

With Mary Taylor Simeti as your guide, roam the streets of Sicily during *I Morti*—literally, "The Dead," officially, "All Souls' Day." To a Sicilian child this is a festival to rival an American youngster's Christmas, with colorful decorations, processions, and gifts of toys and *marzipan*.

Or smell the almond blossoms as early spring breathes new life into the countryside:

The roadsides are thick with tiny flowers . . . The wild calendula speckle with orange the snowfall of camomile that spreads its miniature daisies throughout the vineyards while great swaths of brilliant lemon yellow mark the advance of the wood sorrel.

And join the whole family for *vendemmia*, the grape harvest, in late summer:

. . . the afternoon is cooled by a breeze that brushes away the insects, and the dark purple grapes, heaped in the blue plastic buckets until they dangle over the rim, are beautiful . . . We whistle for Francesco, who drives down the hill to pick them up . . . As we walk up the hill, the sun setting at our backs turns the eastern mountains to copper and paints a ruddy bloom on the grapes that are bouncing up the hill ahead of us.

Simeti is eminently qualified to lead this journey of discovery. Upon graduation from Radcliffe, she left to spend "a year or two" working with the Dolci Center in Sicily. Two decades later she was still in Sicily, married and the mother of two children; **On Persephone's Island** is the journal of her twentieth year there. Her descriptions of the patterns and events of their lives throughout the year presents a fresh look at an island that, she says, is greatly misunderstood.

(North Point, 1986, ISBN 0-86547-282-3, softcover, 336 pages, $11.95)

Sicilian Carousel
Lawrence Durrell

It seems only fitting that the writer who coined the word "islomane" should investigate the largest island in the Mediterranean. Since Lawrence Durrell takes credit for the first, he felt obliged to perform the second. And so he climbed aboard the "Sicilian Carousel," a tour bus that encircles the beautiful historically- and archaeologically-rich island.

At first the idea of a tour was anathema. Durrell recoiled at the prospect of being cooped up in a bus for two weeks with such fellow passengers as "the Anglican Bishop who had developed Doubts, the timid young archaeologist, the American dentist who had eloped with his most glamourous patient, the French couple of a vaguely diplomatic persuasion . . ." But as the bus careened counter-clockwise around the island, from Catania to Syracuse, Agrigento, Palermo, and Taormina, these strange bus fellows developed rapport while they became immersed in the region's culture and history. In Syracuse a guide lectured them on their good fortune in visiting Sicily, one of the only places where the Roman and Greek cultural worlds are set side by side:

"Here you can study both predispositions as if they were historically co-existent while in fact they are separated by centuries," [said the guide]. It was astute and highly suggestive as a way of looking at these now shadowy monuments of a lost world . . . But what is astonishing is the speed with which the exact nature and function of things becomes forgotten; the archaeologist tries to read a sort of palimpsest of superimposed cultures, one displacing or deforming the other—and then tries to ascribe a raison d'etre, function, to what he sees. [But] the ruins keep their secret. The monuments have been worn down like the teeth of an ancient jawbone . . . yet sitting in this old Roman theatre it takes no great act of the imagination to reconstruct the crowds, themselves now swallowed up by the centuries, as they watched the sports offered to them by the state—sports of blood.

With his typical wit and style, Durrell ruminates, reflects, and recounts— moving with agility through the years, with ease through the culture. His account brims with humor, insight and intellect, paying homage to "the fairest garden of the Mediterranean."

(Viking, 1977, ISBN 0-670-64362-9, hardcover, 223 pages, $13.95)

The Stones of Florence
Mary McCarthy

Travelers are often put off by Florence, notes author Mary McCarthy in her travel-essay classic **The Stones of Florence.** She enumerates the reasons: "the noise, the traffic, the heat . . . and something else besides . . . something [the tourist] hesitates to mention, in view of former raptures: the fact that Florence seems to him dull, drab, provincial."

But for those willing to look, the captivating Florentine charm is abundantly evident in its art, architecture, science, literature, and music. McCarthy writes of the giants of the artistic media: Leonardo, Donatello, Brunelleschi; she admires the magnificent churches: the Duomo, Santa Croce, Santa Maria Novella. And her perceptive observations on the Florentines' character permeate the book.

" 'Stingy, envious and proud,' the Florentines were possessed by a ferocious independence and rivalry, a determination to be outdone by no one," she writes. It was this determination that inspired every thirteenth-century landowner to build a tower taller than his neighbor's, until some of them reached more than two hundred feet. In 1250, in a democratizing effort, the towers were required to be reduced by two-thirds—"and enough material is supposed to have been left from this to build the city walls beyond the Arno [River]."

Since this book first appeared in 1959 some of McCarthy's observations have become dated; on the whole, however, it remains as entertaining and enlightening as ever. This edition is a handsome, oversized work lavishly illustrated with black-and-white and color photographs of some of Florence's finest artistic and archaeological works.

(Harcourt Brace Jovanovich, 1987, ISBN 0-15-685081-8, softcover, oversized, 129 pages, $19.95)

A Traveller in Italy
A Traveller in Rome
A Traveller in Southern Italy
H. V. Morton

Traveling with H. V. Morton as a guide is like touring with a well-educated uncle—one who although slightly stuffy can occasionally be persuaded to tell wonderfully witty stories. His three books about Italy, written over a span of twelve years, all provide a characteristic mix of historical anecdote and personal reflection that renders them ageless.

Morton wandered the streets and byways of the capital city in the 1950s and shared his knowledge and his experiences at the Roman Forum, on the Spanish Steps, at the Trevi Fountain, at St. Peter's, and the Vatican in **A Traveller in Rome.** Nearly ten years later he enlarged his scope and produced **A Traveller in Italy**, in which he described his journey through the regions of Lombardy, Emilia, Veneto and Tuscany.

Then, when the Autostrada del Sole was completed southwards from Naples, an Italian friend urged him to explore the southern regions of Italy—Abruzzi, Campania, Apulia, Basilicata and Calabria—the area "whose cities were famous for their wealth and luxury before anyone had heard of Rome." Morton took his friend's advice, headed south, and began gathering experiences for **A Traveller in Southern Italy.**

He found all that his friend had said he would—"that thousands of southern Italians worship in Norman cathedrals, that the ruins of Norman castles still crown a hundred hill-tops, that the peasants still remember the paladini—the knights, the paladins—that memories of King Arthur and Morgan le Fay are still alive"—and much more besides.

In the old town of Bari, he witnessed a three-day celebration for St. Nicholas of Myra (Father Christmas) during which the fishermen take the saint's statue out on a fishing boat to spend the day at sea, "in the belief that the patron saint of sailors would enjoy a day on the water." He dined in the shadow of the Castel dell'Ovo in Naples, so named because in the Middle Ages it was believed that Virgil had built the castle upon an egg (it actually was built by William I of Sicily, and its dungeons witnessed as many tragic stories as did those of the Tower of London). And he caught a glimpse of a *tarantolata*, a woman dancing the *tarantella* to cure a tarantula bite. He found out later she "might dance for days until completely exhausted, to expel the poison."

No matter what part of Italy he's describing, Morton is knowledgeable and articulate. And no matter which of Morton's books is appropriate for a particular Italian journey, it's probably best to take the advice of *The Times:* "Read it first, but do not leave it behind either."

(Dodd, Mead, softcover; A Traveller in Italy: 1964, 1984, ISBN 0-396-08046-4, 636 pages, $14.95; A Traveller in Rome: 1957, 1984, ISBN 0-396-08345-5, 432 pages, $12.95; A Traveller in Southern Italy: 1969, 1983, ISBN 0-396-08926-7, 420 pages, $14.95)

Vidal in Venice
Gore Vidal

Venice is "the most beautiful cliché on earth," says Gore Vidal in his intensely personal look at the land of his ancestors. While searching for his own roots he studied those of this incomparable city, exploring its history from its founding by barbarian tribes fleeing the Roman Empire up to present times. In the resulting book he portrays Venice's varied images—pictorially in a profusion of stunning color photographs by Tore Gill and verbally in his inimitable style, ripe with cynicism and biting wit. He comments:

The Venetians never wanted an empire. They just wanted to do business—and make money. Although there were fewer than 50,000 Venetians when the eastern Roman Empire fell to the Crusaders, the Venetians managed to end up with three-eighths of what remained of the old empire as well as exclusive trading rights throughout the entire eastern Mediterranean. It was a marvellous deal for the inhabitants of a few mudflats in an out-of-the-way lagoon.

and:

Napoleon just walked into Venice . . . Although the Venetians had been independent longer than any other people in the world, they welcomed the little dictator who had said, "I shall be a second Atilla to Venice" . . . As for the thousand-year-old Republic, it ended when the 120th Doge removed the doge's hat and gave it to his valet, remarking, "I suppose I won't be needing this anymore" . . . *Napoleon then gave Venice to Austria, delighting neither.*

Vidal makes a perceptive and provocative guide to the city that, he says, was "once a world capital. Now it is a sort of Disneyland."

(Summit Books, 1985, ISBN 0-671-64536-6, softcover, 160 pages, $14.95)

ANTHROPOLOGY AND ARCHAEOLOGY

Greek and Roman Life
Ian Jenkins

See Greece—Anthropology and Archaeology

The House That Giacomo Built
Donald S. Pitkin

"I married a good man," says Maria Rossi. "There are times when I wish my life could be different. I would like to ease away from the struggle, rest, maybe even go somewhere with Giacomo, although heaven only knows where we would go . . . [But] I am truly one of the fortunate ones. Before me lies, God willing, years of joy with our blessed family that we have created in this corner of the world."

Maria's corner of the world is a small village in central Italy, a place where she grew up, married, raised four children and, most likely, will die. She and her husband, Giacomo, first met author Donald Pitkin when he came to Valmonte as a young anthropologist in 1951. They have maintained their relationship ever since. And here Pitkin tells the story of their lives.

He focuses on the Rossi family, from the time of their marriage on February 13, 1953, until the birth of their first grandchild on September 16, 1978. Yet, to provide "an essential temporal perspective" he dips back into family history and details also the lives of Maria's parents, Giovanni and Giulia Tassoni.

Often Giacomo, Maria, and other members of the family speak for themselves in direct statements taken from notes and tapes. At other times

Pitkin relates their tale, telling of work and unemployment, birth and death, success and failure. In 1966 for example, Giacomo won seven acres in a lottery and built a house for his growing family: "At first Maria could not get beyond the idea that what she wanted was a larger kitchen, a larger bedroom for the six of them. Only at Giacomo's insistence did she imagine two bedrooms and a living room." In later years he added on to this house and built another nearby, keeping his family close and enjoying the benefits of living together as an extended family.

The House That Giacomo Built shows an Italy where well-being is measured by the strength of family ties rather than by money. It is, as its author states, "a love story," albeit one cloaked in anthropological trappings.

(Cambridge, 1985, ISBN 0-521-30168-8, hardcover, 243 pages, $29.95)

The Mute Stones Speak
Paul MacKendrick

If the mute stones of a thousand generations could whisper their secrets, what stories would they tell us of early man and his civilization? Paul MacKendrick asked this question and listened carefully to the answers. Here, in **The Mute Stones Speak**, he provides an account of the major modern archaeological finds on the Italian Peninsula.

He begins at the end of World War II, when two R.A.F. officers stationed in Southern Italy combined training flights with air reconnaisance of potential archaeological sites. The officers were both trained archaeologists, and their findings profoundly changed the archaeological map of Italy, doubling the existing number of known prehistoric sites in the region of Tavoliere, near the heel of the Italian boot.

"Modern archaeological excavation is neither haphazard nor a treasure hunt. It is a scientific business, preceded by careful survey, conducted with minute attention to levels and strata," MacKendrick states. Aided by photographs and maps, he shows how "the potsherd is the archaeologist's best friend . . . Comparison with pots of similar shape and decoration . . . yields precious information about dates, imports, exports, trade routes, and the aesthetic taste of the pot's maker and user."

Through archaeologists' interpretations the mute stones, potsherds, stone axes, and querns (handmills) tell of early man and of the "rich, energetic and mysterious" Etruscans, forebears of the powerful Roman civilization. It is a tale that proves "scientific business" can be as exciting as a detective story.

(Norton, 1960, 1983, 0-393-30119-2, softcover, 491 pages, $10.95)

Sicilian Lives
Danilo Dolci

Danilo Dolci spent three decades among the impoverished villagers of Trappeto, living and working among them and talking with them about their daily lives. In his compelling collection of oral history, the impoverished people of Sicily paint a stirring self-portrait.

We come to know Rosario, 55-year-old gatherer of greens and snails:

You get up in the morning, four, three, five, depends on the season and where you go ... You go out into the country, do six, seven miles, then plunge right into the fields looking for greens ... When I sell to the middleman I get a nickel or four cents a bunch ...

and Bastiano, who recognizes some of the village's problems but feels incapable of solving them:

The land around here can't be developed. There's just no water ... All it takes is for the government to build a dam on the Bruca. Why don't they do it?

and Grandma Nedda, a 75-year-old matriarch who always dresses in traditional black garb:

Of course a husband can beat his wife. At least when he's in the right. That's fair, no? Like if she gabs or talks back.

Dolci came to Sicily not just to record, but to change and reform. His efforts repeatedly landed him in jail, but because of his work Trappeto now has paved streets, sewers, and a drugstore—and the people have the satisfaction of knowing that the outside world has heard their stories.

(Pantheon, 1981, ISBN 0-394-74938-3, softcover, 306 pages, $6.95)

Spello: Life Today in Ancient Umbria
John and Adeline Hartcup

English authors John and Adeline Hartcup, intrigued by the medieval appearance of the backroads villages of Italy, wondered: how do people of these towns actually live? How much have their lives been changed by the twentieth century? So the couple spent six months in the hill town of Spello in the center of Umbria, *il cuore verde d'Italia*—the green heart of Italy—talking with and living among the villagers.

Family life, they found, is an amalgam of modern demands and traditional customs. "The age-long pattern of rural Mediterranean life still holds: several generations living together in the same house, working together for the family farm or business." Yet the relationship between parent and child reflects less authoritarianism than in the past. "We used to say children should be brought up *con amore e timore*, with love and fear," comments one resident. "There is not much *timore* now!"

Spello was once the heart of a rich agricultural region, with few *padroni* (rich employers) and many *contadini*(peasants). Now the farming business is no longer economically viable ("the politicians' fault"), so the villagers must seek other work. However, as a schoolteacher notes, "there are no more *contadini*. They have all become *padroni*."

Weddings and funerals, food and drink, art, education, the church—nearly every aspect of village life is revaled through the Hartcups' anecdotal accounts. Their book, a fusion of observation and conversation, is the next best thing to actually living there.

(Allison & Busby Ltd., London, from Pantheon/Schocken, 1985, ISBN 0-85031-611-1, hardcover, 168 pages, $13.95)

ART AND ARCHITECTURE

The Architectural History of Venice
Deborah Howard

"The architecture of Venice is remarkable not only for its ingenious solutions to the technical problems of building in amphibious surroundings. It also embodies artistic achievements of the highest level," states architecture professor Deborah Howard in her introduction to **The Architectural History of Venice**.

She approaches her subject chronologically, offering outstanding examples of each period's architecture—not "typical" buildings of each era "for these are, by definition, distinguished by their ordinariness." Beginning with the Byzantine age, when "the foundations of Venetian architecture were laid, both literally and conceptually," she proceeds through the Medieval, Gothic, early Renaissance, "Roman" Renaissance, and Baroque periods as well as Palladianism and Neoclassicism, before concluding with the years since the fall of the Republic.

Her discussion of architecture is laced with vignettes of social history, and the whole is illustrated with black-and-white photographs and drawings. This is a concise yet thorough overview for the layman.

(Holmes & Meier, 1981, ISBN 0-8419-1142-8, softcover, 263 pages, $44.50)

Classic Art: An Introduction to the Italian Renaissance
Heinrich Wolfflin

First published in 1899, **Classic Art** remains a highly influential work of art history. Author Heinrich Wolfflin (1864-1945) was a forceful critic, boldly offering his opinions on some of the world's greatest art. A pioneer who introduced a new discipline to the study of art, he "found art criticism a subjective chaos and left it a science," says Herbert Read in his introduction. "There is no art critic of importance after his time who has not, consciously or unconsciously, been influenced by him."

Beginning with antecedents of the Renaissance (Giotto—"he it was who loosened the tongue of art"—Donatello and Verrocchio, among others), Wolfflin devotes the majority of his book to the giants of the period. There is a chapter each on Leonardo ("a born aristocrat among painters"), the young Michelangelo ("like a mighty mountain torrent, at once fertilising and destructive"), Raphael ("open, serene, friendly"), Fra Bartolommeo ("a feeling for the significant, for nobility of gesture, for the splendour of a rhythmic contour"), Andrea del Sarto ("a soft, almost sleepy beauty"), and the older Michelangelo ("he seems not to have reached the zenith of his powers until the second half of his life, when he created the Medici tombs, the *Last Judgment*, and St. Peter's"). The remainder of the book deals with concepts developed by the Renaissance: New Ideals, New Beauty, and New Pictorial Form. It is illustrated throughout with black-and-white photographs.

Wolfflin has been criticized for over-emphasizing del Sarto and neglecting the Venetians; certainly he reflects Victorian-era tastes more than those of the modern day. Nonetheless, his opinions are worthy of serious consideration.

(Cornell, 1980, ISBN 0-8014-9193-2, softcover, 294 pages, $13.95)

Florence: The City and Its Art
Luciano Berti

Of all the fairest Cities of the Earth
None is so fair as Florence. 'Tis a gem
Of purest ray; and what a light broke forth,
When it emerged from darkness! Search within,
Without; all is enchantment! 'Tis the Past
Contending with the Present; and in turn
Each has the mastery.

–Samuel Rogers, *Italy*, 1830

More than 150 years have passed since Samuel Rogers wrote his panegyric to Florence, and even a quick glance at Luciano Berti's *Florence* proves that the enchantment remains to this day. Brimming with richly-detailed full-color photographs, the book is a superb introduction to the city that was home to Dante, the Medici, and Michelangelo and that houses some of the world's greatest art and architecture.

Beginning with early Christian times author Luciano Berti succinctly traces the history of Florence through medieval days, the Renaissance, and into the present. He then traverses the city, giving the historical background of the most significant architectural and artistic sites and noting their stylistic and technical details. Architectural wonders such as the Palazzo Vecchio and Piazza della Signoria, the Pitti Palace and Boboli Gardens, San Marco and San Lorenzo, and paintings by masters including Michelangelo, Giotto, Donatello, and Titian come alive through Berti's vivid descriptions and photos.

The Florentines, Berti concludes, are the "heirs of the civilisation" and their city one in which, as in Rogers's day, the past contends with the present.

(Instituto Fotografico Editoriale, Firenze, from Scala, 1979, ISBN 0-935748, softcover, 159 pages $13.95)

Venice: A Thousand Years of Culture and Civilization
Venice Preserved
Peter Lauritzen

Venice . . . is apparently a city belonging only to her past, an empty shell of former glories. Its native population diminishes constantly . . . Its last remaining industry makes baubles for the tourists who come in droves to stay on a statistical average of about eighteen hours . . . [yet] the discriminating, the connoisseurs and the devotees sense the peace of Venice and its supreme beauty.

Author Peter Lauritzen, obviously a connoisseur and devotee of Venice, had lived in the city for more than a decade when he wrote **Venice: A Thousand Years**—"long enough to have been accepted as a *cittadino* under the Republic." His book is an affectionate history and one that places Venetian works and artists against their proper background, for Lauritzen firmly believes that in order to fully appreciate a work of art it is necessary to understand the history behind it. "The Titians in a museum, the lace in a Medici portrait or the Vivaldi concerto in a concert hall should be approached bearing in mind the environment that produced them."

Designed for the general reader, his book concisely covers the entire span of this man-made city from its founding in the early fourth century through its rise to become a world capital in the sixteenth, and on to its present-day status of a decaying tourist site.

Because he had become so enthralled with Venice and her art, this decay appalled Lauritzen to the point that he became involved in cataloging restorations effected by UNESCO over the past twenty years. "But the long and fascinating tale of cleaning paintings, repairing buildings and restoring statuary since 1966 is still only part of the story," he asserts, and so he set out to record the full drama of what needed to be done, and why, and what progress has been achieved. The result is **Venice Preserved**, a remarkable tale of private and public sectors working together in a monumental effort to overcome the results of the hazards, both natural and man-made, that threaten the city's very existence. Illustrated with more than two hundred photographs, half of them in full color, this book, as well as his previous one, pays beautiful tribute to the Queen City of the Adriatic.

(Venice: A Thousand Years; Atheneum, 1981, ISBN 0-689-70603-0, softcover, 232 pages, $6.95; Venice Preserved: Adler and Adler, 1986, ISBN 0-917561-17-1, hardcover, oversized, 176 pages, $29.95)

CUISINE

Foods of Italy
Giuliano Bugialli

This is not a cookbook—at least not in the traditional sense. It is more at home displayed on a coffee table than propped up on a kitchen counter where it might get splashed by spaghetti sauce.

That's not to say, however, that it is not full of mouth-watering recipes. Italian culinary authority and award-winning author Giuliano Bugialli has prepared 125 recipes especially for this book: *Verdure con zabaione secco* (vegetable compote with dry zabaione), *Triangoli di pesce* (pasta triangles stuffed with fish) and *Involtini di tacchino* (rolled stuffed turkey cutlets), to mention just a few.

But the real charm of **Foods of Italy** lies in its anecdotes and photographs. Bugialli intersperses his recipes with tales about their origins and information about the growing, harvesting, and preparation of the ingredients. For example, in a discussion of vegetables—which, we learn, "even more than pasta, are the cornerstone of Italian cooking"—he tells us that "one summer day, while I was searching through the ancient town of Cremona and its countryside for the special regional dishes of the area . . . all the local people I asked told me that one couldn't find Cremona's characteristic dishes at that time of year because of the Italian's passion for fresh vegetables in season."

Veteran photographer John Dominis, who for years was on the staff of *Life* magazine and has been picture editor of *People* and *Sports Illustrated*, portrays the finished dishes against the scenic backdrop of Italy's famous architecture and rolling countryside. These full-color photographs (250 in all) join with the text to create a feast in which history, culture and cuisine are simmered together to a rich, delectable perfection.

(Stewart, Tabori & Chang, 1984, ISBN 0-941434-52-4, hardcover, oversized, $45.00)

The Gourmet's Tour of Italy
Antonio Piccinardi and James M. Johnson

Antonio Piccinardi and James Johnson, noted authorities on European cuisine, must have had a grand time writing this book. They traveled throughout Italy—looking, dining, tasting—and finally chose thirty restaurants where food and surroundings blended into an experience *eccellente*.

Here are Cà Peo in Liguria, Il Sole in Lombardy, Enoteca Pinchiorri in Tuscany. From Florence, Venice, and Milan to smaller cities and villages such as Palermo and Lecco, the authors talked to chefs, gleaned recipes and photographed restaurants that are among the most elegant and enchanting in the world.

The full-color photographs are beautiful, mouth-watering, intimidating. They show Squid alla Veneziana, Maltagliati Pasta in Duck Sauce with Black Olives, Scallops in Pastry with Broccoli Sauce—all cooked and arranged with precision and care. They show crisp white tablecloths, meticulously-arranged wine cellars, relaxed smiling chefs, well-dressed sated diners and breathtaking surroundings.

Accompanying essays profile the owners and chefs, describe each restaurant's history and atmosphere, and conclude with recipes that are intriguing to read and challenging to prepare. Most of us would probably prefer to take advantage of boxed bits of information that give directions to each restaurant as well as the address, phone number, and hours of business!

(New York Graphic Society/Little, Brown, 1987, ISBN 0-8212-1628-7, hardcover, oversized, 176 pages, $29.95)

The Tuscan Year
Elizabeth Romer

The pasta sauce is simmering on the stove, and we are sitting in Silvana Cerotti's kitchen, resting our arms on the heavy wooden table, our fingers outlining the squares on the oil cloth cover. On the wall near the door we see the old stone sink, and opposite the fireplace there is a new gas stove with an electric oven. But Silvana believes food tastes better when prepared over an open flame, so the heart of the kitchen is really the old wood stove.

Silvana's cooking is the happy focus of much of this tale, and the recipes are plentiful. *Minestrone acquacota, sanguinaccio* and *cotechino*—they are all here. And even more important than the recipes is the glimpse we're given of life in the Cerottis's small village. Here, nestled in a valley lying between Tuscany and Umbria, people "live in medieval houses, pray before altarpieces painted by Renaissance masters and prepare their food with the grace and balance instilled into them by hundreds of years of measured civilization."

The pictures of the people and their customs are as rich as Silvana's sauces: "Everyone seasons his own plate with black pepper according to taste, although if anyone has been ill . . . and is therefore eating in *bianco*, nothing but white food, he would naturally forego the black pepper," says Romer, a long-time resident of Tuscany and friend of the Cerottis.

The Tuscan Year is organized according to seasons; we go month by month through the year, from "the traditional pig-killing and preserving of hams in January to the gathering and curing of olives and preparations for Christmas in December." Throughout it all we are given the sights and sounds, as well as the tastes, of a pastoral, half-hidden region of Italy.

(Atheneum, 1985, ISBN 0-689-11568-7, hardcover, 182 pages, $12.95)

FOLKTALES

Italian Folktales
Italo Calvino

For two years Italo Calvino lived in woodlands and enchanted castles. He glimpsed mysterious creatures and monstrous transformations, was bewitched by beautiful maidens and held captive by tyrannical dragons. During this time he was searching, he says, for the Italian equivalents of the tales compiled by the Brothers Grimm.

It is evident in this physically heavy (765 pages) and metaphorically light book that he found what he was looking for. **Italian Folktales** contains two hundred tales of love and enchantment, witchcraft and trickery. It illustrates every variety of folktale and represents every part of Italy, showing regional tastes, attitudes, and customs.

This is not intended to be a book for children, although there is no doubt that youngsters would enjoy the tales, particularly if read aloud to them in front of a crackling fire. It is for all those who wish to absorb the flavor of Italy by immersing themselves in its oral tradition. "Folktales," explains Calvino, "are labeled 'Italian' insofar as they are narrated by the people of Italy . . . but we also classify them as Venetian, Tuscan, Sicilian. [The folktale], regardless of its origin, tends to absorb something of the place where it is narrated—a landscape, a custom, a moral outlook, or else merely a very faint accent or flavor of that locality."

The late Calvino is regarded by many as one of the greatest writers of modern times, and here he exhibits his preeminence both as a raconteur and as a scholar. A lengthy introduction sets forth the parameters of his study; notes at the end document related versions of each tale and help place it in its proper perspective.

Unanimously chosen as one of the *New York Times*'s ten best books of 1980, **Italian Folktales** is "a magic book, and a classic to boot," says *Time* magazine. "To read it is to plant feet in the soil, and to fly."

(Pantheon, 1966, 1980, ISBN 0-394-74909-X, softcover, 765 pages, $9.95)

HISTORY

The House of Medici
Christopher Hibbert

The history of the Medici family is the history of Renaissance Florence—indeed, perhaps of all Italy. At a time when power was usually expressed through violence, intrigue, and physical action, the Medicis were learned humanists whose occasional incidents of cruelty were only momentary lapses in their benevolent rule.

The family's founder, Giovanni de' Medici, was a kind and honest man who wanted nothing more than to live a private life while quietly making money in his growing banking business. On his deathbed he advised his sons, "Be inoffensive to the rich and strong . . . while being consistently charitable to the poor and weak . . . Avoid litigation and political controversy, and always keep out of the public eye." His son Cosimo, although also honest and kind, was more ambitious. While building the family bank into the most successful in Europe, he most determinedly stayed in the public eye, assuming a key role in the political life of Florence as well as becoming an influential patron of the arts.

For generations the family remained an important force in the ruling class of Florence, producing some of the world's most colorful statesmen, scholars, popes, and soldiers. Historian Christopher Hibbert tells the entire story, from Giovanni's time in the fourteenth century to the death of Anna Maria, Electress Palatine, in 1743. Along the way there was Lorenzo (about whom it was said, "if Florence was to have a tyrant she could never have found a better or more delightful one") and a later Giovanni (who as Pope Leo X "took his religious duties seriously and fasted twice a week. He was evidently prepared to be ruthless when the interests of his family were threatened; but how many popes were not?") The tale encompasses the careers of Donatello, Fra Angelico, Michelangelo, and Botticelli, all of whom were supported by the Medicis.

When Tuscany was finally conquered by Austrian troops in 1743, the people of Florence "looked back to the great days of the Medici with pride and a sense of loss . . . They would have given two-thirds of all they possessed to have [them] back." That, as it turned out, was unnecessary; Medici palaces and villas, art treasures and manuscripts will always reside in Florence. Anna Maria, the last member of the family, made that a condition of her will.

(Quill/Morrow, 1974, ISBN 0-688-05339-4, softcover, 364 pages, $12.95)

The Leopard
Giuseppe di Lampedusa

"The Bourbon state of Naples and Sicily, called the Kingdom of the Two Sicilies, was about to end . . . The whole Italian peninsula would soon be one state for the first time since the fall of the Roman Empire," states the historical note at the beginning of Giuseppe di Lampedusa's highly acclaimed novel, **The Leopard**.

Completed in 1957 just a few months before Lampedusa's death and since hailed as a masterpiece of European fiction, **The Leopard** tells the story of Don Fabrizio, a Sicilian prince of vibrant charm. Against the backdrop of political upheaval, Don Fabrizio enjoys his days—benevolently controlling large parcels of land and large numbers of human beings. Rich and poor, male and female—all are magnetized by his dynamic personality.

Lampedusa knows well the life of which he writes. He was born a Sicilian prince in 1896, and **The Leopard** is based on the life of his paternal great-grandfather. With an accuracy that comes from true understanding, he portrays a time when decadent aristocrats first heard the cries of democracy.

(Pantheon, 1960, ISBN 0-394-74949-9, softcover, 322 pages, $7.95)

The Romans
Karl Christ

"Who were 'the Romans'?" asks German author and scholar Karl Christ as he embarks upon his concise distillation of Ancient Rome. "To begin with, they were of course the farmers, shepherds, craftsmen, the small-to-middling landowners who originally lived in the 'city' founded on the Tiber..."

Christ breathes life into these men, and documents their stories as their numbers expanded to incorporate "not only the leading townsmen of Italy but also soldiers of Rome's allies who had distinguished themselves; not only the supporters of the factions in the Roman civil wars but also St. Paul; the wealthy Greek merchant as well as the rhetorician; the Arab tribal prince and the German army leader."

The extraordinary achievements of these people are chronicled in this brief but thorough guide to Roman antiquity. Christ offers a "portrait in miniature" of Roman civilization, detailing historical events as well as the social and cultural systems that made it one of the bases of the modern world. Separate sections discuss ways of earning a living, the role of women, education, housing, clothing, games, and even the disposal and remembrance of the dead. In addition, Christ covers literature, art, science, technology and religion—letting, when possible, the Romans speak for themselves through representative texts.

The Romans, he states, was written for the person "who would like to know about the main features of Roman society, its politics, economics, and culture; for the traveller seeking to place the monuments of the *imperium Romanum* in their historical context; and for the students of those disciplines which were, and still are, built on Roman foundations." By writing with clear and compact precision, including maps and photographs, and preparing a chronological table for easy reference, Christ has succeeded in all he set out to accomplish.

(University of California, 1984, ISBN 0-520-05634-5, softcover, 294 pages, $9.95)

Rome: The Biography of a City
Christopher Hibbert

As we approach Rome, Ancient Italy rushes on the Imagination. Italy has had two lives!
        —Samuel Rogers, *Italian Journal*, 22 November 1818

Christopher Hibbert may well take issue with Rogers; his "biography" of Rome takes the Eternal City through *many* lives as it traverses the years from the days of prehistory, still shrouded in legend, through World War II and (although only briefly) up to the late 1970s.

Hibbert, aided by numerous black-and-white illustrations, conjures up a multitude of images from the city's past: a she-wolf nursing Romulus and Remus, Caesar becoming enchanted with Cleopatra and being betrayed by Brutus, fifty thousand people cheering gladiators in the Colosseum, Michaelangelo painting the Sistine Chapel, Mussolini planning the March on Rome.

A lengthy section of chapter-by-chapter notes on historical sites and works of art becomes, in effect, a sort of guidebook, allowing the visitor to see the sights of the city in their historical context. (The book, however, is a bit hefty to make an ideal travel companion.)

As Churchill declared, "He who holds Rome holds the title-deeds of Italy." In this work Hibbert recreates not only the history of Rome but, in many ways, of Italy as well.

(Norton, 1985, ISBN 0-393-01984-5, hardcover, 387 pages, $25.00)

The Twelve Caesars
Suetonius, translated by Robert Graves

It is fair to assume that the Roman ruler Caligula was a favorite of nobody. "He frequently had trials by torture held in his presence while he was eating . . . and kept an expert headsman in readiness to decapitate the prisoners brought in from the gaol," wrote Suetonius, the great Latin historian who, as chief secretary to the Emperor Hadrian, gathered his information from the Imperial and Senatorial archives of ancient Rome as well as from eyewitness accounts.

Nero deserved hs reputation as a pyromaniac: "Once, in the course of a general conversation," according to Suetonius, "someone quoted the line: 'When I am dead, may fire consume the earth,' but Nero said that the first part of the line should read: 'While I yet live,' . . ."

A true and diligent historian, Suetonius checked his facts carefully and refrained from inserting his own biases. Where he found conflicting evidence, he quoted both. Partially because of this his book has become a classic and a model for biography.

The Twelve Caesars, true to its name, chronicles the lives of the Roman rulers beginning with Julius Caesar, who ruled from 49-44 B.C., through Domitian, who was in power from A.D. 81-96. It depicts each ruler's family history and early life, his public career and his physical appearance. But it is the private lives of these men that fascinated Suetonius, and his book abounds with details of their scandals and vices, their romances and domestic conflicts.

The profuse illustrations, both color and black-and-white, combine with the text to vividly recreate one of the most formative periods in the history of western civilization: the Roman Empire of the first century.

(Penguin, 1957, 1979, 1984, ISBN 0-1400-5416-2, paperback, 281 pages, $18.95)

NATURE

Gardens of the Italian Villas
Marella Agnelli et al.

"Behind each of these gardens," writes Marella Agnelli, "there is a long, long story which interweaves the poetical ideals, the sense of elegance and all the imaginative spirit of the Italian civilization." Agnelli, a renowned interior decorator and designer, coordinated a group of highly talented individuals—botanist Luca Pietromarchi, photographer Robert Emmett Bright, and horticulturalist Federico Forquet—who traveled throughout Italy to reveal thirty-six magnificent **Gardens of the Italian Villas.**

The photographs of Bright and Agnelli explore nature in all its brilliance (the book contains 225 pictures, most in full color and many that are double-page spreads); but the text is equally revealing as it considers the gardens as representations of major cultural trends within Italian artistic tradition. Here are medieval expressions of courtliness and meditation; Renaissance attempts to master nature and explore its mysteries; seventeenth-century compositions on a grand theatrical scale, bubbling with fountains and lush with greenery; geometrically elegant arrangements from the late seventeenth century; romantic landscaping of the eighteenth century; and humanistic, intimate courtyards of modern times. Varied in location as well as style, the gardens span the peninsula from Lombardy's Villa Fogazzaro in the north to Sicily's Villa Camastra in the south.

This book is a boon to the traveler who is also a garden enthusiast, whether to plan an Italian itinerary, to bring a touch of Italy to the reader's own garden, or just to revel in the amazing variety of nature's beauty.

(Rizzoli, 1987, ISBN 0-8478-0825-4, hardcover, oversized, 221 pages, $50.00)

Views from a Tuscan Vineyard
Text by Julian More, photographs by Carey More

As you turn the pages of this very personal photograph album, you'll find yourself magnetically drawn to the enchanting region of Tuscany, where "museums should be approached lightly, and discoveries made personally—with the intuitive pleasure which comes when one is truly touched by what one perceives."

Divided into five sections, the book incorporates the grape-growing cycle into the region's history: Planting (Tuscan Roots), Flowering (The Golden Age of the Medicis), Ripening (The Age of Unreason), Harvest (Paradise of Exiles), and Tasting (The Recent Years).

Carey More's sensitive photographs depict every aspect of the diverse area. The River Arno flows by in the muted tones of a watercolor painting; a gray-haired couple prunes their grape vines amidst a vibrant field of wildflowers; Montecchio, a restored eighth-century castle near Arezzo, stands outlined against the sky in sepia tones; a bicyclist wends his way along a narrow cobbled street in Florence.

Author Julian More's accompanying text touches with deft humor on history, cuisine, climate, music, art, and above all, the unforgettable Tuscan people. He introduces, for instance, octagenarian Contessa Marinetta di Franssineto on her Chianina bull-breeding ranch in Fontarronco. She would love to retire, but she must eat. "So," she declares, "I export semen to America. Bull's semen, you understand. So much cheaper than sending the actual bull."

As he revels in the Italian countryside, More meditates on his good fortune:

How good it is to get out of the museums into fields, gardens, country churches, village piazzas, narrow streets, and vineyards. These vineyards—good year, bad year, come shine or come hail—seem to symbolize Tuscany's continuity, its fitness for survival.

In this father-daughter collaboration, the Mores admirably succeed in evoking the spirit of this resiliant, lusty region.

(Holt, 1987, ISBN 0-8050-027508, hardcover, 143 pages, $19.95)

PERFORMING ARTS

The Golden Century of Italian Opera
William Weaver

The time from the early nineteenth century to the early twentieth—from Rossini's *Barber of Seville*'s premiere performance in 1815 to that of Puccini's *Turandot* in 1926—was a golden century, indeed. And, as William Weaver writes in his introduction, "we know about the composers' lives and about their operas, but too often these have been discussed in isolation, out of their context. The world in which those operas were written, heard, applauded, or jeered, remains only partially known."

But now Weaver gives us an intimate backstage look at the world of Italian opera, citing a plethora of contemporaneous sources to set the stage as it was at the time, rather than viewing it through a 1980s opera glass. The story he tells is an anecdotal, gossipy tale of musical passion and illicit love, personal and professional rivalries, exploitation, intrigue, and jealousy. Reading almost more like soap opera than like the musical variety, the book portrays renowned composers and performers as multi-dimensional human beings who might, as a lark, dress up as female beggars and go out singing in the streets during Carnival (as did Rossini and Paganini) or shock local sensibilities by living openly together without benefit of clergy (as did Verdi and famous soprano Giuseppina Strepponi).

Period photographs and drawings, play-bills, engravings and cartoons fascinate as they bring the past to life. A set of caricatures published in 1869 prove, for example, that human motivations don't change much through the centuries. Answering the question "Who goes to the theatre?" it responds, "He goes to the theatre because he's a subscriber. A man of good society must at least be a Scala subscriber," and "These [foreign tourists] go to the theatre because . . . their guide advises them to go . . ."

Whatever your motivation for attending the opera, Weaver's book will set the mood, transporting you back to the golden days when Italian opera reigned supreme.

(Thames and Hudson, 1988, 1980, ISBN 0-500-27501-7, softcover, oversized, 256 pages, $19.95)

Italian Film in the Light of Neorealism
Millicent Marcus

Millicent Marcus, an associate professor at the University of Texas, Austin, wrote this book in "an attempt to fathom the impact of neorealism on Italian cinema through selective analyses of exemplary works produced between 1945 and 1982."

She discusses seventeen films which she divides into four categories: "Neorealism Proper" (Rossellini's *Open City*, De Santis's *Bitter Rice* and De Sica's *Bicycle Thief* and *Umberto D*), "Transitions" (Comencini's *Bread, Love, and Fantasy*, Felini's *La strada*, Visconti's *Senso*, and Antonioni's *Red Desert*), "Return to Social Commentary" (Olmi's *Ilposto*, Germi's *Seduced and Abandoned*, Pasolini's *Teorema*, and Petri's *Investigation of a Citizen Above Suspicion*), and "Fascism and War Reconsidered" (Bertolucci's *The*

Conformist, Wertmuller's *Love and Anarchy*, Rosi's *Christ Stopped at Eboli*, the Traviani Brothers' *Night of the Shooting Stars*, and Scola's *We All Loved Each Other So Much*).

Neorealism proper, as Marcus admits, "lasted only seven years, generated only twenty-one films, failed at the box office, and fell short of its didactic and aesthetic aspirations." Yet its influence has been so profound that Purdue University's Ben Lawton considers the book to be much more than an exceptional work on Italian cinema. It is also, he says, "must reading for anyone interested in Italian culture in any way."

(Princeton, 1986, ISBN 0-691-10208-2, softcover, 444 pages, $17.50)

YOUNG PEOPLE'S BOOKS

City: A Story of Roman Planning and Construction
David Macaulay
For ages eight and up

For almost two hundred years the wheat and grapes of northern Italy's fertile Po Valley had been collected in small trading villages and shipped to Rome. In 26 B.C. a disastrous spring flood destroyed the villages along the Po riverbanks as well as an important bridge. When news reached the Emperor Augustus he immediately dispatched to the stricken area forty-five military engineers, including planners, architects, surveyors, and construction specialists. They were to supervise the building of a new bridge and new roads and to lay plans for a new city. The city was named Verbonia.

Verbonia is fictitious, but the methods used to build it are not. Through simple text and the detailed line drawings that have become his trademark, David Macaulay takes us to the site of the new town. He lets us watch as first the roads and bridge, then the city wall and aqueduct, next the forum and market, finally the homes and apartments, and at last an amphitheater and theater gradually take shape.

City won praise from educators and architects alike and was named one of the best books of 1974 by the *School Library Journal* and the *New York Times*. Perhaps the best praise, however, comes from his young readers: they keep reading—and buying—his books year after year.

(Houghton Mifflin, 1974, ISBN 0-395-34922-2, softcover, oversized, 112 pages, $6.95)

A Family in Italy
Penny and John Hubley
For ages seven to ten

Eight-year-old Francesca Rossi lives in Grassina, a suburb of Florence, and except for the language, most American youngsters are likely to find her life quite similar to their own. Color pictures show Francesca perched on her bicycle in front of her recently-built apartment house, her teacher strumming a guitar, her father tinkering with the engine of his Fiat, and her mother shopping at a supermarket. There are mouth-watering scenes of a pasta factory and a bakery, and Grandfather Rossi is shown tending his garden and pruning his grapevines. The text tells about daily life and slips in small tidbits of history and geography. It proves that—at least in the case of the Rossis—a family in Italy may be very much like a family in America.

(Lerner, 1986, ISBN 0-8225-1673-X, hardcover, 32 pages, $8.95)

Italy: Balanced on the Edge of Time
Anthony DiFranco
For ages ten to thirteen

Italy, as the subtitle suggests, is on the brink of change:

In one town, men in old-time costumes race on horseback. In another, fast cars speed around a track. Out in the country, children drive oxen in the fields, while in the city they shop in new malls. Think of movie theaters and old temples, shacks and skyscrapers.

Author Anthony DiFranco sorts out the old and the new in a well-rounded look at Italy that covers geography and history, religion and folklore, sports and schools, holidays and foods.

The chapter on food, for example, reveals that pasta, is more than spaghetti and ravioli. It comes in a multitude of shapes such as *bucatini* ("little holes"), *farfalle* ("butterflies") and *agnolotti* ("fat little lambs"). Moreover, the Italian diet doesn't just consist of pasta and pizza. There is Florentine beefsteak, Alpine trout, Parma ham and pork, veal, chicken, and sausage prepared in a great variety of ways, to say nothing of delicacies like snails, octopus, squid, and "pig, goat and calf innards . . . made into tasty snacks."

Italy includes a map, glossary, bibliography, and a list of "Fast Facts about Italy." A generous sprinkling of black-and-white photographs illustrate the text, making the book a pleasant and easy way to gather a wealth of Italian information.

(Dillon, 1983, ISBN 0-87518-229-1, hardcover, 127 pages, $12.95)

Venice: Birth of a City
Piero Ventura
For ages seven to twelve

Not only the birth, but the entire life of this "strangest, most fascinating and perhaps . . . most beautiful" of cities is chronicled here through Piero Ventura's words and pictures. Ventura takes the reader to visit eleventh-century family-run shipyards; to witness the Doge's Procession "proclaiming Venetian pride and self-importance"; and to enjoy Carnival, the exuberant week-long pre-Lenten festival where "everyone, nobles and commoners alike, hid behind the famous *bautta*, (the black or white domino mask that covered the eyes)." He introduces Venice's many craftsmen, mentions some of her best-known artists, and shows the bustling activity behind stage at La Venice Theater.

His detailed, multi-captioned drawings complement the text, and a four-page foldout gives a panoramic aerial view of the city. **Venice**, like the city it describes, captures the imagination of young and old alike.

(Putnam, 1987, ISBN 0-399-21531-X, hardcover, oversized, 40 pages, $13.95)

GERMANY

GENERAL

Born Guilty: Children of Nazi Families
Peter Sichrovsky

Just look at me sitting here in front of you. My face, my eyes, my mouth, my nose. What do I look like to you? Tell me, what do you see? Suppose we were to run into each other at the supermarket on the check-out line. I turn around and you look at me. There's nothing special about me, right? And now here we are, talking about whether I'm the child of murderers—incredible!—Actually, you're the first person willing to talk about it all.

The speaker is Susanne, conceived in 1944, perhaps, she says, "at the very moment your grandmother was killed in a concentration camp." Susanne and the other thirteen people who speak here are the children of former Nazi war criminals, and as such face the burden of "inherited guilt."

Most of these "children" are now in their forties, facing at midlife questions that center on morality, honesty and, often the most troubling, filial loyalty. Some see their parents as murderers and liars, others see them as victims of circumstances, and still others try, as best they can, not to see at all.

When these interviews were published in Germany, they created a tremendous outpouring—catharsis to be sure, but also questioning: are they, the new Germans, really so different from their parents and grandparents? Sichrovsky sees this self-doubt as cause for hope. "Until now," he says, "the people in Germany were convinced that what happened in the past could never happen again. That is no longer true today. Now they say that they want to see the threat in time and defend themselves against it. They say that anything is possible and that therefore they have to be vigilant. And this vigilance is a greater safeguard against a possible fascist resurgence in Germany than the conviction that it cannot happen again."

(Basic Books, 1988, ISBN 0-465-00742-2, hardcover, 178 pages, $17.95)

Dreams and Delusions
Fritz Stern

Germany is complex, controversial and contradictory, a nation of opposites. Here ten essays by German-born Fritz Stern, history professor at Columbia University and a recognized authority on modern German history, address separate topics that combine to form a cohesive overview of German history during the past century.

A piece on "fraternal opposites" Albert Einstein and Fritz Haber examines German accomplishments and dreams through the lives of these preeminent scientists who, says Stern, were good friends despite the fact that Einstein was a pacifist and Haber the inventor of chemical warfare. A chapter on "National Socialism as Temptation" investigates the subliminal motivation as well as the material interests that Nazism used to lead Germany into its national nightmare, while a piece entitled "The Burden of Success" points out that German Jewry was a success story—"partial, embattled, vilified, but triumph nevertheless"—before the rise of Hitler.

Other works deal with the post-war period and Germany's "release from greatness," the country's relationships with her European neighbors and the United States, and her economic condition. Stern's simultaneous involvement and detachment add a compelling personal dimension to the lucid and informative essays.

"Germans deserve friends who feel the burden of the past, as so many of them do, but who have compassion for a people that have had so rich and terrifying a history," he writes. This book should help make many such friends.

(Vintage/Random House, 1988, 0-394-75772-6, softcover, 320 pages, $9.95)

The Germans
Gordon A. Craig

The Germans make everything difficult, both for themselves and for everyone else.
—Goethe

Goethe, of course, made his statement some two hundred years ago; if he had lived during the Holocaust he might have chosen a stronger word than "difficult." Yet, maintains Stanford professor Gordon Craig, we must remember that Germany gave us not only Hitler's military, but also some of the world's great works of science, literature, philosophy, music, and art.

Here Craig assesses this complex and contradictory nation, admitting its faults while honoring its genius. The task he sets for himself is difficult:

. . . to suggest the way in which contemporary German attitudes show the effect of old but stubborn assumptions and prejudices: a religious heritage that has always been ambivalent in its simultaneous tendency toward establishmentarianism and revolt; a respect for hard work and the financial rewards that it brings that is combined with the uneasy knowledge, based on traumatic historical experience, that such rewards are apt to be impermanent; a veneration

of learning and literature that has traditionally been offset by a disinclination to allow them full freedom of expression; a resistance to change and nonconformity and to those who represent it . . . [and] an inconsistent attitude toward modernity which, through most of the modern period, has expressed itself in the eager adoption of technical and economic innovation and a simultaneous reprobation of its social and moral effect, this latter feeling often assuming romantic, racist, and regressive forms.

With the surefootedness that comes from thorough familiarity, Craig dissects the nation's character, investigating various subjects (religion, money, literature, democracy, and nationalism) and segments of the population (Jews, women, professors and students, romantics, soldiers). His study is an interesting and informative portrait of a culture riddled with paradox.

(New American Library, 1982, ISBN 0-452-00622-8, softcover, 350 pages, $9.95)

Germany and the Germans
John Ardagh

"Germany . . . is a land of ghosts which have never been exorcised," says Goronwy Rees (*Encounter*, April 1964), and it is these ghosts that make it different from other European counties. As a nation Germany must deal with the legacy of Nazism and of wartime defeat, with the political division that can't obliterate the common heritage of West and East, with the contradictory nature of a people who desire perfectionism but suffer from insecurity and anxiety. Yet author John Ardagh sees Germany "not just as some peculiar problem child but as a normal modern society, with many of the same pleasures and problems as the rest of us. Forty-plus years after the war's end, that ought now to be possible."

This said, he sets out to explore the psyche as well as the activities of contemporary Germany. With the exception of party politics and foreign policy, there is not much that he omits. He touches upon life in the major cities; the reasons federalism works; industry and labor; the slowly dying forests; the transformation of the German *Hausfrau* into a chic, self-confident woman; the Shop Closure Law that forbids shops to stay open after certain hours; the German devotion to spa-going; schools that "educate the mind, but not so much the character"; and the "New German Cinema" with an analysis of Edgar Reitz's fifteen-and-one-half-hour *Heimat*.

Except for one long seventy-page chapter on the German Democratic Republic, this is a book about West Germany. It is thorough, admiring, honest—and a fine work of solid craftsmanship.

(Harper & Row, 1987, ISBN 0-06-015839-5, hardcover, 478 pages, $24.95)

Germany Today
Walter Laqueur

Walter Laqueur probes the spirit of modern Germany in this thoughtful treatise, composed after visits with hundreds of West Germans. "I went from town to town," he says, "talking to mayors and high-school students, to doctors and booksellers, to factory managers and workers, to small traders and heads of local chambers of commerce."

He asked particularly about the rampant insecurities that many observers have noted lately, leading them to see a troubled country on the verge of collapse. And he did find signs of difficulty, from a generalized feeling of angst to the rise of the anti-establishment Greens. Yet, overall, he feels the outlook for his homeland is promising: "Germany is on the move again, but in what direction? Neither to great glory, nor to collapse . . . There is now not only more freedom in Germany than ever before in her history, but also more common sense and moderation. There is a great deal of hypochondria about, but also an essential toughness, an unwillingness to surrender without a major struggle to the threats facing the country at home and abroad."

Laqueur, a leading student of contemporary Europe, does an excellent job of exposing the character of one of the continent's most contradictory nations.

(Little, Brown, 1985, ISBN 0-316-51453-5, hardcover, 231 pages, $16.95)

A Voice from Germany
Richard von Weizsacker

We possess a unique history and occupy a unique geopolitical situation. Our country lies in the centre of Europe, surrounded by many neighbours. Our history with these neighbours has reciprocally threatened and stimulated both our people and theirs. Beside injustice and suffering stand enrichment and friendship.

So says Richard von Weizsacker, who became president of the Federal Republic of Germany in 1984. **A Voice From Germany** presents six of his speeches, made between 1981 and 1985; all, he says, aim "to contribute to the political self-awareness of the German people in the closing years of the twentieth century."

His inauguration speech is included, as well as remarks commemorating the anniversaries of the assassination attempt on Hitler, the end of World War II, and the building of the Berlin Wall. He addresses some of the major concerns of modern Germany such as the political legacy of Second World War, the question of German guilt for the Holocaust, and the thorn of the two Germanies.

But Weizsacker sums up his recurrent concern in "What Does it Mean to be German?" He maintains that for Germans "a reconciliation of spirit and power, of conscience and act, and a coming to terms with life based on compromise are especially difficult. We wish neither to reawaken the past nor to lose ourselves in dreams of the future, but rather to come to terms with life in the present, in a humane and responsible manner."

These talks, delivered at different times to different audiences, are thoughtful comments by one of the nation's leading spokesmen. As such they give penetrating insight into Germany's history and character.

(Weidenfeld & Nicolson, 1985, ISBN 1-55584-016-7, hardcover, 112 pages, $12.95)

Voices East and West
Edited and translated by Roger C. Norton

"What is a short story?" asks Wolfdietrich Schnurre. "Roughly speaking, it is a piece torn out of life," he answers. Here, for the first time in one volume, are the torn pieces from a group of German authors, representing the best of both the East and the West.

Once there were two children. When they were two years old they hit each other with their fists. When they were twelve they hit each other with sticks and threw stones. When they were twenty-two they shot at each other with guns ... When they were eighty-two they died. They were buried next to each other. A hundred years later, when a worm ate its way into their two graves, it had no idea that two different men were buried there. It was the same earth. All the same earth ...

Wolfgang Borchert, author of the above, is from West Germany. Stefan Heym, author of the following, is from East Germany:

'You knew, of course, Richard, that it is against the law to go over the Wall into West Berlin?' Richard lowered his head.
'Then just tell us once in your own words why you two did it.'
'We wanted to go to the movies ...'

Twenty-six short stories, all written since 1945, many with the dark political shadow of the Second World War in the background, make up this anthology. Yet, for the most part, the authors have freed themselves from "narrow nationalistic goals and resentment against war-time enemies," states Roger Norton, editor and translator of the collection. "The conflict of ideologies proves to be less of a dividing factor than one might have expected."

The stories reflect the concerns of the two Germanies; and in their strong and simple language—sometimes lyrical, often satirical—give an understanding of a country that remains divided against its will.

(Ungar, 1984, ISBN 0-8044-6608-4, softcover, 181 pages, $8.95)

ART AND ARCHITECTURE

Bauhaus
Frank Whitford

"The Bauhaus, the most celebrated art school of modern times, was closed down by the Berlin police acting on the instructions of the new Nazi Government on 11 April 1933." Beginning with the ending, Frank Whitford takes us back through fourteen years to show how "during its brief existence the Bauhaus—for better or worse—precipitated a revolution in art education whose influence is still felt today."

From locomotives to lampshades, from upholstery fabric to housing developments, the influence of the Bauhaus was immediate and far-flung. The names of its most famous participants—Klee and Kandinsky—remain giants in modern art.

Through the book's clear text and over 150 illustrations, Whitford shows how the school realized the all-encompassing nature of its project, running art and architecture studios as well as metal, pottery, weaving, and theatre workshops.

Set against the backdrop of the rise and fall of the Weimar Republic, the daily lives of the artists—often described in their own words—depict the brief, but explosive era. This is a captivating, authoritative history of a school which, as Wolf von Eckardt said, "altered the look of everything from the chair you are sitting in to the page you are reading."

(Thames and Hudson, 1984, ISBN 0-500-20193-5, softcover, 216 pages, $9.95)

German Architecture and the Classical Ideal
David Watkin and Tilman Mellinghoff

The development of classicism in German-speaking Europe took place during a "period of vital political change which led from the enlightened absolutism of the eighteenth century to the parliamentarianism and liberalism of the nineteenth"; from the time of the "the enlightened despot" Frederick the Great to that of "the burgher-king" Friedrich Wilhelm IV. Although there was no "Germany" at this time (European nationalism developed only during the nineteenth century), in the area that is now East and West Germany architecture flourished under a generous patronage system unparalleled elsewhere in Europe.

Throughout the region rulers were rebuilding their capitals, and generous funding was available for the construction of palaces, private houses, and public buildings. David Watkin and Tilman Mellinghoff, professors and authorities on European architectural history, here recount the history of the period and analyze its architectural achievements. Beginning with a discussion of French and English influence, they move on to the development of a Germanic style and the works of Karl Friedrich Schinkel and other neo-classicists. The second half of the book is a gazetteer of important German neo-classical buildings (some still existing, others destroyed) listed by location.

Thoroughly illustrated with color and black-and-white photos, this book documents an important era in German architectural history.

(MIT Press, 1987, ISBN 0-262-23125-5, hardcover, oversized, 296 pages, $50.00)

German Expressionist Painting
Peter Selz

"The expressionist movement," says Peter Selz, "may be seen in part as a reaction against the prevailing values of the deceptively stable society in which the artists grew up." Here he provides thorough documentation of the movement that flourished from 1905 until the outbreak of the War in 1914 and shows how the term "expressionism," originally used to differentiate this type of art from the impressionism of the recent past, slowly "came to mean a specifically German manifestation in painting and sculpture, and shortly in literature and film."

Nolde, Kokoschka, Munch, Kandinsky—their works and influence are explored in this comprehensive, scholarly study. Selz, who began his research in the post World War II years and took ten years to complete it, was able in some cases to discuss the movement with the artists themselves. In other instances he conversed with art critics and historians who had been intimately involved with expressionism in its heyday.

The book contains numerous photographs of the artists' works, some in the vibrant tones typical of the expressionists. Selz has provided an important reference book, one that the *Journal of Aesthetics and Criticism* calls "the final documentation of the Expressionist movement."

(University of California, 1957, ISBN 0-520-02515-6, softcover, 528 pages, $14.95)

German Folk Art
Ernst Schlee

A nutcracker stands at attention, a paper silhouette details a stylized farm scene, and a stoneware plate shows a gaily prancing horse—these items and hundreds of others are shown and discussed in this lavishly illustrated study, **German Folk Art**.

With precision and thoroughness, Ernst Schlee gives an overview of German folk art from the end of the Middle Ages to the mid-1800s, always relating objects to the social and cultural milieu that gave birth to them. He gives a detailed analysis of various art forms: house decoration, both interior and exterior; ceramics; textiles and costumes; and religious items. Salt-boxes, window panes, bakery moulds, cupboards, and panel carvings are all put into artistic and historical perspective.

Printed in oversized format, **German Folk Art** contains thirty color plates, four hundred black-and-white photographs and one map. It is informative and beautiful, a book to be both studied and treasured.

(Kodansha, 1980, ISBN 0-87011-356-9, hardcover, oversized, 316 pages, $75.00)

FOLKTALES

Folktales of Germany
Edited by Kurt Ranke

Kinder und Hausmärchen, known in English as *Grimm's Fairy Tales*, was first published in 1812; and its authors, Jacob and Wilhelm Grimm, immediately regretted placing the word *kinder* (children) in its title. They realized that the violence and sexual overtones of many of the stories made the volume unsuitable for children. In **Folktales of Germany**, the first important collection of German folktales in English to appear since then, Kurt Ranke has collected eighty-two stories that best represent folk narratives of the past one hundred years. There are tales of animals, of spirits, ghosts and giants, of demons, saints and sinners. There are stories of wise men and women and of "stupid ogres" and "numskulls." And while many of them are delightful to read to children, murder occurs in numerous violent forms, infanticide and suicide are not infrequent, and sexual and excretory innuendoes are rife.

Many of the stories have familiar themes. "The Cruel Stepmother" is a version of "Hansel and Gretel" in which the brother is turned into a golden stag, the sister marries a wealthy lord, and both are saved from a conniving servant by the Holy Virgin. In "The Fox and the Hare in Winter" the hare, having been cheated of a basket of eggs he had offered to share with the fox, gets his revenge when he tricks the fox into fishing with his tail in an icy river.

When humor is incorporated, it is frequently directed at the smug and puritanical. In "The Pig in the Church," for instance, the pastor is caught up on the back of a big black sow: "In this fashion he appeared astride her in the middle of the church and shouted to the people, 'People, stick to God; I have to leave with the devil!'"

Each tale is fully documented as to source, origin, and relationship to other countries' folktales. Together, the stories offer entertaining reading and prove the truth of Harvard professor Maria Tatar's statement that folktales are not "the fiction of childhood" but rather "the childhood of fiction."

(University of Chicago, 1966, ISBN 0-226-70440-8, softcover, 257 pages, $5.95)

HISTORY

Before the Deluge: A Portrait of Berlin in the 1920's
Otto Friedrich

- "It was a renaissance," says Sol Hurok. "The greatest renaissance in this century" . . .

- "If you could choose a time to live in, any time, any place, I'd choose the 1920's, in Berlin," says Rabbi Joachim Prinz.

- "I loved Berlin," says Yehudi Menuhin. "Berlin had a most advanced and neurotic society . . . Everything became Experience, with a capital E—and a capital X."

Like Paris during the same decade, Berlin was reckless, hedonistic, full of talent, ferment, and excitement. The third largest city in the world, it attracted and nourished such individuals as Marlene Dietrich and Greta Garbo, Albert Einstein and Adolph Hitler, Kurt Weill and Lotte Lenya. In **Before the Deluge**, Otto Friedrich whisks us back to those dizzying days and tells the story through the eyes of those who lived it.

In his preface Friedrich tells us: "Historians tend to specialize . . . to mistrust any journalistic attempt to include movie stars and generals and bankers and poets in the same chronicle. I think the story of Berlin in the 1920s permits no other approach."

Beginning with the abdication of the Kaiser in 1818, the book takes us year by year through the decade of the '20s and ends with the Nazi takeover in 1933. It is a political, social, and cultural history of the era, filled with thrills and spicy gossip. Today's reader can see the signs of impending tragedy, as well, adding a poignancy to the drama.

Before the Deluge brings an exciting era to life, and invites us all to "Come to the Cabaret, old chum . . . Life is a Cabaret!"

(Fromm International/Harper & Row, 1986, ISBN 0-88064-054-5, softcover, 418 pages, $12.95)

The Berlin Stories
Christopher Isherwood

While Hitler was gathering power in Germany, a young English novelist named Christopher Isherwood lived in Berlin. He turned his experiences into two short novels, *The Last of Mr. Norris* and *Goodbye to Berlin*, which were subsequently published as **The Berlin Stories**. They present the gripping drama of life during an intense and dangerous time—although they also reflect its occasional lighter moments.

Isherwood appears under his own name as a character in the novels, confirming that the works are highly autobiographical. "I had made up my mind that I would one day write about the people I'd met and the experiences I was having," he wrote of his years in Berlin. "So I kept a detailed diary, which in due course provided raw material for all my Berlin stories." The semi-documentary nature of the tales makes all the characters ring true: the Mr. Norris of the title, an unlikely old rake caught in the struggle between Nazis and Communists; the Landauers, a Jewish couple whose fate is inescapable; the durable Sally Bowles, whose life has been recreated on stage and screen by Julie Harris in *I Am a Camera* and by Liza Minelli in *Cabaret*.

In these fictionalized memoirs Isherwood recreates the horror, the gaiety, the charm, and the danger of pre-war Germany in novels as "true" as many histories.

(New Directions, 1935, 1963, ISBN 0-8112-0070-1, softcover, 207 pages, $6.95)

PERFORMING ARTS

Writings of German Composers
Edited by Jost Hermand and James Steakley

If we see Schütz, Bach, and Händel as servants of their respective princes and kings, Mozart and Beethoven as rebellious citoyens of the new Enlightened age, Schumann and Mendelssohn as representatives of the Romantic internalization brought about by the political and economic stagnation of the German middle

*class . . .—only then are we able to apprehend their music in the right spirit
. . . Beyond its emotional quality and artistic craftmanship, it presents itself to
historically informed listeners as a mirror of its time, reflecting not only the
political and intellectual battles but also the emotional conflicts of a given era.*

With this editors Jost Hermand and James Steakley anthologize the writings of forty-four German composers, from Johann Walther (1496-1570) to Hans Werner Henze (b. 1926). These excerpts place the men (and they are all men) in the context of their time, telling of their political, social and economic surroundings—as well as the inner world that gave birth to their genius. Mozart, for example, tells his father why he wishes to marry:

I who from my youth on have never been accustomed to bother about my things, such as laundry, clothes, and so on, cannot think of anything more necessary for me than a wife. I assure you that I often spend money unnecessarily, simply because I don't pay attention to things. I am absolutely convinced that I'd manage better with a wife (on my present income) than I do now.

and Franz Schubert describes his living quarters, a house that appears to resemble a small hotel with an agent and his family, a steward, doctor, surgeon, magistrate, chef, lady's maid, chambermaid, lodgekeeper, two coachmen, two grooms, the Count, the Countess, and an untold number of children:

Our castle is by no means one of the largest, but it is very attractively built. It is surrounded by a lovely garden. I live in the estate agent's house. It is fairly quiet except for some forty geese . . . It is rare for a nobleman's household to run as smoothly as this one.

Hermand and Steakley want readers to hear the composers in a "consciously historical way," and through these letters, journals, and essays it is possible to do just that.

(Continuum, 1984, ISBN 0-8264-0293-3, softcover, 303 pages, $10.95)

YOUNG PEOPLE'S BOOKS

The Cuckoo Clock
Mary Stolz
For ages eight to ten

"Once upon a time, there lived a clockmaker in a village at the edge of the Black Forest in Germany," begins Mary Stolz, award-winning children's author. Her tale tells the story of Erich, an unhappy foundling, who comes under the protection of old Ula, the town's most skillful clockmaker. Together they make a most wondrous clock, one which is not only beautiful but enchanted as well.

Children will be delighted with Stolz's depiction of the Black Forest and of a world both real and imaginary. The forest creatures comes to life through the words of the storyteller as well as through the magic of Ula's hands. Pamela Johnson's pencil sketches add to the charm.

"Come here and listen," says Erich.

And when we do, the little bird "sings all day, as he goes about his house, the thirty-six songs of the birds of the Black Forest, though no one ever hears a note except cuckoo . . . cuckoo . . . cuckoo . . ."

(Godine, 1987, ISBN 0-87923-653-1, hardcover, 86 pages, $12.95)

Don't Say a Word
Barbara Gehrts
For ages twelve and up

Author Barbara Gehrts was still a child when Hitler came into power. There was much she didn't understand. Her father was a high-ranking officer in the Luftwaffe; yet he was fiercely opposed to the Hitler regime. There were days when he left his office early and didn't come home till late. Where had he been? What had he been doing? And there were adults, once respected neighbors, who insulted the mother of her half-Jewish, second-best friend. "Don't say a word," she was told.

Barbara (called Anna in this mostly autobiographical novel) grew up quickly: her first boyfriend was killed on the Russian front; her half-Jewish schoolmate committed suicide; her father was arrested by the Gestapo and charged with treason; her brother was sent to Polajewo in the East; and the Allied bombs rained down upon the house.

> "Many years later in the seventies, I witnessed a debate in a German university between a young liberal professor and some students . . . In this debate one of the students came out with the statement, "What you call freedom is merely the absence of force." I was shocked. The professor replied, 'Man, do you have any idea what you are saying? Merely the absence of force?'
>
> "I could not forget the scene. What kind of young people were these who so little valued the absence of force, who did not understand the difference between freedom and tyranny? At that time I made up my mind to record the experiences of my own childhood, a childhood that came to an end under the symbol of dictatorship and force."

Her story is World War II from a different perspective. It makes the reader think deeply, not only about freedom but about family, about responsibility, about the choice—and cost—of standing up for what one believes. Barbara Gehrts must be proud of her family—and of her book.

(McElderry Books/Macmillan, 1986, ISBN 689-50412-8, hardcover, 169 pages, $12.95)

A Family in West Germany
Ann Adler
For ages seven to ten

Renate Blattner (Reni for short) is eleven years old and lives in Mainburg, Germany. Mainburg is a small town almost forty miles (sixty kilometers) from Munich. She and her brother Christian spend their time in much the same way as do children in the United States. Their school day, homework, and household chores, described in words and plethora of color photos, will strike a familiar chord with their American counterparts. Their father works in an ultra-modern auto plant, and on Sunday their grandparents visit for a typical family get-together.

There are, of course, differences: Reni often wears a Dirndle (traditional Bavarian dress) to church; she and her brother eat sausages and cakes with hard-to-pronounce names like *Weisswurst, Wurstchen* and *Lebkuchenherz*; and they get their allowances in *Deutschemarks*—but spend them on ice cream and soft drinks at cafés with their friends, just as American youngsters do.

With the help of Reni and her family, children learn to appreciate the similarities that oceans can't obliterate—as well as the differences that make one people distinct from another.

(Lerner, 1985, ISBN 0-8225-1658-6, hardcover, 32 pages, $8.95)

Germany: Two Nations, One Heritage
Christine Pfeiffer
For ages ten to thirteen

Germany is a land filled with contrasts. Busy cities and peaceful farm villages, storybook castles and sleek skyscrapers, ancient legends and new scientific ideas, communism and capitalism—somehow they all exist together. These contrasts may not always make life easy for the Germans, but they do make it interesting.

Christine Pfeiffer's exploration of the two Germanys is a sympathetic and straightforward look at a divided country. She examines geography and history before moving on to customs, legends, holidays, home life, education, and recreation—always pointing out the similarities as well as the differences between life in the West and life in the East.

Both color and black-and-white photos are used to amplify the text: two girls looking at a huge cuckoo clock from the Black Forest, students learning to wire printed-circuit boards to prepare for jobs in the electronics industry, a parade in Düsseldorf celebrating Carnival, a family having afternoon coffee at a *Konditorei* in West Berlin.

Pfeiffer's book provides a thorough overview of a country that, as she says, "can be called Europe's center in more ways than one—not only because it is in the geographic middle of the continent, but because of its central role in the progress and problems of Europe throughout history."

(Dillon, 1987, ISBN 0-87518-361-1, hardcover, 192 pages, $12.95)

SCANDINAVIA

GENERAL

An Everyday Story: Norwegian Women's Fiction
Edited by Katherine Hanson

Twenty-four Norwegian women, thirty short stories, over 120 years—Katherine Hanson has blended these elements into an anthology that is both universal and specific. The writers speak of concerns that are important to women everywhere, yet their voices nearly always reflect their Scandinavian heritage.

Gro Holm writes of rural life during the second half of the nineteenth century:

The farmyard ran like a corridor with buildings above and below. On the upper side the dwelling houses and storehouses, cookhouses and smithies were lined up one after the other. On the lower side were the barns . . . Those of us who lived so far from the church had to take our children with us and pack food for the whole day. Lars took a small tub of butter so he could get money to pay the minister.
—Life on the Løstøl Farm

Ingeborg Refling Hagen borrows themes from old folk tales as she tells of a region of rich farmland and vast forests in eastern Norway:

It was during that time when wolves and bears resided in the forests. When trolls lived in the mountains, elves in barns and stables, and hillfolk in every self-respecting mound . . . The cottage was situated on bedrock, with a narrow strip of earth in front and a desolate expanse of wilderness behind. A dark grove of spruce cast its shadow over the house.
—Borrowing Fire

And Karen Sveen speaks of working-class life in post-war Norway:

Sitting around the round table, Olaf and five or six other men are reading pamphlets out loud, passing books across the tablecloth and leafing through papers; smoke is pouring out of the kerosene lamp that's hanging by a chain between their heads . . . Out in the kitchen her mother is watching the coffee pot and sitting on the wood box in her brown Sunday skirt, chewing on granules of coffee.
—A Good Heart

The writing of these women, along with that of their colleagues, has been molded by the legends and ballads of Norway, shaped by the rhythms of alternating seasons, and strengthened by the ruggedness of mountainous terrain and bottomless fjords.

(Seal Press, 1984, ISBN 0-931188-22-9, softcover, 249 pages, $8.95)

Finland in the Twentieth Century
D. G. Kirby

In the mid-1970s the Finns were asked a simple question: which values or things are worth defending if Finland should be attacked? The overwhelming response was "national independence and the right to self-determination."

Since Finland is situated like a fly on the forehead of the Soviet Bear but has historically close ties to Sweden as well, this answer is especially interesting. While the Finns recognize the benefits (as well as the necessity) of maintaining a friendly relationship with the Soviets, the gigantic shadow cast by their eastern neighbor tends to undermine Finnish confidence.

David G. Kirby, a lecturer on Baltic history in the School of Slavonic Studies, University of London, explores the fine line the Finns must tread and discusses their need for and quest for a strong national identity. His book, **Finland in the Twentieth Century**, is a clear and detailed study of Finland's complex political history. As such it is a welcome addition to the scant information available about this small but strategically important country.

(University of Minnesota, 1979, ISBN 0-8166-0895-4, hardcover, 253 pages, $22.50)

Iceland Breakthrough
Paul Vander-Molen

Paul Vander-Molen had a dream. He wanted to explore the Jökulsa a Fjöllum, the Icelandic river that is considered to be one of the most fearsome in the world. As it leaves the geothermal springs under the Vatnajökull, the largest glacier in Iceland, it "twists and turns, becoming colder and ever more violent as it fights its way through one of the most active volcanic zones in the world, an area so desolate it was used by American Astronauts prior to the first moon landing."

To realize his dream Vander-Molen developed an innovative form of transport: a combination of kayak and microlight. With these vehicles his twelve-man team was able to navigate one of the river's greatest challenges: Dettifoss, Iceland's answer to Niagra Falls.

Not only do we learn a smattering of Icelandic words—*jökulhlaup*, for instance, means "glacier burst"—but we shiver with cold as the breathtaking full-color photos transport us to the land of "Ice and Fire." Thanks to French prize-winning cameraman Bruno Cusa and three expedition members who provided total pictorial coverage, we soar above the foaming waterfalls in the microlight, kayak through the icebergs, and abseil down into the Kverkfjöll Ice Caves.

For the fearless, Vander-Molen gives an "Equipment Taken" Appendix listing everything from Buoyancy Bags (four per boat) to Glacier Cream (categorized as a "survival aid"). For the rest of us, **Iceland Breakthrough** is a genuine adventure story and an all-too-rare glimpse of a land which remains cloaked in mystery.

(Oxford Illustrated Press, England, from Interbrook, 1985, ISBN 0-94660-924-1, hardcover, oversized, 139 pages, $17.95)

Letters Written During a Short Residence in Sweden, Norway, and Denmark
Mary Wollstonecraft

Mary Wollstonecraft visited Scandinavia during the summer of 1795. It was not an entirely happy visit. Her American Don Juan had sent her away, ostensibly to act as his business envoy but in reality to give her a chance to come to terms with his philandering. Her letters, addressed to this lover, contain personal reflections; they also abound with commentary on her experiences. For example, she comments on Swedish climate:

The severity of the long Swedish winter tends to render the people sluggish; for, though this season has its peculiar pleasures, too much time is employed to guard against its inclemency. Still, as warm clothing is absolutely necessary, the women spin, and the men weave.

Norwegian activities:

The people of every class are constant in their attendance at church; they are very fond of dancing: and the Sunday evenings in Norway . . . are spent in exercises which exhilerate the spirits, without vitiating the heart.

and Danish laws:

If any alteration of old customs is thought of, the opinion of the whole country is required, and maturely considered. I have several times had occasion to observe, that fearing to appear tyrannical, laws are allowed to become obsolete, which ought to be put in force.

The difficulties of eighteenth-century travel, unequal treatment of women, the state of prisons, methods of child rearing—all are duly noted. Her letters provide a wide-ranging picture of Scandinavian life nearly two hundred years ago, and while it is fascinating to note the changes brought by time, it is even more interesting to speculate on the many similarities that remain.

(University of Nebraska, 1976, ISBN 0-8032-5832-1, softcover, 201 pages, $4.95)

Of Danish Ways
I. MacHaffie and M. Nielsen

Of Finnish Ways
Aini Rajanen

Of Norwegian Ways
Bent Vangerg

Of Swedish Ways
Lilly Lorenzen

Why does a Swedish grandmother quote a proverb when settling an argument? Why do Norwegians hiss when they shake hands? And why do Danish farmers keep their pigs inside a barn?

The answers to questions like these are found in the **Of . . . Ways** books, a small series that gives brief, chatty introductions to a variety of countries. Each book touches on the history, traditions, educational system, handicrafts, music, literature, theater, and holidays of a specific country.

In **Of Danish Ways**, for example, the chapter on "Food and Hospitality" gives a sampling of recipes for Danish Meat Balls, Red Cabbage, and other delicacies while the section on "The Spoken and Written Word" highlights well-known authors Hans Christian Andersen and Karen Blixen (Isak Dinesen).

Norwegians, we're told in **Of Norwegian Ways**, invented the modern ski binding and also obtained the first patent ever issued for "transmission of pictures, still as well as moving, without the necessity of putting it on film." In short, the Norwegians developed the first television—as well as hydraulic low-pressure winches, the cheese slicer, and the paper clip.

Of Swedish Ways recalls the days when superstition (*skrock*) was supreme and trolls and fairies roamed the land. Even today, says the author, a Swede wishes a person luck by throwing a pair of old shoes at him or by playfully kicking him in the back.

And in **Of Finnish Ways** we learn the favorite home cures for a hangover (raw egg, pickles, buttermilk, or more alcohol) and find out how to take an authentic Scandinavian sauna.

The **Of . . . Ways** books are not perfect. They were written some years ago (note the copyrights) and could benefit from updates, and the tone is sometimes condescending. Yet they are conversational, informative, and easy to read, and considering the dearth of material on the Scandinavian nations, they are more than worth the price.

(Barnes & Noble, softcover; Of Danish Ways: 1976, ISBN 0-06-464075-2, 250 pages, $5.95; Of Finnish Ways: 1981, ISBN 0-06-464077-9, 224 pages, $5.95; Of Norwegian Ways: 1970, ISBN 0-06-464078-7, 228 pages, $6.95; Of Swedish Ways: 1964, ISBN 0-06-464021-3, 276 pages, $6.95)

Sweden: The Middle Way on Trial
Marquis W. Childs

Award-winning journalist Marquis W. Childs wrote his first book on Sweden more than fifty years ago, at a time when Sweden had started forth on the carefully paved path between collectivism and individualism. Now, in **Sweden: The Middle Way on Trial**, written in 1980 and containing a 1983 update, he examines the road through a rear-view mirror.

Including discussions of key political figures and touching on topics like technology, immigration, equality of the sexes, international relations, environment, and nuclear energy, the book provides a political and economic overview of modern Sweden.

Childs is an obvious supporter of the Swedish, seeing them as concerned citizens of the world as well as masters at combining the innovative and the realistic. Yet he is also able to take the middle way. His book is balanced and even-handed, assessing the problems as well as the successes of a mature welfare state.

(Yale, 1980, 1983, ISBN 0-300-03181-5, softcover, 179 pages, $7.95)

There is Something Wonderful in the State of Denmark
Arne Melchior

"There has never been a revolution in Denmark," says Arne Melchior, Minister of Transport, Communication and Public Works. Why? "The Dane must have his hot dinner at the latest by six-thirty—and if you are not finished with the revolution by dinner time, you might as well let it go!"

In this unabashedly biased view of his country, Melchior takes a look at the Danish temperament (as cool as the weather), government (democratically ideal), beliefs (religiously lukewarm), and lifestyle (relaxed). His colleagues contribute special chapters on their areas of expertise: the Minister of Social Affairs pronounces the social system to be "one of the best in the world"; the Minister of Culture states that "in art, culture, and recreation the teamwork between professionals and amateurs thrives to the benefit, joy, and mutual inspiration of all parties"; and the Minister of Education is confident that Danish schools for the young are "far and away the most expensive, splendid and best staffed in the entire world."

All of this reads something like an excerpt from a government-produced travel brochure. The print is big, the reading easy, and the tone enthusiastic. Yet Melchior and cohorts provide information and insight, including some that is intended specifically for a visitor: say thank you a lot, look sincerely into the other person's eyes when you are *skåling* (drinking) together, and don't tip since "service people are fairly paid nowadays, which makes tips appear patronizing." And that certainly proves Melchior is correct when he says, "there is something wonderful in the state of Denmark!"

(Lyle Stuart, 1987, ISBN 0-8184-0429-9, hardcover, 136 pages, $14.95)

ANTHROPOLOGY AND ARCHAEOLOGY

An African in Greenland
Tété-Michel Kpomassie

It's hard to imagine two countries more different than Togo and Greenland. To travel from a small country in West Africa, not far north of the equator, to the largest island in the world, almost entirely within the Arctic Circle, is indeed a giant step. Yet that is the journey Tété-Michel Kpomassie undertakes, becoming the first black man the Inuit have ever seen.

His arrival is quite possibly the most exciting thing that's happened in some time and he becomes something of a pop hero. Greenlanders afffectionately begin calling him "Mikilissuâk (Michel the Giant)," while he starts to consider Greenland "my country." He is charmed by the people, by their hospitality, their friendliness, their *nuanni* (love of life). In Upernavik on the western coast of Greenland he stays in an old earthen hut, one of the last of its kind, sleeping with Robert Mattaaq, his wife, daughter, and son on a small sleeping platform. "It's warmer that way!" says Robert. And in Rodebay he learns how to eat seal (raw) with Hans, Cecilia, Augustina, and Jørgensen.

Although over two-thirds of **An African in Greenland** takes place on the Arctic island, Kpomassie's frame of reference is, of course, West African. Jean Malaurie, Director of the Center of Arctic Studies, points out in the introduction that Kpomassie is fascinated by the "funeral rites, the legends, the taboos on menstrual blood, the horror of incest, and everything that reminds him of African 'witchcraft.'" His book is a fascinating foray into layman's anthropology; it is also a glimpse of two peoples whose surface differences only mask important similarities.

(Harcourt Brace Jovanovich, 1981, ISBN 0-15-105589-0, hardcover, 298 pages, $14.95)

The Last Kings of Thule
Jean Malaurie

For thousands of years the Polar Eskimos in northern Greenland lived on the very edge of survival, almost totally isolated by snow and ice. Then in 1950 the United States built an airbase in their midst, transforming their lives.

Anthropologist Jean Malaurie had documented their pre-airbase life, having spent fourteen months in the northern hinterlands making "a return to the Stone Age, or more exactly, a return to the seal age." He returned twenty years later to witness the changes wrought by the coming of the Americans, and rewrote his study, **The Last Kings of Thule**, to encompass the transformation when "men who lived by the harpoon found themselves in the atomic age."

During his first visit Malaurie lived as did the Eskimos, hunting for food and depending on a dog team for transportation. He discovered the *perlerorneq* (hysteria) caused by the long months of darkness, washed his face in water so icy it had to be warmed by mouth, and sat near seal-oil lamps listening to stories of how the first men were born. Gradually the people accepted him; he in turn admired them and learned to respect the simplicity and honesty of their life.

Now catapulted into modernity, the Inuit find both pleasure and problems. There are movies at the airbase that entertain; there is chewing gum that causes decay and lost teeth. And there are the young people who, attracted by a glimpse of the outer world, leave their homeland. "We need doctors, engineers, too. So it's good they go to Denmark," says a hunter from Qeqertaq. But, he adds, "they don't come back."

The Last Kings of Thule is aptly named; the "kings" are fast disappearing. Malaurie's book is a poignant and illuminating look at their culture and a sympathetic projection of what the future holds:

A new Greenland is searching for itself . . . Greenlanders seek to build a new Inuit society balanced between a liberal capitalism all too eager to devour them, and a bureaucratic and totalitarian socialist state that most of them completely reject.

Equal parts anthropological study, Arctic adventure, and travel book, **The Last Kings of Thule** entertains, informs, and unsettles its reader at the same time.

(University of Chicago, 1982, 1985, ISBN 0-226-50284-8, softcover, 489 pages, $17.50)

Runes
R. I. Page

Wandering through the fields of a small market town in Jylland, Denmark, you walk past a small, plain stone. Just as you pass, your eyes are caught by some strange lines scratched into the rock's surface, and you return for a closer look. These marks were obviously put there for a purpose; they look rather like some form of writing. You puzzle over how they got there and wonder if there is any meaning to them—and then you stroll on.

It's small wonder you couldn't quite understand what the stone was telling you. It was a Viking who carefully inscribed those marks, or runes, around the year A.D. 700, as a monument to his "wife Thorvi, Denmark's adornment."

When were runes developed? Who used them, and why? How did they contribute to the development of modern language? Many questions remain unanswered, despite intense study by archaeologists, linguists, and historians. Here R. I. Page, professor of Anglo-Saxon at the University of Cambridge, sheds a great deal of light on these mysterious marks. In **Runes**, one of the "Reading the Past" series, he discusses the locations in Scandinavia, Ireland, and England where runestones can still be found and notes that much Anglo-Saxon history was recorded in this manner. Although part of the text goes into linguistic detail, the interested layperson will find the discussion highly readable.

If you're curious about deciphering the past, this short course in the Anglo-Saxon equivalent of cuneiform and hieroglyphs is just what you need.

(University of California/British Museum, 1987, ISBN 0-520-06114-4, softcover, 64 pages, $6.95)

ART AND ARCHITECTURE

The Decorative Arts of Sweden
Iona Plath

"To study Swedish textiles is to study Sweden—history, customs, traditions, the people, and even the land itself," says author Iona Plath. She might well have included in this statement all of Sweden's decorative arts—not only textiles, but also ceramics, metal, glass, wood, and wall paintings—for while the arts vary as to the type of material and craftsmanship, they each reflect Sweden's peasant past.

The arts, explains Plath, "are evidence of the high esteem in which the Swedish people hold the home and everything pertaining to the home." During the long, cold winters activity in the rural areas centers indoors; the women weave and embroider, the men whittle and carve, and the home shows the results of these labors. Various textiles hang on the walls, and on occasion, a large piece of decorative material appropriately called a "ceiling dress" is fastened to the ceiling. These hangings hark back to early days when maidens whiled away the hours at their looms as their Viking heroes explored the world.

Plath traces many of the crafts back to their origins, explaining, for example, how the famous Swedish *rya* rugs originated as heavy bed covers, necessary for warmth, and how the three-legged chair is reminiscent of ancient stools formed by the branches and trunk of a tree.

Originally written in 1948 and updated in 1966, **The Decorative Arts of Sweden** remains one of the most comprehensive books on this subject. It is abundantly illustrated with over four hundred black-and-white photos that, in conjunction with the text, give a fascinating glimpse into the customs and traditions of the Swedes.

(Dover, 1966, ISBN 486-21478-8, softcover, 218 pages, $8.95)

The Folk Arts of Norway
Janice S. Stewart

A wooden chest dating from 1756 displays an intricate pattern of chip carving. An ale bowl features a beautiful rosemaling design and an inscription that translates, "Thank the Lord first, [then] quench your thirst." Huge detailed tapestries, delicate embroidered linens, and colorful Norse costumes show the careful work for which the Norwegians are famed.

Author Janice Stewart makes use of over two hundred photographs (twenty of which are in color) to show the wonderful variety of Norwegian folk art. She concentrates on six main types—carving, rosemaling, weaving, embroidery, costumes, and silverwork—and shows the historical and artistic development of each. Weaving, for example, can be traced back to prehistoric days, and long strips of tapestry were found on the remains of Viking ships. Stewart speculates on the types of looms (if any) used for these early pieces and then examines different materials, techniques, colors, and motifs that identify the art of various regions and periods. Rosemaling, on the other hand, is a fairly recent art, originating about 1700. While it bears a resemblance to Swedish *blomstermålning*, Russian decorative painting, and Pennsylvania Dutch art, it is distinctly Norwegian and has its own standards and forms.

The **Folk Arts of Norway** is exactly what its title suggests—a straightforward, unembellished explanation of an intriguing subject. It inspires admiration for the generations of ordinary folk who have steadfastly passed the long winter months by making items of use and beauty.
(Dover, 1953, 1972, ISBN 0-486-22811-8, softcover, 246 pages, $8.95)

The Frozen Image
Introduced by Martin Friedman

"Photography," says Martin Friedman of the Walker Art Center in Minneapolis, "is emerging as a major art expression in Scandinavia." Here, in an oversized book deserving a leisurely perusal, are photographs that span the years: an 1888 depiction of a late afternoon stroll, a self-portrait of Edvard Munch done in the early days of this century, a goalie flying for the ball in a shot taken in 1934, a beach scene in 1967. Spanning the countries, as well, there are photographs of Knud Knudsen's Norway, Carl Curman's Sweden, Thomas Neergaard Krabbe's Denmark, Olafur Lárusson's Iceland, and Into Konrad Inha's Finland.

What, asks Friedman, makes these pictures different? What makes them quintessentially Scandinavian? "Photography in the Nordic countries seemed to us an art of stillness," he answers.

Naturally, 19th-century visions of frozen landscapes under cloudless skies are quiescent, but, to generalize, even Scandinavian photographs of dramatic events seemed to us psychologically remote from their subjects: events are frozen in time. Here formal issues—spatial relationships, contours of forms, tonalities—seem to dominate, yet this cool facade should not mislead us . . . In these images, things aren't always what they appear to be . . . It is the tension between form and feeling that gives vibrancy to the artistic phenomenon of photography in Scandinavia.

Essays by eighteen Scandinavian writers delve into the photography of specific artists, and a brief history of the region adds welcome background. Friedman, who helped gather these pictures for a major photographic exhibition, worked with Mildred Friedman and William Ewing to compile a stunning book of frozen images that reflect an oft-frozen countryside.
(Abbeville, 1982, ISBN 0-89659-312-6, paperback, oversized, 208 pages, $24.95)

Manor Houses and Castles of Sweden
Maita di Niscemi

King Gustav Vasa was perhaps the first to construct a castle in Sweden in the late Middle Ages ("in the common sense of the word—that is, a stone house with one or more corners or central towers"). The idea caught on quickly:

During the Renaissance, the Vasa kings and the ever more powerful nobles competed with one another to achieve the heights of magnificence, recruiting foreign architects, artists, and craftsmen who introduced the latest styles from the European capitals.

This large, lavish book offers glimpses of the grand manors and castles that Sweden produced over five centuries. The tour is organized by region, starting with Stockholm and its coast, moving to Svealand, North of Stockholm, Götaland and Skåne. In all, it visits more than fifty buildings; each is pictured inside and out through beautiful color photographs by Nicolas Sapieha and Frandesco Venturi, and its history and features are discussed by historian Maita di Niscemi.

A wonderful blend of architecture, art, interior and landscape design, and history, **Manor Houses and Castles of Sweden** is a delight for the eyes as well as the intellect.

(Scala/Harper & Row, 1988, ISBN 0-935748-73-3, hardcover, oversized, 216 pages, $50.00)

Modern Norwegian Architecture
Christian Norberg-Schulz

The outbreak of World War I in 1914 not only marked the end of a political and economic era but also changed a way of life and the arts. Age old customs and expressive forms were destroyed and by the end of the war in 1918, the dream of a new world was the only hope. This dream included the longing for a new environment, in other words, for a 'new architecture.'

Architects throughout the world worked to mold this dream but, for the most part, Norwegian architects worked in silence. Indeed the massive Macmillan Encyclopedia of Architects (1982) mentions not a single Norwegian name. Yet, architect/author Christian Norberg-Schulz assures us, "Modern Norwegian architecture has much to offer."

Here, in a slim volume published by the Norwegian University Press, he traces the development of Norwegian architecture from the national romanticism of the early twentieth century to the new styles of the 1980s. Black-and-white photos show the clean lines traditionally associated with Scandinavian design, and along with Norberg-Schulz's text they illuminate this previously neglected topic.

(Norwegian University Press, Oslo, from Oxford, 1986, ISBN 82-00-07696-2, hardcover, 160 pages, $26.00)

Scandinavia: Living Design
Elizabeth Gaynor

There's a characteristic Swedish living room, swathed in blue-and-white cotton prints bathed in light from a large ivy-framed window, and an early twentieth-century octagonal cottage of neoclassical style on the coast of Denmark. There's a grouping of carved folk objects from Finland that display striking motifs: a nineteenth-century clock, a pair of decorative V-shaped yokes for draft horses, cooking utensils, and wooden boxes. In short, there's a comprehensive and enchanting sampling of architecture and design in this ambitious and beautiful book.

The Scandinavian countries are largely isolated from the rest of Europe. Limited natural resources and a harsh physical environment have always influenced Nordic design. As author Elizabeth Gaynor comments, "The winter season, when the sun does not shine for weeks at a time in the northernmost areas, is countered by a summer unequaled for its lush greenery and intense light. Coping with winter fosters ingenuity; the unspoiled summer environment is a seasonal reward."

Despite, or perhaps because of, all these factors, Scandinavian design is considered among the world's finest. More than four hundred color photographs by acclaimed photographer Kari Haavisto were taken specifically for this book to illustrate some outstanding examples of the art. Accompanying text by Gaynor, a writer and editor who specializes in design, explains and adds historical and cultural notes. Arranged by terrain (From the Forest, By the Water, Across the Meadows, In Town, and Great Escapes) rather than by country or by style, the book emphasizes the constant effort to achieve harmony between designer and nature.

Scandinavia: Living Design is an inspiring tour that both reveals and celebrates the charm and beauty that have sprung from a region of contrasts.

(Stewart, Tabori & Chang, 1987, ISBN 1-55670-009-1, hardcover, oversized, 255 pages, $35.00)

Stave Churches in Norway
Dan Lindholm

Along the edges of fjords, in isolated valleys, or high on hilltops overlooking small villages stand the last few stave churches, relics from the eleventh century when Christianity spread across Norway.

[They are] built entirely of wood, with gable roofs piled steeply one on top of another; the wood is dark shiny black, pitch brown, or ochre yellow. Dragon heads project from the many gables as if in exclamation. Fretted decorative

boards like combs surmount the ridges. Roofs and outer walls are covered with a scaly skin of wooden shingles; there are no windows. The whole building has the appearance of a legendary animal of mythical times transformed into a house.

Stave churches are like nothing else in Western art; they more closely resemble Far Eastern architecture than European Gothic or Romanesque styles. Strongly linked with both the mythical world of dragons and heroes and the heritage of Viking shipbuilders, they show the influence of both in their construction and decoration, says Dan Lindholm in **Stave Churches in Norway**.

The book includes numerous drawings as well as 110 vivid photographs by Walther Roggenkamp that give overall views of many of the churches as well as rich details of carved wood and forged iron. A list of the buildings still in existence is appended, each with a brief description and illustration. There is also a map showing their locations.

Stave churches, so at home in the austere northern landscape, are a stirring reminder of Norway's past—a past that Lindholm brings to life.

(Rudolph Steiner Press, London, from Anthroposophic Press, 1969, ISBN 85440-205-5, hardcover, 208 pages, $17.95)

The Triumph of Light and Nature
Neil Kent

Atmospheric conditions in the Nordic countries and their geographical position in very high latitudes produce unique effects of light. The "blue hour" at twilight on a midsummer evening, when the sun barely sets below the horizon, pervades the Nordic sky like a gentle mist. In the winter, the pale and weak rays of the sun fall on the snow-covered landscape of Scandinavia in a way that seems evocative.

Joined by environment, heritage, and history, the five Nordic countries have produced a definable artistic style, one enhanced, says art historian Neil Kent, by the special quality of light in Scandinavia. Here he surveys the art from approximately 1740, when the first native artists emerged, up to about 1940, when modernism began to dominate western art.

The peace and prosperity of the mid- to late-eighteenth century allowed a surge of royal patronage of the arts; painters such as Carl Gustaf Pilo and Alexander Roslin in Sweden and Nilokai Abilgaard and Jens Juel in Denmark became established as the first truly Nordic artists during this period. By about 1830 Finland and Norway experienced an "awakening of national art"; and as the nineteenth century drew to a close the fascination with the light that is a hallmark of Nordic painting began to dominate the work of Scandinavian artists. Bruno Liljefors, Anders Zorn, and Vilhelm Hammershøi were among those whose paintings were imbued with the unique effects of this light—landscapes and interior settings alike. From the beginning of the twentieth century until the outbreak of World War II artists including Edvard Munch, Isaac Grünewald, and Nils von Dardel drew inspiration from continental tradition, incorporating it into a distinctive Scandinavian style.

Kent, in setting the art of these two centuries against their political and social backdrop, provides a thorough study, one that is beautifully illustrated with more than two hundred photographs (thirty-nine of which are in color). Together, text and pictures reveal the distinctive flair of Scandinavian art, always reflecting Nordic emphasis on light and nature.

(Thames and Hudson, 1987, ISBN 0-500-23491-4, hardcover, oversized, $35.00)

Viking Art
David M. Wilson and Ole Klindt-Jensen

For a people who were considered barbarians by their comtemporaries, the Vikings left behind a wealth of highly original and vital art—"evidence of a civilization singularly sure of itself," according to historian Marc Bloch.

During the period from A.D. 800 to 1100 the Vikings brought back booty in the form of goods and customs from the rest of the world. However, archaeologists David Wilson and Ole Klindt-Jensen theorize that rather than merely mimicking the artifacts from abroad, Viking craftsmen adapted foreign influences into native styles. Their art, while rooted in pagan Scandinavia, spread far and wide until "its last flickering brilliancy in Christian Britain." It influenced some of the finest West European art and, say the authors, "when it finally surrendered it was to an art attuned to Viking taste—Romanesque art: solid, sculptural, and occasionally grotesque, the latter element of which must have been particularly appealing to the Viking palette."

The book devotes considerable attention to "the greatest of all Viking Age discoveries—the Oseberg ship burial." This grave, twenty feet high and 130 feet long, yielded a wealth of magnificent artifacts, dwarfing the less generous finds of subsequent stylistic periods (the Borre, Jellinge, Mammen, Ringerike, and Urnes). Eighty photographs and sixty-nine line drawings accompany the text.

The influence of Viking art is still visible today in the wooden furniture and folk-art of Scandinavia, where the intricate carvings serve as reminders of an adventurous past.

(University of Minnesota, 1980, ISBN 0-8166-0977-2, softcover, 173 pages, $12.95)

CUISINE

Classic Scandinavian Cooking
Nika Hazelton

"Like a family, Scandinavia is worth getting to know as a unit and then again for its individual members." In this updated version of her previous work, *The Art of Scandinavian Cooking*, Nika Hazelton shows she is well acquainted with (and very fond of) the entire family. "Denmark and Sweden . . . have a past of rich and splendid courts, whose tastes filtered down into the population; they also had the natural resources, such as meats and dairy products, for fine dishes." The foods of Norway, on the other hand, "are those of a poor, rustic country, though this does not make them less tasty."

From appetizer to dessert, from Sweden to Iceland, Hazelton makes everything sound delicious. She advises on how to put together a smorgasbord (the Swedish table groaning with many small dishes) or smørrebrød (Danish open-faced sandwiches). Although they look exotic, Hazelton claims they're actually "a convenient way to make tidbits go a long way." She offers a wealth of creative recipes for fish, a staple in the Scandinavian diet; for birds and meat; and for wonderfully rich (but "worth every bite") desserts.

Now tailored to reflect changes in both American and Scandinavian tastes, the recipes are lower in fat and sugar than were those in the earlier book, and more vegetable dishes are included. As before, however, the foods are high in appeal and are offered garnished with local history, folklore, and personal anecdotes. Finnish cooks used to bake in enormous quantities, Hazelton says, because heating the oven was such a chore:

The old-time ovens used to be built into the wall behind the stove like a tunnel, about a yard wide and sometimes as deep as six feet. At baking time, a wood fire was lit in the oven, and when it had burned down to red and glowing embers, these were raked forward into the stove with a long pole that ended in a kind of iron shovel. The oven was then cleaned with a broom dipped in water. A ventilator at the back of the stove drew off the smoke, and was closed as the fire was raked out. A damper regulated the heat.

With Nika Hazelton's recipes and tips, an American cook should be able to come close to duplicating most Scandinavian delicacies, even without the advantage of the same applicances!

(Scribner's, 1965, 1987, ISBN 0-684-18636-5, hardcover, 258 pages, $18.95)

FOLKTALES

Folktales of Norway
Edited by Reidar Christiansen

You can't ordinarily see them but they're everywhere in Norway, roaming the hills and forests, living under the cattle barn or in the cellar of your house. *Huldre-folk* (hidden people), trolls, giants, and *oskorei* (groups of evil spirits) are lurking about, waiting for the right opportunity to steal a sleeping infant and leave their deformed one in its place, causing crops to fail, wooing human women. If you're fortunate, however, there is a *nisse* protecting your home. This small creature wearing a red cap with a tassel will staunchly defend his hosts' welfare.

This delightful collection of a hundred Norwegian tales tells of all these supernatural beings and their activities. There are historical legends, like that of King Olav, the national saint, and the hidden treasure of Rakbjorg. Thre are myths of magic and witchcraft, ghosts and shapeshifting; stories of household spirits; and nature tales that tell of the sea, lakes and rivers, the air, mountains, and forests.

The stories themselves are entertaining for adults or to read aloud to children. Beyond their sheer amusement value, however, they shed light on Norway's history and culture. A foreword by Richard M. Dorson, an introduction by the author, and detailed source material with each tale provide an abundance of information about the origins of the stories and the parallels between these myths and those of other countries.

But even if you read this book as a scholarly endeavor, listen carefully as you do so. Those small creaking noises you hear may be one of the *huldre-folk* just waiting to cause you mischief!

(University of Chicago, 1964, ISBN 0-226-10510-5, softcover, 284 pages, $9.00)

HISTORY

A History of Scandinavia
T. K. Derry

"Scandinavian historians in general confine their attention to their own particular nation," remarks historian T. K. Derry in his introduction to **A History of Scandinavia**. "Yet in these days of closer international relationships it seems worthwhile also to examine the development of these five small peoples in terms of the unity which underlies their surface divisions."

And so he does, emphasizing the common heritage shared by Norway, Sweden, Denmark, Finland, and Iceland as well as touching upon their individual stories. He examines the Stone and Bronze ages and the Viking era, peruses the rise and expansion of the monarchy, but devotes the majority of his book to highlighting the more recent events of the nineteenth and twentieth centuries. Interwoven through the study of history is a look at traditions, lifestyles, and artistic contributions. The Parallel Table of Events, a chronological list of important happenings in each of the five countries, shows the similar though individual pathways traveled by the Nordic peoples.

As the *Library Journal* says, "Derry has achieved a near miracle in condensation." Although he covers a large amount of material, he carefully retains the integrity of each strand and weaves them together into a satisfying whole.

(University of Minnesota, 1979, ISBN 0-8166-0936-5, softcover, 447 pages, $14.95)

A History of the Vikings
Gwyn Jones

In the waning years of the eighth century the people of Western Europe inhabited a relatively secure and ordered world. The Roman Empire had collapsed five hundred years before; after a period of strife and turmoil the populace finally had found peace among the crumbling relics that stood on on all sides. Farmers, craftsmen, and monks followed their respective callings in the slow, steady rhythm of medieval life.

That tranquillity ended with the arrival of bearded giants from the North who worshiped strange gods and sought glory in death rather than serenity in life. The Vikings raided so relentlessly that they maintained undisputed control of the seas for three hundred years.

A History of the Vikings follows the development of these Scandinavian peoples from their earliest myth-shrouded beginnings through the height of their power and on to the defeat of Harald Hardradi in 1066, bringing to a close the Viking Age. Gwyn Jones, Professor Emeritus of English Language and Literature at University College, Cardiff, describes the Vikings—their art and religion as well as the economic conditions that led to their overseas exploits. He traces Viking accomplishments in war and expansion: raids on Britain and Western Europe, trade ventures with Eastern Europe, and the colonization of Iceland, Greenland and North America.

When the book was first published it was considered a classic work on its topic, and this revised edition has upheld its reputation. It contains thirty plates, fifty-eight figures in the text, and fifteen maps, all of which contribute to making it an outstanding, highly readable record of Viking civilization.

(Oxford, 1968, 1984, ISBN 0-19-285139-X, softcover, 504 pages, $9.95)

Kristin Lavransdatter
Sigrid Undset

Winner of the 1928 Nobel Prize, this trilogy of fifteenth-century Norway was hailed at its introduction as the finest historical novel of the twentieth century. Epic in length and scope, the books trace the life of spirited Kristin Lavrandsdatter. Beginning with *The Bridal Wreath* in which Kristin is forced to choose between her father's honor and her own feelings of love, continuing with *The Mistress of Husaby* in which she is married and begins life in a once-splendid manor house, and concluding with *The Cross* in which the Black Death devastates her world, the tales evoke the traditions and activities of long-ago Norway.

Everyday life, for example, is recreated in *The Mistress of Husaby* as Kristin reminisces about her childhood home:

This was the time of year when her mother and the serving-maids were wont to sit of evenings in the weaving-house. And her father and the men too would come in and sit down by the women with their own tasks—mending leather gear and farm tools, and carving in wood ... There would be someone who could say forth a snatch of some saga ... Or her father would tell them, as he sat at his wood-carving, tales of knighthood ... Ulvhild and Astrid would sing ... Then Ulvhild would lay from her wheel and spindle and press her hands to her back.

And the details of costume are revealed in *The Bridal Wreath*:

... Lavrans came back to the farm—along with the other harvesters. He was clad much like his workmen in an undyed wadmal coat cut off at the knees and loose breeches reaching to the ankles; he walked barefoot, with his scythe over his shoulder. There was naught in his dress to mark him off from the serving-men, save the leathern shoulder-piece that made a perch for the hawk he bore on his left shoulder.

Author Sigrid Undset recreates a time and a place with masterly strokes, and medieval Norway becomes familiar through the unforgettable character of Kristin Lavrandsdatter.

(Vintage, 1986, $6.95 each; The Bridal Wreath: ISBN 0-394-75299-6, softcover 276 pages; The Mistress of Husaby: ISBN 0-394-75293-7, softcover, 476 pages; The Cross: ISBN 0-394-75291-0, softcover, 402 pages)

NATURE

Aurora Borealis: The Amazing Northern Lights
S.-I. Akasofu

At first a white arc, a giant colorless rainbow arches across the sky. Colors emerge and lights shimmer, twisting and gyrating. Then, suddenly, unexpectedly, they drop earthward, forming a great curtain in the heavens. This—delicate, ethereal, iridescent—is the *aurora borealis*, the northern lights.

S.-I. Akasofu, geophysics professor at the University of Alaska and one of the world's leading authorities on auroras, weaves history, science, and legend into a colorful investigation of the auroral mystery. He begins with ancient Viking, Indian, and Eskimo legends—"these lights shine forth from the fires that encircle the outer ocean," suggested a Norwegian tale of the thirteenth century—and then discusses the beliefs of polar explorers such as Sir William E. Parry, Roald Amundsen, and Capt. James Cook. Robert F. Scott, for instance, probed the frigid waters and wondered "why history does not tell us of 'aurora' worshippers, so easily could the phenomena be considered the manifestation of 'god' or 'demon'." Settlers, traders, and miners had other ideas about the lights: gold miners were convinced they were an illuminated vapor from a mysterious mine.

Against these imaginative legends comes an authoritative examination of scientific theory. Akasofu explains the lights as a phenomenon that occurs when the high-speed plasma flow of solar or stellar wind interacts with the electro-magnetic field of a celestial body. Dramatic photos taken from satellites give a universe-eye view of the Aurora, and those from land show the rainbow-hued display in its many forms.

Polar explorer William H. Hooper commented, "Language is vain in the attempt to describe its ever varying and gorgeous phases; no pen or pencil can portray its fickle hues, its radiance, and its grandeur." True enough; but in words, photographs, and drawings this book pays worthy tribute.

(Alaska Geographic Society, 1979, ISBN 0-88240-124-6, softcover, 96 pages, $7.95)

PERFORMING ARTS

Ibsen's Drama
Einar Haugen
Ibsen's Forsaken Merman
Per Schelde Jacobsen and Barbara Fass Leavy

Norway's best-known playwright, Henrik Ibsen, is truly a product of his beloved Norway, and frequently set his dramas on his native soil: *A Doll's House* in an apartment in Christiania, *Ghosts* on a country estate near Bergen, *Peer Gynt* in Gudbrandsdal and the mountains around it.

In **Ibsen's Drama** Einer Haugen, Harvard Professor of Scandinavian and Linguistics, takes an in-depth look at the playwright's life and work, examining the influences on his writing and his communication with his audiences. It's a thorough and readable analysis that can be appreciated by students and playgoers alike. Synopses of all of Ibsen's plays are given in one appendix and a chronology of his life in another.

Folklorist Barbara Leavy and cultural anthropologist Per Jacobsen delve into Ibsen's work from a different perspective in **Ibsen's Forsaken Merman**. Ibsen, they tell us, was an avid student of native myths and traveled throughout Norway collecting tales, which he subsequently drew upon for his writing. Focusing on seven of his later plays, they show the rich vein of meaning contributed by Norse mythological heritage, and how it reveals Scandinavian culture and history.

Ibsen wrote with universal appeal, yet his Nordic background pervades his work and proves once again that voyages of the imagination often begin in the familiar territory of the artist's homeland.

(Ibsen's Drama: University of Minnesota, 1979, ISBN 0-8166-0896-2, softcover, 185 pages, $7.95; Ibsen's Forsaken Merman: New York University, 1987, ISBN 0-8147-4169-X, hardcover, 288 pages, $42.50)

YOUNG PEOPLE'S BOOKS

An Eskimo Family
Bryan and Cherry Alexander
For ages seven to ten

For four months every year there is no sun at all in the small Eskimo village where Otto Simigak lives with his parents. It's cold there—so cold you get shivers reading about it—and so cold that even the sea freezes over. Boats can only travel to Siorapaluk for a short period during the summer. The rest of the time the Eskimo family must find their own food and arrange for their own entertainment.

Siorapaluk, the world's northernmost village, is in Greenland, but Eskimos also live in Canada, Alaska, and Russia. Many, like Otto and his family, still follow the traditional way of life.

Bryan and Cherry Alexander provide a fascinating glimpse of this life: Otto hunting for walrus and seals, camping on the ice, and riding a sled pulled by dogs. The full-color pictures show smiling people, hungry huskies, and lots and lots of snow!

(Lerner, 1985, ISBN 0-8225-1656-X, hardcover, 32 pages, $8.95)

If You Didn't Have Me
Ulf Nilsson
For ages seven to ten

While his parents are building a house in town, a young Swedish boy and his little brother are left to stay with their grandmother, Aunt Anna, and Uncle Gustav at their farm in the south of Sweden. Grandma and the other relatives are too busy to spend much time with the boys, so the young protagonist is often left to his own diversions. Short episodic chapters relate the boy's adventures as he tries to convince himself he is an important member of the family. Through them all he sings his invented song, whose theme is "if you didn't have me . . ."

He once finds himself held captive on the fence between a flock of hungry chickens on one side and squealing pigs on the other, an experience which convinces him that feeding farm animals is most definitely not a "baby job." In other episodes he encounters bullies, discovers some harsh realities when a pig is butchered, and learns how to read, thus opening new worlds for his imaginative mind.

Whether youngsters read **If You Didn't Have Me** for themselves or have it read aloud to them, they'll feel empathy for this clever, resiliant boy and, as an added bonus, will enjoy their vicarious vacation on a Swedish farm.

(McElderry Books/Macmillan, 1987, ISBN 0-689-504-603, hardcover, 113 pages, $9.95)

Old Lars
Erica Magnus
For ages two to four

Lovely paintings rich with color make the cold Norwegian countryside seem bright and friendly as Old Lars gathers firewood in the mountain forest. He passes children skiing and sledding and animals leaving pawprints in the snow. At last he sets about his work, loading his sleigh with wood too heavy for his poor old workhorse, Blakken.

Old Lars is based on a Norwegian folktale that author/illustrator Erica Magnus loved as a child. Her rendition was selected for exhibit at the Biennale of Illustrations Bratislava in 1985 and received the *Parents' Choice* award for illustration in 1984.

(Carolrhoda, 1984, ISBN 0-87614-253-6, hardcover, 32 pages, $12.95)

Sweden: A Good Life for All
Kari Olsson
For ages ten to twelve

- In Sweden so many people have similar names that the phone book lists people's jobs along with their names. "If your friend teaches school, you must look for teacher Carl Peterson. He will be listed after carpenter John Peterson but before travel agent Albert Peterson," explains author Kari Olsson.

- Many of Sweden's rivers have been dammed to produce electricity. But because the people miss the beauty of their waterfalls, one day a year the floodgates are opened for Waterfall Day.

Bursting with such facts, this lively book presents a wealth of information about Sweden and its people. One chapter discusses "the middle way," the concept of striking a balance between private and government ownership of business. Another recounts Sweden's history, from the times of the early herdsmen through the Viking era to modern times. And another presents some of the folktales and myths that are so integral to Swedish culture.

Festivals, schooling, sports, and even recipes are included in **Sweden**, a book that gives preteens a well-rounded look at the Land of the Midnight Sun.

(Dillon, 1983, ISBN 0-87518-231-3, hardcover, 144 pages, $12.95)

ALPINE AND LOW COUNTRIES

GENERAL

La Place de la Concorde Suisse
John McPhee

There are six hundred thousand assault rifles in Swiss homes. It is said that this is a very good thing, for while a father cleans his rifle at the kitchen table his son is watching, and 'the boy gets close to the weapon.'

This statement was made about modern-day Switzerland, land of staid bankers, reliable clocks, and good chocolate. In this "neutral" nation, every one of the 650,000 citizens is ready to mobilize within forty-eight hours. In fact, contends author John McPhee, "the Israeli Army is a copy of the Swiss Army."

McPhee goes on a bivouac with a *Section de Renseignments*—a group of civilian-soldiers embarking on a military refresher course—and compares his newfound compatriots to members of a swank gentlemen's club. "If you understand the New York Yacht Club, the Cosmos Club, the Metropolitan Club, the Century Club, the Piedmont Driving Club, you would understand the Swiss Army." Captain Rumpf is typical: "He likes sunsets, snow-covered couloirs, vines in fruit, and Switzerland. He tends to treat the army itself as if it were a military secret."

La Place de la Concorde Suisse offers a tantalizing and unusual taste of an extraordinary country, every bit as delectable as the chocolate pears the officers eat after one of their days on assignment—sweet and surprising.

(Farrar, Straus and Giroux, 1984, ISBN 0-374-51932, softcover, 150 pages, $6.95)

Of Dutch Ways
Helen Colijn

Helen Colijn, born and raised in the Netherlands and a current resident of California, often led groups of American tourists through her native land. In need of a general-interest book on Holland "—something that explains the Eighty Years War and the House of Orange, and how we came by all those marvelous paintings, and why we have subsidized schools for different religious groups"—she decided to write one. **Of Dutch Ways** is the result.

Boterham (bread), we learn, may be eaten with a knife and fork; and potatoes are purchased already peeled. Road traffic must give way to water traffic; a "uniquely Dutch sport," known as *wadlopen*, is a form of mud-hiking; and Dutch homes are considered "empty" without a *bloemetje* of flowers. In an easy-to-read format Colijn surveys Dutch history and culture, reminding us that "there is more to the Netherlands than wooden shoes, windmills, and tulips."

(Barnes & Noble, 1980, ISBN 0-06-464076-0, softcover, 240 pages, $5.95)

ART

Dutch Painting
R. H. Fuchs

Van Eyck, Rembrandt, Van Gogh, Mondrian—some of the world's greatest artists came from the small country of the Netherlands. From the somber realism of the fifteenth century to the stark modernism of the twentieth, the works of these men and their compatriots have been a powerful force in determining the direction of international art. Here R. H. Fuchs, prominent art historian and museum director, examines their influence in a chronological tour that details Dutch painting for the past five hundred years.

Aided by a plethora of photographs in both color and black-and-white, Fuchs discusses themes, styles, and techniques while placing the art in its proper economic, social, and political setting. He is particularly proficient when interpreting the symbolic details that appear in many of the works; these are often drawn from Dutch literature and culture with which Fuchs, a native Dutchman, is thoroughly familiar.

For example he shows how Jan van Eyck reveals the "culturally and sociologically delicate relationship between man and woman" in his 1431 marriage portrait, *Giovanni Arnolfini and his Wife*. "The expression of the more prominent position of the husband, in relation to the wife, was already the major compositional motive," he says. "In this picture Arnolfini is presented almost frontally; he seems to be stepping forward, asserting his presence . . . [The wife], however, is looking at him, her head slightly bowed; in fact her attitude as a whole is towards him, submissive and deferential."

As is the case with all of the books in the "World of Art" series, **Dutch Painting** is concise, comprehensive, and a bargain at under ten dollars.

(Thames and Hudson, 1978, ISBN 0-500-20167-6, softcover, 216 pages, $9.95)

HISTORY

The Embarrassment of Riches
Simon Schama

"It is the peculiar genius of the Dutch," writes historian Simon Schama, "to seem, at the same time, familiar and incomprehensible." In **The Embarrassment of Riches** he explores the dualities of this complex culture by examining the brief seventeenth-century period of the "golden age" during which the Dutch virtually created themselves. "Above all, I have wanted to discover how the Dutch made themselves up as they went along. What animated their sense of community; what generated their allegiance; what crystallized the set of manners that became recognizably their own?"

In the beginning the Dutch Republic was nothing but a loose collection of towns and villages; the people were content with Spanish rule over their simple daily lives. When they were finally driven to rebel against a fanatical monarchy and achieved independence in 1579, these hard-working country folk began an amazing metamorphosis that resulted in the wealthy, metropolitan "new Tyre" of Rembrandt and Van Dyck.

Long steeped in stern Calvinist doctrine, however, the Dutch had been taught that wealth was given as a test of moral strength. This "ordeal of prosperity," Schama says, was the dominant force that shaped the essential Dutch character. In looking at the everyday routine of virtuous housewives and the shocking behavior of their more worldly sisters, at "the differentiation of food into honest necessities and morally contaminated luxuries," and at the problems of being both "Christian" and "merchant," Schama points out the predicament the upright burghers faced because of their new-found wealth.

The book takes place "in the moral geography of the Dutch mind, adrift between the fear of the deluge and the hope of moral salvage, in the tidal ebb and flow between worldliness and homeliness, between the gratification of appetite and its denial, between the conditional consecration of wealth and perdition in its surfeit. By the very nature of things . . . there could be no reconciliation of these dilemmas." Although the dilemmas remain unresolved, Schama's book illuminates the subject in a highly enjoyable manner.

(University of California, 1988, ISBN 0-520-06147-0, softcover, 698 pages, $15.95)

Fin-de-Siecle Vienna
Carl E. Schorske
Vienna's Golden Autumn
Hilde Spiel

Vienna in the fin de siecle, with its acutely felt tremors of social and political disintegration, proved one of the most fertile breeding grounds of our century's a-historical culture. Its great intellectual innovators—in music and philosophy, in economics and architecture, and, of course, in psychoanalysis—all broke, more or less deliberately, their ties to the historical outlook central to the nineteenth century liberal culture in which they had been reared.

–Carl Schorske

Turn-of-the-century Vienna was bewildering, confounding, chaotic. But out of that political and social disintegration emerged much that is vital to modern art and thought. Carl Schorske, former Director of European Cultural Studies at Princeton University, and Hilde Spiel, award-winning writer and art critic (whom *The Times Literary Supplement* termed "a female Proust") provide informative and entertaining views of these heady years.

Schorske's **Fin-de-Siecle Vienna**, the more scholarly of the two works, is a collection of seven essays, the topics of which illustrate the ferment of the era: politics and psyche, the birth of urban modernism, politics in a new key, politics and patricide (on Freud), painting and the crisis of the liberal ego. Each essay can stand alone on its own merits; considered together they provide an integrated look at this vibrant period, unified by the theme of the interaction of politics and culture.

Spiel steps back farther and presents a more general overview of the period that extended from the Battle of Königgrätz in 1866 to Hitler's Anschluss in 1938. Beginning with a summary of historical, political, and economic background, she uses events of the turn-of-the-century period to illustrate the fundamental dichotomies of the Viennese people. Despite the gaity of the world of operas and parties, she says, there lurked a profound melancholy; this polarity erupted in the "golden autumn" of achievement in the arts and sciences. Although occasionally careless about details, as a native Austrian she is able to offer insights made possible only by lifelong association with the culture.

The events of nearly a century ago still echo today, for out of that turn-of-the-century chaos came many of today's achievements. Each of these books, generously illustrated with wonderful period photographs, paintings, and drawings (many in full color), does its part to illuminate the era and its legacy.

(Fin-de-Siecle Vienna: Vintage, 1961, 1981, ISBN 0-394-74478-0, softcover, 378 pages, $10.95; Vienna's Golden Autumn: Weidenfeld & Nicolson, 1987, ISBN 1-55584-136-8, hardcover, 248 pages, $22.50)

Modern Austria: Empire & Republic
Barbara Jelavich

"Over the centuries Austria has produced more than its share of historical events," proclaims an Austrian travel advertisement, circa 1980, and these events are placed into proper perspective by historian Barbara Jelavich. In clear, direct prose she traces the years since 1800 when the Archduchy of Austria was the most important state in the Holy Roman Empire through 1980 when the country was, as *The Economist* termed it, "a small house in order."

Although her intent is to emphasize the years since 1918 when the Habsburgs were overthrown and Austria became a republic, she devotes a nearly equal portion of her book to the previous century, delving into matters and institutions that affected German-speaking Austrians. The bulk of the work is chronological, a compilation of succinct descriptions of monarchs and chancellors, treaties and alliances. Yet no history of Austria would be complete without a chapter on the cultural milieu, and a thirty-page central section touches on Viennese music, literature, art, and architecture from the late eighteenth century to the interwar period.

Finally, after careful examination of nearly two centuries of turbulence, Jelavich gives Austria quiet praise for skillfully pursuing its own path despite its location between the two great-power blocs. "In the mid-1980s," she says, "Austria was a fine example of a successful adaptation by a state to modern realities."

(Cambridge University Press, 1987, ISBN 0-521-31625-1, softcover, 256 pages, $12.95)

NATURE

Scrambles Amongst the Alps
Edward Whymper

When Edward Whymper was commissioned in 1860 to make sketches of the Alps, he "had not even seen—much less set foot upon—a mountain." Yet he quickly found that he enjoyed mountain climbing—"The mountain air did *not* act as an emetic; the sky did *not* look black, instead of blue; nor did I feel tempted to throw myself over precipices"—and for the next five years he engaged in a series of "scrambles in the Alps."

He was especially enticed by the grandeur of the Matterhorn and returned, year after year, determined to make his way to the top. On July

11, 1865, he achieved his dream, only to see his triumph turn to tragedy as four members of his party plunged to their deaths during the descent.

His 1936 book telling of his experiences in the Alps became a classic of climbing literature. This fiftieth anniversary edition contains Whymper's original engravings and new photographs by John Cleare, making it a visual treat as well. Whymper would approve highly, for as he was the first to admit,

the ablest pens have failed, and I think must always fail, to give a true idea of the grandeur of the Alps. The most minute descriptions of the greatest writers do nothing more than convey impressions that are entirely erroneous—the reader conjures up visions, it may be magnificent ones, but they are infinitely inferior to the reality.

(Gibbs Smith, 1986, ISBN 0-87905-239-2, hardcover, oversized, 262 pages, $24.95)

PERFORMING ARTS

A History of the Salzburg Festival
Stephen Gallup

On 22 August 1920, at precisely five o'clock in the afternoon, the Domplatz in Salzburg was filled to overflowing with Austrians and Bavarians, some sitting on hard wooden benches, others standing, while still more people were jostling for space far away at the back of the square, almost out of earshot of the dramatic event which was to take place on the makeshift stage in front of the Cathedral doors. All the excitement was for the première performance of Jedermann, *an adaptation by the Austrian poet Hugo von Hofmannsthal of [a] medieval English morality play, . . . directed by Max Reinhardt . . .*

The performance was also the première of what was to become the renowned Salzburg Festival, an extravaganza that fills the town's hotels and jams her cafés for five weeks each summer. The idea of a yearly musical celebration had been born years earlier; Salzburg had long wanted to honor her native son, Wolfgang Amadeus Mozart. Finally, through the genius and perseverance of Reinhardt, Hofmannsthal, and Richard Strauss, that first performance took place. Although it was highly successful, developing the event as an annaul fête was not easy:

The Festival's fortunes in many ways mirrored those of the Republic: depression and fear in the early Twenties, growing hope and prosperity at the end of the decade, the brutality of the effects of the Wall Street Crash in 1929, the fearful consequences of Hitler's coming to power in 1933 and the final solution to the Austrian problem, the Anschluss of 1938.

Yet it did survive and has showcased nearly every great musician of this century—Arturo Toscanini, Herbert von Karajan, Wilhelm Furtängler, Elisabeth Schwarzkopf, Bruno Walter, Lotte Lehmann, Vladimir Horowitz, to name but a few. Their impeccable performances provide a perfect foil for Austria's—and the festival's—vicissitudes. Stephen Gallup tells the turbulent story with scholarly detail and a music lover's delight.

(Salem House, 1987, ISBN 0-88162-315-6, hardcover, 210 pages, $24.95)

The Vienna Opera
Edited by Andrea Seebohm

In a lavishly illustrated, oversized volume, musicologist Andrea Seebohm and five authorities in related fields explore the glamorous world of the Vienna Opera. Seebohm begins with a historical overview of Viennese musical theater before the opening of the grand Opera House in 1869 and then turns to architect Wilhelm Holzbauer for an essay on the Opera House's design:

It must be the most typically Viennese of all the buildings on the Ring—less classical than the Parliament building, less monumental than the Burgtheater, less dramatic than the Neue Hofburg. One thing is certain: it is not merely the function and physical reality of the building that makes the Viennese consider the State Opera, after St. Stephen's Cathedral, to be the embodiment of all that is most cherished about the Viennese way of life.

Egon Seefehlner, former director of the Vienna State Opera, introduces each director and ensemble, beginning with Franz von Dingelstedt and including Gustav Mahler, Richard Strauss, Karl Böhm, and Herbert von Karajan. Wolfgang Greisenegger, professor of theater studies at the University of Vienna, comments on stage design and costume, remarking that "the story of scenery and costume design at the Court and State Opera is also the history of Viennese taste." Riki Rabb, who danced at the Court Opera, discusses the Vienna Opera Ballet which "though often feared dead . . . is as alive as ever before," and violinist Otto Strasser speaks of "probably the only opera orchestra that has managed to achieve recognition as one of the world's leading orchestras."

Photographs and other illustrations (both color and black-and-white) show the Opera House, performers and performances, set designs and costumes, and reproductions of representative art from every era. These images enliven the text and join with it to produce a splendid panorama of Viennese Opera.

(Rizzoli, 1987, ISBN 0-8478-0811-4, hardcover, oversized, 275 pages, $65.00)

YOUNG PEOPLE'S BOOKS

The Boy Who Held Back The Sea
Paintings by Thomas Locker, retelling by Lenny Hort
For ages four to six

"Jan wasn't really a bad boy, but you couldn't call him a good boy either," says Grandmother, launching into the familiar tale of the boy who saves Holland from flooding by putting his finger in the hole in the dike. Here the legend itself is overwhelmed by Thomas Locker's luminous paintings, oils in the style of Rembrandt and Vermeer. The scenery—complete with a windmill and skies so vivid they have a personality of their own—is magnificent; the atmosphere, rich and heavy. Poor Jan gets a bit lost amidst the cloudy skies, and Hort passes quickly over the damage that an unchecked leak might cause. Parents can rescue the meaning by inserting a few well-chosen words of their own; and in the meantime the children can absorb the style of the great Dutch masters.

(Dial Books for Young Readers/Dutton, 1987, ISBN 0-8037-0406-2, hardcover, 28 pages, $15.00)

CENTRAL EUROPE

Note: Many of the books discussed in the chapter "Germany" include information on the German Democratic Republic as well as on the Federal Republic of Germany.

GENERAL

Black Lamb and Grey Falcon
Rebecca West

"Is it so wonderful there?" he asked. "It is more wonderful than I can tell you," I answered. "But how?" he said. I could not tell him at all clearly. I said, "Well, there is everything there. Except what we have. But that seems very little." . . . "In Yugoslavia," suggested my husband, smiling, "everybody is happy." "No, no," I said, "Not at all, but . . ." The thing I wanted to tell him could not be told, however, because it was manifold and nothing like what one is accustomed to communicate by words . . . In a panic I said, "I must go back to Yugoslavia, this time next year, in the spring, for Easter."

With that Rebecca West and her husband, Henry Andrews, set out for Yugoslavia. It was 1937 and all Europe was feeling the tremors of impending war; yet West and Andrews journeyed throughout the country, studying history, cultures, religions, and politics. The resulting work, a massive 1150 pages of text plus bibliography and index, is a penetrating political study of Yugoslavia and the other Balkan nations.

The "black lamb and grey falcon" of the book's title relate to a belief that "doom [is] honourable for innocent things," and it foreshadows Yugoslav resistance, brief though it was, to the German army in the early days of World War II. "In the Yugoslavia of 1941," explains West, "there was no one who would have bought his personal salvation by consenting to the subjugation of his people, and no one who would not have preferred to be victorious over the Nazis if that had been possible. It was their resistance, not their defeat, which appeared to them as the sacred element in their ordeal."

West called her magnum opus an "inventory of a foreign country," and it remains one of the most substantial and distinguished works on this part of the world. (In addition, it is an excellent buy at less than 1.3¢ per page!)

(Penguin, 1940, 1969, ISBN 0-1400-6355-2, softcover, 1181 pages, $14.95)

Budapest
Domokos Varga

Along the shores of the Danube the two towns of Buda and Pest existed for centuries, Buda on the forested hills of the right bank, Pest on the low-lying plain of the left bank. They were officially united as Budapest in 1872 to become the capital of Hungary. Yet to the present day each has retained its own character: Buda, the stately site of the royal castle, government offices, and homes of the old Magyar families; Pest, the commercial and industrial center humming with activity and vitality.

Domokos Varga's pictorial essay tells the story of this two-in-one city, with special emphasis on its art and architecture. Color plates from more than thirty photographers highlight ruins from the Roman era, spires of early Magyar inner city structures, Turkish domes, baroque estates of the German Hapsburgs, and traces of Art Nouveau decadence, before arriving at modern rationalistic design. The accompanying text provides historical notes, anecdotes, and Varga's personal insights into his native city's paintings and statues, domes and mansions, parks and people.

Budapest is an affectionate portrait of a city that is, says Varga, "neither young nor old; its situation has not predestined it for either. It may yet see difficult times, but its sources of strength are inexhaustible."

(Overlook Press, 1985, 1988 [U.S.], ISBN 0-87951-288-1, hardcover, oversized, 136 pages, $27.50)

The Issa Valley
Czeslaw Milosz

Thomas grew up in the peaceful Issa Valley, where

from almost any hilltop you can glimpse a blue sheet of lake with a white, barely perceptible splotch of grebe, with a string of ducks winging over the reeds. The marshlands abound in every species of waterfowl, and in spring the pale sky reverberates with the whir of snipe—a whew-whew-whew—made by the air in their tail feathers as they perform their monotonous acrobatics, signifying love.

Not that everything was always peaceful. There were those weeks when the ghost of Magdalena, who had committed suicide over a love affair with the village priest, kept the whole town on edge until a group of villagers finally exorcised her spirit and everyone could sleep again. Then there was the time Thomas woke up to find a hole in his windowpane and an unaccountably unexploded grenade under his bed.

Yet on the whole, village life revolved serenely and dependably around the progression of the seasons, and Czeslaw Milosz's lyrical and sensitive memoir of rural boyhood charmingly evokes the time and place. His descriptions of the local countryside and his penetrating insight into the character of the people bespeak a warm familiarity.

First published in Polish in 1955, **The Issa Valley** was translated into English in 1978 and won the Nobel Prize for Literature in 1980. In it, Milosz has immortalized an innocent, pastoral way of life.

(Farrar, Straus and Giroux, 1955, 1981, ISBN 0-374-51695-2, softcover, 288 pages, $8.25)

Journey to Kars
Phillip Glazebrook

"What was the impulse," wondered novelist Phillip Glazebrook, "which drove middle-class Victorians to leave the country they loved so chauvinistically, and the company of the race they considered God's last word in breeding, to travel in discomfort, danger, illness, filth and misery amongst Asiatics whose morals and habits they despised, in lands which, at best, reminded them of Scotland?"

To find out for himself, he set out on his own voyage of discovery—traveling first through Yugoslavia, Greece, and Turkey to Kars on the Russian border, and then visiting Istanbul before returning via Bulgaria, Rumania, and Hungary. Here he tells of his journey, lacing his narrative with historical digressions and frequent quotations from those travelers of earlier times, sometimes taking them to task for their haughty attitudes and blasé airs.

Glazebrook, in contrast to his world-weary predecessors, possesses an adventurer's zest that makes **Journey to Kars** a wonderfully captivating and satisfying account told with a novelist's skill and a scholar's background.

(Holt, Rinehart and Winston, 1984, ISBN 0-03-005607-1, softcover, 246 pages, $7.95)

Land Without Justice
Milovan Djilas

"The story of a family can also portray the soul of a land," says Milovan Djilas in his autobiography, a tale inextricably tied to the history of his country. Djilas was one of the four chief founders of Communism in Yugoslavia—yet he became one of its most outspoken critics, and in 1957 was imprisoned for "slandering" the party he helped to create and bring to power. His moving book tells the dual story of his life (up through his college graduation) and that of Yugoslavia in the first part of this century.

Born in Montenegro, Djilas was seven years old in 1918 when his region united with the the Serbs, Croats, and Slovenes to form Yugoslavia. Through this unsettled time pride, heroism, and strong family bonds were the enduring values that shaped his life. "The story of any Montenegrin family is made up of traditions about the lives of ancestors who distinguished themselves in some special way, most frequently through heroism," Djilas asserts.

His heritage was one of personal, racial and political feuds, which he recounts, as the *New Yorker* says, "with a sinister beauty." In remembering the lost world of his childhood he proves that, as is almost always the case, "the child is father of the man."

(Harcourt Brace Jovanovich, 1958, ISBN 0-15-648117-0, softcover, 366 pages, $8.95)

Poland Under Black Light
Janusz Anderman

"The country is fading on the maps, bit by bit withering away," states Janusz Anderman in "Freeze-frame One," his opening vignette on modern Poland. "Patches of steel-coloured paint on the cold walls of the houses cover the slogans of an earlier time. People sneak out at night with buckets of bright paint to liquidate those grey patches of bad conscience, a constant reminder of the slogans underneath," he continues a bit later, in "Freeze-frame Nine."

Freeze-frames, often less than a page in length, alternate with longer stories to provide a pointillistic portrait of modern-day Poland. A feeling of suffocation permeates the stories:

The town is gasping for breath . . . —Freeze-frame One

. . . *well, so they covered my face with a mask, I couldn't speak, 'cos I mean I had my face covered* . . . —Sinking Wells

. . . *that odious front will rise to meet you, will expand and will overshadow you* . . . *it will engulf you and crush you* . . . *Every step will catch in your throat* . . .
—Return Visit

Anderman's world is devoid of optimism; in lieu of hope he presents gallows humor. Yet, as Harvard University's Stanislaw Baranczak says, "Face to face with hopelessness Anderman finds the only solution within a writer's reach, the only solution worthy of a writer: hopelessness must first be called by name. The problem of what is to happen next begins outside literature."

(Readers International, 1988, ISBN 0-930523-14-8, softcover, 131 pages, $6.95)

The Private Poland
Janine Wedel

Janine Wedel arrived in Poland in early 1982, bringing with her eleven suitcases full of canned tuna, dishcloths, toilet paper, fur-lined boots, and cooking utensils—everything, in short, that she thought she would need for a year's stay in a country that had just fallen under military rule.

"My first impression of martial law Poland was that it looked much like the somewhat sullen but intriguing place I had visited previously," she says. "As one friend put it, 'Martial law was relatively bloodless. People only lost their last hope.'"

Wedel went to Poland as a Fulbright scholar. With a Ph.D. in social anthropology from the University of California, Berkeley, and an extensive network of friends in Poland, she was able to penetrate "the private Poland." She quotes a Polish lawyer: "'Everything is so impossible that we have to avoid the law. We have to be more intelligent' . . . One moral code is reserved for the private world of family and friends, another one for the public." And, despite the fact that Poland is Communist, Wedel tells of meeting a group of 'millionaires.' "They earned upwards of 20,000 zloty daily, more than the average monthly salary."

She speaks of political beliefs as well: "Poles are easily persuaded that 'an enemy of my enemy is my friend.' Staunchly anti-Soviet and anticommunist, many Poles see the United States as savior . . . A friend related his observation: 'How do Poles imagine that American Pershing rockets fly over Poland? In a zigzag course. They avoid Poles, but hit Communists!'"

Wedel is obviously at ease in the cultures of both Poland and the United States; her book is easy to read yet well researched and authoritative. It's a first-hand look at a people who throughout history have often been forced to adapt but have never lost their spirit.

(Facts on File, 1986, ISBN 0-8160-1197-4, hardcover, 229 pages, $17.95)

Stealing From a Deep Place: Travels in Southeastern Europe
Brian Hall

Brian Hall was terrified. He was standing on a country road in Romania about to sit down for a bread-and-sausage lunch. Suddenly two farmhands appeared, headed straight for him. "Dark, sweat-begrimed, and muscular . . . they were big. In the four glowering eyes I could read, I felt sure, a murderous intent. The Hungarians had warned me repeatedly about physical violence in Romania, and I had not listened. They had told me to buy a knife to protect myself, and I had scoffed." Paralyzed with fear, Hall watched as they stopped six yards from him and began stamping on the road and cursing. Then he understood. With a stick, they held up the bloody carcasses of two snakes, exclaiming, *"Vipera!"* "The Hungarians had warned me about the vipers, too," Hall added. "But they hadn't told me that the Romanians would protect me from them."

As he travels on his bicycle through Romania, Bulgaria, and Hungary, Hall's experiences offer surprises both positive and negative. He is befriended by a gentlemanly black marketeer when his bike breaks down; he dines with the Polish Minister of Tourism who has come to Bulgaria to gather new ideas; and he learns the formula of street-naming: "In a Communist country . . . a third of the street names [are] of people who had been executed, the second third [are] of the people who had executed the first third, and the last third [are] the dates on which the second third had executed the first third."

Hall paints intimate portraits of the people he meets en route and offers perspective as well, placing the countries of today against their historical background. His is an intelligent and sympathetic two-wheeled tour of southeastern Europe.

(Hill and Wang, 1988, ISBN 0-8090-8835-5, hardcover, 271 pages, $18.95)

Travels with My Sketchbook
Nicholas Garland

"Ventilate your mind!" was the enthusiastic response of the editor at *The Daily Telegraph* when political cartoonist Nicholas Garland asked for permission to travel in Russia and Eastern Europe. And so Garland set off, once in 1981 and again in 1985, taking along his sketchpad, a sharp eye, and an inquisitive mind.

His traveling companion was his friend Harry, who not only had a magical way of clearing up seemingly insurmountable problems—from obtaining the proper champagne to getting an exit visa from Russia to Poland—but also spoke fluent Russian. With Harry as translator, Garland was able to converse with the local people. He found that many things are "forbidden—but only a little bit forbidden." In Hungary, for example, all patients pay the doctors whatever they can, trying to obtain the best possible care—"they don't have to and they [aren't] supposed to but they [do]"—and because everyone knows this, doctors' offical salaries are shockingly low. In Czechoslovakia, he was told, most people hold two jobs, "an official one and a more lucrative unofficial one." As one woman explained, "we are forced to break laws. The laws are bad and often unkeepable—nevertheless breaking them makes you feel bad. We suffer from a permanent sense of guilt."

Travels with My Sketchbook is based on journals Garland kept on his journeys through Russia, Poland, Hungary, and Czechoslovakia, illustrated with his evocative line drawings. Both drawings and text are done with style and perception and show a view of life behind the Iron Curtain that is by turns chilling, amusing, and heartwarming.

(Harrap, London, from Cupress, Ltd., 1987, ISBN 0-245-54528-X, hardcover, 222 pages, $24.95)

The Unbearable Lightness of Being
Milan Kundera

The Unbearable Lightness of Being is, on the surface, a love story: Tereza loves Tomas. Tomas loves Tereza—and nearly every other woman he meets. Sabina is one of Tomas's mistresses; she is also Tereza's best friend . . .

Romance and eroticism are paramount in **Unbearable Lightness**, yet it is also a book of philosophical ruminations and, since it takes place in Czechoslovakia, perhaps inevitably a book of politics. Using an innovative and unorthodox style Czech author Milan Kundera alternates voices, speaking at times through his characters, at times through an outside narrator. In this scene Tomas struggles with life in a police state and ponders political questions. The narrator speaks:

Let us concede that a Czech public prosecutor in the early fifties who called for the death of an innocent man was deceived by the Russian secret police and the government of his own country. But now that we all know the accusations to have been absurd and the executed to have been innocent, how can that selfsame public prosecutor defend his purity of heart by beating himself on the chest and proclaiming, My conscience is clear! I didn't know! . . .

Tomas relates this to the tale of Oedipus: Oedipus did not know he was sleeping with his own mother, yet when he realized what had happened, he did not feel innocent. Unable to stand the sight of the misfortunes he had wrought by "not knowing," he put out his eyes and wandered, blind, away from Thebes. And the narrator continues:

When Tomas heard Communists shouting in defense of their inner purity, he said to himself, As a result of your 'not knowing,' this country has lost its freedom, lost it for centuries, perhaps, and you shout that you feel no guilt? . . . Have you no eyes to see? If you had eyes, you would have to put them out and wander away from Thebes!

Kundera's novel is boldly unconventional, uncompromisingly thought provoking, totally captivating. Pronounced one of the fifteen best books of 1984 by the *New York Times Books Review*, it inspired a 1988 movie that, like the book, blends the politics of government and the intrigues of love, seeing them both as twin-edged swords, able to inflict pain or pleasure with a single stroke.

(Harper & Row, 1984, 1985, ISBN 0-06-091252-9, softcover, 314 pages, $7.95)

A Way of Hope: An Autobiography
Lech Walesa

For five hundred days in 1980 and '81 it seemed as though Poland's luck was changing. Invaded and partitioned throughout history, it looked as if perhaps, for a change, the Polish people would regain some control over their destiny. But on December 31, 1981, Lech Walesa, the man who personified the independent Solidarity movement that had briefly transformed Polish life and politics, was arrested and martial law reinstated.

Here, in his own words, he relates the story of those heady days preceding his arrest and the events that led up to them. He recalls his childhood on a small farm southeast of Gdansk and tells how, as a young shipyard worker, he became aware of local conditions. In describing the growth of free trade unions he says:

It is difficult to say precisely where a river begins. It seldom springs from a single source. More often than not, it starts as a number of small mountain streams, which join together to flow downstream . . . During the seventies, Gdansk was like the network of streams, whose ideas would later merge to form a powerful current.

Walesa harnessed the current and for a short time it looked as if he had tamed it.

If I were looking for a metaphor to illustrate the situation Poland confronted after Solidarity was legalized in the late summer of 1980, I would compare Polish society to a pauper who, for most of his life, occupied a small corner of a fine house only to learn, quite suddenly, that he is in fact master of the house, not its tenant.

He draws on his "action journal," started at the beginning of 1983, as well as on his letters, notes, speeches and interviews, to present the truth as he sees it: the story of modern Poland from the viewpoint of one who not only lived in it but who tried to transform it.

(Holt, 1987, ISBN 0-8050-0668-0, hardcover, 325 pages, $19.95)

ART

Contemporary Polish Folk Artists
Hans-Joachim Schauss

Wladyslawa Wlodarzewska was seventy-eight-years old when Hans-Joachim Schauss visited her small cottage in the village of Swiatkowice. He admired the walls and ceilings that were decorated in traditional fashion with brightly colored floral ornaments. Later he sent Wlodarzewska some paints and, in return, was invited for a second visit.

When we arrived at her home one evening she pulled a sack filled with large drawings from under the mattress. Our eyes feasted on a host of astounding pictures . . . All the pictures had but one subject—the fine lady. No doubt about it—an old woman, who had spent her long life toiling in the farmyard and on the fields, had projected her constant unattainable dream, her youthful yearning to transfigure herself with pretty clothes, hats and finery, and to escape into another world.

Schauss visited many such folk artists who work quietly to fill an inner need and, in so doing, create items of great vitality and beauty. These men and women use different materials—generally wood, clay, or paint—and depict a wide variety of subjects, often concentrating on religious themes, everyday activities, or historical events. For the most part Schauss lets the artists speak for themselves. "I revel in painting," says Wlodarzewska. "When my poor head hurt I used to paint—and my headache went away. When I paint the headache goes. And when I don't paint for a long time my head aches."

Black-and-white photos show the artists; their work is presented in both black-and-white and color. It is unpretentious, revealing, and totally delightful.

(Hippocrene, 1987, ISBN 0-87052-295-7, hardcover, oversized, 209 pages, $20.00)

Treasures of Thrace
Gerda von Bulow

A silver drinking vessel portrays Dionysus, the god of wine, with a wreath of ivy in his hair and a cup in his hand. He is wedding Ariadne, the princess from Crete who helped Theseus slay the Minotaur and escape from the labyrinth; the nuptual pair are surrounded by nymphs, satyrs, dancers, and musicians who have been revelling since the first half of the fourth century B.C.

Gold and silver vessels, jewelry, armor and weapons—all are part of the rich finds dating from the flowering of the Bronze Age in the region known in antiquity as Thrace on what is now called the Balkan peninsula. The first of these artifacts were unearthed by chance at a construction site in the Bulgarian city of Varna in 1972; over the next ten years more than two hundred graves were excavated, yielding a priceless treasure trove of artifacts and offering an unprecedented look at ancient Thracian culture.

These finds, and those from other digs on the peninsula, are documented in this splendid volume by Gerda von Bulow of the German Democratic Republic Academy of Sciences. More than a hundred full-color plates show the meticulous craftsmanship of the ancient Thracian metalworkers while the text gives historical background and comments on artistic style and technique.

"The good state of preservation and wide variety of the objects from the necropolis at Varna have enabled us to gather vital information concerning various aspects of the life of the people in the 4th millennium B.C.," says von Bulow. Her matter-of-fact style contrasts with the glitter of the treasure; yet it concisely reveals previously unknown facts about a nation that was immensely important in ancient times.

(St. Martin's Press, 1987, 0-312-81649-9, hardcover, 143 pages, $14.95)

The Velvet Prison: Artists Under State Socialism
Miklós Haraszti

George Orwell once suggested that a modern dictatorship could find it "just as possible to produce a breed of men who do not wish for liberty as to produce a breed of hornless cows." **The Velvet Prison**, a disturbing exposé by the co-editor of a Hungarian journal of dissent, suggests that Orwell's vision may have come to pass in Central Europe.

Artists and government dance a tango of complicity, suggests Haraszti, with painters and writers following the lead of those that rule them. "Traditional censorship," he says, "presupposes the inherent opposition of creators and censors; the new censorship strives to eliminate this antagonism. The artist and the censor—the two faces of official culture—diligently and cheerfully cultivate the gardens of art together. This new culture is the result not of raging censorship but of its steady disappearance. Censorship professes itself to be freedom because it acts, like morality, as the common spirit of both the rulers and the ruled."

Haraszti examines this "new culture" and asks important questions: "Who makes this culture? Why? How? Why is it so durable? Is the presence of overt or covert terror a sufficient reason for its survival? Is freedom really necessary for art to flourish?"

His essay is a chilling and thought-provoking depiction of artistic life in a place where the unspoken taboos of a "directed culture" may do the work of heavy-handed censors.

(Basic Books/A New Republic Book, 1983, 1987, ISBN 0-465-09800-2, hardcover, 165 pages, $14.95)

HISTORY

Cry Hungary!
Reg Gadney

It looked for a short while as if David's sling might once again defeat Goliath but then Goliath jumped into a tank and smashed David.
—George Mikes, Introduction

October 1956. The Hungarian people rose up against the Soviet occupation of their country and for thirteen days fought for freedom. When it was over, Stalin's statue lay in pieces on the street, hundreds of Hungarians were dead, and Janos Kadar, faithful Communist, was in Budapest.

Reg Gadney tells the story of these days using photographs, radio transcripts, and eyewitness testimony to give immediacy and poignancy to his account. Here's a Polish woman, kerchiefed head held high, carrying flowers to put beneath statues of Hungarian heroes; Erno Gero being hanged in effigy; children playing with an anti-tank gun near the Opera House; the corpses of the hated secret police being spat upon . . .

The days, as Mikes says, were "days of rejoicing, exhilarating and intoxicating happiness." And then the tanks came. Gadney quotes Peter Fryer's first-person account: "Corpses still lie in the streets—streets that are ploughed up by tanks and strewn with the detritus of a bloody war: rubble, glass and bricks, spent cartridges and shell-cases. Despite their formidable losses in the first phase of the Hungarian revolution, Budapest's citizens put up a desperate, gallant, but doomed resistance to the Soviet onslaught."

Cry Hungary! pays tribute to "a decisively important moment in modern history . . . But for the Hungarian Revolution Janos Kadar could never have afforded to turn Hungary into the reasonably liberal and well-to-do tourist resort it is today; in other words he could not have rediscovered the blessings of capitalism under another name."

(Atheneum, 1986, ISBN 0-689-11698-5, hardcover, 320 pages, $18.95)

The First Polka
September Light
Time Without Bells
A series by Horst Bienek

"The characters and events in this book are fictitous—or perhaps not," says Horst Bienek, speaking enigmatically of the first book in his series on life in Upper Silesia, a region which has at various times been Prussian, Austrian, German, Polish, Silesian, and Moravian. Now, as World War II approaches, this most bandied-about of lands is about to become part of the Third Reich.

The residents of Gleiwitz, Upper Silesia, prefer not to dwell on the impending war. In **The First Polka** they go steadfastly about their daily chores: sending out wedding invitations, closing a real estate deal, deciding on the proper white collar for a certain brown dress. Bienek depicts everyday middle-class life in the days when "ordinary" was a meaningful word.

By **September Light**, which takes place a mere month later, World War II has begun. At 2:00 A.M. on September 1, 1939, the Nazis attack the radio station at Gleiwitz. Bombs are exploding, but the hapless victims-to-be concentrate on the funeral of Leo Maria Piontek. Yet the clarity of the September light brings a recognition of forces beyond control.

Time Without Bells opens on Good Friday, 1943, as the villagers set out for church. They arrive to find that the Wehrmacht has ordered the removal of the bells. "When the bells go, faith goes too," says Anna Ossadnik as Bienek continues his portrait of a culture that, once again, is about to lose itself to a "higher authority."

"Bienek is one of the most exciting writers of our generation," says Jan Kott *(New York Times Book Review)*, speaking of the man who has won three of Germany's most coveted literary prizes. Others have compared him to Marcel Proust and William Faulkner. Here, in this series, he uses his skills to present a memorable picture of his homeland.

(The First Polka: Fjord, 1978, ISBN 0-940242-07-9, softcover, 326 pages, $7.95; September Light: Atheneum, 1987, ISBN 0-689-11848-1, hardcover, 352 pages, $17.95; Time Without Bells: Atheneum, 1987, ISBN 0-689-11930-5, 352 pages, $18.95)

Poland
James A. Michener

"Poland is a paradise," [said Bukowski]. "Everyone else knows it, and you better not forget." At this, the farmers fell silent, for each knew that of all the Iron Curtain countries, Poland was the one that was relatively free . . .

Opening his story in a small Polish farm community in the days just preceding the 1981 uprising, James Michener looks back over eight centuries, gradually revealing Poland's story in a long flashback. With the masterly blend of fact and fiction that has become his trademark, he unfolds the panorama of Polish history from the time of Genghis Khan and the Tatars through conflicts with the Germans, Swedes, Turks, and Russians. The Poles fought gallantly but often in vain, and by the end of the eighteenth century the country no longer appeared on the maps of Europe.

Yet the people remained and the battles continued. A new Poland, created at the end of the First World War, fell first to the Nazis and then to the Communists—whereupon Michener brings his story full circle, back to the small village where Bukowski spoke in 1981. As in other Michener novels, the story is told through the lives of several families: Bukowski represents the gentry, the Lubonskis depict the nobility, and the Buks bear the burdens of the peasantry. Although the characters from these families are fictional, they often interact with historical figures such as Emperor Franz Josef and Polish prime minister Ignacy Paderewski, and the social strata they represent accurately reflect Polish society of their time. To clear up possible misconceptions as to where truth ends and fiction begins, Michener includes a chapter-by-chapter summary of historical and fictional characters and events.

As lusty in their pursuit of pleasure as they are heroic in conflict, the Polish people portrayed here possess tremendous exuberance and zest for life. Romance and intrigue permeate their story, showing that Michener's creative imagination equals his painstaking research.

(Fawcett Crest/Ballantine, 1983, ISBN 0-449-20587-8, softcover, 616 pages, $4.95)

Rise and Fall
Milovan Djilas

"Arrange your affairs so you can do both," said Tito when one of his closest aides confessed a desire to escape politics and become a writer. And Milovan Djilas tried, but for a while it was no use. "Politics, especially if one takes it seriously, is all-absorbing," he says.

As one of Tito's three most trusted advisors when the Communists gained control in Yugoslavia, Djilas helped determine the course of his nation. But when he openly opposed the one-party system and suggested allowing another party to exist, he was "[exiled] into damnation and loneliness" and imprisoned for most of the next decade.

At least there was time to write (although much of the writing was done on toilet paper as he was deprived of the more conventional kind), and he wrote voluminously: critical studies of communism, a biography, short stories and novels. And he told his own story in a multi-volume autobiography of which **Rise and Fall** is (presumably) the finale.

Beginning with the postwar Communist takeover of Yugoslavia and continuing through 1966, Djilas tells the story of his country. His book is divided into three parts:

"Power":

The consolidation of the new regime and new land and property laws—the continuation of the revolutionary process—found expression more in Tito's prominence than in that of the Communist party itself . . . [This "cult of Tito"] was the product of a certain mood among the people, a people led by a single totalitarian party and accustomed to charismatic monarchs.

"Confrontation":

The unforeseen, fateful menace of the Soviet Union and Stalin loomed over our party and our country. But if our ideological kinship with Moscow had blinded us to the dangers lurking in our devotion, still less did we suspect the energies the confrontation would release, and the heightened awareness it would generate.

and "Rebellion":

With moving, irrefutable finality it dawned on me that there was no other way out of the bondage to the whims of dictators and oligarchs than by the existence of another party, socialist or Communist. At the same time, and no less unavoidably, there had to be criticism of Leninism and Leninist Communism.

Memoir and history are inextricably interwoven in a book that is as personal as it is factual. Djilas is remarkably even-handed when he speaks of the men and government that subjected him to so much pain, and upon his release from prison in 1966 he muses that "everything was better and worse than it might have been. The hour was late, but the road I was on was of my own choosing."

(Harcourt Brace Jovanovich, 1986, ISBN 0-15-676708-2, softcover, 432 pages, $8.95)

MYTHOLOGY

The Goddesses and Gods of Old Europe: Myths and Cult Images
Marija Gimbutas

Long before Greek and Judaeo-Christian civilization emerged—indeed, before the patriarchal Indo-European culture developed—a peaceful, agrarian, matriarchal society flourished in southeastern Europe. Marija Gimbutas, curator at the University of California, Los Angeles Museum of Cultural Study, reveals this civilization through its paintings and figurine art in **The Goddesses and Gods of Old Europe**.

Gimbutas's study covers the period from 7000 to 3500 B.C. in the area that runs from the Aegean and Adriatic (including the islands) north to what is now Czechoslovakia, southern Poland, and western Ukraine. Old European civilization, she says, was not merely an echo of neighboring Eastern societies, but a distinct and unique culture. At its center was a Goddess that incarnated the creative principle as Source and Giver of All:

The seed must have been recognized as the cause of germination and growth, and the pregnant belly of a woman must have been assimilated to field fertility in the infancy of agriculture. As a result, there arose an image of a pregnant goddess . . . almost universally in European folklore . . . A pregnant woman has magical influence on grain . . .

By looking at representative artifacts, which are the only surviving documentation of the culture of this era, Gimbutas illustrates a link between man and the images of his time; this mythical imagery in turn reveals much about the society's beliefs. What was man's concept of the universe? What was his place in it? What roles did male and female play?

In answering these question Gimbutas has created a delightful find for the reader who is interested in exposing the roots of East European culture.

(University of California, 1982, ISBN 0-520-04655-2, softcover, 304 pages, $14.95)

PERFORMING ARTS

DramaContemporary: Czechoslovakia
Edited by Marketa Goetz-Stankiewicz

Part of the DramaContemporary series, this volume presents six examples of Czech theatre—which, editor Marketa Goetz-Stankiewicz points out, "does not exist in Czechoslovakia itself." Although there is a rich selection of plays performed nightly in Prague, they do not include any by Czechoslovakians, for the best contemporary playwrights "have become publicly invisible in their own country." Across the borders, in Munich and Vienna for instance, their works are regularly produced, reviewed, and discussed. "Within the range of a hundred miles, they are simultaneously secret and famous, condemned and celebrated . . . Yet this is the kind of ironic stuff of which the plays themselves are made."

The works included here are by six leading Czech authors: Milan Kundera (*Jacques and His Master*), Václav Havel (*Protest*), Pavel Kohout (*Fire in the Basement*), Milan Uhde (*A Blue Angel*), Pavel Landovsky (*The Detour*), and Ivan Klíma (*Games*). The plays, which span the decade of the seventies, were chosen to illustrate dominant themes of Czech drama such as realism, humor (often tragi-comic), and the weighing of ethical questions. As editor Goetz-Stankiewicz puts it, Franz Kafka's shadow "moves through all these plays."

It can't help but give the American reader pause to realize that he can easily pick up these plays at the corner bookstore, whereas a Czech must find an underground copy to read surreptitiously. This fact alone lays the groundwork for understanding, appreciating, and admiring these works that deal with "modern man's confusion and fear, his resiliance and humor, his determination to recognize and speak the truth."

(Performing Arts Journal, Farrar, Straus and Giroux, 1985, ISBN 0-933826-76-1, softcover, 222 pages, $9.95)

YOUNG PEOPLE'S BOOKS

Poland: Land of Freedom Fighters
Christine Pfeiffer
For ages ten to thirteen

"What makes Poles Polish?" asks author Christine Pfeiffer, beginning her overview of this "romantic, religious people." She concludes that Poles are honest, hard workers; have strong feelings of love and beauty that are often expressed through the arts; generally believe in Roman Catholicism; speak a language that looks more difficult than it really is; and have a profound love for their country.

As the subtitle suggests, much of this book is devoted to Poland's troubled history, including its disappearance from the map for more than a century. Pfeiffer reaches back to earliest history and brings the story up to date through 1982 when martial law ended and the government declared amnesty for political prisoners. Then she turns to the customs and traditions of Poland, discussing mythology, holidays, food, education, and sports and illustrating them all with photographs in both color and black-and-white. **Poland** is full of facts, and its lively prose is designed to hold young readers' attention while it increases their knowledge.

(Dillon, 1984, ISBN 0-87518-254-1, hardcover, 175 pages, $12.95)

GREECE AND TURKEY

GENERAL

Atlas of the Greek World
Peter Levi

The history of mankind had a crisis in the 5th century B.C., *an explosion of light which affected everything and still does so today. Europe is the result and Greece is the key. What happened in Greece in the 5th century was part of a long process.*

Peter Levi examines this "long process" which produced Greece's Classical Age in **Atlas of the Greek World**, a beautiful, oversized book that encompasses the entire physical, spiritual, and mental world of the ancient Greeks. Levi includes history, philosophy, science, art, architecture, theater, literature, economy, and law in his study, making extensive use of maps, photographs, and drawings to illustrate his points.

After an initial overview of ancient Greece and a look at its geography, the book is arranged chronologically. Beginning with the Bronze Age, it progresses through the Age of Tyranny, the Age of Pericles, and the Age of Alexander, concluding with the Fate of Hellenism. Special two-page pictorial features treat subjects as varied as mother goddesses, music, the royal tombs of Macedon, and the development of vase painting.

Although the subject is weighty, the prose is provocative and highly readable, a rarity in reference works. The author states, "it is meant . . . to excite, engage and amuse. There are libraries of books about the classics more sober than this one, though few, I believe, more seriously intended." Excite, engage, and amuse it does—and inform as well.

(Facts on File, ISBN 0-87196-448-1, hardcover, oversized, 239 pages, $40.00)

Bitter Lemons
Lawrence Durrell

Celebrated author Lawrence Durrell fell under the spell of Cyprus when he went to that Mediterranean island as a visitor in 1953:

Spring was on us and the green fields about the village, still spotted with dancing yellow oranges and tangerines, were thick with a treasury of wild flowers such as not even spring in Rhodes can show.

Wanting to put down roots, he bought a home and tried teaching school:

To achieve silence was impossible . . . I tried, as an experiment, sending talkers out of the room one by one, in order to see at what stage the class became controllable. I was left at last with three students.

and finally served as Press Advisor to the government, which by then was on the verge of revolution:

'They don't mean any harm,' said a Greek grocer dodging adroitly as a brickbat whizzed past him into a shop-window. 'It is just the people expressing themselves.' Then getting down under a counter he added, 'They are very polite people really, but they want self-determination.'

He paints vivid images of picturesque villages nestled between mountain and sea; of colorful people like Frangos, a musician who gets lackadaisically drunk every time there's a Name Day in his family, and Sabri Tahir, the Turkish real estate agent to whom Durrell is always "my dear." He shares acute and sympathetic perceptions of the cultural and political scene; and with his sharp eye and impeccable writing style, he creates a lasting image of this "sun-bruised" island.

(Dutton, 1957, ISBN 0-525-48236-9, softcover, 256 pages, $8.95)

The Colossus of Maroussi
Henry Miller

Henry Miller, lured by the repeated invitations of Lawrence Durrell *(Bitter Lemons, The Greek Islands)*, visited Greece just before the outbreak of World War II. He was enchanted from the moment he arrived:

Marvellous things happen to one in Greece—marvellous good things which can happen to one nowhere else on earth. Somehow, almost as if He were nodding, Greece still remains under the protection of the Creator. Men may go about their puny, ineffectual bedevilment, even in Greece, but God's magic is still at work and, no matter what the race of man may do or try to do, Greece is still a sacred precinct—and my belief is it will remain so until the end of time.

He went to Knossos ("suggests the splendor and sanity and opulence of a powerful and peaceful people") and Athens ("anomalous, straggling, thoroughly individualistic and eclectic"), and camped on a sandy beach where "time was completely blotted out . . . Each morning [we would take] a quick plunge into the sea where we would watch the goats clambering up the precipitous slopes of the cliffs." To satisfy his endless curiosity he talked with everyone—from government dignitaries to refugee soothsayers—and soon learned to love this "enthusiastic, curious-minded, passionate" people.

He especially admired Katsimbalis, to whom he alludes in the title:

My friend Katsimbalis ... will I hope forgive me for having exaggerated his proportions to that of a Colossus. Those who know Amaroussion (Katsimbalis's home) *will realize that there is nothing grandoise about the place. Neither is there anything grandiose about Katsimbalis. Neither, in the ultimate, is there anything grandiose about the entire history of Greece. But there is something colossal about any human figure when that individual becomes truly and thoroughly human.*

Greece, Miller finds, is the most human of places, one where even the gods are of human proportion. Through his prose, this "man-sized world" attains the stature of myth.

(New Directions, 1941, ISBN 0-8112-0109-0, softcover, 245 pages, $5.95)

Crete: Its Past, Present & People
Adam Hopkins

"Almost anything anybody says or thinks in Crete is said or thought against a background of mountains," writes Adam Hopkins. "They dominate the landscape everywhere and nothing in Crete makes sense without them." Having begun with geography Hopkins provides a "companion to the Minoan civilisation," taking the reader beneath the island's many layers of medieval and modern history to expose the land eulogized by travel writer William Lithgow as "the garden of the whole Universe."

He weaves a historical tale of truth and fantasy that dates back to the days of Homer. Led by his narrative, we visit the wealth of archaeological sites that reveal the ancient Minoan civilization: pre-eminent Knosses, Malia, Zakros, and a host of others. Hopkins points out evidence of the periods of Byzantine and Venetian rule, and of the 250 years of harsh Turkish domination. Maps, line drawings, and charts illustrate the text.

In its reconstruction of the past, **Crete** doesn't neglect the present. The latter part of the book is devoted to the people of modern Crete and to present-day life in the countryside, in small villages and in towns like Khania, where some of the old ways survive to charm modern-day visitors.

(Faber and Faber, 1977, ISBN 0-571-11361-3, softcover, 249 pages, $7.95)

Deep into Mani: Journey to the Southern Tip of Greece
Peter Greenhalgh and Edward Eliopoulos

Despite Mani's remote location—a finger of the Peloponnese jutting into the Mediterranean—it occupies a strategic position between Greece and North Africa and between Italy and the Levant. Thus it was fated to have a rich and interesting history. The authors write in their introduction:

Mani's history is a loose thread, interweaving itself with the multi-coloured strands from Sparta, Rome and Byzantium, the Franks, Venetians and Turks, but always creating a unique design of its own on the fringe of the main Greek pattern. It is a land of caves, churches and strange towers, of fortified villages on bare mountain-sides, of Byzantine art and architecture of an extraordinary richness and importance, of feuds, fasting and lamentation.

Professor Peter Greenhalgh is an author and historian; Edward Eliopoulos is a renowned photographer and expert on the area. Here they combine their knowledge and talents to bring us Mani's story in compelling narrative and vivid color photographs. **Deep Into Mani** is in part a guidebook that retraces the authors' 1980 journey through the region; rather than offering listings of hotels, restaurants, and tourist attractions, however, they tell us about history, customs, art, and religion as well as introducing us to people they meet en route.

Blending keen observation, historical anecdote, and poetic description, the authors paint a perceptive portrait of the Peloponnese—of the days long ago when Helen and Paris left the coasts of Mani to sail for Troy and of today when toothless old women, dressed in black and bent double under mounds of hay tied to their backs, struggle up the cobbled paths of small villages.

(Faber and Faber, 1985, ISBN 0-571-13524-2, softcover, 171 pages)

The Greek Islands
Lawrence Durrell

When Lawrence Durrell's editor asked him to write this book, the assignment was straightforward: "The modern tourist is richly provided with guides and works of reference, particularly about Greece. The idea [is] not to compete in this field, but simply to endeavour to answer two questions. What would you have been glad to know when you were on the spot? What would you feel sorry to have missed while you were there?"

The result is this book—"A guide, yes," says Durrell, "but a very personal one." His commentary takes us throughout the Greek Islands and adroitly gambols among the disciplines of architecture and archaeology, mythology and history. He tells us of places to visit, to be sure. Mykonos, for example, "*must* be seen, cannot be missed out or scamped . . . [Walking about] you feel that only paradise could be composed like this, so haphazardly and yet so harmoniously."

But Durrell's greatest charm is his ability to look at Greece's present and find within it traces of the past. He walks across ruins and sees in them the architectural splendors of another age; he watches peasants drinking in a café and is reminded of the gods of Mount Olympus. His essay wanders through the centuries, touching on Homer and Hippocrates, on Demosthenes and Alexander the Great. He tells of the archaeologists Schliemann and Evans, and he recalls the civilizations they uncovered.

Despite his intentions, Durrell has not written a guide as much as a paean to the country and culture he knows so well. Accompanied by over a hundred photographs, many in full color, his text stunningly captures the spirit and history of the "sun-washed, history-laden" Greek Islands.

(Penguin, 1978, 1984, ISBN 0-1400-56610, softcover, oversized, 287 pages, $14.95)

Hellas: A Portrait of Greece
Nicholas Gage

"In one way or another, at some time or other, we have all been [in Greece], even if only in a dream," wrote Henry Miller. For Nicholas Gage the dream was reality, partly a childhood spent in the bosom of a close-knit family, partly a nightmare from which it would take him years to awaken. That story, the story of Greece during the civil war of the 1940s, is eloquently told in his prize-winning best-seller *Eleni*; here, in **Hellas**, he paints the background, dipping into his palette of memory and research to brush the broad strokes of Greek life, past and present.

"It all started with the land," he says:

The red, unpromising soil was sown with stones, but it brought forth the gods, the heroes, and the philosophers, the literature, the architecture, and the art . . . Yet when you walk among the stones of Greece and experience that combination of light and water and earth that is the Greek landscape, it all becomes inevitable. No other land could have produced such a people, and this land could have produced nothing else.

Exploring the inevitability of Greece, he delves into "the heart and spirit of the ancients," and finds that today's Greek has "the same restless curiosity, the shrewdness, the love of adventure, the capacity for suffering. He shares the same tendency to use strong words and violent gestures; he has the same warm heart, the disdain for time, and the delight in life lived fully, with all the senses awake."

From the plight of women to the complexities of the language, from the "brief and brilliant flashes of lightning" that sparked the skies of Greek history to the religion that sustained the people during times of strife, from the salty paté of *taramosalata* and the Pernod-like drink of *ouzo* to the energy and vitality of the *pedecto* dances, the essence of Greece and the Greeks is captured in Gage's ode to his native land.

Originally written in 1971 but substantially revised in 1986, **Hellas** is obviously the work of a man proud of his heritage. "For all those who love the light of reason and the joy of life, who strive for the best in themselves, and who value truth and freedom, Greece is home," he says—a statement that is echoed, not only by Miller, but by all the beneficiaries of Western civilization.

(Villard/Random, 1971, 1987, ISBN 0-394-55694-1, hardcover, 247 pages, $17.95)

Istanbul: A Travellers' Companion
Selected and introduced by Laurence Kelly

The multi-layered history of a great city comes to life in **Istanbul: A Travellers' Companion**, a collection of extracts from diaries, letters, memoirs, histories, and novels written during the last fourteen centuries. Laurence Kelly's introduction sets the stage by concentrating on specific themes that help interpret the city's past; the excerpts themselves recount most of the major events in the region's history. The anthology begins with Byzantine Constantinople:

The city which preserved Greek learning, maintained Roman justice, sounded the depths of religious thought, and gave to Art new forms of beauty, was no mean city, and had reason to be proud of her record.
—Byzantine Constantinople *by Alexander van Millingren, 1899*

moves on to Ottoman times:

It is a changing mosaic of races and religions that is composed and scattered continually with a rapidity that the eye can scarcely follow. It is amusing to look only at the passing feet and see all the foot-coverings in the world go by, from that of Adam up to the last fashion in Parisian boots—yellow Turkish babouches, red Armenian, blue Greek and black Jewish shoes; sandals, great boots from Turkestan, Albanian gaiters, low cut slippers, leg-pieces of many colors, belonging to horsemen from Asia Minor, gold embroidered shoes, Spanish alporgatos, shoes of satin, of twine, of rags, of wood, so many, that while you look at one you catch a glimpse of a hundred more.
—Constantinople *by Edmondo de Amicis, 1878*

studies the waterways that approach the city:

To be seen in all its beauty, the Bosphorus should be looked upon by moonlight. Then it is that the occupants of the spacious mansions which are mirrored in its

waters, enjoy to the fullest perfection the magnificence of the scene around them.
  —The City of the Sultan and the Domestic Manner of the Turks
  in 1936 *by Julia Pardoe*

and looks at life, customs and morals:

The number of [coffee-houses] in Constantinople is quite fabulous. They have the happiest tact for locality, seeking movement, strategic corners, open prospects, the company of water and trees. No quarter is so miserable or so remote as to be without one.
  —Constantinople, Setting and Traits *by H. G. Dwight, 1927*

Kelly has captured the past by using the words of those who lived it, and his book is a wonderfully impressionistic history, one that recreates a legendary world.

(Atheneum, 1987, ISBN 0-689-70716-9, softcover, 390 pages, $14.95)

Memed, My Hawk
Yashar Kemal

The wildly beautiful Turkish Mediterranean coast is the scene for the heroic and haunting story of **Memed, My Hawk**, considered by many to be the most important novel to come out of modern Turkey. The tale is that of Ince Memed, adventurer and rebel, who flees from his harsh Agha (lord) to live in the nearby mountains. Assuming the trappings of a present-day Robin Hood, he evolves from Memed the Outlaw to Memed the Hawk, protector of his people. Paralleling his adventure is the romance: Memed's tender love for Hatche, his childhood sweetheart, who has been betrothed to the Agha's nephew.

Not the least of the charm of Kemal's story is the lyrical descriptive language, rich in sensory imagery. Describing the countryside surrounding Memed's village, he writes:

Only beyond the low hilltops crowned with heavy-scented myrtle do the rocks suddenly begin to appear, and with them the pine trees. The crystal-bright drops of resin ooze from the trunks and trickle down to the ground. Beyond the pines are plateaus where the soil is gray and arid. From here it looks as if the snow-capped peaks of the Taurus are very close, almost within arm's reach.

The drama, heroism, and romance of the tale combine with a vivid sense of the land to give the reader an experience that puts Kemal's native country "almost within arm's reach."

(Pantheon, 1961, ISBN 0-394-71016-9, softcover, 371 pages, $6.95)

My Family and Other Animals
Gerald Durrell

Combine Quasimodo the pigeon, Ulysses the owl, and the puppies Widdle and Puke with the splendor and gaity of the Greek island of Corfu, and you have the setting for **My Family and Other Animals**. Master storyteller Gerald Durrell here recounts the years he and his family spent on Corfu when he was a boy.

His early animal-collecting experiences resulted in a houseful of creatures, each with its own eccentric personality. They all gleefully romped their way into the heart of the Durrell family, which we come to know nearly as well as our own. We meet, too, the local inhabitants, whose joyful goodwill and deeply-rooted traditions somehow survive the family's boisterous exploits.

The book is rich in poetic descriptions of the beautiful Greek surroundings. When he writes of the approach to the island, his tone changes from the jocular voice with which he portrays his family to a quality of hushed reverence:

The sky was pale and stained with yellow on the eastern horizon. Ahead lay a chocolate-brown smudge of land huddled in the mist, with a frill of foam at its base. This was Corfu.

"You pay a penalty for leaving Corfu," Durrell remembers being told, and this book shows that in his heart he never really left at all.

(Penguin, 1956, 1980, ISBN 0-1400-1399-7, softcover, 301 pages, $4.95)

A Poet's Bazaar
Hans Christian Andersen

In 1840 Hans Christian Andersen left the land of ice and snow and journeyed to the sunnier climes of Greece and Turkey, riding a "magic horse" (as he called the train) and experiencing a harrowing boat trip up the Danube. His memoirs of this trip, revealing a man who observes with wide-eyed wonder, are at last available in this country.

Andersen found a Greece that had only recently gained its freedom from the Ottoman Empire, and he marveled at seeing the birthplace of Western civilization:

As in the great days of Athens, one now hurries from Piraeus through the great olive wood. Before us lay the Acropolis, which I had so often seen in pictures, but now it was there in reality! Steep Lykabettos with its shining white hermitage stood out very distinctly—I could see Athens! A few steps from the city, close by the road on the right, stands the Temple of Theseus, so unspoiled and grand with its beautiful marble columns which have become golden brown with age. I actually saw it!

In Turkey he waxed enthusiastic about Whirling Dervishes and the marketplace:

First of all in Constantinople the foreigner should visit the bazaars—for there, in an instant, he is in the heart of this incredible city. One is overwhelmed by the sights, the splendor and the tumult. It is a beehive one enters, but every bee is a Persian, an Armenian, an Egyptian, a Greek . . . Such a throng, such variety of costume, and such a diversity of goods for sale is seen nowhere else.

And despite perilous waters and a ten-day quarantine, he rhapsodized about the scenery along the Danube:

The countryside . . . surpasses the Rhine in its beauty. By Plavisovicza, where the Kazan Narrows are found, the Danube runs between vertical cliffs; the road has been cut into the mountain, the rockmasses hang over the traveler's head like a smoothed ceiling. For a long stretch there is one large cave after another—one of them is so deep that, I was told, it takes an hour and a half to go through it and then one comes out into a valley on the outher side of the mountain.

His views have survived the passage of time, and he remains a storyteller who charms and enchants adults as well as children.

(Michael Kesend, 1988, ISBN 0-935576-23-1, hardcover, 207 pages, $21.95)

The Way to Greece
Harold and Joan Melcher

Harold and Joan Melcher, used to the "polite, careful existence of New England," surprised their friends, neighbors—and themselves—and moved to Greece for a year. They spent time in Athens, in small villages and on remote islands, but wherever they were they tried to live as much as possible in the traditional Greek way, immersing themselves in Greek ways and culture.

It wasn't the ancient ruins that made the adventure—though they were a part of it—but rather the encounters with people of an entirely different culture. The sights and sounds, the smells and tastes, the Greek language—its very alphabet— assailed and delighted us. The exposed layers of history, the ethnic mix, the customs and attitudes cried out for exploration.

They learned to watch not only for buses and cars when crossing the street in Athens, but also for the occasional shepherd driving his flock of sheep. And along with adapting to local customs they began to understand Greek concepts like that of "honor":

The daily papers report items like these: Demetrios K., charged with the murder of Iannis B., pleads he did it for honor. Iannis had seduced his sister, he claims. The verdict? Not guilty! And the women in the court clap and weep, for Demetrios is a handsome lad. Georgios P. murders his wife for honor. Sentence: one year (he is not so handsome).

The Way to Greece is a refreshing look at life in another world as seen through an American family's eyes. As the Melchers put it, "we never arrived; our experience was a journey whose constant destination was Greece."

(William L. Bauhan, 1984, ISBN 0-87233-077-X, softcover, 113 pages, $7.95)

Zorba the Greek
Nikos Kazantzakis

Who is Zorba? "He is Everyman with a Greek accent," says *Time* magazine. "He is Sinbad crossed with Sancho Panza. He is the Shavian Life Force poured into a long, lean, fierce-mustached Greek whose 65 years have neither dimmed his hawk eyes nor dulled his pagan laughter." And his story, told in the words of a rather stuffy and repressed Engish writer who comes to Crete on an ill-focused quest, is passionate, earthy, and refreshing. When the narrator encounters the remarkable Greek, he begins to realize that book learning doesn't begin to teach everything a person must know:

That man has not been to school, I thought, and his brains have not been perverted ... All the problems which we find so complicated or insoluble he cuts through as if with a sword, like Alexander the Great cutting the Gordian knot ... [The serpent] knows [the earth's secrets] with its belly, with its tail, with its head. It is always in contact or mingled with the Mother. The same is true of Zorba.

With Zorba as his friend, employee, and teacher, the Englishman learns how to risk his life in a lignite mine and his life's savings on a zany scheme for an overhead timber chute. He finds compassion for an over-the-hill cabaret singer and comes to understand that grief and sorrow are so interwoven into the fabric of life they cannot be avoided.

The first of Nikos Kazantzakis's novels to be published in America, **Zorba the Greek** has become a classic, enjoyed by millions in its book form, as a stage play and movie. Zorba, like the nation he represents, is immortal.

(Touchstone/Simon and Schuster, 1953, 1971, ISBN 0-671-21132-3, softcover, 346 pages, $7.95)

ANTHROPOLOGY AND ARCHAEOLOGY

The Archaeology of Greece
William R. Biers

William R. Biers, professor of art history and archaeology at the University of Missouri, explores the ruins of Greece in this archaeological overview for general readers and beginning students.

After a brief survey of the discipline of archaeology, the bulk of the book covers the Minoans and Mycenaeans, the Dark Ages, and succeeding periods through the Hellenistic Age. Each of these sections begins with a discussion of the social, political, and economic background of the era. Then Biers examines the major architectural and artistic achievements of the time, as exemplified in buildings and artifacts. The text is illustrated with a profusion of black-and-white photographs and drawings, and a few color photographs; a glossary and bibliography are appended.

The Archaeology of Greece is well organized and well written; it is complete without being overwhelming and thorough without being technical.

(Cornell, 1980, 1987, ISBN 0-8014-9406-0, softcover, oversized, 346 pages, $17.50)

The Athenian Agora
John M. Camp

"The reader perhaps trembles at the name of Athens, but let him take courage. I promise to let him off easily," said J. L. Stephens in his 1839 book, *Incidents of Travel in the Russian and Turkish Empires.*

John Camp treats the reader with similar consideration in this 1986 exploration of "the heart of classical Athens." Camp, who has been associated with the excavation for over twenty years, presents his material chronologically and renders it easily comprehensible for the archaeology buff.

The Athenian Agora tells of the uncovering of the civic center of ancient Athens, that public square at the foot of the Acropolis where administrative, legislative, judicial, commercial, social, and religious activities took place. "If Classical archaeology can be defined as the study of ancient history and culture through physical remains, then the discovery of the agora of a Greek city should be one of the primary goals of the excavator," says

Camp, "for there he will learn most about the history, social institutions, commerce, art, technology, and cults of a site."

Illustrations abound: 183 in black-and-white, eleven in full color. They help tell the story of a project that began in 1931 and continues today, one that has cost millions of dollars and involved hundreds of people. Camp communicates the excitement, as well as the details, of that project.

(Thames and Hudson, 1986, ISBN 0-500-39021-5, hardcover, 231 pages, $29.95)

Eleni
Nicholas Gage

On August 28, 1948, at about twelve-thirty on a hot, windless day, some peasant women with firewood on their backs were descending a steep path above the Greek village of Lia, a cluster of gray stone houses on a mountainside just below the Albanian border. As the women came into view of the village below them, they encountered a grim procession . . . At the front and rear, carrying rifles, were several of the Communist guerrillas who had occupied their village for the past nine months of the Greek civil war. They were guarding thirteen prisoners . . .

And Eleni Gatzoyiannis, age forty-one, was among them. Eleni was one of 600,000 Greeks who were killed during that nine-year civil war, but she might have survived had she blended in, gone along, become invisible. Instead she arranged for the escape of her four children. "She died so I could live," writes her son Nicola.

Nicola, now Nicholas Gage, a top *New York Times* investigative reporter, pays tribute to his mother in a detailed and passionate book of "faction." He recreates the world of his childhood—not just the rocky terrain and small stone huts but also the villagers whose days and lives were molded by age-old traditions and rituals. Here is Eleni, staying in Lia to care for her aged parents while her husband carves out a life in America; Fotini, bringing malewort from the witches and brewing it into a bitter tea to help her daughter-in-law produce a male child; and Vasilo, tending the goats and saying "Good day" to the ghosts.

"The world in which Eleni lived and died," says Gage, "has been reconstructed in this book not only from the memories of myself and my sisters but also from the recollections of scores of people . . . Some of those interviewed possess a remarkable memory and were able to describe not only incidents but also how the people involved dressed, moved and spoke . . . All the names, places and dates are real."

And, because of Gage's meticulous research and his gift of writing, his mother's world remains real and his mother's memory lives on.

(Ballantine, 1984, ISBN 0-345-32494-3, softcover, 640 pages, $4.95)

Greek and Roman Life
Ian Jenkins

In ancient Greece and Rome the home "was the nucleus of all social, economic and, indeed, political activity," writes historian Ian Jenkins. "Both peoples were deeply conscious of the boundaries, social as well as physical, that divided public from private life. Most houses, Greek as well as Roman, large and small, town and country, were built to an inward-looking design with rooms arranged around a central courtyard, the chief considerations being privacy and security."

Details of home design and decoration are just the beginning in this brief but informative book that complements the British Museum's exhibit of Greek and Roman daily life. Focusing on the domestic, it provides a look at marriage and the family, children and education, the role of women, dress, athletic events, drama, work, slavery, and death. In many cases Greek and Roman social structure were similar or identical; often, however, there were major differences, and Jenkins points these out.

This glimpse at the intimate side of Classical antiquity is amply illustrated with photographs, both full color and black-and-white. Sculptures, drawings, and artifacts depict everyday activities: a bridal party graces a cosmetic box; women spin and weave in a scene painted on an oil flask; a boy grows from infancy to school age on the panels of a relief. All these items from the British Museum are reproduced here, allowing them to reach a much wider audience.

The life of the ancient Greeks and Romans is brought into sharper focus through this look at their possessions, and antiquity falls into personal perspective.

(Harvard University, 1986, ISBN 0-674-36307-8, softcover, 72 pages, $7.95)

The Greek Treasure
Irving Stone

"Am I addressing a genius or a fool?" wondered Georgios Engastromenos as he spoke with his daughter's future husband. It was a question that many asked themselves upon first meeting Henry Schliemann. Schliemann, who had already proved himself to be no fool when it came to amassing fortunes, was now determined to discover the entire city of Priam, Homer's "sacred Troy," buried for some three thousand years. Yet the Greeks were convinced there was no Troy; the city was fiction, they felt, a mythical spot created by a gifted poet. Perhaps there had not even been a Homer, but rather a series of bards who over the centuries wove the stories of *The Iliad* and *The Odyssey*. Perhaps Henry Schliemann was crazy.

Crazy? Maybe. Enthusiastic? Determined? Clever? Definitely. And passionately in love with his young wife, Sophia Engastromenos. Irving Stone tells the story of the Schliemanns, and along with it the story of Greece, in one of his best biographical novels. The archaeological expeditions are hampered by bureaucracy, weather, and bruised egos, yet Henry perseveres. His story combines archaeology and romance, education and entertainment. **The Greek Treasure** is fictionalized history at its best.

(Signet/New American Library, 1976, ISBN 0-451-13457-5, softcover, 499 pages, $4.50)

In Search of the Trojan War
Michael Wood

It is irrelevant how many centuries may separate us from a bygone age. What matters is the importance of the past to our intellectual and spiritual existence.
—Ernst Curtius

The ghosts of Troy inhabit the imaginations of all of us who read the *Iliad* and the *Odyssey* in literature class. Now Michael Wood has come along to dust off our memories and give us the historical underpinnings of Ancient Troy. Was there ever an actual siege of Troy? Was there a Helen, an Agamemnon, or a Paris? And what about the assertions of the archaeologists, Heinrich Schliemann and Arthur Evans in particular, who claimed to find verification for the ancient tales?

Michael Wood, Oxford graduate and BBC journalist, travels through archaeological sites and historical records as he searches for the answers. A genial host on both the television screen and the written page, he communicates his fascination with archaeology when he calls it "the most romantic of sciences because it brings back lost time." Reading his book is a two-fold experience: "on one level it is a tale of heroes, adventure and buried treasure; on another it is a fascinating scholarly search into the world of Bronze-Age Greece, where new discoveries are constantly adding to our knowledge."

Written as an accompaniment to the BBC television series of the same name, **In Search of the Trojan War** contains nearly 150 illustrations, thirty-four in full color. It returns to our consciousness the enchantment of the Homeric sagas and, this time around, we get the facts as well.

(Plume/New American Library, 1987, ISBN 0-452-25960-6, softcover, 272 pages, $12.95)

ART AND ARCHITECTURE

A Handbook of Greek Art
Gisela M. A. Richter

"We are lovers of the beautiful yet simple in our tastes, and we cultivate the mind without loss of manliness," said Thucydides in *The Peloponnesian War*, c. 400 B.C. Over two thousand years later the "beautiful yet simple" style of the Ancient Greeks has yet to be surpassed.

A Handbook of Greek Art pays homage to this tradition in an informative account that spans roughly a millennium, from the tenth century B.C. through the Hellenistic period. Gisela M. A. Richter, former Curator of Greek and Roman art at the Metropolitan Museum of Art, New York, arranges the surviving masterpieces according to subject matter and, within this framework, discusses each art form chronologically. She begins with architecture:

It seems proper to begin an account of Greek art with architecture, for in ancient times sculpture was largely architectural, paintings decorated the walls of public and private buildings, and the 'minor' arts, such as pottery and furniture, served their chief functions in private houses.

Then she systematically continues through the other arts: large sculpture, statuettes, paintings and mosaics, gems, coins, jewelry, pottery and vase painting, furniture, textiles, glass, ornament, and epigraphy. A chronology of Greek sculptural works is appended.

The text is amply illustrated with black-and-white photographs, and together words and pictures provide a record of the early days of Western civilization.

(Da Capo, 1959, 1987, ISBN 0-306-80298-8, softcover, 431 pages, $17.95)

The Parthenon and Its Sculptures
John Boardman

"In a way the story of the Parthenon begins with the arrival of Greeks in Greece, with the Greek land itself. It embraces the beginnings of organized religious life in Greece and of Greek religion (not the same thing); the absorption into Greek life and thought of foreign ideas and arts; the history of architecture and sculpture; the development of the narrative and symbolic functions of myth; the physical, political, economic, social and military history of Athens itself." So explains John Boardman as he outlines the task he has set for himself in this book.

His approach is three-tiered. First are full-page photographs of the Parthenon (in both black-and-white and duotone) by David Finn. Beginning at a distance but then moving in for close-up shots of the sculpture and reliefs, Finn breathes life into the famous building.

Next is narrative provided by Boardman, professor of classical archaeology and art at the University of Oxford. He gives an "account not only of the Parthenon's final appearance, its planning and construction, but also for the fifty years which preceded the first work upon the building, since within these years we may hope to uncover much that goes to explain its purpose and its meaning."

Then at the back of the book, for those who wish a more complete discussion, is "The Evidence." In this section Boardman surveys in greater depth such topics as the history of both Athens and the Parthenon, the great Panathenaic Festival, the architecture of the Parthenon, and the sculptures themselves.

The combination of photos, overview, and detail pays homage to a building that, to many, exemplifies "the high point in the development of the most influential tradition of Western sculpture."

(University of Texas, 1985, ISBN 0-292-76498-7, hardcover, oversized, 256 pages, $35.00)

HISTORY

Alexander's Path
Freya Stark

"No part of the world can be more beautiful than the western and southern coasts of Turkey," said Freya Stark as she set out more than thirty years ago to trace the footsteps of Alexander the Great. She followed his path in reverse, traveling through the "immense natural fortress . . . whose bastions are toilsome capes that dip, one after another, to the sea," recreating events of the Turkish winter of 333 B.C. and quoting writers from Alexander's time to her own to piece together the puzzle of his route. By jeep and horseback this intrepid, erudite traveler ventured into remote valleys and treeless plateaus, ever alert for clues in her search:

I was driving along the plain, dark under the sunset, with pointed ranges round it thick like cut paper against the clear pale sky. Looking, as Alexander must have looked, at the easy space on my right that seemed to lead to open valleys, and at the opposite heavy high outlines of Termessus threatening in the west: "why," I asked myself, "should he have wished to turn west at all and attack such a difficult position, when his aim was all towards Gordium in the north?"

Such historical questions determined her itinerary, but she was not so engrossed in the past that she couldn't enjoy the Turkey of her day. She took obvious delight in meeting villagers along her route, even a group of soldiers who insisted on searching all five pieces of her luggage on the hot, dusty plain:

They tried in a pathetic way to help me pack. They had done their destruction with no malice—no official sadism—merely an anxiety to Do Right—an awful thing in Men of Action uninfluenced by Words! I spurned them, and worked on by myself moaning "zahme, zahme, sorrow, sorrow," as I did so: but when all was over, and the luggage tied on to the roof again, we were reconciled.

Well-versed in classical history, Stark makes a knowledgeable and enthusiastic guide. Her narrative is a vivid portrait of country, a history lesson and a philosophical treatise all rolled into one.

(Overlook, 1958, 1988, ISBN 0-87951-309-8, 283 pages, hardcover, $17.95)

The Ancient Greeks
The World of Odysseus
M. I. Finley

"If it is true that European history began with the Greeks," says historian M. I. Finley, "it is equally true that Greek history began with the world of Odysseus." In two books that probe the world of ancient Greece, Finley goes back to Homer's epic poems and moves through archaic and classical Greece (roughly the eighth to the fourth centuries B.C.) to bring the beginnings of Western Civilization into sharper focus.

Homer, he explains in **The World of Odysseus**, "was [for the Greeks] their pre-eminent symbol of nationhood, the unimpeachable authority on their earliest history, and a decisive figure in the creation of their pantheon . . . Plato tells us that there were Greeks who firmly believed that Homer 'educated Hellas and that he deserves to be taken up as an instructor in the management and culture of human affairs, and that a man ought to regulate the whole of his life by following this poet.'" Subsequent chapters on bards and heroes, wealth and labor, home and community, morals and values look at the material, social, political, and cultural underpinnings of ancient Greece, citing weaknesses as well as its strengths.

The Ancient Greeks continues the story but emphasizes the classical period that saw the rise and fall of the great city-states and the crucial conflict betwen Anthens and Sparta. This was an era in which arts and sciences reached new heights: the age of Aeschuylus, Sophocles, and Euripides who, among them, wrote approximately three hundred tragedies; of Aristophanes the master of comedy, Herodotus the historian, and Aristotle the philosopher. It was the time when Hippocrates devised his school of medicine, Euclid fathered geometry, Archimedes discovered specific gravity, and Eratosthenes estimated the diameter of the earth with astonishing accuracy; when Socrates and Plato left their words and thoughts for future generations; when art and architecture flourished.

Both books are overviews, concise but thorough, readable yet not simplistic, and they bring to life some of the finest moments of Greek civilization.

(Penguin, Ancient Greeks: 1977, ISBN 0-14-020812-7, softcover, 176 pages, $5.95; World of Odysseus: 1979, ISBN 0-14-020570-5, softcover, 176 pages, $6.95)

The Last of the Wine
Mary Renault

This accurate and sensitive historical novel depicts everyday life in ancient Athens from the perspective of its narrator, Alexias. The only son of a well-established Athenian citizen, Alexias grows to early manhood during the final years of the Peloponnesian War. He and another youth, Lysis, support each other both through combat and their own personal struggles as they learn to cope with the trauma of war and a changing society.

Although **The Last of the Wine** is fictional, the backdrop features historical figures such as Socrates, and many of the events described actually took place. Mary Renault, who studied at Oxford University, smoothly blends historical fact with both modern and ancient issues, including a sensible and informed presentation of Athenian society and sexuality. Through Alexias's mother Renault gives a reliable account of the treatment of women, who, for the most part, were not active members in Greek society but were confined to household tasks and child rearing. She illustrates how young men looked to one another, rather than to women, for emotional companionship and assurance.

The book abounds with such details as the type of food the Greeks ate and the athletic competitions they held. Adding to the historical ambiance are a map of Greece and the Aegean in the fifth century B.C., a glossary of terms and a brief chronological table. Historical precision and an intriguing plot combine in a novel that is both highly educational and wonderfully readable.

(Vintage/Random, 1956, 1975, ISBN 0-394-71653-1, softcover, 447 pages, $4.95)

The Living Past of Greece
A. R. and Mary Burn

Whether they are directing us to the finest frescoes in a church, debunking the Atlantis myth, or describing the excavation of Thera, A. R. and Mary Burn are ideal guides to bring along on a trip to Greece. Concentrating on over seventy of the sites that best illustrate Greek history, they evoke the past in both authoritative prose and vivid drawings and photographs, pointing out details and providing background information that gives meaning to otherwise lifeless stone.

We learn how the famous Venus "de Milo" statue was found in Melos and how it came to be smuggled to France where it is now on exhibit at the Louvre. We visit the foundations of the Mycenaean palace of Nestor on "Sandy Pylos" (as Homer dubbed the island), and consider the strategy that resulted in Leonidas sacrificing his life to save two-thirds of his army during the Persian War. A date chart, bibliography, and glossary are appended.

The Living Past of Greece is a journey through antiquity, with stopovers at all the most interesting spots.

(Pantheon/Schocken, 1986, ISBN 0-8052-0779-1, softcover, 288 pages, $9.95)

Modern Greece
C. M. Woodhouse

Defining the scope of history is never easy, remarks C. M. Woodhouse. Is the subject that of "a people, a race, a country, a language, a religion, a culture, an idea?" He concludes that simplicity is the best policy. This then is "the history of the Greek people—those who called themselves Greeks and thought of themselves as Greeks—during the sixteen centuries which separate the foundation of the Greek Empire from the present day."

History, he notes, ebbs and flows more or less continually with only rare abrupt breaks in continuity. "Such a moment came with the accession to power of Constantine the Great early in the 4th century A.D." This powerful figure not only founded the new capital of the Roman Empire, Constantinople, but also initiated the melding of the Hellenistic, Roman, and Christian cultures into the Byzantine Empire. Woodhouse traces the rise and fall of Byzantium and probes Greece's "Dark Age," which lasted from the middle of the fifteenth century until approximately 1800, when a Greek renaissance and independence movement emerged.

About two-thirds of the book deals with developments during the nineteenth and twentieth centuries, ending with the results of the presidential and parliamentary elections of 1985:

The democracy restored by Karamanlis had now passed its first major test by making possible, without adverse reaction, the election and consolidation of Greece's first government committed to socialism. It remained to be seen whether it would also make possible, at a later election, the return of a government committed to the opposite course; or whether socialism, once fully established, would prove itself irreversible.

Woodhouse's study thoroughly yet concisely recapitulates the story of the Greece that arose after Ulysses, Pericles, and Alexander had perished.

(Faber and Faber, 1986, ISBN 0-571-13827-6, softcover, 352 pages, $8.95)

Ten Days to Destiny: The Battle for Crete, 1941
G. C. Kiriakopoulos

In the early predawn hours of Tuesday, May 20, Kapetan Vasili Kasantsakis untied his fishing boat from its mooring post in the small harbor of Khania. As he left the harbor behind him, the first brilliant rays of the ascending sun scattered the shadows of night. It looked as if it would be another bright and cloudless day. A stillness prevailed over the whole expanse of the island. To the Kapetan, it was a foreboding silence—the calm that proclaimed the approach of a storm.

That morning at six o'clock the Germans attacked. For ten days Cretan civilians battled shoulder to shoulder with the British army in a defense so magnificent that it cost the Wehrmacht more men than the rest of the war had since its beginning. The Germans won the battle—but, G. C. Kiriakopoulos contends, because of the delay it caused in the launch of Hitler's campaign against Russia, the battle over Crete was instrumental in Germany's eventual defeat. "If the events that culminated in the battle of Stalingrad marked the beginning of the end for Adolph Hitler," he writes, "then the events that took place on Crete in May 1941 marked the end of the beginning."

Kiriakopoulos, professor at Columbia University and author of many articles on World War II, reconstructed this heroic story through painstaking personal research and firsthand interviews. His account illuminates an important segment of history, all the while brimming with drama, suspense and terror.

(Franklin Watts, 1985, ISBN 0-531-09785-4, hardcover, 408 pages, $18.95)

NATURE

Travels with a Wildlife Artist
Peter and Susan Barrett

Peter and Susan Barrett spent ten years in Greece, traveling the length and breadth of the mainland and throughout the islands. During their last three years in their adopted land they became absorbed in learning about its wildlife and began to keep notebooks and sketches, hoping that the fragments would "somehow be shaken like a kaleidoscope so that, however ordinary each piece is, a pattern will emerge."

This book displays the pattern that appeared, a blend of his delicate pictures and her deft prose. Together they present the range of Greek nature from the profusion of wildflowers on Crete to the wild boar, bears, and wolves in the northern Greek mountains.

Peter sometimes uses color as when he portrays the fish of the Aegean, the wildflowers in Vikos gorge, or the small birds that warble in the olive groves; other times he makes soft pencil sketches that show summer's dried thistles, a Turkish gecko, or cows strolling along a cobbled alleyway.

And Susan's words create their own spell, as for example, she sits on a hill overlooking Delphi and writes: "it is easier to feel the magic of the place, a magic which cannot be erased no matter how many of us trudge, hot and tired, up and down its paths . . . The terraces are smothered in flowers, clumps of golden and purple honeywort, yellow alkana, white umbellifers, scarlet poppies . . . Everything seems to have a sound of its own . . . the olives, with their silver-sided leaves noticing a breeze that nothing else can feel, are plucked harps."

Travels with a Wildlife Artist is, as Susan states, "a personal selection of places seen with the eyes of an artist interested in nature and a novelist interested in everything."

(Columbus Books, London, from Cupress Ltd., 1986, ISBN 0-86287-285-5, hardcover, 160 pages, $29.95)

YOUNG PEOPLE'S BOOKS

Greek Myths: Gods, Heroes and Monsters
Ellen Switzer
For ages twelve and over

Every culture on earth has produced a body of tales to answer the universal questions about life and death, light and darkness, the blessings of abundance and the curse of disaster. But the Greek approach to mythology, contends Ellen Switzer, is different:

Greek mythology is unique in that it is so totally earthbound. In today's Greece, any tourist who asks the right questions will be shown the cave (though some say it was a hut) where Odysseus hid before entering Ithica, the spot where the priestess of Apollo pronounced the oracles, the hill on which Agamemnon's palace stood, with the overhang on which Clytemnestra waited for the husband she planned to murder. Occasionally someone will even explain exactly which mountaintop in the Atlas range is Olympus.

In **Greek Myths**, Switzer and Greek-born photographer Costas take this "earthbound" approach and make the tales come alive through vivid text accompanied by black-and-white photographs, many of them on-site in Greece. These photos show, for example, the entrance to the maze at Knossos, the cave in which Odysseus is said to have hidden when he returned from the Trojan War, and a statue of Aphrodite holding the golden apple.

The only disappointment is that many of the photographs are of statues that are currently not in Greece but rather in Florence, Paris, or even New York. Although this emphasizes the wide-spread influence of Greek mythology in Western culture, it would have been more interesting for the traveler were all the sites visible in Greece.

Nonetheless, Switzer's approach is refreshing, and although the book is intended for teens it makes an excellent refresher course for adults. It's an entertaining way to brush up on the doings of gods such as Zeus, Hera, and Hades; heroes like Prometheus, Oedipus, and Antigone; and legends including those of Midas and of Orpheus and Eurydice.

(Macmillan, 1988, ISBN 0-689-31253-9, hardcover, 208 pages, $16.95)

SOVIET UNION

GENERAL

The Anti-Soviet Soviet Union
Vladimir Voinovich

Russia, says Vladimir Voinovich, is a barrel of stagnant water and the Soviet people are like beetles, secure in their cylindrical world:

We are born, we live, and we die in a barrel . . . No matter how different our backgrounds, after years in that barrel, all come to have a shared view of the world . . . The most freedom-loving ones try to escape; they climb up the barrel's rusty sides, fall back down, then climb up again. The most persistent either lose their lives or make it to the rim. And suddenly a new, never-seen and many-colored world opens before them . . . A boundless world. But everyone must obtain his food and everyone has to take care not to be trampled, bitten, or swallowed. Good God, what's going on here? Quick, back in the barrel!

Voinovich, who now lives in West Germany, divides his book into three sections. Part One, entitled "Our Daily Bread—Pictures of Soviet Life," is a commentary on topics from sacred cows to defectors, from money to medicine. Part Two, "Shut Up and Eat!," touches on a subject of great importance to Voinovich: the official and unofficial regulations that govern literature and writers in the Soviet Union; and Part Three, "Abracadabra, Absurdity and Soviet Life" thus seems to follow quite naturally. Throughout his book Voinovich uses humor to make serious points:

I had lived 48 years in the Soviet Union and had stood in lines that, if set end to end, would reach from Moscow to Vladivostok. I remember the lines for bread, for hot water at railroad stations, for some meaningless document or other in governmental institutions . . . Now, with the increase in prosperity, people stand in line for beer, detergent, gloves, toothpaste, toilet paper, and even Rubik's cubes.

The Anti-Soviet Soviet Union ends as Gorbachev takes power. Voinovich is hopeful but skeptical as well for as he says, "no serious changes . . . are genuinely possible without giving people more freedom."

(Harcourt Brace Jovanovich, 1985, ISBN 0-15-107840-8, hardcover, 325 pages, $19.95)

The Burn
The Island of Crimea
In Search of Melancholy Baby
Vassily Aksyonov

Vassily Aksyonov didn't intend to emigrate to the United States; he was visiting here when the Russians stripped him of his citizenship. **The Burn** had been published in Italy, and the Soviets were not amused at his re-creation of his childhood years in Stalinist Siberia and his portrayal of 1960s Moscow:

In Europe there are frivolous democracies with mild climates, where an intellectual spends his life flitting from a dentist's drill to the wheel of a Citroën, from a computer to an espresso bar, from the conductor's podium to a woman's bed ... Russia, with its six-month winter, its tsarism, Marxism, and Stalinism, is not like that. What we like is some heavy, masochistic problem, which we can prod with a tired, exhausted, not very clean but very honest finger. That is what we need, and it is not our fault. Not our fault? Really? But who let the genie out of the bottle, who cut themselves off from the people, who groveled before the people, who grew fat on the backs of the people, who ... submitted obediently to dim-witted dictators? We did that—we, the Russian intelligentsia.

Following his forced move to Washington D.C. Aksyonov continued his exploration of contemporary Russian life with **The Island of Crimea**, a fantasy laced with political overtones. "What if Crimea really were an island?" he asks. "What if, as a result, the White Army had been able to defend Crimea from the Reds in 1920? What if Crimea had developed as a Russian, yet Western, democracy along the totalitarian mainland?"

Finally, in 1987 Aksyonov turned his satirical eye towards his new homeland with a work that reveals Russia as it focuses on America. **In Search of Melancholy Baby** is his wide-eyed look at the United States—the jogging politicians, the big cars, the newscasts that verify the American problems (unemployment and homelessness) that the Soviets so like to point out. The most telling difference between the two countries is obvious from Aksyonov's conclusion: "I see more than the bright windows of my new home," he writes. "I see its mildewed corners as well. I trust that if I point them out my *new* country won't throw me out."

Not a chance.

(Vintage, The Burn: 1980, 1985, ISBN 0-394-74174-6, softcover, 530 pages, $9.95; The Island of Crimea: 1981, 1984, ISBN 0-394-72765-7, softcover, 369 pages, $8.95; In Search of Melancholy Baby: 1984, ISBN 0-394-75992-3, softcover, 227 pages, $6.95)

Cogs in the Wheel: The Formation of Soviet Man
Mikhail Heller

In our Soviet Union people are not born. What are born are organisms. We turn them into people—tractor drivers, engine drivers, academicians, scholars and so forth.

–Trofim Lysenko
quoted by Aleksei Adzhubei in
Komsomolskaya Pravda, May 17, 1986

Organisms into people. People into cogs. *Homo sapiens* into *Homo sovieticus*. This is the aim of the Soviet regime—now and in the past. It is the way to change society, and it is the underlying goal of the Soviet rulers.

So says Mikhail Heller in this trenchant and powerful analysis of the meaning behind the words, the reasons behind the actions of leaders from Lenin to Gorbachev. The Soviets, he contends, desire to change the very essence of human nature; and they will use both fear and force to achieve their goal.

Heller delves into literary and artistic sources as well as political ones to arrive at his assessment of the government's strategy: Infantilization (treat the citizens as children, educating them with "propaganda and persuasion"), Nationalization of Time ("Soviet-type planning is not intended as an instrument for forecasting economic development, but as a powerful tool for remolding human consciousness"), and Ideologization (using the psychological powers of totalitarianism—miracle, mystery and authority—to retain complete control).

Comparing the Soviet instruments of control with those described by Orwell, Heller discusses the means by which a totalitarian regime can shape a "New Man": fear, labor, corruption, education, culture, and language. These methods, he proposes, are being used in the Soviet Union today, despite the veneer of *glasnost* and *perestroika*.

In fact, suggests Heller, much of the Gorbachev revolution is an updated replay of the past. Stalin's words—"I drink to the simple people, *ordinary* and modest, to the 'cogs,' who keep our great state machine in motion"—are still the overriding philosophy of the Soviet Union, and Gorbachev has no intention of allowing these cogs an independent existence.

(Knopf, 1988, ISBN 0-394-56926-1, hardcover, 293 pages, $22.95)

Fellow Travelers
Alex Beam

Fictional American journalist Nick Perkins considered a year in Moscow to be a year in exile, and he only grudgingly accepted the transfer that took him away from the bright lights of New York. His arrival in Russia didn't improve his attitude:

The view was Village Modern. The homogeneous apartment blocks provided the ideal backdrop for the planned society, but the extras hadn't seen the script. In a parking lot between two high-rises, a man and a woman were scuffling next to a beer stall. The lot was empty because a truck had dumped a load of melons across the entrance. While a line of cars honked madly, an old grandmother in a gray apron was calmly selling off the stack of melons to a long line of customers. Consumerism, Soviet style.

At first, life was unbearably lonely. Although he spoke some Russian, foreign journalists were suspect, and his hesitant overtures were rebuffed. But eventually he met Andrei and Lilya, through whom he glimpsed the real Russia: warm-hearted people who live in crowded apartments and wait patiently in endless queues, who weekend in dachas in the country and "sandwich dutiful work binges in between mornings and afternoons of visiting with friends," and who love their country fiercely.

Nick's outlook changed rapidly, and as he prepared to return home, he had difficulty saying good-bye to his newfound friends:

"I think you're wonderful. I love you—" I couldn't finish the sentence. I burst into tears . . .

In this skillfully crafted novel Alex Beam recreates the interaction between American and Soviet cultures and shows the paradox of an irrepressible people governed by a harsh political system. His story is amusing, heart-warming, tragic, and always entertaining.

(St. Martin's Press, 1987, ISBN 0-312-00001-4, 296 pages, $17.95)

From the Yaroslavsky Station: Russia Perceived
Elizabeth Pond

Journalist Elizabeth Pond boarded the Trans-Siberian Railroad ("that monument, instrument, fable and epitaph of Russia") at Moscow's Yaroslavsky Station on a Monday. The following Sunday, after traveling more than 8,500 km., she arrived at Vladivostok. Her long trip—through eleven time zones and across the homeland of 150 distinct nationalities—gave her time to describe the Russia she had come to know during her tenure as Moscow bureau chief for *The Christian Science Monitor*.

Written in the form of a journal, each day's entry contains Pond's observations of the countryside and depictions of her fellow passengers as well as a thoughtful essay on some aspect of Russian life—the intelligentsia on Tuesday, the economy on Wednesday, nationalities on Thursday, Russia's relationship with the rest of the world on Friday and its leaders on Saturday:

Gorbachev is now compelled to produce swift answers to existential questions—questions that his generation admit are far more intractable than their elders ever acknowledged. It would be rash to prophesy what solutions will be favoured by men in their mid-50s who have waited so long for the septuagenarians to relinquish their monopoloy on power.

She draws her compartment-mate, Tanya, into conversation, delighted to meet "the real Russia . . . In the capital all I meet are intellectuals, propagandists and drunks." After some initial reluctance, Tanya found the exchange unexpectedly easy, remarking, "You know . . . this is the first time I ever met a foreigner personally. I thought it would be complicated. But we found out we had the same interests. We have much in common—literature, music and so forth."

Pond's ability to hurdle cultural barriers, her far-ranging knowledge and reporter's zest for uncovering a story make this a wonderfully revealing look at Soviet institutions and people.

(Universe Books, 1981, 1984, ISBN 0-87663-853-1, softcover, 300 pages, $9.75)

Galina: A Russian Story
Galina Vishnevskaya

Writing with the sweep and passion of *Gone With the Wind*, Galina Vishnevskaya, Russia's most celebrated diva, relates her life story. It is dramatic, romantic, and factual: from a childhood of extreme poverty she rises to stardom, experiencing along the way deprivation and disillusionment, love and success.

Her cast of characters resembles a *Who's Who* of Russian art and politics. She accompanied, for example, the first Soviet delegation to Yugoslavia since the break between Stalin and Tito. All the important players were present:

The atmosphere at the table was tense . . . Tito was exaggeratedly calm and reserved . . . Mikoyan proposed toasts like a toastmaster; Bulganin tried to keep the conversation at the sophisticated level; and Khruschev, for all the world like some kind of hail-fellow-well-met, kept trying to kiss everybody.

In later years Galina and her husband, cellist Mstislav Rostropovich, shared their home with dissident writer Alexander Solzhenitsyn while he wrote *August 1914*. This friendship introduced them to the world of KGB surveillance and party control, and eventually cost them their Russian citizenships.

It's all here—the glittering world of the Bolshoi as well as the drab society of Stalinist Russia, the leaders of Russian government and the stars of Russian art. Galina Vishnevskaya's life story is one of insight and emotion, art and politics, blood and vodka—a very Russian story indeed.

(Harcourt Brace Jovanovich, 1984, ISBN 0-15-634320-7, softcover, 519 pages, $10.95)

Klass: How Russians Really Live
David K. Willis

"Ideology is for the dry pages of *Pravda*," says David Willis. "Reality is that each social rank, or class, is so tangible, so evident, that the Party recognizes it and awards it specific privileges not available to the class or subclass below. To the bulk of Soviet citizens, Marx and Lenin are yesterday's theory. *Klass* is today's reality."

As Moscow correspondent for the *Christian Science Monitor* Willis, along with his wife and three children, lived in Russia from August 1976 to January 1981. During that time he learned that Soviet society provides the basic necessities—"hot water, a roof, minimum space, free (but overloaded) education and health care, potatoes, cabbage"—and that *klass* provides the rest. *Klasszi*, for example, is a ticket to the Bolshoi, a duplex apartment with a live-in maid, a son in Moscow's prestigious Fourth School of Physics and Mathematics. It is watching a porn film from Finland, listening to music played on a Japanese tape deck, or having, when necessary, a vial of American medicine.

Willis divides Soviet society into five groups: the Top Class of Party chiefs and government officials; the Military Officer Class of generals "not senior enough to edge into the Top Class"; and the Urban and Rural Classes that comprise the "toiling and struggling masses." His examination is wide-ranging—from money ("it doesn't talk as loud") to women ("the statusless sex"), from medicine ("a matter of privilege") to commodes ("a symbol of prestige"). **Klass** looks both analytically and anecdotally at a country that is experiencing a second Revolution; only this one is "fought not with guns but with Western jeans . . . not with iron tanks but with bright cotton tank tops."

(Avon, 1985, ISBN 0-380-70263-0, softcover, 355 pages, $4.50)

Moscow: A Travellers' Companion
Selected and introduced by Laurence Kelly

Rich in personal observation and diverse in viewpoint, this "topical anthology" brings together examples of the most evocative writing about

Moscow, a city that, as Marquis de Custine said in 1839, "is neither Europe nor Asia; it is Russia—and it is Russia's heart."

The selections, which are arranged geographically, come from many contemporary sources: novels, biographies, letters, poems, and diaries. Nearly half are devoted to the Kremlin; others cover Moscow beyond the Kremlin; areas outside of Moscow; and Muscovite life, customs and morals. Each section proceeds chronologically, beginning with legends about the founding of the Kremlin c. 1147 and ending with Lenin's triumphant arrival in 1918.

The fearsome reign of Ivan the Terrible; Peter the Great's bloody reprisals following the musketeers' riot in 1698; the burning of the the city and Napoleon's ignominious retreat in 1812; and the flourishing of art, theatre, and dance in the early twentieth century—these milestones and more make up the "tumultuous, often sanguinary, and always enthralling life of Moscow." And as Kelly says, a knowledge of the city's history lays the groundwork for appreciating its present:

It is no accident that Ivan the Terrible was one of Stalin's favorite models . . . or that Soviet schoolchildren are taught to regard Lermontov's Borodino *as the quintessence of patriotism. The exploration of the past provides unexpected ways to understanding today's Muscovite.*

(Atheneum, 1983, ISBN 0-689-70670-7, softcover, 328 pages, $9.95)

My Russia
Peter Ustinov

"I was born in London, and yet I was conceived in Leningrad, and let no one tell me this is without importance," says Peter Ustinov, a man whom millions of Americans honor as a brilliant playwright, author, actor, and director.

In this rather gentle history of his land of conception, Ustinov tries to give us "a detective story to the roots of a national character which often frightens and often mystifies, but the roots of which lie in the humanity and inhumanity which are common to all mankind."

Russia, you say, is a huge country, a sleeping giant. Not at all, says Ustinov. "People forget that Russia was once very small at a time when Poland and Lithuania were very large . . . She has been invaded far more often than she invaded, and lost far more sons and daughters on her own soil than she has lost sons on foreign fields."

Yes, but she is a predator, an aggressor. No more so than the free world, exclaims Ustinov, equating Soviet tanks in Budapest and Prague with American participation in Viet Nam and Kampuchea, Russian invasion of Afghanistan with the United States' "cantankerous and mischievous policies of Israel."

If statements such as these are going to upset you, you'd best avoid this book. At times Ustinov seems to bend quite far backwards in his efforts to be fair. Yet **My Russia**, interspersed with numerous pictures in both color and black-and-white, provides an easy-to-read version of a country's long and complicated history.

"No system is perfect," says Ustinov, "yet all peoples in a troubled world feel constrained at times to defend their system as though it is . . . Are we fundamentally so different from each other that we can afford to evoke the elements which divide us as an excuse for a hostility graver than mere disagreement?"

(Atlantic Monthly, 1983, ISBN 0-316-89052-9, hardcover, 224 pages, $19.95)

Portrait of the Soviet Union
Fitzroy Maclean

"Russia has two faces, an Asiatic face which looks always towards Europe, and a European face which looks always towards Asia," said Benjamin Disraeli. Here Fitzroy Maclean, long-time Sovietologist, paints a picture of both sides of the Soviet countenance.

Russia, he reminds us, is but one of fifteen different Soviet Socialist Republics, yet because it is European and because it is the largest republic, many Americans have but a hazy notion of the rest of this vast country. **Portrait of the Soviet Union**, a companion to Turner Broadcasting's seven-part television series, remedies this by exploring all of the Soviet Union, both geographically and culturally. Maclean traverses the nation that spreads into two continents, visiting the European cities of Moscow, Kiev, and Leningrad as well as the Asiatic ones of Tashkent, Irkutsk, and Vladivostok. His discussions range from architecture to religion, from daily lifestyles to natural wonders. A sprinkling of photos, both color and black-and-white, provide added interest.

And as Maclean examines the past and explains the present, he also tries to foresee the future for, as he quotes Russian revolutionary Alexander Ivanovich Herzen, through "achieving a greater awareness of the past, we clarify the present, digging deeper into the significance of what has gone before, we discover the meaning of the future; looking backwards, we move forwards."

(Holt, 1988, ISBN 0-8050-0891-8, hardcover, 230 pages, $23.95)

Pushkin House
Andrei Bitov

Pushkin House is not an easy novel. Even its author admits that ". . . on putting aside the novel, you might read a fresh or stale newspaper and suppose that what is happening now in the newspaper—and consequently, to some extent, in the world at large—is happening in the time of the novel. And, vice versa, on putting aside the newspaper and returning to the novel, you might suppose that you hadn't broke off reading the novel but had reread the introduction once more, in order to clarify a few trifling points about the author's intentions. Since we hope for this kind of effect, since we count on the inevitable collaboration and coauthorship of time and environment, there is much that we probably will not spell out at length or in detail, believing that all these things are mutually known, from the experience of author and reader."

On one level Andrei Bitov tells the story of Lyova Odoevtsev, a philologist who works at Pushkin House, a literary center in Leningrad, and whose daily existence is similar to that of the average Russian. But on a metaphorical level he inhabits the center of Russian literature, and here Bitov interjects both history and literature (alluding frequently to Pushkin, Dostoyevsky, and Tolstoy, among others).

Currently unpublishable in the Soviet Union, **Pushkin House** was translated into English in 1987 by Susan Brownsberger. Most readers would be well advised to read her "Afterword" before beginning the novel. "The Western reader does not really need to know Russian literature in order to follow the story and understand the deeper levels of **Pushkin House**," she says, "[but] the surface play of wit and irony . . . may be less accessible to Western readers." For that reason she includes a brief listing of relevant facts that serve to remind the reader of Russian literary and, to a lesser extent, political history.

Andrei Bitov has constructed a Russian Hall of Mirrors in which he fuses life and literature, fact and fiction. A journey through his maze may disorient the reader as reality and reflection intermingle, but the rewards for completion are, as Brownsberger says, "to experience the wild paradoxes lived by a contemporary Soviet intellectual [and] that experience is shared, in varying degree, by all thinking citizens of the modern world."

(Farrar, Straus and Giroux, 1987, ISBN 0-374-23934-7, hardcover, 372 pages, $22.50)

The Siberians
Farley Mowat

"The life is good out here. The people are the finest in the world . . . All that talk about the terrible hardship and isolation in Siberia was old woman's talk . . . On my first 'three-year holiday,' we went back to Leningrad and to the Black Sea . . . then, with the holiday only half spent, we returned to Siberia." So speaks Dmitri Maslov, a Soviet engineer who voluntarily moved from Leningrad to Siberia.

Most "English language sources" depict the Soviet arctic and subarctic as a vast wilderness of trackless forest and snow-covered tundra "inhabited mainly by ravening wolves and doomed political prisoners." Farley Mowat discovered otherwise. As he traveled across Soviet Siberia, from the Ural Mountains to the Sea of Okhotsk, from the Mongolian border to the Arctic Ocean he met the Siberians—reindeer herders, poets, dissidents—who welcomed him with mare's milk and vodka, good humor and love for their frigid homeland.

For more than thirty years Mowat has written of the Northern Lands with compassion and understanding. In fact, he has said of himself, "I am a Northers man . . . my chief concern is with the tales of men, and other animals, living under conditions of natural adversity." In **The Siberians** he shows that he is indeed a kindred spirit.

(Bantam, 1971, 1982, ISBN 0-553-24896-0, softcover, 286 pages, $3.95)

The Soviet Union Today: An Interpretive Guide
Edited by James Cracraft

"This is a book for anyone wanting to understand the Soviet Union today," promises James Cracraft, research fellow at the Russian Research Center, Harvard University. To this end he and twenty-nine other specialists write on their areas of expertise and provide a book that is "concerned less with 'covering' the subject than with responding to the questions most commonly asked of experts."

Divided into sections on history, politics, the armed forces, physical context, the economy, science and technology, culture and society, **The Soviet Union Today** is designed to flow chronologically and thematically from topic to topic, although each essay can stand on its own. Individual chapters investigate topics from the Lenin cult to architecture and urban planning, from military strategy in the nuclear age to the role of women. New chapters added for this revised and expanded edition discuss Soviet cinema, mass media, foreign trade, arms control, and the legal system. The resulting overview is thorough, readable, and stimulating.

"Understanding the Union of Soviet Socialist Republics, the biggest country in the world and one of its two most powerful, is no easy task," Cracraft says in a moment of understatement. Anyone who has ever wanted to pick the brains of leading Soviet experts now has their chance.

(University of Chicago, 1983, 1988, ISBN 0-226-11663-8, softcover, 382 pages, $12.50)

Two Lives, One Russia
Nicholas Daniloff

On August 24, 1986, the Russian agent Gennadi Zakharov was arrested in the United States. Nicholas Daniloff, completing a five-year stint in Moscow as correspondent for *U.S. News and World Report*, was wary, knowing that the KGB frequently made retaliatory arrests; still he was entirely unprepared when he found himself charged with espionage and taken to Lefortovo Prison. He later noted:

Had I been able to reflect clearly, I would have realized that my difficulties with the Soviet authorities did not begin that day, or even the week before . . . My troubles flowed from my Russian grandmother and from an antique iron ring, lined with gold, which my father wore on the fourth finger of his left hand . . . [from] Nicholas I's couriers seizing Alexander Frolov in February 1826 in the Ukrainian town of Zhitomir.

Two Lives, One Russia interweaves two intriguing and suspenseful tales, alternating between the contemporary story of Daniloff's arrest, imprisonment, and interrogation and that of the nineteenth-century Russia of Daniloff's ancestors, revealed as he describes the search for his family heritage. The dual stories illuminate the parallels, as well as the differences, between the two eras, resulting in a dramatic, compelling, and often chilling work. The experience left Daniloff wiser and sadder, but not bitter:

As for myself, my Lefortovo experience has not changed my views of the Soviet Union. The Soviet people are generous and talented and deserve a more responsive government than the one they have. I personally wish Mikhail Gorbachev success with his reforms . . .

This is a statement which even those of us who have never seen the inside of a Soviet prison can heartily agree.

(Houghton Mifflin, 1988, ISBN 0-395-44601-5, hardcover, 320 pages, $19.95)

USSR: From an Original Idea by Karl Marx
Marc Polonsky and Russell Taylor

"The artificial word *effektivy* [efficiency], considered to be both linguistically and conceptually German in origin, is associated with thrift and embryonic fascism, and is thus regarded with suspicion [in Russia]," explain authors Marc Polonsky and Russell Taylor. This, of course, makes it easier to understand the Soviet public transport system. Riding a Russian trolley or tram should be "at least a once-in-a-lifetime experience, especially for those without a first-hand acquaintanceship with the Black Hole of Calcutta," they say.

Polansky and Taylor are familiar with Russian transportation, having both lived in the Soviet Union and run an English travel company specializing in 'real life' tours to the USSR. Their book is a tongue-in-cheek guide to this country, one that teaches "basic survival skills," such as how to bribe your way into a restaurant or how to behave when visiting Lenin's mausoleum.

In the introduction the authors state that they portray "Soviets neither as SS-toting bogeymen, nor as lantern-jawed proletarians, but as human beings." It's sometimes difficult to decide if they like these human beings; their humor can become a bit heavy-handed. Yet their book does help to sort out a country that can seem "endearingly chaotic" and "utterly bewildering" to the unprepared visitor, and it does so with a sharp wit.

(Faber and Faber, 1986, ISBN 0-571-13842-X, softcover, 178 pages, $8.95)

Ustinov in Russia
Peter Ustinov

In 1985 the well-known actor Peter Ustinov obtained *carte blanche* to travel throughout Russia to film a documentary television series. This book chronicles his trip and displays more than a hundred vivid color photographs, taken by him and photographer John McGreevy.

Ustinov toured with an open mind and a keen eye and found that the spirit of *glasnost* predated Gorbachev:

> *During our expedition to Russia, which began before the arrival of Mr. Gorbachev, we shot 77 hours of film taken in various parts of the country. When we left the Soviet Union, the authorities did not ask to see one single foot of it. Out of courtesy we showed them a two-hour rough that we had cobbled together, but though they expressed polite interest they kept on looking at the time because they were busy officials with many more important matters to look into.*

He compares American and Russian cultures:

> The peoples in the United States are rather like the drinks in an American bar. The racial bottles are tipped into the cocktail shaker and something gaudy, mixed and surprising is produced . . . But in the Russian bar, every bottle is kept separate with its label firmly attached. There are the liquors of the Baltic states, the heavy wines of Georgia, the vodka from Moscow, and whatever fiery potions are brewed in Tashkent, Alma Ata, Irkutsk, or on the Siberian shores of the River Lena.

And he confutes some stereotypes. For instance, there are indeed lines and shortages in some parts of the country but in others, like Tbilsi, "there is everything in abundance, from fruit and flowers, to meat and groceries."

The book teems with historical notes, observations, philosophical comments, and thumbnail sketches of the people. Ustinov, a great proponent of person-to-person diplomacy, writes that "common humanity and good manners, if nothing else, suggest that it might be a better idea to bombard our neighbours with questions and intellectual curiosity rather than with nuclear missiles." His warm and entertaining book personifies his philosophy.

(Summit Books/Simon and Schuster, 1987, ISBN 0-671-65954-5, hardcover, oversized, $22.95)

A Vanished Present
Alexander Pasternak

A Vanished Present is difficult to classify. Is it history? Yes, as it evokes the bygone days just before and after the revolution. Is it literature? Yes, in that a goodly portion of it is about the childhood Alexander shared with brother Boris, the poet and author of *Dr. Zhivago*. And it is "architecture" since Alexander grew up to be a prominent architect whose descriptions of Russian streets and squares reflect a keen and a trained eye. In a lesser sense these memoirs also touch on art and music, for Alexander's father was the Impressionist painter Leonid Pasternak and his mother, Rosa Koffmann, was a concert pianist.

Alexander's niece, Ann Pasternak Slater, edited and translated the book. Her introductory protrait is revealing:

> *Alexander Pasternak was an enchanting man, with a mischievous slant to his sly greenish-blue eyes and wicked smile. He did everything with a neatness he must have inherited from his mother, quietly dapper at breakfast-time in his threadbare Muscovite clothes . . . The big board by the window which served as his desk was always kept clear, but for a few precious objects—an old majolica tile, picked up from the rubble of one of Moscow's many demolished churches; a plaster cast of a classic head; a little bronze statuette of a boy . . . All objects rescued from the old world; relics, I now see, reflecting the tastes of this memoir.*

This is a book warm with memories, rich with detailed recollections, and fascinating as a picture of one of Russia's most cultured families.

(Harcourt Brace Jovanovich, 1985, ISBN 0-15-193364-2, 240 pages, $17.95)

Where Nights Are Longest
Colin Thubron

In 1980 British writer Colin Thubron received Intourist permission to travel, alone and by car, throughout the western part of the Soviet Union. His ten-thousand-mile journey covered virtually all roads then accessible to tourists and took him to Moscow and Leningrad, to the Baltic and Black Seas, to Armenia and Kiev. Although he was technically allowed to travel without supervision, each evening when he arrived at his campsite, he found that he was expected—"and this foreknowledge struck me always with the unease of clairvoyance."

Yet his relative freedom gave him ample opportunity to talk with the people. He spoke, for instance, to Olga, a widow who "lived with a bored daughter in one of those faceless apartment blocks which ring the northern suburbs of Moscow." Olga's conversation was nervous, "as if I were posing her unspoken questions and embarrassments":

"I don't mean that I should like to live in Britain. Not at all. Your television's lovely, of course," Her toes wriggled in anguish. "But no, I wouldn't live there. It's too cold—the people, I mean." She looked faintly confused. "It's hard to talk. I can't say."

In Leningrad he met with a group of "callow men and soft-eyed girls" who distribute *samizdat* (underground) art and literature:

They lived in a garden of ideas, passions, possibilities still unfrustrated. They talked with all the brightness of their long, unknown futures . . . One man here was reading out some politically risqué poetry, another planning a dissident sculpture exhibition. The room vibrated with a half-adolescent excitement at the forbidden and the initiate. I felt afraid for them.

When it was time for Thubron to leave the Soviet Union, immigration officers inspected his luggage for over four hours; they summoned an interpreter to translate and explain his diary. "At last," says Thubron, "the shoulders of the immigration officer (if that is what he was) heaved with a kind of dejected relief . . . For a minute more he ruminated in silence, then a tiny resigned smile opened in his face, and he handed back to me the notes from which this book has been composed." We owe that immigration officer our thanks.

(Atlantic Monthly, 1984, ISBN 0-87113-167-6, softcover, 212 pages, $7.95)

Women and Russia
Edited by Tatyana Mamonova

"According to the mass media, everything in the Soviet Union is wonderful," says Vera Golubeva. "But people's expressions reveal worry, depression, or complete indifference... Women are particularly dissatisfied."

"Children's day care centers and nursery schools are the most destructive institutions in the U.S.S.R.'s health care system," says Natasha Maltseva. "Most of [the personnel] are guided by mercenary aims."

"Vera Golubeva" and "Natasha Maltseva" are pseudonyms. Indeed, of the twenty-seven women who contributed to this book, all but six use disguised names. "The continued harassment by the KGB of feminist activists in the Soviet Union has made secrecy necessary," says editor Tatyana Mamonova.

Mamonova's own story is illustrative. In 1979 she edited the first feminist underground publication in Russia, *Women and Russia: An Almanac to Women about Women*. There were ten copies. On December 10, 1979—Russian Human Rights Day—she was notified she would be arrested if a second issue appeared.

A second issue did appear, albeit under another name. Mamonova's home was watched; her mail and phone calls were intercepted. She and her husband were interrogated. But she was lucky. In August 1980 she managed to go to Vienna to confer with feminists from other countries. The resulting publicity, including a trip to the U.S. sponsored by *Ms.* magazine, provided her a bit of protection.

Kari Unksova was not as fortunate. A talented writer, she went into hiding after being sentenced to fifteen days' forced labor. Finally offered an exit visa, she was killed by a hit-and-run driver shortly before she was to leave the Soviet Union. It is clear Mamonova does not think her killing was an accident.

Women and Russia is an angry book; it is also a brave one. It deserves to be read by everyone who wants to understand the plight of women in today's Russia.

(Beacon, 1984, ISBN 0-8070-6709-1, softcover, 273 pages, $10.95)

ART AND ARCHITECTURE

Gold in Azure
William Craft Brumfield

Glittering gold stars on azure, onion-shaped domes typifies Russian architecture to many of us, but its entire spectrum from wooden churches to gilt-laden mosques embodies even greater richness. In this handsome volume we see the thousand-year panorama of Russian architecture—a discipline that, says William Brumfield, has been "suspended between art history and Russian studies." Here he singles it out, analyzing the history and design of hundreds of structures, interspersing the discussion with social history and illustrating it with eight photographs in full color and nearly three hundred in black-and-white.

He tells of the reign of Yaroslav the Wise and the extensive collection of Kievian mosaics that still survive in his Cathedral of Saint Sophia; of Novgorod which rose to artistic and architectural preeminence during the twelfth century and retained its status until the 1700s; and of Suzdal, now a museum of Russian architecture where tourists can stay in medieval monasteries.

He speaks too of Vladimir, whose founder also established a number of settlements—"among them a small fortified post called Moscow"; and finally he visits Saint Petersburg to explore both baroque architecture and the neoclassicism that Catherine the Great introduced in the late 1700s. Catherine, notes Brumfield, "possessed an abiding interest in architecture, but her tastes ran counter to the rococo fancies of the reign of her predecessor." She encouraged a more restrained style which persisted for nearly a hundred years until it was superseded by eclecticism. A chapter on twentieth century architecture rounds out the discussion and brings us up to date on *style moderne*, rationalism, constructivism, and functionalism.

Boris Pasternak wrote of the Russian "craving for the superlative." **Gold in Azure** both reflects and satisfies this craving. As readable as it is beautiful, its combination of substantial text and wonderful illustrations make it well worth the price.

(Godine, 1983, ISBN 0-87923-436-9, hardcover, oversized, 429 pages, $60.00)

A History of Russian Painting
Alan Bird

From the icons of earliest times to the mid-twentieth century, distinguished art historian Alan Bird presents a comprehensive look at the entire span of Russian painting. He leads us through the maze of artists, paintings, styles, and movements that characterized each successive era, presenting each in clear and succinct style.

Icons, he tells us, arose from the "craving by the ordinary people for an intimate and personal image." These images painted on wooden panels were believed to be imbued with miraculous powers and were not only hung in churches and homes, but on stable doors, well-heads, and at crossroads as well.

Although the characteristic Russian artform for centuries, icons dwindled in importance as foreign artists were atrracted in large numbers to the court of Peter the Great. These men strongly influenced Russian art and contributed to its dramatic flourishing; by the eighteenth century such Russian painters as Levitsky, Rokotov, and Borovikovsky were the equal of contemporary European artists.

Bird continues his narrative through an Academy revolt in the second half of the nineteenth century; the profusion of *fin-de-siècle* and early twentieth-century movements (Suprematists, Rayonists, Constructivists, Cubo-Futurists); the "proletarian episode" and Socialist realism; and ends with a look at Russian art of the 1950s and 60s. He emphasizes the artists and their work rather than general concepts and theories, and he depicts the artwork in more than 150 illustrations—sixteen of which are in color.

There is a growing "recognition that the artistic genius of Russia stands level with its triumphs in music and literature," says Bird, and his thorough history of its painting can only help to further this recognition.

(G. K. Hall, 1987, ISBN 0-8161-8911-0, hardcover, oversized, 303 pages, $50.00)

The Kremlin and Its Treasures
Irina Rodimzeva, et al.

Gold. It's stamped on the cover, glitters from the jacket, and nearly overwhelms on the inside pages. **The Kremlin and Its Treasures** is a sumptuous book, depicting the political and cultural center of the Soviet Union in opulent splendor.

Irina Rodimzeva, director of the Department of Museums in the Ministry for Culture of the USSR, together with internationally renowned photographer Nikolai Rachmanov and art historian Alfons Raimann, presents an overview of the architectural complex that represents six centuries of Russian history.

The book is divided into four sections: On the History of the Kremlin, On Cathedral Square, Palaces and Residences, and The Armory. The text is clear and direct and is accompanied by nearly three hundred photographs (almost all in color) that are startling in their brilliance.

Here are paintings from all the leading Russian art centers, icon paintings from Byzantium, masterpieces of Russian gold and silver jewelry, hunting weapons, armor, frescos, church vestments . . . In short, the Kremlin, in its architectural glory, houses some of the world's greatest art treasures, treasures which inspired the Executive Committee of Soviets, following the 1917 October Revolution, to exclaim:

Citizens! A gigantic inheritance has been left behind which now belongs to the entire people . . . Protect this inheritance . . . they are an expression of your and your ancestors' intellectual prowess . . . Protect monuments, buildings, objects, and documents from former times. All of these are your history and your pride. Remember that this is the basis upon which our new art shall flourish!

The Kremlin is impressive: its size, its grandeur, its importance. This book does it justice in all respects.

(Rizzoli, 1987, ISBN 0-8478-0856-4, hardcover, oversized, 356 pages, $75.00)

The Pure Spring: Craft and Craftsmen of the USSR
Alexander Milovsky

Bright spring colours are splashed about in whatever direction you care to look from Anna Bobyak's cottage windows . . . But the sudden coming of spring never catches Anna unaware. During the last few days she has gradually selected the largest and whitest eggs from her most prized layers, put bits of black beeswax taken from the hives in autumn into a tin, and assembled her special minature work tools—the tiny copper-foil funnels with wooden handles she uses for painting eggs.

The resulting *pisanki*—intricately painted Easter eggs—are the fragile bearers of a heavy load of folklore and symbolism. The egg itself represents the regeneration of spring, and each stylized design is fraught with its own meaning: an ear of corn symbolizes a good harvest; a netting pattern foretells a bountiful catch of fish. All these are expressed with painstaking craftsmanship passed down from mother to daughter. The repetitive process of drawing designs in wax, then dipping the egg in baths of progressively darker dyes can take several hours for each egg, says Anna, but the basket of rainbow-hued eggs eloquently affirms that it is time well spent.

Alexander Milovsky celebrates the U.S.S.R.'s rich vein of folk art by taking the crafts one by one and, as in the case of the *pisanki*, talking with artists to learn the background and technique of their craft. Stone and wood carving, pottery, yurt-building, embroidery, knitting, and weaving are just a few of the art forms he explores, letting a generous sprinkling of color photographs illustrate the stories that he and the craftspeople tell.

By juxtaposing the history, mythology, and symbolism of the arts with their technical aspects and the lives of the artists who create them, Milovsky offers a well-rounded and satisfying view of these dwindling folk arts. And, although machines now fill many of the artists' functions, Milovsky observes that "there are still plenty of places in the multinational Soviet Union, in the North or Central Asia, the Baltic republics, the Caucasus, Siberia, and the Carpathian Mountains where old folk arts and crafts have kept their secrets and succeeded in competing with much cheaper and more accessible mass-produced goods."

(Raduga Publishers, Moscow, from Imported Publications, 1987, ISBN 0-8285-3590-6, hardcover, 255 pages, $13.95)

CUISINE

The Art of Russian Cuisine
Anne Volokh

"To paraphrase a well-known biblical truism, there is a time to count calories and a time to make *bliny*," declares *Izvestia*'s former food editor Anne Volokh as she launches into an explanation of the appropriate time for bliny (February, during the festival of *Maslenitsa*), their proper size ("medium-thin pancakes, that is, slightly thicker than crêpes but thinner than ordinary breakfast pancakes") and the fine points of serving them ("some American cookbooks and restaurants suggest serving bliny with caviar *and* sour cream. In Russia this combination would be as appealing as shrimp with caramel custard!")

With her book at hand, you can make not only bliny but also fragrant dark rye breads, savory meat pies such as *pirozhki*, and hearty soups like Ukrainian *borscht* ("so thick with vegetables that . . . a wooden spoon will stand upright when stuck into the pot"). And along with the culinary expertise comes a wealth of anecdotes that offer insights into the culture that produced the cuisine.

For instance, she offers a possible explanation for the elaborate *zakuski* (appetizer) ceremony—"the equivalent of a whole first movement in a formal Russian dinner." Country estates, she suggests, were so far apart that guests, "who had been traveling on poor roads, often in cold weather, were first treated to a number of hors d'oeuvre, which did not take long to make, while they waited for dinner to be prepared." She adds, however, that "a cynical observer may think the bounty of *zakuski* is merely a pretext for drinking vodka." And speaking of the national beverage, she claims that the Polar Star is the preferred Russian cocktail: "take ½ glass of vodka, add another ½ glass of vodka, and stir thoroughly."

Volokh's book is a perfectly blended stew including more than five hundred tested recipes with clear directions and explanations of cooking techniques. She offers serving suggestions, menus for every occasion, and information on where to get unusual ingredients. Her wit and humor season the concoction perfectly and result in an exemplary feast.

(Macmillan, 1983, ISBN 0-02-622090-3, hardcover, 632 pages, $24.95)

HISTORY

A History of Russia
Nicholas V. Riasanovsky

It would seem that in many respects the Soviet Union is neither a stable . . . nor a happy country. Moreover, its economy and society continue to evolve. Profound alterations in the very foundations of the Soviet system appear, therefore, likely in the not-too-distant-future. But the problem of change in the Soviet Union has quite a special character.

So that we may better understand that special character and what the future might hold for Russia, eminent Russian historian Nicholas Riasanovsky here presents a penetrating investigation of its past.

After a brief overview of Russia's geography and pre-history, he divides his examination into five parts, beginning with Kievan Russia. This era started with the ninth-century arrival of the Scandinavian Rus tribe (from whom the country derived its name) and concluded with the fall of Kiev to the Mongols in 1240. It was followed by "Appanage" Russia, a time when the land was parceled into appanages (the separate holdings of individual princes). "Subdivision followed upon subdivision, destroying the tenuous political unity of the land," writes Riasanovsky, who marks the end of this period with the accession of Ivan the Terrible in 1533. The next era, Muscovite Russia, lasted until Peter the Great ushered in Imperial Russia, which in turn was followed by the Revolutions of 1917 and Soviet Russia. Riasanovsky continues his story to the death of Leonid Brezhnev in 1982.

Each section provides a well-rounded view of political, economic and social history, drawing on quotations from a number of historical figures and Russian scholars who both support and contradict the author's opinions. Thirty maps, more than fifty black-and-white photographs, charts of Russian rulers and political subdivisions, and tables of statistics combine with the text to offer an authoritative look at Russian history.

(Oxford, 1963, 1984, ISBN 0-19-503361-2, hardcover, 695 pages, $29.95)

Nicholas and Alexandra
Peter the Great
Robert K. Massie

Two monumental works—**Nicholas and Alexandra**, which was published in 1967, and **Peter the Great**, which appeared thirteen years later—have irrevocably linked the name of Robert K. Massie with the subject of Russian history. A history student at both Yale and Oxford and later a writer for several major magazines, Massie became interested in Russia because of an unfortunate personal trauma: his oldest child, Bobby, was born with hemophilia.

"For Bobby, what could I do?" writes the distraught father in *Journey*, a book he co-authored with his wife Suzanne. "I was helpless . . . The only thing I could do was to write about it." And so he wrote an article about hemophilia for *The Saturday Evening Post* and included a brief sketch on "The Most Famous Hemophiliac," Tsarevich Alexis, heir-apparent of Nicholas II, the last Tsar of Russia. As it turned out, *The Post* never printed his portrait of Alexis, but Massie was hooked. For three years he researched, wrote, edited, and rewrote. The resulting book became a bestseller, setting forth the history of early twentieth-century Russia in human terms.

The illness of young Alexis, says Massie, indirectly brought down the Romanov dynasty and profoundly altered the course of Russian history. "In an effort to deal with the agonies hemophilia inflicted on her son, [Empress Alexandra] turned to Gregory Rasputin, the remarkable Siberian mystagogue," he writes in his introduction. "Thereafter, Rasputin's presence near the throne—his influence on the Empress and, through her, on the government of Russia—brought about or at least helped to speed the fall of the dynasty."

Several years later Robert, still under the spell of Russia, probed more distant history and recreated the world of Tsar Peter I ("the Great") who ruled from 1682-1725. Peter was ferocious, tender, zealous, and imperial. He was, says Massie, " a force of nature, and perhaps for this reason no final judgment will ever be delivered. How does one judge the endless roll of the ocean or the mighty power of the whirlwind?"

Yet Massie tries—not to judge, perhaps, but to explain—and he succeeds admirably. His book won a Pulitzer Prize and as with its predecessor, **Peter the Great** gives a panoramic sweep of Russia at a critical point in her development.

Russia may be, as Winston Churchill once said, "a riddle wrapped in a mystery inside an enigma," but Massie unravels many of the layers in his two epics on the Russian past.

(Nicholas and Alexandra: Dell, 1985, ISBN 0-440-36358-6, softcover, 624 pages, $6.95; Peter the Great: Ballantine, 1980, ISBN 0-345-33619-4, softcover, 939 pages, $5.95)

The Shadow of the Winter Palace
Edward Crankshaw

The day was December 14, 1825; the place, St. Petersburg, Russia; the event, the accession of Tsar Nicholas I. Three thousand revolutionaries gathered in the Senate Square—"firing, sporadically, loosely, but dangerously." The heartfelt but disorganized Decembrist uprising ended quickly, an ill-fated, bloody failure—but it marked the first step down the long road toward the Revolution of 1917.

[The Decembrist attack] *was the first truly political movement ever to be directed against the established system. Tsars had been struck down before . . . but always in the course of palace revolutions, designed to replace the reigning sovereign with another. Peasant revolts there had been in plenty . . . but always blind convulsions of rage by downtrodden slaves who had been driven too hard. In these there was never any popular movement against the Tsar.*

Journalist Edward Crankshaw's riveting account analyzes the accomplishments and the decline of the Romanovs throughout the reign of Nicholas I as well as those of Alexander II and III and Nicholas II. He presents military, economic, and social aspects of the period, giving a thorough picture of, as the subtitle states, "Russia's drift to revolution." A chronological table sets the events into the perspective of both political and cultural developments in other parts of the world.

Crankshaw concludes that "Imperial Russia simply rotted away from the centre outwards until the shell fell in." His colorful cast of characters and unfailing sense of drama portray this decay and foreshadow the future soviet state.

(Penguin, 1976, 1978, ISBN 0-670-004622-4, softcover, 429 pages, $5.95)

The Tolstoys: Twenty-four Generations of Russian History
Nikolai Tolstoy

Like an epic Russian novel, this book sweeps through four centuries of history, giving the reader some of everything—romance, violence, sex, suspense, laughter, and tears. Nikolai Tolstoy chronicles his family's past vividly, drawing from an enormous wealth of family and historical records and illustrating it with portraits that help identify the enormous cast of characters.

For most Americans the best-known Tolstoy was Count Lev Nikolaevich Tolstoy, otherwise known as Leo Tolstoy, the author of *War and Peace*. Yet his relatives were equally interesting. In the early eighteenth century the Tsarevich Alexei "cursed Tolstoy and all his house to the twenty-fifth generation, and foretold that each of those generations would produce men of pre-eminent ability—but also mad and witless individuals."

Although the family is now scattered throughout the world, the Tolstoys were outstanding personages, each generation supplying a key figure in some phase of Russian life—politics, literature, the military. They were passionate, eccentric and fascinating; and through them we can see the panorama of Russian history.

(Morrow, 1983, ISBN 0-688-06674-7, softcover, 368 pages, $10.95)

NATURE

The Natural History of the USSR
Algirdas Knystautas

The Soviet Union accounts for one-sixth of the world's land mass; it straddles two-thirds of the globe and occupies 8.5 million square miles. Professor V. E. Flint, eminent ornithologist and conservationist, reminds us in his foreword to this beautiful book: "When the inhabitants of Moscow and Leningrad are about to eat breakfast, their fellow countrymen on the Chukotka Peninsula are already getting ready for bed. When in the south they are beginning to harvest the wheat, in the north the ground is still snow-covered and there are blizzards blowing." It's no wonder the Soviet Union is home to such rich variety of animal and plant life.

In clear, readable text and 275 superb color photographs **The Natural History of the USSR** provides a wonderful overview of its vast subject. Algirdas Knystautas, freelance writer and photographer who specializes in natural history and conservation, begins with a look at the country's geography and climate and the evolution of its wildlife. In the second chapter he discusses the distribution of flora and fauna; and in the third he explores conservation, a topic of great concern as many of the U.S.S.R.'s animal and plant species are rare or endangered. The rest of the book is devoted to a region-by-region survey of vegetation and wildlife, showing in text and illustration the terrain and its inhabitants.

From the Horsfield's Tortoise patiently crossing a sand dune in the Tau-Kum Desert to the huge and fearsome Siberian Tiger, from the thick conifer forests of the Taiga to the alpine meadows of the Ural Mountains, this comprehensive study covers the entire range of nature. The book is an impressive accomplishment, beautiful and informative; moreover it is an inspiration to visit these wonders first-hand.

(McGraw-Hill, 1987, ISBN 0-07-035409-X, hardcover, oversized, 224 pages, $29.95)

PERFORMING ARTS

The Birth of the Ballets-Russes
Prince Peter Lieven

The ghosts of Nijinsky, Stravinsky, Diaghileff, Pavlova, and Karsavina dance stunningly through the pages of this captivating history of the Ballets-Russes. Prince Peter Lieven, who witnessed the company's founding and growth and who knew its stars personally, choreographs an informative and entertaining narrative that begins in Paris in 1909 with a performance by an unpretentious Russian ballet troupe led by Serge Diaghileff:

> *If you meet anyone who remembers the Paris season of 1909, the talk will inevitably centre round the ballet performances, and not the operas, which are scarcely remembered. Even* Prince Igor *is memorable only for its "Polovetz" dances . . . Diaghileff and his friends found their true vocation, and their future was decided by this season.*

Each year saw increased acclaim for the troupe, which staged such works as Stravinsky's *Firebird, Petrushka,* and the *Rite of Spring,* in which Nijinsky achieved his world-famous gravity-defying leaps. The revolutionary composition, however, was so shocking that the audience lost its aplomb:

> *Almost from the first notes of the music, hissing and protests were heard and the noise, the shouting and vituperation did not cease for a single moment during the whole of the half-hour performance. Members of the audience jumped on their seats and yelled; there was almost a free fight . . . Even the orchestra could not be heard above the noise.*

Lieven offers both a front row center view of the performances and a fascinating backstage peep into the lives of the performers: their scandals, feuds, struggles, and triumphs. He muses, "Will there be found in this book even a few words which will bring to life before the young reader some of the romanticism of those long dead years?" He needn't have been concerned; in his prose and a charming collection of black-and-white photographs and drawings, all the famous artists pirouette brilliantly across history's stage.

(Dover, 1973, ISBN 0-486-22962-9, softcover, 377 pages, $6.95)

The New Grove Russian Masters: Volume I
David Brown, et al.
The New Grove Russian Masters: Volume II
Gerald Abraham, et al.

In the middle years of the nineteenth century Mikhail Ivanovich Glinka founded the great tradition of Russian music with his "bold and original concepts of musical language and form," states musicologist David Brown. Glinka exerted a strong influence on Mily Balakirev, who in turn was mentor to Alexander Borodin and Modest Mussorgsky. These four distinguished musicians, along with the preeminent Pyotr Il'yich Tchaikovsky (who, although "standing outside the nationalist circle of composers around Balakirev . . . nevertheless dominates 19th-century Russian music as its greatest talent") are portrayed in Volume I of **The New Grove Russian Masters**.

Volume II steps into the twentieth century, beginning with renowned orchestrator Nicolai Rimsky-Korsakov. The authors go on to discuss the mysterious Aleksandr Skryabin and the moody Sergei Rakhmaninov, musical theater maestro Sergei Prokofiev and virtuoso symphonist Dmitri Shostakovich.

Both books were adapted from *The New Grove Dictionary of Music and Musicians* and the entries enlarged and updated for this **Masters** series. They are basically reference works, confining their information to factual material—a brief biography and discussion of style, major works, and influence—rather than critical analysis. There is also a comprehensive worklist and extensive bibliography for each composer. Brief yet complete and authoritative, this pair of books highlights the brightest stars in the Russian musical firmament over the past two centuries.

(Norton, 1980, 1986, softcover, 260 pages, $9.95 each; Vol. I: ISBN 0-393-30102-8; Vol. II: ISBN 0-393-30103-6)

Red and Hot: The Fate of Jazz in the Soviet Union
S. Frederick Starr

S. Frederick Starr had two major interests: the Soviet Union and jazz. As an associate of the Kennan Institute for Advanced Russian Studies and a professional jazz musician, he was knowledgeable on both subjects; but for years he could see no connection between the two. After all, didn't the Russians consider jazz to be a "particularly decadent manifestation of dying capitalism?"

Fortunately, through interviews with colleagues, musicians, and friends on both sides of the Iron Curtain, Starr overcame his block and was able to write **Red and Hot**, the story of jazz under the Commissars.

"There's nothing quite like [it]," says Harrison Salisbury. ". . . Starr's scholarship is impeccable and the story he puts together of the efforts of Stalin and his heirs to keep the Russians from substituting boogie-woogie and hard rock for the melancholy strains of the Volga Boatman is a minor epic."

Starr begins in 1917 and carries his tale of the Russian infatuation with jazz up to the present day. He shows through it all that the Russian people are not quite the docile and malleable folk that Americans often believe them to be, and their government is not quite as successfully organized and capable of molding popular tastes as it pretends it is.

"The present young adult generation is the first in Soviet history to share fully in European and American popular culture. When, in the future, members of this generation gather together to reminisce about their youth, they will dredge up many of the same 'golden oldies' that would come to mind at a similar session in Hamburg, Lyons, Birmingham, or Milwaukee," concludes Starr. Perhaps in jazz, of all things, lies the foundation for better communication and understanding.

(Limelight Editions/Harper and Row, 1985, ISBN 0-87910-026-5, softcover, 368 pages, $9.95)

YOUNG PEOPLE'S BOOKS

Count Your Way Through Russia
Jim Haskins
For ages six to ten

Count Your Way Through Russia imparts bits of Russian lore in counting-book format via words by Jim Haskins and illustrations by Vera Mednikov. Together they show and tell, for instance, that "a Russian sleigh drawn by three horses that are side by side is called a *troika*, and in the Soviet Union a three-part form of government is also known as a *troika*," or "it takes **five** people to dance the *Pereplyas*, a popular folk dance."

Each number appears in numeric form and in the Cyrillic alphabet, along with its pronunciation. Although the format appears designed to appeal to the young child just learning to count, the text is sophisticated enough to interest the American counterpart of the young Russian who "at the age of **ten** . . . may join the Young Pioneers, a youth organization that offers recreational activities and encourages patriotism."

(Carolrhoda, 1987, ISBN 0-87614-303-6, hardcover, 24 pages, $10.95)

Siberia
Madelyn Klein Anderson
For ages eleven and over

Siberia, says Madelyn Anderson, is "far more than a place—it is a state of mind." Even as a place, however, it is difficult to define. It is not one of the U.S.S.R.'s fifteen Republics or any other political or administrative entity. By general agreement it comprises most of the Asian portion of the Soviet Union—and its name is synonymous with barren wasteland, with prison camps and gulags.

The history of Siberia is one of conflict and strife. Genghis Khan and his Mongol tribesmen "thundered out of Siberia to take on half the known world." Cossack raiders terrorized the countryside, Ivan the Terrible annexed Siberia and first used it as a place of exile, wars were waged over trade and railroad rights-of-way. And Lenin and Stalin, both in Siberian exile themselves at various times in their lives, formed the infamous "corrective labor camps" for dissidents on the frozen tundra.

Yet its grim history isn't Siberia's whole story. This vast area is rich in natural resources: rivers that produce hydroelectric power, minerals so plentiful that generations of Soviet school children have joked that "if you are asked to name the source of any mineral, always answer 'the Urals,' for it's almost sure to be there," and billions of acres of agricultrual and grazing land. Today's Russian leaders are concerned with developing this area so that it can realize its potential as well as increase their Pacific military presence. And tourism is encouraged, too; visitors can ride the Trans-Siberian railway to Lake Baikal to view the only fresh-water seals in the world and Russian bears fishing through holes cut in the ice by sympathetic humans.

"Every leader of the Soviet Union has promised great things for Siberia—one day," writes Anderson. "Perhaps . . . Mikhail Gorbachev, and his policy of 'glasnost' . . . will make today that day. Or tomorrow."

(Dodd, Mead, 1987, ISBN 0-396-08662-4, hardcover, 148 pages, $13.95)

The Soviet Union: The World's Largest Country
John Gillies
For ages ten to thirteen

Just how large is the Soviet Union? John Gillies puts it into perspective when he writes:

Let's say an Estonian student is finishing breakfast in Tallinn, getting ready to go to school. Tallinn is near the Baltic Sea, just across from Sweden. At the same time, one of her friends, in Providenya, just across from Alaska, would be putting away the supper dishes and ready to do some homework. To visit her friend, the Estonian student would have to cross eleven different time zones.

He continues to explain about the geography and people of the U.S.S.R., its history and folktales, family life, holiday celebrations, schools and sports. He tells why the most important holiday, The Great October Revolution Day, is celebrated in November (because of a change from Julian to Gregorian Calendar); how to make *borscht* (a beet or vegetable soup) and *kugel* (a potato dish) and why "Red" is sometimes used to refer to Russia (the Russian word for "beautiful," *krasnaya*, also means "red").

The book is well illustrated with color and black-and-white photographs that show that the Soviet Union is as old as the Kremlin and as current as cosmonaut Yuri Gagarin. A map, "Fast Facts," and such aids as a glossary and the Cyrillic alphabet offer additional information about this giant of a country.

(Dillon, 1985, ISBN 0-87518-290-9, hardcover, 160 pages, $12.95)

TITLE INDEX

African in Greenland, An, 219
Afternoon Tea Book, The, 32
Alexander's Path, 281
Alhambra, The, 146
All-Italy, 166
Ancient Greek, The, 282
Anti-Soviet Soviet Union, 290
Any Four Women Could Rob the Bank of Italy, 166
Apple's Europe: An Uncommon Guide, 2
Archaeology of Greece, The, 276
Architectural History of Venice, The, 180
Argyle, 80
Art of Russian Cuisine, The, 309
Art Works Itself into a Region, 119
At Home in Scotland, 68
Athenian Agora, The, 276
Atlas of the Greek World, 266
Aurora Borealis, 232

Ballet Shoes, 53
Baron Philippe, 110
Bauhaus, 203
Before the Deluge, 207
Belfast Diary, 84
Berlin Stories, The, 207
Best of Irish Wit and Wisdom, 84
Best of James Herriot, The, 16
Between Meals, 123
Birth of France, The, 127
Birth of the Ballet-Russes, The, 313
Bitter Lemons, 266
Black Lamb and Grey Falcon, 248
Blood of Spain, 159
Blue Trout and Black Truffles, 124
Book of the Medieval Knight, The, 11
Born Guilty, 198
Boy Who Held Back the Sea, 245
Brit-Think, Ameri-Think, 17
British Art Since 1900, 28
British Cookery, 33
British Design Since 1880, 29
Budapest, 249
Burn, The, 291

Castle, 80
Castles in Spain, 154
Castles of Ireland, 93
Cathedral: The Story of Its Construction, 141
Chambers Guide to Traditional Crafts of Scotland, 69
Chateau, The, 111
Churches of Portugal, 155
City as a Work of Art: London, Paris, Vienna, The, 2

City: A Story of Roman Planning and Construction, 193
Classic Art, 181
Classic Scandinavian Cooking, 228
Coasting: A Private Voyage, 18
Cogs in the Wheel, 292
Colossus of Maroussi, 267
Concise History of Irish Art, A, 94
Concise History of Scotland, 75
Confessions of a Concierge, 128
Contemporary Irish Art, 95
Contemporary Polish Folk Artists, 256
Contentious French, 129
Count Your Way Through Russia, 315
Country Diary of an Edwardian Lady, The, 48
Country House Garden, 48
Country Manors of Portugal, 155
Course of French History, The, 129
Crazy Years, The, 130
Crete: Its Past, Present & People, 268
Crofter and the Laird, The, 58
Cry Hungary!, 258
Cuckoo Clock, The, 208
Cut & Assemble a Medieval Castle, 80

D.H. Lawrence Album, A, 42
Daily Life in Johnson's London, 37
Dangerous Summer, The, 146
Decorative Arts of Sweden, The, 221
Deep into Mani, 268
Dickens's England, 43
Dining in France, 125
Discovering London, 54
Discovering Scotland, 81
Discovering Shakespeare Country, 54
Discovering the Tower of London, 54
Discovery of King Arthur, The, 35
Distant Mirror, A, 131
Don't Say a Word, 209
DramaContemporary: Czechoslovakia, 263
DramaContemporary: France, 137
DramaContemporary: Spain, 161
Dreams and Delusions, 198
Druids, The, 24
Dublin, 101
Dutch Painting, 239

Edinburgh, 75
Edinburgh Portraits, 76
Eleni, 277
Embarrassment of Riches, The, 240
England of William Shakespeare, The, 44
English Architecture: A Concise History, 29
English Channel, The, 19
English Painting: A Concise History, 30

Title Index

English Style, 30
Enigma of Loch Ness, The, 58
Eskimo Family, An, 233
Europe 101, 4
Europe: A Tapestry of Nations, 3
Europeans, The, 4
Everyday Story, An, 214
Exploits of Don Quixote, 163

Faber Guide to Twentieth Century Architecture, The, 10
Fabled Shore, 147
Fairy & Folk Tales of Ireland, 100
Family in France, A, 141
Family in Ireland, A, 107
Family in Italy, A, 194
Family in West Germany, A, 210
Farewell Spain, 148
Fellow Travelers, 292
Fin-de-Siecle Vienna, 241
Finland in the Twentieth Century, 215
First Polka, The, 259
Florence: A Traveller's Companion, 167
Florence: The City and Its Art, 181
Folies Bergère, The, 138
Folk Arts of Norway, The, 222
Folk Heroes of Britain, 36
Folktales of France, 126
Folktales of Germany, 205
Folktales of Norway, 229
Food of Portugal, The, 157
Foods of Italy, 182
Footsteps: Adventures of a Romantic Biographer, 5
France High-Tech, 111
France: The Crossroads of Europe, 142
French Cinema, 139
French Style, 120
French, The, 112
From the Yaroslavsky Station, 293
Frozen Image, The, 223

Galina, 294
Gardens of Ireland, The, 105
Gardens of Provence and the French Riviera, 136
Gardens of the Italian Villas, 190
German Architecture and the Classical Ideal, 203
German Expressionist Painting, 204
German Folk Art, 204
Germans, The, 199
Germany and the Germans, 200
Germany Today, 201
Germany: Two Nations, One Heritage, 210
Glasgow, 77
God's Acre, 49
Goddesses and Gods of Old Europe, 262

Gold in Azure, 305
Golden Century of Italian Opera, The, 191
Gourmet's Tour of Italy, The, 184
Great Cat Massacre, 131
Great New British Cooking, 33
Great Theatres of London, The, 51
Greek and Roman Life, 278
Greek Islands, The, 269
Greek Myths, 287
Greek Treasure, The, 278
Guns of August, The, 11
Gypsy Folk Tales, 73

Handbook of Greek Art, 280
Harrods Book of Traditional English Cookery, 34
Haunted England, 36
Heidi's Alp, 6
Hellas, 270
Hill Towns of Italy, The, 168
Historic Architecture of Wales, The, 70
History of London, A, 38
History of Russia, A, 310
History of Russian Painting, A, 305
History of Scandinavia, A, 229
History of the Salzburg Festival, A, 243
History of the Vikings, A, 230
Homage to Catalonia, 159
Horse of Pride, The, 118
House of Medici, The, 186
House that Giacomo Built, The, 177
Houses of Ireland, The, 96
How Green Was My Valley, 59

Iberia, 149
Ibsen's Drama, 233
Ibsen's Forsaken Merman, 233
Iceland Breakthrough, 215
If You Didn't Have Me, 234
Illustrated Counties of England, The, 20
Illustrated Handbook of Vernacular Architecture, 31
Illustrated History of England, An, 39
Impressionists at First Hand, 120
In Search of Ireland, 85
In Search of Melancholy Baby, 291
In Search of Modern Ireland, 85
In Search of the Trojan War, 279
In the Footsteps of Johnson and Boswell, 60
Inspector Maigret Stories, 112
Ireland, 86
Ireland's Traditional Crafts, 96
Ireland: A Concise History, 102
Ireland: Land of Mist and Magic, 107
Irish Country Cooking, 98
Irish Life and Traditions, 87
Irish Spinning, Dyeing and Weaving, 97
Irish Traditional Music, 106

Title Index

Island, 61
Island of Crimea, The, 291
Issa Valley, The, 249
Istanbul: A Travellers' Companion, 271
Italian Film in the Light of Neorealism, 193
Italian Folktales, 185
Italian Hours, 169
Italian Journey, 170
Italian Labyrinth, 171
Italians, The, 172
Italy: Balanced on the Edge of Time, 194

John Prebble's Scotland, 62
Journey to Kars, 250
Joyce of Cooking, The, 99

Kinkell, 71
Klass, 295
Knowth, 91
Kremlin and Its Treasures, The, 306
Kristin Lavransdatter, 231

Land Without Justice, 251
Last Kings of Thule, The, 220
Last of the Wine, The, 283
Learning to Dream, 51
Leopard, The, 187
Letters Written During a Short Residence, 216
Linnea in Monet's Garden, 142
Little Tour in France, A, 114
Living Isles, The, 50
Living Past of Greece, The, 284
Loch Ness Mystery Solved, The, 58
Louis XIV's Versailles, 121

Mackintosh Architecture, 72
Manor Houses and Castles of Sweden, 223
Matador, 150
Matter of Wales, The, 62
Mean Feat, 7
Memed, My Hawk, 272
Memories of Mistresses, 172
Mermaids of Chenonceaux, The, 8
Modern Austria, 242
Modern Greece, 284
Modern Norwegian Architecture, 224
Mont Saint Michel and Chartres, 122
Montaillou: The Promised Land of Error, 132
More Myterious Wales, 74
Moscow: A Travellers' Companion, 295
Mute Stones Speak, The, 178
My Family and Other Animals, 273
My Russia, 296
My Small Country Living, 78

Nan, 92
Natural History of the USSR, 312

New Grove Russian Masters, Vol. I, 314
New Grove Russian Masters, Vol. II, 314
New Grove Twentieth-Century English Masters, 52
New Grove Twentieth-Century French Masters, 140
Nicholas and Alexandra, 310
No Country For Young Men, 87
No. 10 Downing Street, 39
Nothing Happens in Carmincross, 88
Now I Remember, 40

O Come Ye Back to Ireland, 89
Of Danish Ways, 217
Of Dutch Ways, 238
Of Finnish Ways, 217
Of Norwegian Ways, 217
Of Swedish Ways, 217
Old Lars, 235
Old Regime and the French Revolution, The, 133
On Living in an Old Country, 21
On Persephone's Island, 173
100 Irish Ballads, 106
One Summer at Grandmother's House, 143
Out of the Past, 162

Painted in Blood: Understanding Europeans, 9
Painting in Scotland, 72
Panther Book of Scottish Short Stories, The, 63
Paris Arts on the Seine, 123
Paris: A Literary Companion, 134
Paris: The Musical Kaleidoscope, 139
Parthenon and Its Sculptures, The, 280
Peig, 92
Permanent Parisians, 114
Peter the Great, 310
Pillar of the Sky, 25
Place de la Concorde Suisse, La, 238
Pleasures of the Belle Epoque, 134
Poet's Bazaar, A, 273
Poland, 263
Poland: Land of Freedom Fighters, 259
Poland Under Black Light, 251
Portrait of the Soviet Union, 297
Prehistoric Avebury, 25
Private Poland, The, 252
Proud Tower, The, 11
Pure Spring, The, 308
Pushkin House, 298

Radiant Way, The, 22
Red and Hot, 315
Red Balloon, The, 143
Red Doll, 150
Rise and Fall, 260
Road Wet, the Wind Close, The, 102

Title Index

Robin Hood: His Life and Legend, 54
Romans, The, 188
Rome: The Biography of a City, 188
Round Ireland in Low Gear, 89
Runes, 221

Sarum, 41
Scandinavia: Living Design, 225
Scotland: An Anthology, 64
Scotland: Archaeology and Early History, 68
Scotland Forever Home, 65
Scotland's Story, 77
Scrambles Amongst the Alps, 242
Selling of the Royal Family, The, 22
September Light, 259
Shadow of a Bull, 164
Shadow of the Winter Palace, The, 311
Sherlock Holmes's London, 44
Siberia, 316
Siberians, The, 299
Sicilian Carousel, 173
Sicilian Lives, 179
Sixth Continent, The, 45
Social History of England, A, 41
South of France, The, 115
Soviet Union: The World's Largest Country, The, 317
Soviet Union Today, The, 299
Spain, 151
Spain, 152
Spain: A Shining New Democracy, 164
Spain: The Root and the Flower, 160
Spanish Folk Ceramics, 156
Spello, 179
Stave Churches in Norway, 225
Stealing from a Deep Place, 252
Stonehenge Complete, 27
Stones of Florence, The, 174
Story of a Castle, The, 55
Story of a Main Street, The, 55
Story of an English Village, The, 55
Stranger in Spain, A, 152
Sweden: A Good Life for All, 235
Sweden: the Middle Way on Trial, 218

Talking of Wales, 65
Taste of France, The, 125
Ten Days to Destiny, 285
There is Something Wonderful in the State of Denmark, 218
Through Parisian Eyes, 115
Time Without Bells, 259
Tolstoys, The, 311
Tower of London, The, 56
Traditional Dancing in Scotland, 79

Traveller in Italy, A, 175
Traveller in Rome, A, 175
Traveller in Southern Italy, A, 175
Travels with a Wildlife Artist, 286
Travels with My Sketchbook, 253
Treasures of Thrace, 256
Trinity, 103
Triumph of Light and Nature, The, 226
Tuscan Year, The, 185
Tuscany: An Anthology, 167
Twelve Caesars, The, 189
Two Lives, One Russia, 300
Two Towns in Provence, 116

Unbearable Lightness of Being, The, 254
USSR: From an Original Idea by Karl Marx, 301
Ustinov in Russia, 301

Vanished Present, A, 302
Velvet Prison, The, 257
Venice: A Thousand Years of Culture and Civilization, 182
Venice: Birth of a City, 195
Venice Preserved, 182
Very Best of British, The, 23
Vidal in Venice, 176
Vienna Opera, The, 244
Vienna's Golden Autumn, 241
Views from a French Farmhouse, 137
Views from a Tuscan Vineyard, 190
Viking Art, 227
Voice from Germany, A, 202
Voices East and West, 202
Voices of Northern Ireland, 108

Wales: The Imagined Nation, 66
Way of Hope, A, 255
Way to Greece, The, 274
Welsh Dylan, 67
When in France, 117
Where Nights Are Longest, 303
White Wall of Spain, 153
Who's Who in the Ancient World, 12
Wiltshire Village, 27
Wine and Food of Spain, The, 158
Women and Russia, 304
Wordsworth & the Lake District, 46
World of Odysseus, The, 282
Writer's Ireland, A, 104
Writers at Home, 47
Writings of German Composers, 207

Zorba the Greek, 275

AUTHOR INDEX

Abraham, Gerald, 314
Ackerman, John, 67
Acton, Harold, 167
Adams, Henry, 122
Adler, Ann, 210
Agnelli, Marella, 190
Akasofu, S.-I., 232
Aksyonov, Vassily, 291
Alexander, Bryan, 233
Alexander, Cherry, 233
Anderman, Janusz, 251
Andersen, Hans Christian, 273
Anderson, Jean, 157
Anderson, Madelyn Klein, 316
Apple, R.W., 2
Ardagh, John, 200
Armes, Roy, 139
Armstrong, Alison, 99
Arnold, Bruce, 94
Artigas, J. LL., 156
Ashe, Geoffrey, 35
Astair, Lesley, 68

Balderi, Susan, 142
Barber, Chris, 74
Barrett, Peter, 286
Barrett, Susan, 286
Barzini, Luigi, 4, 172
Bauer, Henry, 58
Beam, Alex, 292
Bergan, Ronald, 51
Berti, Luciano, 182
Bianco, Frank, 166
Bienek, Horst, 259
Biers, William R., 276
Binney, Marcus, 155
Binns, Ronald, 58
Bird, Alan, 305
Bishop, James, 20
Bitov, Andrei, 298
Björk, Christina, 142
Boardman, John, 280
Bowe, Patrick, 105
Breen, Christine, 89
Briggs, Asa, 41
Brody, Elaine, 139
Brown, David, 314
Brumfield, William Craft, 305
Brunskill, R.W., 31
Bugialli, Giuliano, 182
Bulow, Gerda, von, 256
Burke, John, 39
Burl, Aubrey, 25
Burn, A.R., 284
Burn, Mary, 284

Calder, Nigel, 19
Calvino, Italo, 185
Camp, John M., 276
Campbell, James, 63
Carson, Ciaran, 106
Carter, Jenny, 69
Castle, Charles, 138
Cebrián, Juan Luis, 150
Childs, Marquis W., 218
Chippindale, Christopher, 27
Christ, Karl, 188
Christiansen, Reidar, 229
Cliff, Stafford, 30,120
Colijn, Helen, 238
Conrad, Barnaby, 150
Conroy, John, 84
Cooper, Jackie, 72
Cornelisen, Ann, 166
Courtney, Nicholas, 24
Cracraft, James, 299
Craig, Gordon A., 199
Crankshaw, Edward, 311
Crawford, Peter, 50
Crow, John A., 160
Culbertson, Judi, 114
Curtis, Tony, 66

Daiches, David, 75, 77
Daniloff, Nicholas, 300
Darnton, Robert, 131
Davis, Michael, 44
de Azevedo, Carlos, 155
de Breffny, Brian, 93, 96
Denvir, Bernard, 120
Derry, T.K., 229
DiFranco, Anthony, 194
Djilas, Milovan, 251, 260
Dolci, Danilo, 179
Drabble, Margaret, 22
Durrell, Gerald, 273
Durrell, Lawrence, 173, 266, 269

Eliopoulos, Edward, 268
Eogan, George, 91

ffolliott, Rosemary, 96
Field, Carol, 168
Finlayson, Iain, 45
Finley, M.I., 282
Fisher, Leonard, 56
Fisher, M.F.K., 116
Fishlock, Trevor, 65
Flett, J.P., 79
Fox, Levi, 54
Fraser, Ronald, 159

Freson, Robert, 125
Frétard, Dominique, 119
Friedman, Martin, 223
Friedrich, Otto, 207
Fuchs, R.H., 239

Gadney, Reg, 258
Gage, Nicholas, 270, 277
Gallup, Stephen, 243
Garland, Nicholas, 253
Garmey, Jane, 33
Gaunt, William, 30
Gaynor, Elizabeth, 225
Gehrts, Barbara, 209
George, Michael, 105
Gillies, John, 317
Gimbutas, Marija, 262
Glazebrook, Phillip, 250
Gmelch, Sharon, 87, 92
Goethe, Johann Wolfgang, von, 170
Goetz-Stankiewicz, Marketa, 263
Goitia, Fernando Chueca, 154
Goodall, John, 55
Goulbert, Pierre, 129
Gray, Robert, 38
Greenhalgh, Peter, 268
Greenoak, Francesca, 49
Grigson, Jane, 33

Hall, Brian, 252
Hamilton, Ronald, 40
Hammond, Peter, 54
Hanson, Katherine, 214
Haraszti, Miklós, 257
Hardy, George, 42
Hardyment, Christina, 6
Harris, Nathaniel, 42
Harris, Paul, 64
Hartcup, Adeline, 179
Hartcup, John, 179
Haskins, Jim, 315
Haugen, Einar, 233
Haycroft, John, 171
Hazelton, Nika, 228
Hélias, Pierre-Jakez, 118
Heller, Mikhail, 292
Hemingway, Ernest, 146
Hermand, Jost, 207
Herriot, James, 16
Hibbert, Christopher, 186, 188
Hilling, John, 70
Holden, Edith, 48
Holland, Cecilia, 25
Holmes, Richard, 5
Holt, Marion Peter, 161
Hopewell, John, 162
Hopkins, Adam, 268
Hort, Lenny, 245

Howard, Deborah, 180
Hubley, John, 194
Hubley, Penny, 194
Hunter, Mark, 111

Irving, Washington, 146
Isherwood, Christopher, 207

Jackson-Stops, Gervase, 47, 48
Jacobsen, Per Schelde, 233
James, Henry, 114, 169
Jelavich, Barbara, 242
Jenkins, Ian, 278
Johnson, Hugh, 158
Johnson, James M., 184
Johnson, Paul, 102
Jones, Christopher, 39
Jones, Gwyn, 230
Josephs, Allen, 153

Kazantzakis, Nikos, 151, 275
Kelly, Laurence, 271, 295
Kemal, Yashar, 272
Kent, Neil, 226
Kiely, Benedict, 88
Kightly, Charles, 36
Kirby, D.G., 215
Kiriakopoulos, G.C., 285
Klindt-Jensen, Ole, 227
Knobel, Lance, 10
Knowles, Roderic, 95
Knystautas, Algirdas, 312
Kobayashi, T., 44
Kpomassie, Tété-Michel, 219
Kundera, Milan, 254

Ladurie, Emmanuel, 132
Laing, Gerald, 71
Lamorisse, A., 143
Lampedusa, Giuseppe, di, 187
Laqueur, Walter, 201
Laurence, Kelly, 271
Lauritzen, Peter, 182
Leavy, Barbara Fass, 233
Levi, Peter, 266
Lewis, Flora, 3
Liebling, A.J., 124
Lieven, Prince Peter, 313
Lindholm, Dan, 225
Littlewood, Ian, 134
Littlewood, Joan, 110
Llewellyn, Richard, 59
Lorenzen, Lilly, 217
Lynch, Tony, 43

Macaulay, David, 80, 141, 193
Macaulay, Rose, 147
MacCarthy, Fiona, 29

Author Index

MacGregor, Geddes, 65
McHaffie, I., 217
MacKendrick, Paul, 178
Maclean, Fitzroy, 75, 297
Macmillan, Duncan, 72
Magnus, Erica, 235
Mahder, William, 123
Malaurie, Jean, 220
Mamonova, Tatyana, 304
Manjón, Maite, 158
Marcus, Millicent, 193
Martine, Roddy, 68
Massie, Robert K., 310
Massignon, Geneviève, 126
Matheos, J.C., 156
Maxwell, William, 111
McCarthy, John, 84
McCarthy, Mary, 174
McCormick, Malachi, 98
McCracken, David, 46
McMullen, Jeanine, 78
McPhee, John, 58, 238
Melcher, Harold, 274
Melcher, Joan, 274
Melchior, Arne, 218
Mellinghoff, Tilman, 203
Melvin, Eric, 81
Meras, Phyllis, 8
Meyer, Carolyn, 108
Meyer, Kathleen, 107
Michener, James, 149, 259
Miles, Bernard, 54
Millau, Christian, 125
Miller, Henry, 267
Miller, Stuart, 9
Milosz, Czeslaw, 249
Milovsky, Alexander, 308
Mitchell, Lillias, 97
Montaufier, Poupa, 143
Moran, Tom, 107
More, Julian, 137, 190
Morris, Jan, 62, 152
Morton, H.V., 85, 152, 175
Mowat, Farley, 299
Moyes, John, 54
Murphy, Dervla, 86

Nectoux, Jean-Michel, 140
Newby, Eric, 89
Nielsen, M., 217
Nilsson, Ulf, 234
Niscemi, Maita, di, 223
Norbeg-Schulz, Christian, 224
Norton, Roger C., 202

O'Brien, Kate, 148
O'Faolain, Julia, 87
Olson, Donald, 2

Olsson, Kari, 235
Openshaw, Gene, 4
Orwell, George, 159

Page, R.I., 221
Park, James, 51
Pasternak, Alexander, 302
Pearson, John, 22
Pfeiffer, Christine, 210, 263
Piccinardi, Antonio, 184
Piggott, Stuart, 24
Pipkin, James, 48
Pitkin, Donald S., 177
Plath, Iona, 221
Polonsky, Marc, 301
Pond, Elizabeth, 293
Porter, Melinda, 115
Prebble, John, 62

Raban, Jonathan, 18
Racine, Michel, 136
Radice, Betty, 12
Rae, Janet, 69
Raison, Laura, 115, 167
Rajanen, Aini, 217
Randall, Tom, 114
Ranke, Kurt, 205
Read, Jan, 158
Rearick, Charles, 134
Reeves, James, 163
Regan, Mary, 141
Renault, Mary, 283
Riasanovsky, Nicholas V., 310
Richter, Gisela M.A., 280
Ritchie, Graham, 68
Rodimzeva, Irina, 306
Romer, Elizabeth, 185
Rothschild, Baron Philippe, de, 110
Roy, James, 102
Rutherfurd, Edward, 41

Sadie, Stanley, 52
Sampson, John, 73
Sayers, Peig, 92
Schama, Simon, 240
Schauss, Hans-Joachim, 256
Scherman, Katharine, 127
Schlee, Ernst, 204
Schorske, Carl E., 241
Schwartz, Richard, 37
Seebohm, Andrea, 244
Selz, Peter, 204
Shaw-Smith, David, 96
Shenker, Israel, 60
Sichrovsky, Peter, 198
Simenon, Georges, 112
Simenti, Mary Taylor, 173
Sinclair-Stevenson, Christopher, 117

Slesin, Suzanne, 30, 120
Smith, A.G., 80
Smith, Bonnie, 128
Smith, Michael, 32
Somerville-Large, Peter, 101
Spalding, Frances, 28
Spiel, Hilde, 241
Stark, Freya, 281
Starr, S. Frederick, 315
Steakley, James, 207
Steel, Tom, 77
Stern, Fritz, 198
Steves, Rick, 4
Stewart, Janice S., 222
Stolz, Mary, 208
Stone, Irving, 278
Streatfeild, Noel, 53
Suetonius, 189
Switzer, Ellen, 287

Tanner, Heather, 27
Taylor, Russell, 301
Thubron, Colin, 303
Tilly, Charles, 129
Tocqueville, Alexis, de, 133
Tolstoy, Nikolai, 311
Trevor, William, 104
Tuchman, Barbara, 11, 131
Turnbull, Michael, 76
Turnbull, Stephen, 11

Undset, Sigrid, 231
Uris, Leon, 103
Ustinov, Peter, 296, 301

Vander-Molen, Paul, 215
Vangerg, Bent, 217
Varga, Domokos, 249
Ventura, Piero, 195

Vidal, Gore, 176
Vishnevskaya, Galina, 294
Voinovich, Vladimir, 290
Volokh, Anne, 309

Waite, Garth, 61
Waite, John, 7
Walden, Hilary, 34
Walesa, Lech, 255
Wallace, Barbara, 80
Walmsley, Jane, 17
Walton, Guy, 121
Watkin, David, 29, 203
Weaver, William, 191
Webster, Bryce, 85
Wechsberg, Joseph, 124
Wedel, Janine, 252
Wehle, Philippa, 137
Weizsacker, Richard, von, 202
West, Rebecca, 248
Whitaker, Terence, 36
Whitford, Frank, 203
Whymper, Edward, 242
Williams, Niall, 89
Willis, David K., 295
Wilson, David M., 227
Wiser, William, 130
Wojciechowska, Maia, 164
Wolfflin, Heinrich, 181
Wollstonecraft, Mary, 216
Wood, Michael, 279
Woodhouse, C.M., 284
Woods, Geraldine, 164
Wright, Patrick, 21

Yeats, W.G., 100

Zeldin, Theodore, 112